Photograph of bearer
Martha G. Hemingway
AMERICAN
ULAR SERVICE
This passport, properly visaed, is valid for travel in all countries unless otherwise restricted.
This passport, unless limited to a shorter period, is valid for two years from its date of issue and may be renewed upon payment of a fee of $5 but the final date of expiration shall not be more than four years from the original date of issue.
See page 17
MISS MARTHA GELLHORN
WAR COR.
COLLIERS WEEKLY
HQ P.R.O. UK BASE
APO 413 C/O POSTMASTER
NEW YORK
BRONXVILLE, N.Y.
FEB 12
7-PM
1945
AIR MAIL
UNITED STATES OF AMERICA
MARTHA
A MERRY
CHRISTMAS
AND A
HAPPY
NEW YEAR
D. E.
beating one into a sodden pulp and making
than sun-bathing an impossibility.
you left, so our games will stay
On Friday I'm going up
in their cosy little cast
his hotel for a dri
situation. Well,
the Washington
krauts. What
successful an
James was i
D1192367

Praise for
Yours, for Probably Always:
Martha Gellhorn's Letters of Love & War
1930–1949

"Somerville makes an impressive book debut with a life of novelist, journalist, and intrepid war correspondent Martha Gellhorn (1908-1998), told through a captivating selection of her letters to friends, family, husbands, and lovers... An engrossing collection that burnishes Gellhorn's reputation as an astute observer, insightful writer, and uniquely brave woman."

~ *Kirkus Reviews*, Starred

"*Yours, for Probably Always* is a rich resource about an extraordinary life well-lived. The literary stream-of-consciousness letters, uncensored and intimate, read like a novel. There are dramatic flashpoints, but also revelations of everyday existence that are equally absorbing. The book provides genuine insight about Martha Gellhorn and how real she was."

~**Wayson Choy**, author of *Paper Shadows*

"The remarkable Martha Gellhorn leaps from the pages of these vivid, witty, deeply human and humane letters. Through her loving curation and attention, Janet Somerville gives voice to a 20th century literary pioneer, too long in shadow."

~**Charles Foran**, author of *Mordecai: The Life & Times*

"I loved this book. It is astonishing to realize that the courageous war journalist, Martha Gellhorn, was born in 1908, for the letters read as totally contemporary. How can you know everyone from Eleanor Roosevelt to Colette? The only woman to leave Hemingway and say—keep the champagne glasses! *Yours, for Probably Always* is totally mesmerizing and Somerville is easily as urbane, knowledgeable and well-informed as Gellhorn. It was a huge job to pull this all together and make it read smoothly when you are covering so much territory and Janet Somerville did that with perfect aplomb. She chose wisely so you see Gellhorn's wit, her charisma, but also her hard work and dedication to mankind."

~**Catherine Gildiner**, author of *Too Close to the Falls*

"As much as any woman in the twentieth century, Martha Gellhorn succeeded in her ambition to 'go everywhere and see everything and sometimes write about it.' It is wonderful to have this compendious new collection of letters from and to her, a few newly discovered. Janet Somerville has carefully set each group of correspondence in its historical context and further enriched them with photographs which even longtime Gellhorn admirers will not have seen."

~**Adam Hochschild**, author of *Spain in Our Hearts:*
Americans in the Spanish Civil War, 1936-1939

"*Yours, for Probably Always* is an essential book, a ticket into the past, a life spent wildly, often bravely, sometimes not so wisely… The great writer: presented in full throat, the real thing. Read in full, as the careful writer would do, can light an afternoon. Janet Somerville has done a marvelous job with marvelous material. Bravo."

~**Ward Just**, author of *American Romantic* and
An Unfinished Season

"Martha Gellhorn was courageous and committed in love and war. What a pleasure reading her correspondence and being reminded of how beautifully she wrote, filled with passion and insight."

~**Azar Nafisi**, author of *Reading Lolita in Tehran* and
The Republic of Imagination

"Martha Gellhorn was a force of nature. She more than deserves this rekindled recognition in *Yours, for Probably Always*. Janet Somerville has done the almost unimaginable: brought Gellhorn back to life. The timing couldn't be more serendipitous or, more aptly, prescient. Gellhorn should be a beacon of hope, because she trailblazed the future. She was a singular talent."

~**Rex Pickett**, author of *The Archivist*

Yours,
for probably
always

Yours, for probably always

Martha Gellhorn's
Letters of Love & War

1930–1949

JANET SOMERVILLE

FIREFLY BOOKS

A FIREFLY BOOK

Published by Firefly Books Ltd., 2019

Text © 2019 Janet Somerville and the Estate of Martha Gellhorn and respective correspondents

Copyright © 2019 Firefly Books Ltd.

First printing

Library of Congress Control Number: 2019933683

Library and Archives Canada Cataloguing in Publication

Title: Yours, for probably always : Martha Gellhorn's letters of love & war, 1930-1949 / Janet Somerville.

Other titles: Correspondence. Selections | Martha Gellhorn's letters of love & war, 1930-1949

Names: Gellhorn, Martha, 1908-1998, author. | Somerville, Janet, 1966- editor.

Description: Compiled by Janet Somerville. | Includes bibliographical references and index.

Identifiers: Canadiana 20190065222 | ISBN 9780228101864 (hardcover)

Subjects: LCSH: Gellhorn, Martha, 1908-1998—Correspondence. | LCSH: Authors, American—20th century—
Correspondence. | LCSH: Novelists, American—20th century—Correspondence. | LCSH: Journalists—
United States—Correspondence. | LCGFT: Personal correspondence.

Classification: LCC PS3513.E46 Z48 2019 | DDC 813/.52—dc23

Published in Canada by
Firefly Books Ltd.
50 Staples Avenue, Unit 1
Richmond Hill, Ontario
L4B 0A7

Published in the United States by
Firefly Books (U.S.) Inc.
P.O. Box 1338, Ellicott Station
Buffalo, New York
14205

Printed in Canada

 We acknowledge the financial support
of the Government of Canada.

Martha Gellhorn's letters are located in the Martha Gellhorn Personal Papers, Howard Gotlieb Archival Research Center, Boston University, the Archives of Charles Scribner's Sons, Princeton University, and the Ernest Hemingway Personal Papers, JFK Library, Boston and reprinted here courtesy of Dr. Alexander Matthews.

Letters from Eleanor Roosevelt and Franklin Delano Roosevelt to Martha Gellhorn are reprinted here courtesy of the Estates of Eleanor Roosevelt and Franklin Delano Roosevelt.

The Author and the Publisher have made every effort to locate the copyright holders of all material in this book and to provide proper credit. Any omissions brought to the attention of the Publisher will be corrected in future editions.

For my parents

CONTENTS

Foreword

Martha Gellhorn was my stepmother. She married my father after she
divorced Ernest Hemingway. Martha used to tell me that her inspiration
for writing a letter was a heartfelt complaint. That was her dynamo. And
when she started to write it, she wrote it to someone, person to person.
That way she could focus her complaint in a more direct way that didn't
have a scattergun effect and dissipate the emotion in her letters.

She always claimed not to be an intellectual. But there was a contra-
diction in her here because she loved ideas. She was also very much
against what she called 'navel inspection' and yet her heartfelt letters
often included an analysis of a relationship or the person she was
writing to.

Martha and I started off on the left foot. I had been airlifted from my very
comfortable, seemingly successful life in Princeton, living with an aunt,
into an exciting, grey, post-war London, where I didn't seem to fit very
well. But then we had a geneticist who came to visit us at our school in
Devon and he said that we will go to a party in maybe thirty-five years
and not know who is man-made and who isn't. The thought horrified
me and I wrote to Martha about it. Instead of saying "get on with your
studies," she wrote right back and said "yes, isn't it terrible?" I replied
that, as far as I could see, we were living like one-eyed cyclops and
Hollywood was the opiate of the masses. And, in the meantime, the

wool was being pulled over our eyes by a few scientists, who were taking the responsibility for the future, and how dare they, and how could they, and so on and so forth. And Martha wrote right back fulsomely and with growing concern.

We then cemented our friendship on anti-nuclear campaigning, she with her magnificent book, *The Face of War* (cf. the 1986 introduction), which, in my view, is the best thing she ever wrote. I went on anti-nuclear marches, which she supported avidly. This is how we became pen pals and created our friendship through letters.

Her letters delve deeper into her, I think, in some ways better than her presence. She nearly always had a party face and made the best of whatever company she was in and that served to hide away the true Martha. Only in her letters did her feelings emerge … and with gusto. She opened her heart to you and it was a great compliment and privilege and treat to be in on such a display. It presaged affection and trust and they were an education. I probably got more out of Martha's letters than I did out of my schooling.

Janet Somerville has painstakingly put together a rich collection of Martha's letters for you, the reader, to enjoy. And then there are the replies from her friends. People who helped to shape the 1930s and 1940s. What you are getting in this book is a very articulate account of those fascinating times. Not just the history but the feelings, thoughts and aspirations of those who shaped the history of the time. Janet Somerville has done a wonderful job. I invite you to enjoy the fruits of her labor of love.

Sandy Matthews
Devon, England

Prologue

"The only way I can make it seem real to me is to write."
—Martha Gellhorn

Reflecting back on her life as a journalist, Martha Gellhorn insisted, "All I wanted to do was go everywhere and see everything and sometimes write about it. I suppose you're born with curiosity. I certainly wasn't trained. I spent my childhood riding the streetcars of St. Louis telling myself I was going to Samarkand. All the exotic names. So, I think I have always wanted to travel and I have always been curious." Writing about what she saw and heard for newspapers and magazines was her passport to adventure. She hoped "in a humble and fairly hopeless way" that something she wrote "would make people notice, think a bit, affect how they reacted." The idea that her work might "change minds" was a stretch, but Gellhorn nevertheless believed that her words might be able to "wake minds" so they would "know what's happening in the world." Her public self and her private self were the same, an authenticity that remains remarkable decades later. Martha Gellhorn was a fascinating, pioneering woman of her time, and her enduring legacy of words is for all time.

ONE

Nothing Ever Happens

"I think one can only afford to be poor alone:
poor *à deux* is a disaster."

—Martha Gellhorn

Much to the chagrin of her progressive parents, in 1929 Gellhorn left Bryn Mawr after her junior year, only one year shy of her degree. She would later say of her parents, "they didn't do any instructing. They just lived and were." Her mother Edna was a suffragette and a founder of the National League of Women Voters. She had a great sense of civic duty and what things should be made better. Her father George was a doctor, "half of whose work was charity work," a man who "cared a great deal more about his poor patients." She grew up watching two extremely generous, talented and charming people live their lives with a moral code grounded in social justice.

Her co-ed days behind her, Gellhorn got work first as a fact checker at *The New Republic* in New York City. There, she wrote a profile of heartthrob Rudy Vallée published in August, observing that "his shy, I-can't-imagine-why-I'm-here pose is tiring." She almost decided to return home to St. Louis because the NYC skyline "plunged [her] into despair." That September, she moved upstate and took a job as a cub reporter for the *Times Union* in Albany, where she covered streetcar crashes and the mortuary beat. Her first real story, never published, was about a child custody case. Gellhorn thought it would be "a chance to be Don Quixote on a newspaper." She hoped her reporting might be able to "direct public opinion… to help the underdog." Waiting for her editor's indignation about the unfairness of the situation to match hers, she was repelled by his response that "a lot of lousy middle class muckers" knocked each other around. Besides, they couldn't print the truth: the judge would haul the newspaper up "for contempt of court." While on the mortuary beat for the Albany *Times Union* during the winter of 1930, Gellhorn reported on the death of a prostitute in "a particularly frowsy brothel on south birch street [sic]" on which the coroner "gave a verdict of suicide." Instructed by her editor to look for marks on the body which "might contradict the coroner's verdict," Gellhorn was shown the corpses of three women. She found herself growing cold, shaking, wanting "to scream that it was all too ghoulish to be true." The undertaker showed her the woman she was there to observe and she noted, "a grey, marcelled bob, matted, narrow shoulders. Her breast was sore and red," resolving that the "death that the poets are always muttering about, something lovely and calm, hell, they better shut up." Back at the *Times Union* office, she "stayed a polite number of hours," excused herself, took a big breath, lit a cigarette and "marched off through the slush."

It was in Albany that she began her friendship with Mrs. Roosevelt, a close acquaintance of Edna's through the National League of Women Voters. Her spouse Franklin was then Governor of New York. Eleanor Roosevelt would become one of Martha's most intimate friends, a woman about whom she'd write, "the finest conscience in America, the most effective one too, a woman incapable of a smallness or cheapness, and fearless… Heroes, on the whole, do not stand up well to the repeated tests of time and life, but she does triumphantly. They use the word 'great' in America to describe anything from a toothpaste to the latest least book; Mrs. Roosevelt was great. It is a word that should be used with infinite caution and only correctly."

But Albany, like New York City, could not engage Gellhorn for long. Europe was where she "wanted to be; more than that, had to be," and the "green coast of France was a door opening into the lovely grab-bag world." She thought that, perhaps, she had always had "a very slight capacity or desire for belonging, and was only meant to move about and look." She contacted a steamship company who provided "steerage passage" from New York to France "in exchange for a couple of publicity stories about the joy of travelling on their line." In March 1930, at the age of 21, Martha had arrived in Paris, chasing her dream of becoming a foreign correspondent. It was what she wanted to do, so she did it. She was "frightfully poor which was instructive and valuable." And, though "those hardship years were in a way fake" because she could always have been bailed out by her family, she wasn't bailed out, and she said she would "rather have died" than have asked them "for any money."

She introduced herself to Percy Philip, Paris bureau chief of the *New York Times*, declaring herself available for work. He laughed a great deal and took her out to lunch. When he asked her where she lived and she told him, he laughed even harder. Martha was delighted with her room near the Place de la Madeleine because it was so cheap. Every morning she bought violets at the flower stalls, "violets instead of breakfast." She thought "the mirrors on the ceiling and all the noise in the corridors, well, it's French, it's their business." It was "a *maison de passe*, where you rent a room for an hour to have a good sexual time." Philip thought it was both funny and scandalous and that Martha should get out of there. So she moved to a little hotel on Rue de l'Université, which turned out to be a hotel for homosexuals, where her neighbours had passionate shouting matches and wept playing Chopin on the hallway piano. She was happy there in her two rooms that she shared with her friend Lydia, "where the doors were of curtained glass" and they had a weekly bath four floors below, "*service compris* for something less than six dollars a week."

Gellhorn's first job was writing copy for Dorland Advertising Agency, located on the Avenue des Champs-Elysées. Decades later she could only remember one piece, "a lyrical composition in praise of a thinning bubble bath," a product that perplexed her because she could not understand "why anyone would want to get thin since the aim was to get enough to eat." Her next job was with the United Press, taking messages over the telephone, "delivered in machine gun French by provincial rag-pickers who gathered scraps of useless information." When the telephone "kept saying; René Henri Émile Irene Marie Suzanne," she hung up, eventually decoding that "some poor soul was calling from Rheims," spelling out the city with the first initial of each person's name. Stuck in this shabby office on the Boulevard des Italiens, Gellhorn was frustrated because she knew what she wanted to do with her life: "to go everywhere and see and everything," writing her way.

In her journal she notes that on July 14th she met Bertrand de Jouvenel, a French socialist and journalist, who would become her companion for the next several years. Through him, she would meet the celebrated French novelist Colette.

Martha returned to St. Louis, "ill and pregnant," in time for Christmas 1930. She had her first abortion in Chicago in January 1931. During the rest of the year, she wrote journalism pieces stateside and took a train trip to Mexico where she interviewed Diego Rivera as he painted his extraordinary mural dedicated to the people of Mexico City. At the end of September, Martha met Bertrand in New York, where he'd arrived on the *Île de France*. They bought a khaki-colored ancient Dodge for $25 and drove through the Southern states, where they met men on their way to a lynching. Martha would write about this experience five years later in a piece called "Justice at Night," one that H.G. Wells helped her place in *The Spectator.*

Campbell Becket was a lifelong friend who would oversee Gellhorn's divorce from Ernest Hemingway, provide financial advice, and manage her publishing contracts. She first met him in New York City in 1929, "when he walked into a flat" where she was dining "on his hands." He had "apparently come up all four flights in this manner, and found it good and unusual exercise." Their friendship was warmly affectionate for more than 60 years. Of her relationship with Becket she'd write, "I was the spoilt friend, the taker," because Cam "looked after people."

March 1930
                                                     Paris

Cam my dear,

I am in bed again. I begin to wonder, rather unhappily, why I ever get up—as I only get up in order to lie down all over again. (Odd sentence)

I am pretty damn weary of this perpetual nameless sickness. I have acquired a new trick which consists in being unable to stand up and therefore fainting without losing consciousness.

The American odyssey was well smashed by a cable from the *North German Lloyd* rejecting my articles. Today I was going to the Balearic Islands to pull myself together with a little sun and no more city. But I'm in bed instead.

Audrey has spent three hours talking to me. Yesterday Gi spent three; the day before Win had his turn. They insist that I go home. Gi wants to take me to Madeira for three months but hasn't the money. People seem wildly worried about me. I do look like Gorgonzola cheese.

And I'm so bitterly discouraged about everything, so damned indifferent that I don't care where I am. But I know that if I go home my family will take one look at me and Europe will be settled for a long time. And I'll be well-disciplined with green vegetables and sleep and tonics. And I still love Europe. I love it despite incessant rain, despite Paris, despite personal despair and frustration.

But I have a feeling that I will be put on a boat, about December 7, and told to stay in St. Louis until I look, feel, & think like a human being.

Because God knows I am not a human being now.

But I am afraid of months in St. Louis—afraid of loneliness and a frustration even greater than what I now feel.

I don't know what to do. I only know that I'm tired—terribly, terribly tired—and contemptuous of myself—and betrayed by my rotten, aching body.

So you may see me very soon. And may not.

What a life.

Love—Marty

Martha's relationship with her father, Dr. George Gellhorn, was a complicated one. He was a well-established, beloved obstetrician/gynecologist who not only taught at St. Louis University School of Medicine, but was also the founder of the Gynecological Clinic, Barnard Free Skin and Cancer Hospital. He pioneered trans-vaginal hysterectomies because that radical surgical approach was preferable to the abdominal route and better for the recovery of his patients. Although her father was progressive in his parenting during Martha's early years—he always taught her to believe that she was equal in talent and intelligence to her three brothers—Dr. Gellhorn became judgemental when she fell in love in her early 20s with Bertrand de Jouvenel, a married man. To her then, he said, "there are two kinds of women and you are the other kind." She believed he thought she was "some unserious and rackety character." Dr. Gellhorn's opinion of his only daughter darkened her life for years and Martha regretted that they "did not have enough time to become friends."

Her father died in 1936 before "anything good" of her writing was published. When her first novel *What Mad Pursuit* was published in 1934, her father said, "I cannot believe anybody would publish this." Decades later Gellhorn would proclaim "he was right" about that "baby novel" she disowned and refused to list among her books. Gellhorn never permitted subsequent print runs of that *bildungsroman*, a coming-of-age novel in which she was beginning to find her narrative voice.[1]

George Gellhorn to MG

April 5, 1930
St. Louis

Dearest Girl,

This afternoon I wrote you a letter, but as I had to write between patients, it turned out so jerky that I tore it up and am now trying a second time. It's a red letter day whenever a letter comes from you, and we smile happily when you at the time of writing were on top of the wave, and we look forward to the next change, when you happen to be in a despondent mood. Well, the last two letters seem to have left you fairly content, though some of your predilections for the French appear to have undergone a change. Witness, "they are smiling and polite as long as they expect their three franc tip, and are cruel and hard when the silver is not forthcoming."

… Are you going to send us some specimens of your writing? Can we get hold of your articles for the *North German Lloyd*? And what did you write for the *Post-Dispatch*? You've left us in the dark as to the exact work you are doing at present. Is it advertising, modeling or reporting?

… How is *your* accent? How do you pronounce cliché?—Oh, sweetest, I love you so much and miss your clinches and your chatter and your tempestuous vivacity.

The enclosed check represents a recent dividend of one of your bonds. It isn't much, but may help keep the wolf from the door until your own earned checks come pouring in.

Good night, my Beloved. I am off to play bridge with Grandmother *et al.*

Devotedly,
Dad

In April, Cam Becket, her lawyer friend to whom she'd been writing back in New York, showed up in Paris and invited her to travel with him to Tunis. For the short excursion she packed a purple-flowered dress, "the sort of garment a cheerful but dingy French housewife might have worn," sneakers and "a tight taffeta sheath of deep blue with a cascade of ruffles." It didn't occur to her that her clothes "might be too few" or inappropriate for visiting a French military governor and his countess wife in Morocco. It was "a boon granted to youth, this wonderful facility for not noticing." There, to her everlasting mortification and amusement, she got "sudden ptomaine poisoning," fainted in the bath and was carried naked to her bedroom by "two silent Senegalese giants." Gellhorn wrote that "years later" she finally understood that the countess had presumed she and Cam were lovers and that she had catalogued Martha "as a girl who would come to a deservedly bad end."

A piece Gellhorn had written for *The New Republic* to help pay for her cheap, shipboard passage to France, about the express train from NYC to Toronto was published on April 30th. In it, she compared her fellow passengers to more worldly strangers she met on similar journeys in Europe. Here, on the way to Toronto, "they were reading the morning papers… with a sort of deadness about them. They were uniformly the color of the chairs they sat in—a stale gray-green." Not one face "had any apparent interest in living or curiosity of going on a trip."

There were only "two people worth looking at and wondering about." And in the ordinary moment she celebrated, a mark of her style, Gellhorn observed "an old man, with a thin, yellowed beard and skin like a dried apricot stretched over his bones. His eyes are deepset and seem blind, though he is reading a Yiddish paper. Next to him is a woman" with a "coarse auburn mop" contrasting with "her face, lined and uncertain with age, one eye smaller than the other, as if she had already started to die. Her hands are swollen and tired. She says something to him in their dialect. He affects not to hear her, but she looks at him persistently with her head on one side, and suddenly he gives a shaky little laugh. Then she laughs, too. He goes back to reading his paper, vigorously." The woman takes "down a bundle—it is a great handkerchief wrapped around something… and soon they are eating mud-colored sandwiches four inches thick and talking to each other in jerks. They have the expectancy of children on a picnic." They show the European knowledge that going on a journey is a good thing.

Gellhorn then recalled a journey she made from Breslau to Berlin where she felt "that wordless delight in the life that exists in a train." Fellow passengers in her compartment were all reading and it seemed that "being there together was, for no reason, important," and so they "began to talk all at once without any excuse," talking of everything from "the Russian Ballet" to peace. One man remarked that there would be another war. "He said it without hate or haste, without feeling, but as if there were nothing else to say or think." Gellhorn wanted to be able to speak German better to "tell him that he must be wrong," but all she could say was, "No, we won't have it." Then the man "stood up and bowed and smiled at such insistence and said: '*Le flambeau est à vous tous. Portez-le.*' [The torch is yours. Carry it.]"

In contrast, the passengers on the Toronto Express made her think drearily "of queues of people standing in line before movie-palaces on Broadway, and dim, unformed faces in speakeasies, and the blind, hurrying humanity on subways," taking things for granted. She resolved to "look, on one side, at the Hudson, shining and cold in this light, and the stone quarries, derricks, road-gangs and desolate, beautiful forests on the other," noting that perhaps she's being "unduly morose at ten-thirty in the morning."

George Gellhorn to MG

May 3, 1930
Metropolitan Building
St. Louis

My beloved Girl,

Neither Mother nor I can understand how you can possibly complain of being left without letters. Mother has been writing two and three letters a week to you, and we wonder whether you have made any arrangements with your bank to have the letters forwarded to you without delay.

… Your article appeared in *The New Republic*. I assume that its check was the one to save you from immediate starvation. That reminds me of this 10$ [sic] check which I squeezed out of your savings, and I take it that even 10$ [sic] will look quite large soon after a vacation to Corsica and Tunis. Now tell us the truth about this trip. Mother thinks you are just—fabricating. What did you *really* do? And how did you do it? Did you go with young—I find I have forgotten his name. Is he now my prospective son-in-law, your seducer or merely your traveling and strictly platonic traveling companion? You must admit that even in 1930 a father who is—blessed with highly progressive offspring, has a mild interest in learning some of the accompanying details. Beyond it, I am naturally interested in your impressions, if you *really* did go south beyond let us say, Tour!

… Good bye, Dearest. I am looking forward eagerly to your next and all following letters. I have just been through a siege of "bubbles" [acid reflux] and feel like eighty.

Lovingly,
Dad

Early in June, Gellhorn travelled from Paris to St. Tropez where she settled into a cheap pension to work on her first novel, *What Mad Pursuit*. Despair set in so, "having a low tolerance for despair, and also having learned that the way to lose it is to walk away from it," she "took to the roads," paying her way by writing fashion articles for American newspapers and magazines for $25 each, including one she fabricated about "the latest fashion in men's pajamas in Paris." Twenty-five dollars would finance her for two frugal weeks, travelling around with a knapsack.

By June 20th she'd reached Andorra, "a small pink patch, the size of a thumbnail" on her map, a place she'd never heard of. To get there she climbed over a snow-capped Pyrenees mountain, bloodying her feet in her cheap, street-market boots from Perpignan in the process. That day's trip was "the only piece of physical prowess" in her life "and it was accidental." After "bouncing down the mountainside in the dark," she was found by a shepherd out retrieving his animals, and he took her back to his home where she stayed with his family until her feet healed.

"Heading back for the coast," Gellhorn discovered a rash on her chest. "Never having had prickly heat," she "decided this was syphilis acquired, as every informed person knew, by using dirty drinking glasses or dirty towels," of which she had had a large supply. In Marseille, she went to a clinic where "a bearded doctor laughed so hard he had to sit down at his desk and wipe his eyes" when she told him her suspicion. He prescribed calamine lotion and told her not to walk around the port alone at night.

Before returning to Paris at the beginning of July, she "walked and swam and ate bread and cheese and wrote in a copy-book inflated descriptions of nature and profound thoughts, and was happy." She figured, however, that "real life, obviously, concerned other people, many people, hordes of people," not only herself with a knapsack.

Edna Gellhorn to MG

June 21, 1930
4366 McPherson Avenue
St. Louis

Dearest Marty,

… There are a number of famous M.D.s in town for some sort of pow-wow… Dr. Dock… came straight up to me saying, "I read every word Martha writes, if I know where to find it. I have enjoyed her *New Republic* things a lot. I read them aloud to my wife and tell her that I knew that young lady as a child. I am waiting for her novel. Tell her I am for her the whole way."

… As I bring home each fresh installment of "light literature" from the Library, hoping to find something to entertain Dad, he exclaims, "why they print this stuff I can't imagine. I'd better wait for Martha's book." So all of us wait, but that thought need not worry you. We'll wait until you say you are satisfied with what you have done, or perhaps "satisfied" is not the word. I remember it is not one of your favorites.

Does it distress you when sometimes a line slips into my letters saying that we miss you? I do not mean that it should, and I am not sorry that you are doing what you are but it would be unnatural wouldn't it did we not miss you?

… The greatest problem we are facing as a nation today is unemployment. It is terrifying to go down-town, the stores are empty, the lines before the newspapers are hopeless men waiting to read any stray advertisement that may appear in the next edition.

Love to you, old dear. May your days bring you plenty of inspiration and some pleasure of achievement.

Mother

Claiming "it was singularly hard to get into real life" back in Paris, she went to stay with her friend Gi, "who had been loaned a grisly little house in the suburbs" where Martha returned to writing "the Great American Novel." She felt she had plenty to say and that she might be "a spokesman for a generation." Gellhorn would later insist about *What Mad Pursuit* that she "never worked so hard on anything else, nor so long," even though it read "as if an ignorant and fairly illiterate young person (correct) had dashed it off in a week or two, just the time necessary for hands to move over the typewriter."

According to her journal, on July 14th Gellhorn met Bertrand de Jouvenel, a French socialist and journalist who had scandalously lost his virginity to his father's second wife, a woman more famous than all of them: Colette. In her unpublished *Memoirs: A Bare Beginning*, Gellhorn recalled the summer of 1930, when "[a] new French friend presented himself on the shores of Lake Annecy, like Lochnivar, except standing in the prow of a motor boat." She determined that Bertrand, five years her senior, had "lived a misspent life… among famous rich nasty elders" and had been deprived of the freedom of travelling with a knapsack so he joined her "as a disciple." They hiked through "Nietzsche country, Sils Maria, the freezing dark green lake and those bony stone mountains." They "plodded through that scenery, discussing Life [sic]." She figured she must have been "a windy bore, full of the windiness of Nietzsche with touches" of her own.

At Lake Lugano, after dark, they waded in, knapsacks on their backs, "boots hanging by their laces" around their necks. When the water met their chins, they "realized that wading was out." Bertrand, who could not swim, began to sink "in gales of laughter." Luckily, his knapsack "turned into a life-saver, floated" and he got back to shore. They laughed at their foolishness of ruining their passports and her mother's check. Gellhorn was especially amused that the dip "had a blurring effect on the notebook" in which she scribbled her "profound thoughts."

In September 1930, Gellhorn travelled to Geneva to write articles for the *St. Louis Post-Dispatch* about the women who had important positions in the League of Nations.

Sitting in the press gallery one day, she heard "a squat, strong-looking man, with a mane of grey-white hair, say something: the whole assembly burst into volcanic applause." Fearing she was "missing a moment of history," she asked her nearest neighbour to tell her what former Prime Minister of France and 1926 Nobel Peace Prize Laureate Aristide Briand had just said. His declaration, "*Tant que je suis ou je suis, il n'y aura plus jamais de guerre* [As long as I exist, there will never be war again]," left her "aglow with solidarity." Briand's emotional statement remained true enough as he died in 1932.

After the session, Gellhorn saw Briand "in the corridors and went to congratulate him on what he had said and to tell him how right and good he was." She recalled that she had no fear of being rejected by him, noting "people are always kinder than they seem." Briand "declared himself delighted" and asked her to dinner with Nicolae Titulescu, who was then President of the General Assembly of the League of Nations. That evening was her "first hint that the Great [sic] were, when you got up close, only people too."

In Geneva during those couple of weeks, Gellhorn was "enchanted to become a cohort, in a café perhaps called the Lutetia, of the grown-up authentic, genuine foreign correspondents." Percy Philip, Paris bureau chief for the *New York Times*, whom she had met in March, seemed to her "the most glorious of the lot." For years she dumped her "woes, indignations, confusions and jokes in his lap, and he attended to them all by laughing most kindly." She "wanted to be one of them, deep in real life, seeing everything, understanding everything, and writing it so that all of the world could know." For a very long time, Gellhorn believed "that if everyone knew the truth, justice would be done." In her 80s, she'd implore in a radio interview that she hoped her writing would "wake minds" to what was happening in the world.

During those hand-to-mouth days, Gellhorn received windfalls from her family including a $100 check her maternal grandmother sent on her own birthday, a gesture she extended to all of her grandchildren. There were occasional gifts of $10 from her mother or father, "disguised by them as being something due" her, something that was essentially hers. In 1930 France, $10 would cover a week's living expenses. And, although grateful for this boon, as a matter of pride and principle, Gellhorn refused ongoing financial support.

Back in Paris in November, where Bertrand had been recalled from his September excursion to Florence with Martha by his wife Marcelle, who claimed to be pregnant, Gellhorn was fired from a temporary job at the *United Press* and made plans to return to America on a "bargain boat" that bobbed "like a cork on the waves." She felt she was "limping back (in a tub, seasick)." She was also pregnant, believing herself "to be old and failed" (she was 22), that her life had "come to nothing," as she returned to her family home in St. Louis for Christmas.

MG to Bertrand de Jouvenel

Fall 1930
Villa Noria
France

Dear love,

There is four inches of snow. Joke. I've re-written the first chapter [*What Mad Pursuit*] with what pain and I'll never be content with that chapter (the most re-done of the lot). It moves slowly, setting no key-note and I just can't make it jell. I'll have the second re-done before I go to bed. I see the book pretty clearly up until the end and then I don't know what to do. Of course it's all going to be much more banal when I'm done with it; lots of the fire has flickered out.

I walked five miles in the wind today and my head hurt from the cold. I'm losing my appetite which is a good thing; why didn't you tell me I was plain fat these days. I shall come back to you as usual thinner and with gobs of discipline which I'll lose the instant I lay hands on you (I meant lay eyes on you but there you are—the subconscious coming out)…

I listen for the telephone hoping it will be you and then I'm glad it's not because if you phoned I'd be tempted to come home at once and I must stay until I finish this damn thing. I love you passionately as you no doubt know by now.

I'm reading *Tragic America* and I love that old goofer Dreiser for all his cheap journalistic style: he's angry and alive and that's pretty rare these days. On the other hand I think Hemingway is pretty bum from what he did in *In Our Time*: the story about skiing is written about an ex-beau of mine who used to ski with him. Hemingway makes him inarticulate simply because Hemingway simply doesn't know how to talk, as a matter of fact that guy can talk in 9 syllable words all night long. So I'm not impressed. Anyway Hemingway has affected my style which is really too bad; but there you are.

Dearest you'll be very cool and stern with Marcelle [Bertrand's wife] won't you? I want so terribly to go to St. Louis with you. Oh God if only that female will crash through with a divorce; she's hideously hopeful, isn't she?

Sixty seven [sic] kisses and a friendly greeting to the dog.
Marty

Gellhorn travelled to Chicago in January 1931, where she had her first abortion. In her journal the occasion is noted matter-of-factly: "Jan: St. Louis (abortion in Chicago)." She did, however, write an unpublished short story that addresses how emotionally complicated the abortion was for her. In that piece, "Requiem," as the unnamed protagonist takes the elevator to the clinic, she thinks, "How vile being afraid that someone will guess. How sordid it is. No use thinking about that. The real thing is: get my lies straight." She continues to fret, stopping "to despise herself. Don't make drama out of it, she instructed herself; low and lousy it is, to be sure, but some things sometimes happen this way. Stop thinking; you're a spineless idiot." She chastises herself further: "you fool. This is your own mess; try to behave with some courage. Do you suppose soldiers got hysterical about their wounds?"

When the nurse removes the dressing, it seems "endlessly long. Its ends were twined around her heart." The doctor appears and "the walls bent in on her," her breath beating "her lungs like a whip." She hears herself "scream through a red haze of madness, pain, that knife."

On the way out of the clinic hours later, she notices the nurse and doctor eating lunch off the operating table, where "heavy, fat sandwiches and two bottles of milk stood on the leather surface." In the mirror between the elevator doors she looks at herself: "Like wearing a mask, she thought; I'd recognize the face, but I'd say, 'Dear, dear, how that girl has changed.'"

This early fiction that often reads like nonfiction is typical of the way she would blend and blur those genres for the rest of her writing life.[2] Of those years, Gellhorn wrote in her diary, "I swallowed the world around me whole and it came out in words."

Recovering from the abortion at her parents' St. Louis home, Gellhorn corresponded with Cam Becket about Bertrand—to whom Becket referred as "the Jewish candidate" for Martha's affection—and their shared need to find meaning in life, and she made plans to tour the western United States alone to write pieces about interesting Americans for the *St. Louis Post-Dispatch*, travelling by train on the Missouri Pacific Railroad in the early spring.

Cam Becket to MG

February 1931
New York City

Sweet—Sunday morning and in the apartment at an hour which would satisfy the plot of any Horatio Alger novel… Your letter came yesterday morning…

I regret the suffering of mankind and having three meals a day and occasionally a fourth I note the discrepancy… Unless we reconstruct man there shall be castles for the few and no homes for the many. There is no justice… Why should a seventy year old [sic] bum sidle up to me last night and beg for a nickel. It isn't fair; it can't be just…

I mentioned Bertrand. I haven't drawn any conclusions about him which would satisfy a lawyer. Because I don't know him as well as friends of yours whom I have never seen… I can't seem to see that youth married to you and I don't see him living with you. Consequently I try to see him as a stimulus, a mind, a sympathetic support. Who can and does have dreams you understand or at least who understands the dreams you have… Is it possible to fall in love? Do you want to fall in love? Isn't there a mind like Bertrand's, a heart like your own, an affection (may I?) like mine?

I think darling that life as we want to lead it may and must not be formalized. I think that the chart you are preparing is one trademarked M.G.—it won't work for others…

You have a vast sensitiveness, a depth and a field which knows no fixed limits, you are getting to know yourself and to find the picture pleasing—the tendency will be a less sympathetic view of those who are not leading your mental life, your fascinating existence. You will grow a little intolerant, not of mediocrity, for there intolerance is needed, but of those who have never had the opportunities that your own good fortune and birth as well as your own "guts" have afforded you. Remember when you have three francs and a head ache [sic] that there are many people who would give their life to have the same pain were it to be had…

A radio in the corner is very soft and the music ageless and familiar. I am alone. If so I can ever be when you are in my mind and words on the tip of ten fingers (four at least). Sometimes, call it after a long day of eternal dictating, I yearn for the view from the balcony of Tunis, the cliff at Carthage. But only seen with your eyes…

If there's a key to this enigma of life I haven't it—you I know are closer to the secret. Perhaps to have a heart that sings—and bleeds so well—and to be glad that it can bleed. To be terribly alive, grandly, beautifully, tragically. To feel an achieved detachment from all things unworthy and petty and demeaning desire and ideals—until at last, one can claim what once you said Gi called the *"Bonheur intérieure,"* can claim it when crowds are howling, when dreams are fading. You are nearer than I Marty, and nearer than you were...

By the way infant:

Don't marry the Jewish candidate [Bertrand].
(I will if I want)
I know you will, but anyway don't
(Pooh)
A socially responsible outfit I admit, supporters of the arts and charities, brains and a heart.
(All right I won't marry anyone for a while)
Thanks—sweet.

... Farewell my own and may the story etch out as you will it. And if you need some hankies or anything do write as I should like to get abroad sometime before I die...

Quite decidedly YOURS
  Cool
    Sweet
      Wretch
        Etc

MG to Cam Becket

February 26, 1931
4366 McPherson Avenue
St. Louis

Darling,

Too tired to make sentences, but will try literary grunts—on the now or never principle. Because I loved your letter and I won't marry the Jewish suitor [Bertrand] though he's very nice and I am awfully tired of being unmarried and being told by people that I'm a menace.

Darling *such* work. It is making me happy in my mind and driving me nuts with fatigue. From dawn till dusk, dashing to hideous dark holes where humans die patiently in these dreary days. Finding out what they need and getting it to them. I have one family where 3 children are dying at once. I know how doctors feel. But so tired and no writing accomplished. And then at night I flit about with the men "who have discovered" me. It's very annoying. I don't like verbal love making, when the heart is cold and the mind a question mark.

Read Priscilla's letter but don't let her know. It's sweet. As are you. I love you very much. I would like to giggle with you and kiss you and go to sleep on your shoulder.

So wearily,
Martha

In "One Ranger Rules," she wrote about the oil boom in Kilgore, Texas, a place that "became a draw for soldiers of fortune, gamblers, thugs, lease hounds, oil men, restaurant keepers, burlesque actors." There, the population "multiplied with a speed generally attributed only to mosquitoes: in eight weeks, it rocketed from 900 to 25,000. There was money to be made and spent. And ways of doing both."

It's a richly drawn portrait of Texas Ranger Manuel Gonzales, who "is the law itself." His "languid, gentle drawl is pure Texas," but his clothing is unique. His "whipcord breeches and coat seem unaffected by the all-pervading red clay dust. His belt buckle is intricately carved, brightly polished silver." A diamond "Shriner's pin glitters on his lapel, matching the glow of a large octagonal diamond on his little finger. His guns—worth $800, the gift of a grateful ranch owner in west Texas— have bone handles, carved with steers' heads, gold-inlaid, and neatly tricked out with precious stones." When Gonzales arrived in Kilgore four months before, he masqueraded "as a roughneck—a regular, oil-field laborer—wearing an old cap, grease-stained overalls." His performance was so convincing that he was able to gather evidence "to round up 500 people whom he knew as undesirable charac- ters." He herded them into the church that served as a *de facto* jail. "Later, when the number of arrests decreased, the jail was moved to a deserted seed store."

Gellhorn's sly humour is evident when she notes that "the undertaker is the most discouraged person in Kilgore. He complains that business is abnormally light. And announces, disconsolately, that Gonzales spells bankruptcy for him." Wary of mentioning his own accomplishments, the Texas Ranger admits "that he could shoot the heads off matches, split fifty-cent pieces, and keep a snuff box spinning to the staccato beat of bullets."

MG to Cam Becket

May 1931
4366 McPherson Avenue
St. Louis

Dear,
I am home. The word as you know has always had merely dictionary meaning for me. This is no longer true. I am home. It is like saying rest, peace, honorable

things. I love my family; their love for me is an unaccountable blessing. I feel protected from unnecessary ugliness and I feel that there is after all some meaning to my brief transit of this globe...

There are cornflowers in my study and when I return from an insignificant but pooping shopping tour, I find orangeade coolly on my desk. None of this implies vast histories to you. I have traveled so much, lived so thoroughly alone, that these piffling details of comfort and thoughtfulness come as a sweeping surprise.

I would rather not go to Mexico but shall go—in two days. Naturally. One doesn't die on jobs; and besides I shall doubtless be glad of it, as memory, if nothing else.

... A letter from Audrey delights my risible muscles; the girl belongs in Henry James novels, and in music by Couperin. Two letters from Bertrand are almost more than I can stand... I wrote him that we might as well abandon each other because of his wife, I hoped—yes, hoped terribly... And now without meaning to he has so surely finished that hope, and his own blindness, his child-like refusal and inability to see what is what and what can be anything, merely adds to the piteousness and futility of it all. I have talked to Mother about this, and we have arrived at the conclusion—she wisely, I bitterly—that only work heals those stranger wounds, those sick deep wants that clamor in one's memory. I'm not sure I shall do anything more about Russia next year; but probably try to get a job at a local paper; work, work, and home at night quietly. Some sort of anodyne; I have been counting my losses honestly and know that if I am to live with any joy or usefulness, without hideous wastes of days and enthusiasm, I must forget all that B. means. Because he has meant too much. And I have spoiled months of my life already groping backwards, praying, weeping and wondering why I was doomed to this ignominious frustration. Enough about all this too. I am saying several "good-byes to all that" in this letter.

Dearest thank you 1000 times for your sweetness in N.Y. and for giving Kitten a good time, and for being alive, and wise. I like Jean and Robin, and had not expected to and find them pretty splendid news. As for you—well, my old play-mate, you will have to guess.
Write me here.

Yours, for probably always,
M.

In late June, Gellhorn was back on the train, travelling to Mexico, this time with the ardent hope of swinging an interview with Diego Rivera for the Missouri Pacific Railroad, but, as her journal notes on the 21st, she "had the devil's own time" getting into the country, because she could not produce a certificate of vaccination. That dilemma was solved when "a pleasant, myopic man in a white coat appeared, rolled up [her] sleeve, dabbed it dubiously with cotton of faint alcoholic tinge, and stuck a needle with more energy than kindness" into her arm as fellow passengers "beamed happily." No sooner had she been inoculated than the conductor wondered where her "tourist card" was. Offering instead her "passport which was quite deformed and unrecognizable from having fallen into Lago Maggiore last summer," Gellhorn was told nothing but the tourist card would do.

Typed on flimsy yellow paper, "Morning with Rivera" chronicles the next day, June 22nd, 1931, which she spent chatting with the celebrated painter as he worked on his infamous murals in Mexico City's *Palaccio Nacional*. Swinging her legs from the scaffolding as she sat beside Rivera, drinking bottled beer brought to them by his assistant, he told her, "I only need a wall in front of me, and some paint." And Gellhorn noted that "he has now, probably, offers of more walls than he can use; and paint is easily ground. Seeing this man's work, and watching him doing it, are two of the most impressive spectacles one can hope to witness nowadays." Rivera painted as Gellhorn wrote, revealing his visual narrative of "the sufferers of history."

"Morning with Rivera"

This afternoon I went to see Diego Rivera working on his murals in the *Palaccio Nacional*. Arrived there I asked a guard, "Senor Rivera," that being all I could manage in the mother tongue. The guard smiled, made signs of writing, and led me to some scaffolds which covered a vast wall and rose far up to a distant ceiling.

I climbed the stairs. On our left massive figures drawn but not painted move across the white stone of the wall. Ahead there is a fully completed mural; crammed with movement and meaning, almost breathless with life. It shows the early Aztecs before the Conquest. Rivera has used that sturdiness of colour which is his private miracle to its best advantage. The brown bodies of the Aztecs appear child-like, pure, and unspeakably appealing, sit and stroll and work their way across the south wall; wheat ablaze and granite implements for cooking, fruits and baskets are light golds and greys and the earth brown of the people, the innocent white of their clothing... a perfect wealth of faces and forms leaning upon each other staring at each other and nothing, caricatures for the most part, but all sturdy, clean, sharp and alive.

"Ho, Diego!"

From far above our heads, around a corner of the scaffolding, a face looms cordially. A vast face dedicated to the geometric perfection of the circle; round eyes, round nose, cheeks, mouth, round curls on a round head. A smile widens the diameter of some of these circles, contracts others.

We clamber over boards and up the wide, center stone staircase of the *Palaccio Nacional*. On either side, and high to the ceiling, Mexican history unfurls itself. The walls are so crowded with people that one feels elbowed and shoved. Aztecs pounding grain, praying, seeming very simple and beautiful and right, until suddenly the shine of armor introduces the Conquest together with a great deal of action and blood. Farther on, there is the central period of modern Mexican history, Benito Juarez holding some very benevolent looking documents in his hand, a porcine priest, a couple of knotty-faced folks, generals and the like, some Indians carrying burdens, soldiers, everything closely packed and breathing; by its very composition true to the intensity, confusion and beauty of the country. Here Diego Rivera sits, half way between floor and ceiling, working ten or more continuous hours each day…

A very fat and very dusty posterior, surmounted by a much bloused dark blue polka dotted shirt, and tapering to feet which look trifling as a descent from such girth: the painter. His hair is fuzzy and dark and from the back he might be—for no specific reason Amy Lowell. He is talking as he works to a young man, talking and laughing; every so often he stops painting completely and just chortles, a high happy absurdly pleased chortle. A woman with a face like a Greco Madonna is also sitting up there. Neither of the men pay any attention to her. Her face in repose is sad and cadaverous and somehow out of line. The young man with him goes on talking; they are having some pleasant argument or joke or gossip. Meantime, Rivera is finishing the figure of a girl he started by sketching this figure on the dead white plaster. Gently he has traced a pattern on the heavy basket she struggles under. All this when he has a free moment to use his hands, because he is talking and his hands are essential to his conversation too. The girl comes alive, into a world of unhappiness and heavy weights to carry and Reform laws. She becomes not one girl but countless hundreds of oppressed Indians; she becomes in a sense a single figure of suffering and in some obscure special way, she is woman and it would not do to have a young boy carrying that load because only in this female figure could the imagery come so clear.

…We have crawled uneasily up a wobbly ladder and are standing on the planks beside him. Jean Charlot, whose frescoes are close neighbours of Rivera's in the Education Building, introduces me, "*Elle ne sait rien de la peinture.*" [She doesn't know anything about painting.] I agree to this. Rivera is amused, suggests that I sit down on an upturned, paint-smeared box, which I do. He is busy now, curving the bent strained back of the girl. He dips his brush into a can of particularly typhoidal appearing water, mixes this with some black paint on his palette—which is a cheap kitchenware saucer. Charlot and I are hot and speak of beer. Women and children are not allowed in the cafés. I am mildly irritable about this. Rivera gives a peso to one of his helpers (their work is to hand him a clean saucer, or re-fill the battered water can) and instructs him to purchase beer for us. We settle down soon, in the dust of flaked plaster, the smear of paint, our feet hanging over the edge of the scaffolding, with beer and cigarettes.

The conversation settles into steady comment on the country directly north, the celebrated United States of America.

Rivera has just come back from San Francisco. He likes it, "naturally," he explains, "I was never so well treated in my life. The people there are interested in art." When his things were finished everyone talked of them—the poor people as well as the intellectuals. This is because it is your work, I suggest. Nonsense, he replies. I was just an accident. But how does this pleasure in your painting coincide with the much described materialism of America, I ask, the materialism of the West Coast especially. He thinks that rather than bewail materialism one should beware the inadequacy of it. There are too many religions of every sort in America, too much substitution of fake mysticism for realistic thinking.

… As for all the present resentment against America on the part of Americans (artists, writers, musicians, intellectuals), he considers this a mark of weakness. For really, he says, if I live in an ugly house I am constrained to make it beautiful; its very ugliness is a challenge and an incentive. Personally, he continues, he would like to live in the States for that very reason; there is a great stimulus to make beauty where—relatively—so little exists.

... He has a great enthusiasm for the states [sic]. But would he really like to live there permanently? Ah, well, the entire American continent thrills him. Mexico, too, of course. Actually, it makes little difference where he lives as long as there is light over the land and color and forms; these, after all, are everywhere.

Gellhorn spent the rest of July and August 1931 with her family at Fish Creek, a cabin in Wisconsin where they had previously summered, but in September she returned to New York to meet Bertrand. He had come from Paris, leaving behind his wife and baby son Roland, to reunite with Martha and drive through the country with plans "to write a big book, a definitive book, no doubt, about America," while she intended to try to finish "the great American novel." Both of their families objected to them making the journey together; nevertheless, in Trenton, New Jersey, they bought an ancient Dodge for $25 and set off southward, ending up in New Orleans by Christmas, where they both had jobs in a cafeteria for a time. Bertrand was delighted because he "thought this was not only real life, but romance." Martha hated it.

They had very little money and "this was the beginning of a hated concentration on making both ends meet." Although she had never been hampered by a lack of money when travelling alone, Martha was "haunted" by the money that was not there for her and Bertrand. Admitting she did not "understand the mechanics of feeling poor," she however realized that "one can only afford to be poor alone: poor *à deux* is a disaster."

As they drove south in their sagging car, people seemed "persistently unreal, as if they were acting some ill-defined part, living up to some legendary version of themselves which they had not clearly understood." Sitting on crumbling porches in rocking chairs, "looking at dry hopeless land and sad trees, rocking and rocking, in faded rags of clothing, they seem less like people who cannot earn a living than like people out of a play about people who cannot earn a living. When they are brutal, they seem bigger than life, and nasty-fake… copying Southern brutality from the movies."[3]

One night their car broke down, "twenty miles or more from whatever speech-less sunbleached village" they were trying to find. There was nothing to do on that stretch of road but sleep outside as "the mosquitoes arrived, in singing armies." Around midnight "a truck bumped into sight." When Martha explained their position and asked if these strangers would drive them to the next town, the locals said, "not right away" as they were going to a lynching, but they would drop them afterward.

"There were two men in the truck, big men with fair hair and fair skin and heavy faces that looked unfinished." They were aimiable and drunk. Martha and Bertrand went with them, because they "did not know what to do." She felt their "minds stopped." She turned that horrifying experience into a piece called "Justice at Night," short fiction rife with upsetting sensory detail, proof that Gellhorn bore auricular witness for the unjustly hanged man. She knew "what happened from those men, from their faces and their voices." Gellhorn never forgot her own cowardice in that moment. Although "the crowd could not have been stopped," she "could have stood up" and declared herself.[4] Time and again she would look, when others looked away. After another atrocity she would note, "I could not help anyone; I could remember for them."

TWO

What Mad Pursuit

"Ah, my beloved one, it is good to love you as if you were sea
and mountains—and a man."

—Martha Gellhorn, letter to Bertrand de Jouvenel

Shortly after their dismal Christmas in New Orleans, Bertrand and Martha were "rescued by French friends," a playwright who had been "lured to Hollywood to write scripts" and his wife, neither of whom spoke English and "both of whom were withering with homesickness in the California sun." They drove north and west through "often beautiful endlessness, sometimes just land, land to break the heart." When they finally "clanked in," California looked "like a haven and an oasis: green, growing, cultivated, trees with oranges." The ancient Dodge "went to an automobile graveyard" and Bertrand bought its replacement for $25, a "grey Cadillac touring car," christened Jane after Lady Seymour. They moved into a little bungalow in the Garden of Allah, next door to their friends the Leos.[5]

In January and February 1932, Bertrand got work as a Hollywood extra, often cast as a French fop and once as "a Cossack in a tall fur hat, leaning against something." He earned $15 a day for leaning "and adored it," according to Martha. "Dressed in a blue sequin evening gown once having belonged to Myrna Loy, and in shoes once having belonged to Greta Garbo since they were the only ones large enough," Martha failed a screen test for a tiny speaking part in a Harold Lloyd picture. For the test her hair was "marcelled into hard waves, [her] eyebrows were made into a hard black curve and [her] mouth became a black rosebud. Looking like a 40-year-old hostess in a broken down dancehall" she was led to a stage, told to sit upon a table, expose her legs to the knee, and say while being filmed, "Look at me, I'm full of sex" in her "firm, clear Bryn Mawr voice, as if announcing the weather." She didn't get the part and decided she was "meant to be a writer and nothing else," and continued to beaver away on what would become her debut novel, *What Mad Pursuit*.

She rented a little place in Carmel to work in solitude on her book while Bertrand remained in Hollywood in an apartment on Sunset Boulevard, which meant they wrote rambling letters to each other and sent cables for several weeks. They always needed money and in Hollywood then, "if you did not have money, you were diseased, and the disease might be catching." Failure was considered a sickness that Martha felt was "terrible, infuriating, criminally ignorant and against life."

Bertrand returned to Paris at the beginning of May and wrote the first of several frank and deeply felt letters to Martha's mother, Edna. All of the men who mattered to Gellhorn understood that Edna was, as Martha said, her "true north"—a human compass, pointing the way to be in the world—and sought not only her approval but also her advice. At the end of June, Martha was "full of hope and $1000, borrowed at 6% from a friend," the money meant to finance "the final effort on the great American novel, which book, when finished, would automatically return the loan."

On her shipboard journey to Germany, with plans to reunite later with Bertrand in Paris, she developed an earache for which she sought treatment in Munich in early July. Her ear was lanced repeatedly over ten days, after which she fainted and "was bundled into the children's whooping cough ward," waking in a crib with her "legs hanging over the fence of the bed." Medical staff told her she was feeble and that if she "had been a real German Aryan model" she would not have collapsed under such minimal pain. Much later she'd recall of those days, "I did not think I was dying, I only wished I could."

In fall 1932, Bertrand and Martha were living in Paris and working as journalists, Martha at *Vogue* as a general helper on the fashion pages. She called herself a *"femme de ménage littéraire"* [literary maid]. By June 1933, she'd be reporting on the London Economic Conference where she interviewed Hitler's translator Herr Haempstaengl, "known to his friends (and to you and me and everyone else) as Putzi," a man who had rowed for Harvard in 1908, wrote "all the Nazi marches and hymns" and, according to rumor, had "a hand in writing Hitler's speeches." She also debuted the first halter-necked backless evening gown, a gift from Schiaparelli, one of the Paris designers who enjoyed having Gellhorn model her clothes. Biographer Caroline Moorehead noted that after the Depression, "French fashion houses had adopted a number of pretty young women of good background as their unofficial models, lending them evening dresses in return for publicizing their collections."[6]

In January 1933, her debut novel *What Mad Pursuit* was accepted by publishing house Frederick Stokes, her protagonist co-ed Charis Day an analogue for Gellhorn's Bryn Mawr self. Gellhorn remained in France until October 1934, when she broke from Bertrand and returned to the U.S.A., where she got a job reporting to Harry Hopkins, President Roosevelt's right-hand man, on the treatment of the unemployed across the country for the Federal Emergency Relief Administration (FERA).

January 1932
Santa Maria

Dear,

I loved it so, all day. Beautiful, beautiful—shabbily I have tried to tell you how smooth and warm and alive and many these hills are.

Then Lady Jane [gray Cadillac], fat red matron and slow on the towns, screamed like a beast in pain and broke—at 6 pm or so, 13 miles outside the town. I coaxed her here, with prayer and promises. She's broken 2 connecting rods—a hell of an expense—and here I'll be until noon tomorrow. I'll go very slowly, as the road winds trickily; but possibly I shall be at Carmel tomorrow night.

You'd be irritated by my inconsistency if you knew how much I'd thought of you all day—and how much I hoped you weren't thinking of me. Mainly shame: you've given me everything and I've given you in exchange faintly grudging thanks, so little warmth. My dear, forgive me. I wasn't meant for every day consumption: no one's ever been able to stand that great a dose of me—not even mother. I'm a holiday diet; I'm only bearable to myself—in solitude—as ordinary rations. You'll have to think of me as oysters—you wouldn't want oysters everyday for breakfast?

You have been more than gallant. My dear, only a nag—and a dyspeptic one at that—would criticize your manners or question your charm. *Sois rassuré* [rest assured]—I know they don't grow your equal at every corner of Sunset Boulevard.

Somehow—you will think me mad and unkind—I wish you'd have an affair, with someone beautiful, sophisticated, and attentive. I mean that. It would make me realize what I've made you forget—too many things.

I've repaid ardor with impatience and sponged your assurance with icy water. Please be a conqueror for a bit; forget me—I'm a shit face; and make yourself realize again what you knew before I came.

I'll write from Carmel. My dear, my dear—why do you have to be so good and I so mean?

love
m

MG to Bertrand de Jouvenel

Western Union
22 Jan 1932
Bertrand de Jouvenel
8152 Sunset Blvd Hollywood Calif

Darling Jane [car] repairs cost forty-four dollars absolutely *merde* [shit] could not sell her for twenty now so must let mechanics go ahead am miserable we will have to take beautiful trip to get moneys [sic] worth from her wire me California hotel santa maria cant [sic] leave until tonight disgustedly marty

---

MG to Bertrand de Jouvenel

Western Union
26 Jan 1932
Bertrand de Jouvenel
8152 Sunset Blvd Hollywood Calif

Some chickenhearted kidnappers held lady next door I didn't know they were there but apparently the presence of graystoke awed them they cleared out and the witty police thought Jane was their car very funny but nothing disturbing sorry you were worried *quand viens tu je t'embrasse* [when you come, I'll love you]

Marty
Santabarbara Calif 31

MG to Bertrand de Jouvenel

Western Union
January 1932
Count de Jouvenel
8152 Sunset Blvd Hollywood Calif

Je viens vite arriver avant neuf venres petit loque. [I'm coming soon, within nine days, little one.]

Bertrand de Jouvenel to MG

January 29, 1932
Hollywood

My beloved, I am sitting, naked in the hills. At four I have to be at Fox studio and I will earn $7.50.

… In your absence a deaf-and-dumbness sets upon me. When you come back, if you do, I will live again in daily dread of a new separation…

I hope to be able to send you a little money Tuesday. I will have worked on 3 shifts.

The playboy of Central Casting

Bertrand de Jouvenel to MG

May 1932
M.S. Lafayette
À Bord. le

Sweetheart, I feel this is very pointless, this sailing business. I feel silly going to France when my interests lie over here. Silly is a rather apt word. Because just now I don't feel desperate over your not being with me. My packing, getting on board and this rushing to and fro before leaving is just the sort of thing that I am thankful you don't witness. I feel pretty bad tonight. I feel so incomplete. Strangely enough I feel very acutely the lack of your presence when I am with other people. I feel that nobody is here to give me my cues and to but [sic] in at the right moment with the right thing. I feel—I'll tell you how I feel!—I feel like a *"montreur d'ours"* [bear trainer] without his bear. Is that rude?

I suppose saying I feel like a dancer without his usual partner would be nicer. But less exact. I have that habitude of pointing with pride in your direction when you have said something specially brilliant. I always want to go round with my hat in my hand to collect the nickels and dimes of public approval.

I feel very proud of you as of a specially noisy, lusty, fat and pink baby! Are you insulted?

Oh, my tower of strength, I am very happy to love you!

Say listen, kid, you know the way it is with me… there is a book review of a Roy Long book which recounts at great length how many times Hemingway had his 1st stuff turned down by publishers! Yes, the Great God Hemingway! This is cheering in case anything went wrong. But it wont [sic]. Audrey phoned the Knopf dame and she thinks you are the goods.

Take good cheer.

Your letter, my dear, came this morning, and I hold my breath and hardly dare to write to you because I feel that you love me just now and I fear that anything which I may say, proving me to be only ME, will ruin my image. Oh, sweetheart, this building up process, you are going thru [sic] it now.

The poor old bastard will have a hell of a time living up to it when we get together again!

Beloved, I joke because I cannot reply to your letter on the same level on which it was written. I am awed by the perfect beauty of what you wrote. It is the most wonderful thing I ever read because it combines yearning with repose. It is not a feeling of want which [sic] something of hysteria but a sort of joy in the mere act of stretching out your arms, a sense of fulfillment in the very aspiration.

I love you. I love you. Smooch.

Well, we've passed Plymouth. I posted a bulky letter to my beloved. Didn't go to bed this last night. Wrote about plight of American railways. Got immersed in that. Thank God for statistics. Had breakfast at half past five, enjoyed the glory of the morning. Wrote to Cam [Becket] and Walter [Gellhorn]. Packed. Everything in short but think of what's coming. Enclosed, the address of middle-aged lady who was very kind to me. Please look her up when you come to NY. Contrived to lure her into my cabin so that she should see pictures and that I might speak of you. Which I did abundantly, dotingly. Just a few hours to Havre, a few more to Paris. Where will the struggle begin, I wonder.

Nearby, a priest is saying mass on board. The low muttering, the lame piano and the violin of a chance passenger make up a "noise picture."

Oh, write to me, sweetheart.

Send me chapters. Let me have many stray bits of you to cling to.

I am sinking into that queer deaf and dumbness which comes over me when I haven't got you. Come to me, give me joy of life and talent. Oh, my beloved.

B.

Bertrand de Jouvenel to MG   May 12, 1932
                                                              Paris

Beloved, I got your cable three days ago. It called for no reply. You know how much I wanted to clear the way for our lives when we parted. You have no right to think that I wanted it less when I got to Paris, or that I didn't make every effort possible. I failed. I quite understand—I have seen you so worried and miserable, that you should not care to risk a life in common under the only conditions that are now possible. But I cant [sic] excuse the accusation that it is implied in your cable: "You can force it and must." If I could have forced it, I would have. I didn't need to be urged on.

A cable of one word only: NO, would have been far less cruel. I know you well enough to be assured that if you refuse to lead an unlegalized life with me, it isn't through social cowardice, but because you think it has REAL drawbacks, makes work more difficult, makes your family unhappy, weighs upon the mind, and so forth.

But implying that I hadn't tried hard enough was such an insult to my love!

… Have I been gone that long? Have you forgotten how much I love you? Can you misunderstand to that extent? Oh then it was very foolish to part. The transatlantic misunderstanding, how I hoped it would never be renewed! I was very confident that they could not put us on different planets, that we'd never misunderstand. It is worse than not having you, worse than losing you, this proof of the frailty of our faith.

Now maybe I'm misunderstanding. We just want to bear this distance between us, and remain as one. Maybe it isn't human!

I thought you'd know without my telling that it had been hell to discuss with Marcelle, and more hell to be without you. I thought you'd know without my telling how much it cost me to write these letters, bald and cold, urging you to make your choice.

… My dear, I have loved Marcelle badly, and I have been indulgent to her weaknesses; time and again I have spared her, excused her, and my indulgence made her self-indulgent, just as her indulgence towards me made me self-indulgent. We have reaped the reward of that conduct. We have made each other worse than we need have been. We have made ourselves into the worst sort of trouble-makers: those who make trouble through weakness.

I love you too much, and I have learned too much from you, to make the same mistake over again. I love you very harshly indeed. I quite understand how much you must have worried in St. Louis waiting for news. But there is nothing specially beautiful in that kind of worry. In one of my letters I wrote at length of the social and financial drawbacks of living with me without marriage. And I almost thought I was being generous and wise in pointing this out to you and sparing you some discomforts. I wasn't being generous and wise: I was just insulting you.

… If I lose you, my dear, I hope and trust you will do with some other man what you might have done with me: you will live with him, without marriage to the knowledge and scandal of all. And I am not thinking now that this will be useful in that it will open the way for other breakers of whichever commandment it is. I am not concerned with that. I am concerned only with the moral advantages that will accrue to you. You told me once you were glad that you had had the abortion. So am I, now. And the pages it has inspired are but the tangible sign of the moral benefit it has entailed for you. You are built for fights. And you have had but too few occasions of fighting. Too many for anybody else. Too few for your moral build.

You are throwing away an almost unique chance: the chance of a grand fight on both fronts, of a challenge to prejudices as to private behaviour as well as to established interests on the political and social plane. You are similar to those thoroughbred horses that give their full measure only if saddled with a heavy handicap. I know by experience that "the most favourable conditions"—I had them—are not an asset.

We have loved each other for two years under very adverse circumstances, and is it your belief that it has unmade us, or made us?

I am not pleading with you to become mine but to become yourself. Your letters worry me.

… I spare all my time for work, having embarked upon several series of articles, and wrestling almost continuously with them. I took a sip of politics, and it was enough to convince me that, barring the eventuality of serious social unrest, of which there seems to be none today, I will take no part in this childish game. There is a beautiful role to play for which we, as a couple, are cast. It holds in two words: understanding, describing. Not condemning as partisans do: I am amazed to find how much more lenient bitter enemies turn out to be than dispassionate observers. Bitter political enemies have in common with those they denounce the worst traits and so they can only indict their enemies on account of their lesser sins.

My dear, there is so much that we can accomplish. We have learned that we want few things but that we must have them: we want sunburn and talent, independence and insolent youth. In my case I will add: "And I want you." Find out for yourself whether you want me.

I think you do.

B

MG to Bertrand de Jouvenel

Late May 1932
4366 McPherson Avenue
St. Louis

Sunday morning; it is raining. Cam [Becket] reads my novel [*What Mad Pursuit*]. Last night, after the Kings [Hortense Flexner and Wyncie King] went home, I talked to him for hours. Talked? Well, I'm ashamed to say, I sobbed…

Bertrand: even with you, who love me—and whom I love, I have never had such a feeling of complete understanding. Finally, after three hours, I felt cleansed and quieted. And last night I slept.

I began talking about the Russian divorce. I told him he must help me to persuade the family so that they would give their consent gladly; so that they would realize that you were my salvation not my destruction. I told him I could never be happy if I were torn between my love for you and for them: that I needed happiness—or rather peace—because the mind and the body cannot go on forever, in doubt and struggle and uncertainty.

… I explained what it had meant to be a mistress; how you despised me for cowardice and conventionality; how it was—for me—like a Roman Catholic turning atheist. It was in my blood, my upbringing. I explained how I had fought my father's coldness and seen him sag and grow old before me. How I had been bitterly lonely with you, when, the mail arriving, the letters from Marcelle claimed you and unconsciously you turned away from me, giving your sympathy to her, regretting your desertion, and—again, unconsciously—knowing that I was to blame. How I had failed you, being unable to give you complete joy in sexual love—because I was unable to attain that climax; and how I even faked it on occasions when you had tried and I felt your wretchedness at failure. And how I couldn't have pleasure: no mind so tortured by conflicting emotions—my feeling that you didn't really belong to me (there were Marcelle's letters) and that my family were agonizing—could be released and so release the body. And I told him how you had wept that night at Pascagoula, when I had let you swim alone—because I was no longer ME. And I said (listen now; here's the most important truth). "If I am ever again the girl he knew at Annency, at Sils, in Toulon, it will be after years of careful training. I have to be led back to my youth. I have to be melted—as if I were iron—because I have really grown hard and tired and old." That is the thing beloved… I'm no longer Marty who talked to you of Nietzsche at Sils Maria; and walked through life with hope, radiantly; I can't help it—I loved that girl, as you did—more than you did, because to me she was the flowering of old dreams. And she is dead. Do you understand. I shall tell you frankly that I am shop-worn goods now, I'm neither beautiful nor admirable. I'm tired and I'm bruised. Bertrand, I feel sick—spiritually sick. I feel old and bitter, faithless. My feeling for you is deeper than love. You are my only hope in life of being beautiful again; of living beautifully. Will you help me? Will you be patient and loyal and forgiving? It may take years: now, I feel that I am asking you to assume a titanic burden—I am asking you to marry a spiritual invalid.

Marcelle was your destroyer of peace. These last hellish months have been valuable in this respect: you have laid a ghost. Beloved, you wouldn't lie to me please—would you? You are too fine for that. You really mean that you are free of Marcelle, can now go with me, hand in hand, alone—as if she'd never been, as if you were born anew. You won't torture yourself and me with regret and doubt?

And my destroyer of peace was my family. Dearest, you will be free of Marcelle—and I, of my family. We will take each other's hands and make over life. We will learn again that there is joy, and hope, and—peace.

Beloved, do you agree?

Oh, say you understand! Say you love me, forever! Say "Yes."
Marty

MG to Bertrand de Jouvenel

June 1932
4366 McPherson Avenue
St. Louis

Oh my beloved, my beloved: I've booked my passage today. I'm coming. It's going to be all right. Let's spend next winter in the Bavarian Alps—just we two, writing and getting husky… I have over $1000—we needn't worry for a year or so. My love, be at Hamburg on July 1 for the *President Roosevelt*. I'll get off in my walking trip clothes and we'll start. Sweetheart, I've missed you so. I'm going to see a doctor about my lack of sexual reaction tomorrow and maybe I'll be just like a Frenchwoman when you meet me. Dearest, I must stop—I'm doing an article to make more money for us. I shall be keeping you! Three cheers.

Cam is going out to St. Louis this weekend (the angel) to convince them that a Russian divorce will quiet their fears. Of course it's *illegale* in France and America but if they're happy, who cares? Oh my darling, I'm coming; I'm coming; I'm coming.

Do you love me? I'm almost happy for a change—if only these next three weeks don't drag so slowly.

Dearest Smuf

Bertrand de Jouvenel to Edna Gellhorn

June 17, 1932
284 Bld St. Germain
Paris

Dear Mrs. Gellhorn,

I have received in these last three weeks such letters and cables from Marty that I feel I must write to you. I trust I will not be making matters worse, but I have to take that risk. Please make allowances for my being a foreigner, both in my style of writing, and in my style of thinking.

Such love as Marty has for you, and as you have for her is seldom found between a mother and a daughter. Marty's admiration for her father is a beautiful thing. I could quote from her letters to me innumerable instances of her love for both of you; one day, she writes, "Dad has been so adorable these last days that it almost makes me want to weep." She has forwarded to me a penciled note from you, which it was almost sacrilege for me to read, it was so laden with the most intimate and tender love.

These links between Marty and you are very precious and no other love could ever replace for Marty this warmth which surrounds her wherever she goes, that unfaltering solicitude which follows her, and which awaits her.

Forgive me if I make so bold as to say so, but the very strength of the love that lies between you three, seems to have been to all of you a source of misery, not joy, in the last few weeks, maybe in the last two years. You have been tortured by a feeling of unsecurity [sic] about Marty's future and Marty has been tortured by the fear of making you unhappy.

I have called her to me, and you have called her back, and the poor sweet child was torn between us, thinking less of her happiness than of my misery if she didn't come to me, and of your own misery if she did come.

This conflict between two loyalties is destructive to her. Her nerves can't stand such a strain. No decision she can take can relieve that strain. If she comes to me, she will always know that you and her father are unhappy, and that she is responsible for that unhappiness. She won't be able to enjoy under those conditions whatever happiness she might otherwise experience.

The situation results, I will readily grant it, from an initial error or sin of my own. Possibly, I have somewhat aged since I first came into Marty's life, and I trust I have lost some of that selfishness which caused me to crash, so to speak, into her existence, without any thought of the consequences. I believe that now my main concern is her happiness and her work. How can she be happiest and best do her work?

I thought that if I uprooted myself so as to give her all of my life, I could make her happy, and that she could work and do something worth while [sic]. If the union were legal, so much the better, if it were not, we'd make it so perfect in other ways that the legal aspect would never worry us. This may be a Latin way of looking at it. Over here, and in the circles we would have moved in, marriage is more or less out of date. Even old Poincaré [58th Prime Minister of France, 1926–29], not a wild boy by any means, lived for ten years with Mme Poincaré before they got married.

A firm and loyal partnership between man and woman, by whatever name it goes, entails no social condemnation and is not looked upon as a crime, but with whatever measure of respect the feelings and the attitude of the pair command.

However, I do not for a moment deny that marriage is, in principle, preferable, whenever it is attainable. I trust I did manage, when I was privileged to meet you, and also when I spoke to Walter [Gellhorn, MG's brother] and to Cam [Becket], to convey my earnest desire to marry Marty.

Unhappily, I found myself impotent to do as we had planned. Marty and I parted, when she returned to St. Louis, with the understanding that I was returning to France to try my hand at verbal persuasion. I was all the more anxious to succeed that I witnessed Marty's constant distress during the six months we spent together in the States. Almost all of that distress was due to her worrying about your unhappiness. Whereas I may safely conjecture that your own unhappiness was due to the consequences you feared for her.

Loving Marty as I do, I was spurred on to every possible effort by that distress which I had witnessed. When I failed, however, I must admit that I didn't readily accept the idea that since we couldn't be married, we ought not to meet again. However I did write to Marty frankly: "Marcelle will not divorce… show this letter to your family, talk it over with them… I am prepared to remain alone." Of course I hoped that she would answer: "I will come to you irrespective of marriage or no-marriage." But I wanted it to be her choice, and made with your agreement. I had miscalculated, since her letters following upon those news were passionate as to the feelings and yet negative as to coming. They led me to imagine Marty's state of mind as almost desperate. Frankly, when I first realized that because the divorce had failed, Marty wouldn't come, I thought at first mainly of my loss. And my main preoccupation was then to be a good loser. But when I got Marty's letters, it was plain to me that she suffered as much as I did, and hence it all seemed very purposeless. Since we loved each other, why be parted? There was one moment when we might have denied ourselves: that was when we first met, when I was married and ought not, in principle, to have betrayed my wife, when Marty was a young girl who ought, in principle, to have married quietly a lad of her own country, with no complications attached. Our love was too strong then. We broke every tie, we refused to consider the consequences. If we could do that, at the beginning, why should we now give up? So I thought, and I wrote and cabled asking Marty to come.

You, on the other hand, wondered how all this would turn out for Marty: twice she came back to St. Louis, and both times you saw her suffering. I can well understand that you should feel uneasy about letting her associate her life again with someone who has caused her so much suffering. But while she has been with me I think she has been happy, and—this is a point I very much want to make—she has been happy through her work, her intellectual satisfaction, the enjoyment of everyday life, and not because of some wild passion that was satisfied. It cannot be said that she is not herself when she is with me. I think she is more herself every day that she spends with me. She has no wild passion of any description whatsoever for me. But I think I am a suitable companion for her. I am even convinced that, far from being a rash impulse of the body or the heart, her devotion to me has its source mainly in her brain, that she finds life with me interesting because I am concerned with things which interest her, and considering that she lives mainly by her brain, I think I am justified in saying that it is a suitable union for her. However I do not flatter myself that she needs me. She will develop, irrespective of her associations. It remains to see whether it is best for her to deny herself what she has proved through two years of endurance, that she wanted. If it is best for her, I wont [sic] stand in the way.

I can quite well understand that Marty's father should think of me as enticing her time and again out of the straight path, and being a cause of unhappiness to her and of anxiety to both of you. I think I am not a cause of unhappiness to her, when she is with me. But as long as I am a cause of anxiety to both of you, I can never make her really happy; she is too devoted to you to be happy while she knows you are in anguish.

All this is not meant to lead up to anything: I am just typing down my thoughts as they come. To me, and this, maybe, will be to you proof positive of my "Frenchness," there is no problem in all this, but that which is created by your anxiety over Marty's future, anxiety which reacts upon Marty and makes her miserable.

The problem then seems to me: how to alleviate your anxiety about Marty. I understand her going to Germany seems to you a good thing, but you think it unreasonable that she should come and share my life either in Moscow or Paris. I will not discuss whether it is really unreasonable or not. I am perfectly willing to accept your judgment. As Marty cant [sic] be happy as long as you disapprove her actions, her actions should be such as to deserve your approval.

On the other hand, she does like travelling [sic], and going places, and Moscow or Paris might indeed be a prison to her.

All right: let her travel, I will remain in Moscow or Paris. I will see her when she lands, I will even board the ship at Cherbourg and go on to Hamburg with her. And after that, I will turn back and let her go on. I will not try to entice her back with me into the town where I shall have to live for my work. The work I will be doing will give me the means of helping her to go on with her traveling and her work. Please don't think this crude, but the child must live while she writes her books, it will be some time before she makes money, and as I look upon her as my wife, it is natural enough that I should do what little I can do in that direction.

This separation will not be as painful as when the Ocean lies between us. It will answer two purposes: firstly, it will put us both where we can work best, secondly, and mainly, it will, so I hope, alleviate your anxiety. I admit that it cannot pass muster as a permanent settlement, but there seems to be no permanent settlement possible other than

a) living together
b) getting married
c) parting for ever [sic]

Out of these three possibilities, a) seems to you fatal, b) is impossible. You know Marty's mind better than I do: do you recommend c)?

I am sorry to have written at such length. It is amazing how we have all been led to ponder on this problem, whereas the things of the heart are usually not a subject for conferences. I trust that a time will come, and soon, when Marty will be no more; by my fault—a cause of anxiety to you, but—by her own accomplishments—a cause of pride.

I go over my letter, and find nothing there that can appear very satisfactory to you. Maybe it was an error to write.

… Please believe most respectfully yours, and believe also that I am terribly sorry to have caused you so much grief and anxiety.

B.

MG to Bertrand de Jouvenel

October 3, 1932
Gran Hotel
Faraux

I'm sending a cable to Cam and wife in our names. [re: Cam Becket's wedding October 6th]

Beloved,

You've not told me your address—so for a whole week you'll get no mail from me! Oh misery! But anyhow you'll have a fine harvest to reap when you return to your feudal estate in the vast plains of Auteuil.

Listen, beloved, you are quite quite quite mad. I have no intentions of living until Toulouse without seeing you. I'm a pretty active group of longing flesh and blood myself. How about the weekend of October 22? Or anytime during any week? And then dear there's your birthday—October 31. Shall I come and meet you somewhere near Toulouse on that day and we'll have three days [sic] vacation before your nasty congress starts? Say "yes."

Cam is getting married in three days—a very large, society wedding it appears at Greenwich (that's a place like where the Eugene Meyers live) on the Granbergs [sic] estate. Poor Cam, he's too happy he says to be "either too amused or too embarrassed" by the show. Isn't it amazing and wonderful to think of him getting married. I'm so happy for him. I've wanted it for so long. She sounds like a grand gal; I know she'll give him love and warmth—and *sous* [money].

You would be very much in love with your wife [Though Martha and Bertrand never wed because his wife Marcelle refused to grant him a divorce, they considered each other husband and wife and so did their Paris friends.] now—she is a beauteous color—golden, if you see what I mean—and she sleeps 10 or 12 hours a night without drugs (she doesn't eat except *chocolado completo* in the afternoon) and in a day or so, god [sic] willing, she will be diving through the breakers. My ear is momentarily in fine shape. I so wanted you to come this weekend because I shall be a miracle of health.

Beloved, I adore this place and may stay—rain or shine—until Toulouse. We'll have to take a honeymoon here some time—next summer maybe. You never saw such a beach. And I'd reserved the room next to me, for you, on the sea with bath plus meals for 52 francs a day.

And my arms are very empty. (Shame on me! I shouldn't have said that. I know you can't come dearest and I really accept it.)

You may be happy about my health—it's 100% better every day. I'm beginning to feel alive.

Ah my beloved one, it is good to love you as if you were sea and mountains—and a man.

Marty

Bertrand de Jouvenel to Edna Gellhorn
October 21, 1932
1 rue du Cdt Guilbaud
Paris

Dear Mrs. Gellhorn,

I paid a flying visit to Zarauz last week-end [sic]. Marty and I we decided that she would come back to Paris. I am writing this letter because I want to explain why we came to this decision, and because I feel that I made you a promise four months ago, which I am now breaking.

I wrote to you before Marty sailed from the States saying that I would arrange it so that she would live in Germany apart from me. Now I am letting her come back to Paris, to live near me. I am fully aware that in letting her do this, nay in inducing her to do this, I am breaking a promise. But not without good reason.

Let me begin with Marty's arrival in Europe. I understand she was in New York some time before her departure. So that you didn't see what she looked like when she sailed. Nor what she looked like when she came to Havre. As for me, I was more scared than I've ever been. She was so thin, her voice was so broken, she was so weak… I can well understand her father's resentment towards me if he saw this as the result of my coming into her life. On the other hand, I felt that I'd had her fine and healthy in California, that I'd left her in perfect shape, and that separation had wrought that change.

However, the main point was to take care of her. I will not mince words. I hasten to say that she has immeasurably changed for the better. And that I have no such anxiety left. But then I was convinced she had T.B. Hence, my whole point of view was changed. Whereas I had felt that she should come to me, that I needed her, and that I was only thrusting her away to avoid conflict between her love for you and her feelings for me, I now looked upon the situation solely from the point of view of her health. At one fell stroke, all my plans, promises et al, were forgotten in the urgent desire to take care of her. If I could have taken her away with me to some place where she could be cured from her ear and where she would recover her health in general, I would have done it there and then. It wasn't possible for more than two weeks because I had started on the somewhat arduous process of building a material position for myself in Paris, and had to come back there. Hardly had I come back, when Marty was driven there herself by her ear. I don't want to stress the extent of her sufferings. I know how it tortures you to imagine it.

… She is thin and sleeps badly. It's November soon, and the weather every-where is terrible. I thought it well that she should use this rotten month to get her ear once more attended to. That is one reason why I was in favour of her coming back to Paris.

… If it be granted that she should mingle with her contemporaries, feel the drift of the world, where should she do this. I am positive that she can only do this in one of two places: St. Louis, or Paris.

A foreigner never sees the inner side of things, remains ever on the surface. To cut in deep one must be of the country, at home in it. I have always thought that Marty could do amazingly good work in St. Louis. It has never tempted her. Then let it be Paris.

Let her know this country better than she knows her own. Let her learn its past. Let her mingle with what this country has to offer in the way of minds. Let her steep her vagrant soul in stable, uneasily-influenced, obstinate and enduring France.

I can imagine your objection: "Why shouldn't she do this in Germany?" Well I'll answer that very blatantly: "Because in France she has me."

Because I can be her roots.

I will go about the business of introducing her to France very systematically indeed, as proud as one of these priests who were commissioned to educate the king's son, of old.

The easiest part will be to introduce her to the French. You cant [sic] imagine how eagerly she is expected here by the very people she'll most want to know. Either in society, or literature, or in politics, there is no circle where she will not be greeted with enthusiasm. That is nothing. In order to be at home here, she must get the feeling that she has a common culture and formation with these people.

However, I am drifting back from my main purpose. I wanted to justify my having her back here.

Well, to put it plainly, I think she needs me. She may need me intellectually as a link with reality, as I implied already. But she also needs me very humanly, because she loves me. Just as I need her. Because it's simple and natural to be together. Because all this longing and craving and fearing that we've gone through, is all right for adolescence. But the time of maturity comes. When work is the greater part of life and demands the comfort of love, not abstract, but present.

Dear Mrs. Gellhorn, I should not, maybe, add this. But Marty has recently shown herself worried by your letters. They sounded anxious and unhappy, she said. You know how much it matters to her. I have a feeling that the present message may make you easier in your mind about Marty. If not, please let me know. Because your peace of mind commands hers.

Most respectfully yours,
Bertrand

Early in 1933 Gellhorn was again pregnant by Bertrand, as their frank letters confirm. She arranged for her second abortion, this time in Paris, paid for with money she earned as a general factotum at *Vogue*, where she claimed she was grateful for the banal work. Around the same time, she visited Colette, the celebrated novelist who wrote *Cheri*, inspired by her scandalous affair with Bertrand who happened to be her stepson. Colette, nevertheless, provided sage writing advice: believe in your work as you are drafting; you can be critical of it once it is complete.

MG to Bertrand de Jouvenel   Early March 1933
                                                                      France

Belovedest, belovedest, belovedest, and really you know *mon vieux* [my old dear one] I could just go on writing that cute little word for three pages and sign "yours truly" and you'd have a letter which would accurately describe my feelings from a to z.

I haven't written since you left because the old wife has been pooped—so pooped in fact that it took me 2 days to read a thriller. From that you can gather in what decay I find myself.

Last night it [ear infection] burst by God (what a surprise!) and goo-d [sic] all over the compress… after this if anything happens I'm going to murder myself and send me to you in a trunk (cf *The Squeaker* by Edgar Wallace)

… Smuf, a man's first duty is to be a hot water bottle to his wife and I think you better hurry back as I am very mizable [sic] and shivery unless I can bury myself in you like a flea.

… Please lets [sic] go and live on a desert island with a weekly supply of thrillers and chocolate milkshakes and just be two happy little thugs.

I most pashunately [sic], lustfully, animally and all other ways adore you and I am ever thine.

Terpsichorean Turnip

MG to Bertrand de Jouvenel   Early March 1933
                                                                    France

I'm taking quinine hoping that it will stir up my laggard insides. Being fertile is a great handicap. God knows we can't afford young or the extermination of young. We'll have to be wizards of carefulness in the future. Should I need any probing I'm in grand physical condition and that will be an asset.

My dearest heart, come to me; we are a pair of Siamese twins, you and I; when one cuts such twins apart one or the other or both dies. They have taken nourishment through each other and alone they aren't equipped to live. That's us. It's terrible isn't it; if either of us stumbled under a bus or fell for a blonde or a brunette, it wouldn't be merry for the other. But there's no use dwelling on future risks; better to lap up the present and be thankful for it.

I love you. Will you meet me in Lavandou, laddie? Many warm wet kisses, dripped all over your dear little mug.

M.

MG to Bertrand de Jouvenel   Early March 1933

Beloved,

I'm surely having a child so will have to return to Paris the 23rd [March] at latest in order to get fixed up before my job starts… so PLEASE COME QUICK. I miss you too much I can't write a line… just roam around like a dog with colic and no friends. Oh hurry hurry.

Forty-five kisses wherever you want them and I do so love you.

M.

MG to Bertrand de Jouvenel   March 30, 1933
                                                             Paris

These scratchy, useless days—darling darling—it makes me want to scream when I see time wasted. Money is nothing compared to time; there's always more money and even if by some economic miscarriage one is *sans sous* [without a dime], what does it matter. But time; God how valuable it is, and how crazily one lavishes it on the dingy, squirrel-in-a-cage details of life.

Me, I'm feeling like a shoe-string that carries electric current (impossible image.) I've lost 2 kilos in four days—which is fine for my figure and grim for my nerves. I'm pooped and jumpy, wasting my substance as usual. A job will come as a boon; you needn't worry about my efficiency at *Vogue*. I regard my future career as *femme de ménage littéraire* [literary maid] with positive gratitude.

Saw the great Colette yesterday and found her lovable, really so. She is sweet to me, tender I think; she cherishes a strange *rancune* [rancor] against your father—I should never have thought him worth while [sic] as a subject for endless bitterness. We talked of this and that; what impressed me was to come in and find her writing on a book, with such steady, bored persistence, so little flame and fireworks—but just determined weariness of one adding up accounts… What wouldn't I give for that will and discipline. She asked me to come back; I hope she meant it because I should like to go. And she said, after I talked a little with her about my book, '*Je crains que vous êtes trop intélligente.*' [I believe you are very intelligent.] I was properly astounded and slightly *méfiante* [proud]. Then she explained, '*Vous jugez ce que vous faîtes quand vous êtes en train de la faire; c'est fatale. On doit croire dans son travail; vous pouvez le critiquer quand c'est finit.*' [You judge what you're writing while you're in the middle of it; that's fatal. One must believe in one's work; you may criticize it once it's complete.] At the moment, I can't do anything—my brain like my tummy feels desperately unsettled.

Sweetheart, your funny little dusty letters from Rome; bored they are—bored and at a loose end. You are so accustomed to having your own life; to doing your work or playing as and when you like in your own way. Obviously, being courtier—which really only means waiting in ante-rooms and smiling like a well-bred statue and echoing the last three words of what anyone says to you—is no *métier* [profession]. One of the great sillinesses of life is that people like your father always live in places like the Palais Farnese (they might as well live in a metro for all the imagination they bring to life) and that people who would revel in that gilt luxe, and manage to act up to it—being a cross between Cecil de Mille, Eric Stroheim, Oppenheim, and Hans Andersen—always live in small, neat houses in the *banlieu* [suburbs]. However, as I'm not there I can't know how dun-coloured it is, or the extent of your disappointment. And besides I don't long for rococo furniture and footmen in livery; I want flowers and sun and grass to roll in and air to breathe and sun and long, intensely empty days.

My darling my darling. Come back when you can. I shall be so absurdly happy to see you, for I take very little pleasure in life unless I have either you or country; and if I have both I am probably too happy to be decent.

I love you Smuffy.

Kisses, as many as you want.
Marty

In her journal on June 20th, Gellhorn observed that King George V gave a speech at the World Economic Conference in London "in a mild stammery voice," partly in French and read "with a true British schoolboy accent." He sported a "perfectly cut morning coat," a white carnation in his buttonhole.

The labyrinthine Conference Building perplexed Gelhorn so she asked a Hungarian journalist, "who was polishing his monocle with an air of acute cynicism," how to get access to the delegates. He explained, "It's very simple—just think of Dante's Inferno. Up there are the committee rooms—you can just call that Hell."

Having sat in corridors "like a dejected wastebasket," waiting to speak to members of the German delegation, Gellhorn finally cornered Herr Haempstaengl. She observed that he was "even Nazi in his tailoring." In 1921, he "made an acquaintance of an inspired but impoverished young man named Adolf Hitler… and said to himself, 'This man is going to become a great power and I believe in him.'" Among his duties, Haempstaengl composed Nazi marches and hymns. Officially, he was a press liaison officer and translator, interpreting during interviews between Hitler and foreign statesmen or journalists.

MG to Bertrand de Jouvenel

June 1933
Savoy Hotel
London

Beloved,

Heinmann's taking my book! [*What Mad Pursuit*] Can you believe it? Oh *God* I'm happy. Love love.

M.

Gellhorn's debut novel *What Mad Pursuit*, a coming-of-age story about a co-ed named Charis Day, was turned down by four publishers before she revised it by "slashing out sex right and left," obliterating abortion scenes and "tossing syphilis into the wastepaper basket." Charis rages, for example, about "seven negroes sentenced to death because of the accident that they bummed a ride on a freight-train with two white girls. Oh, God, what stinking, rotten injustice!"[7] Gellhorn always made her "squeaking noise" about the wrongness of things for society's most vulnerable and disenfranchised. It is no accident that Charis shakes herself angrily, noting, "it was a privilege to be a witness, not a sacrifice."[8] The narrative voice is vibrant and the characters are emotionally true. Other than a couple of dated references to blotting paper and a Victrola, the novel reads as though it were written today, more than eight decades later. It's unfortunate that Gellhorn never permitted *What Mad Pursuit* to be reprinted, possibly because she believed it to have relied too heavily on her own life. Two years after its publication, nevertheless, esteemed novelist H.G. Wells insisted that the narrative was "all alive."

MG to Bertrand de Jouvenel

June 1933

Dear My [sic] love,

… My fear of war is greater than yours; I'm a real coward for one thing and for another I can't endure pain—hate it passionately—and for another thing I really care selfishly about life; I want all of it—so many things I want to do and see and feel. And then war; if war came you'd take a side and I wouldn't and that would be the first horror. And then you'd be killed and I'd either follow suit or just go on living in an empty world. There mustn't be war; and we both know there will be. So then what?

… if I make a name for myself possibly I can propagandize for peace; propaganda is the novelist's only chance for direct action. But you can't shout if no one will listen to you; therefore I've got to have some books published.

… I think I would be pretty bleak if you met a gal who was prettier, brighter and generally more appetizing (and if there aren't dozens such then it's a poorish world.) I add; should you meet such an [sic] one probably my last noble gesture will be to wish you luck. Meantime I feel desperately monogamous.

Always,
Marty

Of the many letters Edna Gellhorn wrote to Martha on found writing stock (typically from her husband's medical clinic or hotels where she stayed or on League of Women Voters stationery), this letter on the back of Hadley Hemingway's wedding invitation takes the cookie, as Gellhorn would have said looking back with amusement on her mother's friendship with Ernest's first wife.

Edna Gellhorn to MG

June 1933
4366 McPherson Avenue
St. Louis

Hadley Richardson Hemingway
and
Paul Scott Mowrer
announce their marriage
on July the third
nineteen hundred and thirty-three
London

98 Boulevard Auguste-Blanqui, Paris
after September 1st

[Reverse]

Marty, do you know this couple—I've known Hadley Richardson *always*, as you probably remember. Florence Usher, Hadley's sister tells me that Mr. Mowrer is great. What is your opinion.

M.

In July and August 1933, Bertrand and Martha were in Palamos, Spain and then Italy. They stayed with painter José Maria Sert, a friend to Colette. There was talk of the two being married there, but Bertrand had not yet secured an agreement from his wife Marcelle to divorce. However, after that time, Bertrand referred to Martha as his "darling wife" in correspondence and Martha referred to him sometimes as her husband, though she felt he'd been exactly that in spirit since they had become a couple. Sert's sculptor wife Isabelle "Roussy" Mdivani created a bust of Martha during those months.

MG to Edna Gellhorn   Fall 1933
                                                                            Paris

Matie dearest;

Thank you for your letter. It's too bad you did that with the Stixes: because of course I shall just go on being Mrs. and being accepted as such. Presently a diplomatic passport will cinch the matter once and for all. I daresay the news will be in papers sooner or later and why shouldn't it be. It's going to be awkward all round; though the only practical result will be that I can't come back to St. Louis. I do wish to God you and Dad wouldn't hang on so bitterly to woe and lack of confidence. It does seem to me that the years and my satisfaction with them ought to prove to you that this thing works and is what I want and need. Let people infer that you disapprove the match—it wouldn't astonish anybody and is doubtless correct anyhow. We've found the only way out—after some time—of the material awkwardness of unmarriage. Because we really are married, the legal fact of marriage is here accepted without question. The friends in U.S. who've heard the news also accept it. I don't ask you to lie but merely to keep silent, though probably now it's too late as you can't very well go back on that first statement. I'm sorry to be so peevish about this: but it's no joke having my careful building up just easily torn down that way, especially as all our plans for America hang on the veracity of that building up. Added to which it just all goes to prove that you no more understand or believe in us than you did three years ago and that makes me pretty hopeless. It's obviously no use trying either to explain or convince, and you won't let the facts influence you either. I regard B. as my husband and always have; my friends are willing to accept him as such—with or without legal confirmation. If you wish to go on thinking my life is ruined and that I'm a martyr to B's brutal selfishness that's your prerogative—but I have no sympathy with such an attitude. It's false and troublesome, as insulting to me as to B. If I were actually legally married to B. you wouldn't adopt such an attitude even if you felt it. I consider myself married, and resent your point of view towards my husband. I shan't discuss myself and B. anymore with you; it's no use. Also we won't worry you by coming to St. Louis; you apparently aren't willing to accept B. as a permanent factor in my life, and I have no desire to come alone and re-open stupidly a question which I feel to be finally and satisfactorily settled. We've evidently both got our prejudices and we can just go on having them. It's wasteful and painful; but it so happens that I love B. and intend to go on making my life with him; and no one but B. could ever change my purpose, and it's doubtful if he ever will. And finally about the "gossip" which you say will be inevitable in St. Louis: I don't give a damn about it. There's no gossip here: we have lived in such a way that people respect us and don't feel it suitable to whisper and criticize. Every time I came to St. Louis, I felt dirty and afraid: life is easy and proud elsewhere. I'll never come back to that untrue and unwholesome atmosphere of terror and lying; of course people will make up foul stories if they feel one is cringing and apologetic. You and Dad have always felt that I committed mortal sin; the reward for such an attitude is all the gossip one can stomach and then some. I'm sorry for you; it doesn't touch me. Like the old families of the South, St. Louis can go on fighting my civil war long after it's finished and forgotten.

I'm sorry to write this letter; probably silence would have been kinder. But I want you to know how I feel, to know also why in future I shan't attempt to make you understand my life. Please show this letter to Dad, it's for both of you. And it's probably the last letter of its kind you'll ever have to read.

Love,
Marty

Edna Gellhorn to MG

December 31, 1933
4366 McPherson Avenue
St. Louis

Dearest Marty,

In thirty-five minutes it will be Jan 1st 1934. It has been a year and a half since I have seen you—sort of like being the wife of a navy man—it's a long time between visits, but I have a feeling that I shall see you in 1934. I believe in some sort of justice and we've tried to play the game of life as well as we can so I know we'll have a lucky break and land on the same side of the ocean somehow, some-where, some time…

I've grown terribly dull myself these past months. I mean *duller*—and yet I'm very conscious of the exciting times in which we are living. Imagine this—artists are being engaged by the gov't civil works administration to paint pictures at the flat rate of $35 per week. The products belong to the gov't. Joe Jones is among those so engaged. It means security & three meals plus a roof and all time except the 30 hours they work for C.W.A. [Civil Works Administration] belong to them-selves and they can paint for themselves or for problematical purchasers. That's only one excitement of the New Deal.

Good night. Sleep well & dream of our meeting.
Your M

1934

Bertrand de Jouvenel to MG   Early 1934
                                                             Paris

My dear love,

A violent physical incompatibility seems to exist at the moment between us. For which I am entirely responsible. We each and everyone have our sexual distinctive traits, and I seem to have, with loathsome persistence, misunderstood your own. The best course seems to be going away.

I am leaving you for the present because it seems to be the best way of letting you pull your nerves together after my mistreatment of them—Most assuredly I don't propose to "make the most of my freedom" to obtain other physical experi-ences. More than ever I love and desire you, you only. I am a passionate and single minded, though incompetent, lover. I am depriving myself of the multiple joys of our intimacy with the full knowledge of what I'm losing. Life, when sleep is not shared with you, is pretty damn bleak. But if I stay, I'll just exasperate you.

Hence the momentous decision. I'm not going far, anyhow. The Republique is my anchoring ground. And for the sake of economy, I'll try and stay at my mother's.

I adore you, now and ever.

And I feel a bloody blundering fool.

B.

Gellhorn reported on the Stavisky riots in Paris on February 6th, signing the piece "Martha Gellhorn (Mme. Bertrand de Jouvenel)." That day police shot and killed 15 anti-parliamentarian protestors during a siege organized by far-right factions in the Place de la Concorde. She wrote, "as a warning and a menace, every paper carries on its front page two headlines: *Daladier Forms His Government*, and alongside—*Latest Developments in the Stavisky Scandal*." Anti-fascist organizations were created as a result of actions that day.

Gellhorn wrote a scathing little piece called "Politics *à la mode*," insisting that "It is a well-known fact: Frenchwomen prefer femininity to feminism. The reason they haven't got the vote is that they don't want it. They believe in the traditional methods: a woman wearing ruffles (with tears in her eyes) gets more than a woman in a stiff collar (with spectacles and logic to help her)." She continued to observe women discussing politics, "over tea-tables, bridge-tables, dinner-tables; in restaurants, in salons; at clubs, at the coiffeurs, at the races" as "wide hats bend towards each other." She wondered, "Are they studying politics as a patient studies his own fatal disease?"

In a late-in-life interview Gellhorn said she had no faith in politics, that "all governments are bad and some are worse." But they'd be "even worse if their citizens didn't keep their eye on them." For her, the price of freedom was "eternal vigilance;" and the "price of any good government... perpetual nagging."

MG to Bertrand de Jouvenel

February 27, 1934
Sainte-Maxime

Dear heart,

There was your first letter—like a perfectly dazzling moment, when the sun seems more than on fire, seems to be burning with a special intentness and joy. Ah, Smuffy, our week was something too miraculous to be true; I've spent lots of time these last three years dreaming about a week like that.

... For I love you very much—you must know that.

I think, for always
Marty

Bertrand de Jouvenel to MG

Early March 1934
Wednesday night

Little one, as I sit down for an all-night session (I am giving my script tomorrow and three chapters are yet unborn) I get your Ste. Maxime letter. I cant [sic] call you up because I have no provision for interurban calls. I am distressed to feel you so panicky. For God's sake, my darling, pull yourself together. I am a fine one to speak so bravely. Write to the Post Office at Cavallaire and have the letters I wrote you there sent on to you: you'll find I'm no hero. But my needs are simple. I need you, and provided I have you or news from you, I can discharge the simple duties of living.

Speaking of the Post Office at Cavallaire, I sent you money there, and that will have to follow too. I wish I could send more straight to Ste. Maxime but have no more…

Dearest, a sentence in your letter from Cavallaire terrifes me: "This arrival is a perfect replica of my arrival 3 years ago. I had the worst *cafard* [depression] imaginable on this very coast; ending in the St. Tropez incident." For God's sake, my love!

Alas, I worried terribly because I had no news from you. And now that I have some, I worry even More.

"I just want to cry and cry and cry…" Oh, Marty! Remember: nothing ever happens to the brave. But so much happens to others…

Nor do I find anything to say. But this: that writing is not all. That novels may be of little account in a capsizing world. That living is something also. It is not a question of latitude but of ardour. It so happens that you are an unending source of joy to me. If I could be to you, then you would have nothing to complain about. If not, then find someone else…

I wish you were here, and I could bear you down with the weight of my body, press you down with my knees, laugh into your mouth, and though I couldn't make you feel what I felt, I could still shake you and kiss you into warmth and into life.

War? Yes, and before five years. Run away to enjoy the last years of bliss? Is that what aristocracies were made for? Oh darling I'll take my stand. My chosen one, wont [sic] you stand by my side?

Bertrand

MG to Bertrand de Jouvenel

March 20, 1934
South of France

My rabbit,

I too am tired but withal very contented. I haven't had much chance to sleep as yet, having hopped into the bus at six in the morning yesterday to get here, and today to go back to Toulon to give copy… Nevertheless, it would be idle to pretend that I'm not delirious with joy—Stumbling back to the hotel along a path that actually smells of mimosa, is too exciting. There is a sea just in front of my window… It's too big and I'm sort of blind and it's only what I touch with the inside of my hand, and what I feel against my cheek that I'm really conscious of.

Dear heart, you must leave Paris on Tuesday to come here. Don't say no. Tis [sic] an order. Not that I want to see you. Even you I don't want to see. I suffer from a surfeit of humanity. How I've listened to them, how I've answered then: Talk, talk, talk. Willa [sic] dictator, do you think, put a tax on words?

… Dear heart, we're very much linked up, aren't we? I'm not at all in the right mood to undertake to express it better. To hell with expressing things.

But I love you.

YOU START TUESDAY.

Bertrand de Jouvenel to MG

March 23, 1934
Paris

My dear, when I had you on the phone I felt queerly shy. I didn't have anything any more to say to you. Hearing your voice was enough. I might have hung up on you. You know when we're in bed and you're going to sleep, I call you and wake you and you ask: "Yes, what?" and I don't say what, because I just wanted you to speak, and it rather enrages you. Same thing with this phone call.

Also I like to grasp your hand and feel it firm and have it press mine in answer. I don't like not being able to bear you down under my weight and keep you there, just looking into your eyes.

Your absence makes me fidget. It's my sense of touch that misses you most. I don't look at you as much as I did. I want to press my shoulder against yours. Rabbit.

We must in the future only do things that matter to us directly, not indirectly. I refuse to go to dinner with the third cousin of somebody who knows a guy who's believed to be the proprietor of a newspaper in Nicaragua…

I wish I had work to do all day, out in the open. Then I'd feel right at nights. That's what gets me, always, when I'm away in Capri or something like that. There's nothing to tire oneself with but "taking walks." I hate to take walks. That's why I liked Hollywood. I had some common work to do. Only it wasn't physical enough. I'd like to work on the land. I wish we got ourselves a farm somewhere…

I'm sorry I wasn't a boxer. That's a career that might have satisfied me. Only I'd be out of it by now…

It's exhilarating to shit but one doesn't wave the shit in the air for everybody to admire.

Good Bye. I wish you were here to kick me all night: I'd strangle you with my arm in return. That's fun, nice clean fun.

Oh, hell, come on Tuesday!

Bertrand

Bertrand de Jouvenel to MG

April 7, 1934
Palace Hotel
Bruxelles

Dear Love,

I forgot to say we're both invited to a large noisy dinner party at Robert Lange's Thursday night. I don't suppose you'll want to go. Anyhow it's in the new phonebook—28 blvd Raspail I think.

I told you in my telegram I'd leave here Friday 8 o'clock arriving *Gare du Nord* at 230' [sic] or so. I won't be disappointed if you're not there. Go out or leave town or do anything you want. I'll get you a little house by the sea this summer so you won't have to be always homeless. Arrange your plans. My sweetheart—don't consider me—I've been walking for hours thru the town feeling lost, not "O lost!" but "Ah lost!" breathing cold clammy smoke-laden air with a feeling of reaching an impersonal numbness.

How I've watched the many tempers passing on your face! How every mood that showed upon you, swayed my eager anxious heart. There is no freedom, no sense of self as a separate, independent, important entity in such love.

How I love to put my head down between your cheek and your shoulder…

Don't mind what I write… I'm tired but I'm not going to sleep. I have my articles all once in my head but I guess I won't write them. I have no business to be lank like hair and squashy like rotten melon. I am a successful man—have captured as my wife the most beautiful woman in the world—shall be able to take her all summer long travelling round the greens of Scotland and England.

Beloved—the whole of my life depends upon the kind of smile you can give me.

B.

When Gellhorn wrote to Cam Becket from Bertrand's family home in Provence at the end of April, she was trying to sort herself out emotionally. Frequently in her letters to him she was also writing advice to herself, admitting, "I am writing to myself through you." The second book to which she refers is *Ways and Means*, one that was never submitted for publication but remains in her Boston papers with a detailed chapter by chapter outline. It was several more months until Martha broke with Bertrand. She would always love him, but she also understood that he would never be free to be wholly with her. Gellhorn returned stateside in October to work for Harry Hopkins at the Federal Emergency Relief Administration (FERA), beginning the most important work of her life so far.

MG to Cam Becket

April 29, 1934
Villa Noria
France

G. Campbell, dearie:

I write you today just because I must somehow lead my mind back to the type-written word, after four days of barren paralysis with nary a key clicking on the whole peninsula. You see, I have started my second book; and therefore whether I write or not makes a hideous difference; and now I am going to be saddled with this wearying, half-finished, unquiet ache until the damn thing is done—a few years hence no doubt, what with publisher's rewritings and all the misery of trans-porting goods from manufacturer to consumer.

I'm writing about France, my son. France and the French and myself, dismayed and finally cynical amongst them. Or rather I'm writing about the Jouvenels; because I'm far too wise to write about the French. A very hard book to write, since I am trying to do it in the first person singular (a test in technique) and that is no cinch at all. You wouldn't believe how the world narrows in when you have to say *I* instead of *She*. But I must do it; because writing is more than just putting words down on paper to fill the time, hoping for money to come and a dash of fame: more than a job to ease one's conscience with against the empty passing of time. For me, it's my mind's and spirit's purge: there are things to be eternally rid of. There comes a time when one can no longer carry in one's brain, heavily, certain memories, certain aspects of the present. I did that once before: I wrote out of myself a lot of destruc-tion. My father once said: blondes only work under compulsion. It must be true. I know what hell it is to write. I know how everything goes to pieces under the strain of it, the fear of not finishing or finishing badly. It never stops and there is never a moment—until the thing is out of one's hands into alien hands—that is really rest. I am really sated with France; I have had all I want or can bear. And possibly I have had enough of the Jouvenels, the entire clan, for this life.

I don't know what to do about B. [Bertrand] because I have turned coward. Not coward about him; I writhed too much over his pity ever to want to go in for pity myself. I'm sure on that point; pity is the one great crime because it destroys two people sloppily. Besides, his world stands firm around him; he fits in so tightly into his own pattern that nothing I could do would really run him off the rails. And then he's French (and here is where I draw conclusions) and the French are realists as neither you nor I nor members of our feeble Nordic lineage can be. We are people who go mad, or drift into gutters or suicide, from broken hearts. The French, at best, go back to their work, their life, their picture frame of place, position and reality. At worst, they turn hard and scheming and vindictive. But even so, they go on; with an eye to opportunity…

I should hurt him somewhere deeply; but that hurt is part of life and not to be feared. (If one has been hurt oneself and weathered the 'buffeting,' one knows how time soothes all things, and how good an investment pain can be.) But in the end, what—he has a son, and a name which must go on; a place in his world which demands him, a role to play. And even if he doesn't love anyone again quite as he loves me, he may be happier with a smaller love; he will ask little because he has sources of riches elsewhere.

The cowardice concerns myself. I stopped lying or exaggerating to myself a long time ago; and have gotten a certain amount of deadly joy out of knowing myself and where I stand. I am 25 which is not old if one has done something but is not the beginning if one's hands are empty. I have at this moment no name: I am called one thing and recognized unwillingly as such: but my passport says something else. And this is a handicap as only I can know.

I have no money and therefore no freedom. One must not lie about these things: money is the only guarantee of privacy, the only way to operate one's fate. I should have to work—at some job which had nothing to do with me and used up more of this valuable vanishing time. It is laughable but true; I could probably only get work in Paris being a mannequin. They would all love having me: I am considered to be rather beautiful, with a good body—and enough of a lady to give that highly desirable amateur touch which all great dressmakers (the real professionals) so snobbishly seek. What else is there. The ideal is a country where I am not known, where I could stay a few years until my life grew dusty in people's eyes, with the passing of time—and vague in my own mind too. But how? And what else: going home, my mouth buttered with humility and failure, to leach on their generosity? Through ignorance, carelessness, pride and generosity: and the passionate desire to burn all boats, to prove that I had no intention of retreating. I pay for my own acts: mainly for my own pride. Because my own pride has been at the bottom of all this; possibly more than anything. Since I would not admit that I was licked by events or circumstances or people, and so—with my head down—I charged through. I shall pay for that, for a long time.

The root of the trouble is the body. I take it for granted that you would rather be drawn and quartered than share this letter with anyone. You know how I count on you; on your wisdom and loyalty. I am writing you because I want to see for myself; I am writing to myself through you.

It is a mammoth irony; I sailed against the wind, with incredible determination, and brought the whole house of cards down on my head: to sleep with a man—forbidden territory—a married man, and all of this most scandalously, bravely and openly—out of wedlock. So that it must be thought, she is a woman of great passion—with the needs of the body clamouring—and their life together must be a constant feast in honour of Venus. It has never been; that was the great error. The error of my pride—since I chose to give (out of pride—not wanting to save my hide or be afraid, and tenderness for his needs) I would go on giving. But one mustn't make love like that. It's terribly wrong: I—who have such a quiet cool body—know all that. I have a deep respect for what blood calls for, for passion, and satisfaction. Not that these things are mine; but that is my tragedy and my own fault. Bertrand has always, and still most terribly and completely, desired me. I am amazed at myself—amazed at the years that have gone by. Because I have no corresponding desire and have never had. But the years added on other things; he has always touched me more than anyone, I have always found such gayety and nourishment in his mind, and then there is tenderness—gratitude a kind of love that wavers between friendship and maternity. It is strong (foolish to deny that) and coupled with physical passion would make such a love as is rarely seen, and exists in old books and legends. Because I have suffered for him, and he for me, and very much alone we have gone together through endless rough country.

It isn't restlessness which makes this all so clear. I am not turning from Bertrand, looking dimly or pointedly elsewhere. I have no desire for affairs. My body very curiously has no need of that food—not at least now. If anything, I turn away; into greater and greater detachment. I am very happy with myself, with land and trees and the smell of things on the wind; and with my typewriter. I have enough in me to fill my life. But all my life boils and simmers, stews and burns, because something is asked which I cannot truthfully give. And though I would—have and do—give it, when I remember; it is contrary to nature to remember with one's mind what ought to be a joyful instinct. And so, I forget—or don't notice—and then there is storm, rage, misery and a kind of maimed despair. And I can do nothing; because I *know* that it would be useless even to try to fake an instinct. And possibly—oh let me be very honest—there is selfishness deep in this too; the desire to save myself, the order and rhythm of my life, not to harness and throw out of key something which runs so smoothly—alone…

It can't go on; what is there to go on to? He can take mistresses; and now—provided he was graceful enough not to place them before my eyes—I shouldn't mind. How could I? He has a right to these things which I do not—and cannot give him. But what answer is that—more complication, more confusion, more people hurt in the mess, the growing mess. And all the time, he wouldn't really be happy, because in the end it is me that he wants. And we would be acting a life, and because we acted we would only be half-alive. Whereas we have that great talent: we can live—we were made to live… Great God! what an eagerness and energy I have to live; how much living I can stand and must have…

I am not lonely, living this way, because I have given up expecting that loneliness can be blotted out by anyone else; my loneliness is my own cherished possession and probably my only one. I feel, after the waste and nervousness of too many months, a kind of order coming back into my spirit. And I know I shall write— and maybe even write better than before.

The land is gladness to my eyes; I feel positively dizzy with happiness sinking my feet into dirt, grass, sand; the pine forests smell like themselves and somedays the sun is hot and close, over this small corner of the world. Somehow inside me I have protection against passing events, people and circumstance. Somewhere within me, I know what climate I need for my own *vie intérieure* [interior life] and have found it now. And so I live, profoundly glad of each day.

If only one needn't think: next month, next year… Because I don't know, and stumble in ignorance. What can happen next? I don't see any way out. So I shall just go on with my own small garden. There is a book to write. And I shall write it. At the beginning of this letter, I told you how I used writing to purge me of memories; and I also use it as a wall between me and the present and the unpredictable future, and people, and fear…

Have you ever had such a letter?

Love,
Marty

Bertrand de Jouvenel to MG   May 7, 1934
                                                                         Paris

Marty my dear, it is six o'clock in the morning. I have just come in, having walked sixteen miles in five hours, which isn't so bad considering my rotten physical condition. Sixteen miles is the distance between Rocheville and my mother's flat.

This is how it happened yesterday. Yesterday I lunched at my father's with Marcelle, the general purpose being to thrash things out under his guidance. It all went wrong, however, the conversation drifting rapidly to what interested him the most, the political consequences of old Doumer's demise. I left with Marcelle and she drove me to Rocheville to see Roland [his son] who is in perfectly marvelous shape, kicking and giggling. In the evening, I was going to Mantes, to dine with Bergery and attend his final rally. Marcelle wished to come with me, and it was understood that on the way we would have a serious talk. We had. With the usual result. When we left Bergery, it was half past twelve. When we got to St. Germain, it was quarter past one, the last train to Paris had left. Unhappily, I had no money left to go to an [sic] hotel. Marcelle offered that I should spend the night at Rocheville. It would have been innocent enough but would not have seemed so to Byron. And I promised you I would do no such thing. When I declined, Marcelle was enraged. She said it was ridiculous and so forth. Thinking, doubtless, that I was putting myself needlessly at great inconvenience, and resenting this obvious fear of any false step. However, I left her, and as I had no money to hire a taxi, the only thing was to walk back. Of course, I signaled to the few cars that passed me, but this is not America. So I walked, and walked, till I came to the *Porte Maillot*, and there I used my only *franc* on a very welcome cup of coffee. All in all, it was a pleasant experience. And as I walked, I thought. Being hungry, and tired, I thought brutally. And I will put it down as I thought it.

This is the situation: Marcelle wants me to live with her. Well, tough. I don't want to and wont [sic], and that's all there is to it. You want me to divorce. Well, tough. I can't and wont [sic], and that's all there is to that. Now I dismiss these possibilities from my mind, because they have been found impossible, and that if I brood upon them any longer, I will destroy myself. I want to do some work. I want to go on wanting to do it. I have been obsessed by a twofold sense of guilt. I must get rid of it or it will ruin me. It is true that I have duties towards Marcelle and duties towards you. But there is nothing I can do about these duties. So I will think of nothing but duty to myself. I will not let myself be moved by anything. Marcelle's letters worked upon my feelings and tortured me. You know that. You may not be aware, though, that you also worked upon my feelings and tortured me when you stressed the unease and unhappiness you felt because of your situation. I have wanted to end Marcelle's unhappiness, but I can do it only by giving to her a love which is not mine to give. It is given wholly to you. I have wanted to end your unhappiness, but I can do it only by giving you a name which is not mine to give. It belongs to her.

I am powerless. That being the case, the only thing for me to do is to organize my life in function of my work, and first to restore my health and balance which are seriously impaired. I cant [sic] afford to wreck my work. I am going to take two, perhaps three months off, I think in Germany, probably where you said.

I may cycle through Bavaria and down into Tyrol. Afterwards I will go to Russia most probably. I am asking for that Rockefeller purse for this year, my father backing me.

Such are my plans. They are all I have to offer. Will you share it with me?

If so, come very soon, my love.
B

May 1934
4366 McPherson Avenue
St. Louis

Darling Marty, your letter is precious. Oh, my one and only girl child how I long for your complete happiness. The tragedy of motherhood is that it can't protect what it most cherishes or give the joys that it most longs to provide. But I believe that your courage and uprightness is bound to fin [sic] for you the returns I am powerless to give. Don't stop loving me, don't think for one tiniest moment that I do not need your loving devotion. I am as dependent on you for my happiness as any of those who weep and moan about their loneliness. I won't moan (at least not often) but I yearn for all that you are willing to give and rejoice in the ridiculous that is my daughter.

Mate

Edna Gellhorn to Bertrand de Jouvenel   June 1934
Le Paillaret
Mozac-Riom

Dear Bertrand,
    True to the Gellhorn tradition I write on paper "swiped" from any place. (By the way the particular spot from which this blue sheet was removed is a most enchanting retreat—Martha will tell you about it.) Our "honeymoon" has been an unqualified success—it is hard to write the word finer to anything that has been so blissful, and yet it is ridiculous to permit oneself to grow tragic about it-it would be tragic to part were it not for the fact that each of us has her *mate* at the end of the parting. Thro' [sic] al [sic] the hours of our conversations our two men have very naturally been the golden thread on which all other experiences have been strung. Fortunately, this can be so without restraint as Martha understands and loves her father and thro' [sic] Martha I have learned to know and appreciate you. To my great happiness I am carrying away with me quite a complete picture of the life you and Martha share. She has told me with pride of your important role in the France of today and tomorrow. As I read the *N.Y. Times* articles sent over by Philip [Percy, Paris bureau chief] I shall be able feebly to interpret them as they reflect what you think, and the names of your friends will mean something to me.
    Martha has been a marvelous guide and pathfinder. I shall be able to give illustrated lectures on the Côte d'Azure, the Tarn, French Cathedrals, peasants

I have met, Russian princes in exile, almost as varied a repertoire as Walter Lippmann puts out in his daily column. It's been grand fun, these two carefree weeks, and again we thank our two men for their various sacrifices which made them possible.

The Ford has performed admirably—it climbed mountains like the proverbial goat and ate up miles on the level like a seasoned racer. It was also quite restrained in its thirst for gasoline.

I am going back to find the answers to many questions in case you decide to come to the States. Some of them I can find the answers to, others are yours to solve when and as you can.

Perhaps I shall hear in mid-ocean of what happens on the eighth of July. Whatever happens on that day, or on any other, to you will continue to be of tremendous interest to an ever anxious (perhaps you can understand that) grateful (that you surely understand) and appreciating (that word means a lot) woman.

Edna Gellhorn

Bertrand de Jouvenel to MG   June 25, 1934
                                              Paris

Rabbit,

…. Marcelle has concocted a story for the Hearst press about your using her name. And she states with great firmness that she will release it whenever we start proceedings against her. Her lawyer pretends that there is one letter among those you wrote her that will unfailingly land you and probably me in jail. French law is pretty severe about this matter, you know. In other terms, she feels she holds the whip-hand.

Of course, darling, what prevents you from "jumping with me" is that you always feel trapped either by this or by financial considerations. In other terms, I have certainly not laid before you the steaming banquet of life… A loathsome metaphor if you ask me…

I am almost sure you would have loved me quite passionately if you had been properly married and endowed with a reasonable income. But I have given you a life so full of worries that you can hardly be blamed for feeling impatient with it.

The financial situation is, as yet, enshrouded by clouds of a blackish nature.

Dear love, if you drive to Hâvre, I advise the *route des Alpes* which is perfectly beautiful. Do not fail to spend a night at the *Col du Galibier*. There is a hotel there and the view is unforgettable. Do not drive through Lyon. It is absolutely foul. Strike North-East [sic], or even due East [sic] until you get to the Alps. Take the highest *route des Alpes*. The best procedure is to go to Cannes first, then through the *Canyon du Verdon* (splendid stone, like frozen assets), then North [sic].

Will write about our own possibilities whenever I find out what they are.

je t'aime le plus tendrement du monde [I love you the most tenderly of anyone in the world]
B.

Bertrand de Jouvenel to MG   June 29, 1934
                                                                      Paris

My beloved,
    you'll [sic] find this letter at Hâvre, on your way to the pier, and you'll glance through it hurriedly, more concerned about the coming separation with your mother.
    It is important, though. And you'll have to take a half-hour off to ponder over it.
    I got your relation of the shock you unwittingly gave your mother yesterday. I wanted to reply right away but forced myself to sleep over it. And this morning I delved through many of your letters. And, my beloved, I've come to the conclusion that the one sane thing you can do is sail on the *Champlain* with your mother.
    Why?
    Because the material side of our lives is not satisfactorily settled. That the divorce you set so much store upon you will not get. And that a life alternating between travel and tranquil contemplation of a beautiful country I cannot give us.
    There have been these three months. During that time you were not harassed by the need for a legal settlement and you had that sun and sea without social obligations which matters so much to you (as it does to me). And even so, you were unhappy. And I have a letter here saying, "I am sick to death of this house." And I have the memory of that walking trip which was so glamorous to me and all through which you smouldered with an anger I could not understand.
    So, my beloved, when we share the life we both love, even then you are not happy. Probably because there is between us this physical misunderstanding which leaves me half-a-man and you half-a-woman. Because we cannot achieve this *zusammen marchieren* [coming together] of our bodies. And because these wild trembling rushes of mine are wearying to you. And because your denial or amused and patronizing complacency gall me.
    There will be no divorce, my beloved. Nobody in the world can stop Marcelle from attacking you for using her name, if she so choses [sic]. And it would be a perfect suicide for us to take the initiative. It would be something as destructive as when Oscar Wilde attacked Queensberry.

… There isn't enough material satisfaction, moral satisfaction or sentimental satisfaction, in this life that I offer you to make it worth your while. I've said this before. And as I spoke, I watched your face, hoping to see that sudden quick smile which means that there is some deep reasonable reason that keeps two beings together against all logic. But, beloved, I never saw that smile, and you always concluded that the time was not ripe for separation, giving me the impression that it was only a lack of brutality that prevented you from leaving.

My beloved, you are away from me, away from tears and outstretched hands. There is a boat pulling out soon, going to your own country, and your mother is sailing on it. Never will it be so easy again to leave.

Please, do it now.

Because you'll do it anyhow. Because you cant [sic] go on acting with the blindness of passion where there is no passion. Nor can you give up your life to a cause you do not believe in.

If you turn away from that boat, retrace your steps along the pier, you'll be coming back to uncertainty, poverty and misunderstanding. How bitterly you'll regret having come back!

Because, my beloved, you don't love me.

It's such a simple, plain, little fact.

Nobody can help you by making it clear to you. Because you do all the gestures of love. You're loyal, staunch, helpful, kind. But that's not because you love me, it's just because you're a Gallahad. How can they understand that, those others who think one acts in the direction that provides "a maximum of happiness with a minimum of effort."

Dear love, don't you go imagining you love me, just because I'm away, and don't intrude on your image of me. Remember that when we meet again, your lips stumble about, impatient and incapable of meeting mine. You forget. That has been my great asset. You'll always come back to me for a simple reason. I provide you, probably better than most people would, with the raw materials out of which you can fashion the figure of your hero. But, dearest love, well do you know I'm not your hero. I am enclined [sic] to think I'm in the way of finding your hero. That you've got to clear your mind of me, and look around. As long as you are with me, you'll measure others against me; and while they will be superior in many things, they may be inferior in some; which will disqualify them unfairly. That wouldn't happen if you drew a red line across me.

You told me once that I was standing in your sun, keeping its light from you. I remove myself from it, dear love. The world is so limited with me, so wide open, so limitless if you're alone. Take this chance, my little one. Escape.

There is the wet lush welter of leaves, and in the alleys of the *Forêt de Fontainebleu,* birds bathe in every small pool at dusk before they go to sleep. I walked there and turned these things in my mind, and decided that I shouldn't grasp and hold my unwilling love, but let you go, let you scamper away, my rabbit, out of this barren hole where I watched over you so jealously, lest you should escape and leave me empty-handed.

B.

Edna Gellhorn to MG

July 4, 1934
À Bord du
S.S. Champlain

Beloved Marty—

A great deal of the joy of life suddenly is blotted out when I say good bye [sic] to you. That's a fact—yes, sir!!! Our utterly care-free and alone two weeks are as precious to me as they can possibly have been to you—they are this for both of us and I know from your boat letter and I am happy that it is so. As I wrote Bertrand, I am going home with certain satisfactions as well as the joyous experiences of our varied days.

I know that you and B. are bound together by ties that are deep and sacred, that each of you needs the other and is happy in meeting that need. Don't misunderstand that sentence—I do not see either of you as martyrs sacrificing your life for the other fellow. The hurdles you will have to take to make of your life something you can be satisfied with and enjoy are probably many, but as I see it, you are taking them in better and better form with fewer tumbles. Promise me you'll tell me about all of it, your life, I mean—I hunger to know the tiniest detail.

… Are you going to stay healthy till [sic] B. sees you? Or will you get all drag-gled [sic] before he comes from Brussels.

There are several things you said you'd do about sending me material looking to possible lecture courses. You might do this rather soon—and then a file of *La Lutte* to the N.J. office of the League of Nations & to the Midwest office. I've put their addresses on a slip of paper… Another file should go to the library in Chi-Go Regna [sic]. I'd get that address, too.

It is almost seeming a dream, our honeymoon—but unlike real dreams, I can prove it true. a) there's my red rose b) I can redream it at my pleasure, and that will be constantly.

Devotion to you,
M.

July 10, 1934

Dear Bertrand,

I'm glad you wrote to me—I think I knew all you said because Martha has told me much of it, but I'm glad to have it directly from you. All of us have been caught in a whirlpool created by conflicts of loyalties—you with yours to Marcelle and Martha, Martha with hers to you and to us, I with mine to George Gellhorn and to Martha. Being the sort of person I am—uncomplicated and usually serene I can not believe that the conflict will go on for ever [sic]—happy days must be round [sic] the corner—a solvent must be found—my faith in Martha is unwavering. I believe in her to the last ditch. She lacks everything that makes living easy, she possesses most things that make it worthwhile. She means more to my life than anyone else in the world except my husband—Her unhappiness has almost destroyed my usefulness. Please don't think here that I am weighing her happiness for a moment in relation to anything I am or am not, do or do not. No, I mean to say that Martha's happiness is my constant desire. To know that I cannot do much to achieve it for her has been hard.

Just why the Russian plan [to obtain a divorce, of sorts, from Marcelle] was abandoned I cannot guess—unless it was because Martha is not strong enough to go and/or because your work demands that you stay in France. You and Martha will work out your futures as you see best—you will be able to be together and find help that way.

I saw your *New York Times* article two weeks ago—perhaps there will be another after this treacherous Lausanne achievement. Too bad that I can't read the French papers these days.

The flowers you sent when Martha came back after California were very beautiful—for days we looked like a gorgeous Rockefeller palace. We're far from that, in fact, we're very middle class, somewhat conventional, sure that our only usefulness and happiness lies in service, sort of people. I couldn't possibly make you understand us—what would it prove? Nothing. Martha is our child—whether she likes it or not—something of us and our way of looking at life is a part of her and there's the conflict with which we began—

You two will work it out somehow, or it will work itself out—I shall always be glad to hear from you—you probably won't be able to read my answers, but I may send them.

Edna Gellhorn

MG to Cam Becket

G. Campbell dearie,

Have I written you lately—a thick letter full of this and that. Or haven't I? At any rate I got a long, pretty glum letter from you. There is absolutely no answer to make. I could write you ten typed pages full of wisdom and advice. If you did that to me, it would make me mad. When one writes as you wrote me, one does it for a purpose. Simply to put it all down on paper and push it into the post. Far away. And forgotten. I think it's inevitable. For a good many reasons; dreary, truthful reasons. To wit: we are both really very piggy people who are used to living alone and pleasing ourselves. We both expect too much. We are both fool romantics. What else. You know it all anyhow.

As for myself; I have fallen in love with England and a little with an Earl [sic]. I don't know if it can be the Earl [sic] (I only saw him for three days) or if it's his way of life and his land. I'd marry him tomorrow if he asked me. Yes, you guessed it; I would like comfort, security, ease, unanxiety and a good digestion. The Earl [sic] has this great distinction; he is the only man I have ever met in my life who had any of this world's goods who didn't revolt me after five minutes. From which you may gather that he is intelligent and charming. But, I love England anyhow.

I am coming over alone around the 10th of October. I am quite blanched with fear over the whole business. The Unknown [sic] and etc. But it must be done. I think (if I have the guts) that it will be a definite break with France and B. Nothing more can come of this union; it is getting to be destructive in a bad, chipping-off way. Which doesn't mean I'm not fond of B. or that I don't often amuse myself splendidly with him. It only means that the whole biz is sterile. There is no place to go now. I can't have that. I've cared too much about living in my day to give up. So I shall come back. Tell lots of lies and fairy stories—or none at all, and just refuse politely to answer questions—and start over again. It's a bit frightening and a bit hard. But it must be done. I hate death in any of its forms; even relatively pleasant forms. You need speak of this to no one. I count on you. And you must help me when I arrive cheering me up and telling me I'm beautiful and have lots of talent and that the world merely waits to be conquered. All lies. But essential to anyone whose insides are so tremulous and uncertain.

Of course I want money more than anything else extant. I would do deeds fair or foul to get same. I know about money; what it means not to have it. And I'm finished with dependence. Forever. If I ever marry again, I'll have a contract before I start—salary to be paid, and regular hours. As a matter of fact, I doubt whether

I'll be troubled with offers; I also doubt whether my writing will ever go over; I also doubt whether I'll find a job (unless it's being a mannequin). The outlook is not brilliant. I have little hope and less confidence. I feel pretty badly worn-out, if you get what I mean. Still, it has to be done. One can't let things slide just because one is scared out of one's wits by the unpredictable future.

... Are there any jobs for such as me in New York. And if so do they pay more than $30 a week. Or any rich men to marry; who are old enough not to want much. Or scenarios to be written. Or roulette wheels that work. You never can tell.

Blessings on you my dear. We'll be talking over my cigarettes before long. That at least will make me happy.

Love, and until soon.
Marty

Around October 10th, 1934, Gellhorn arrived in NYC on the *Normandie*. Within a few days, she contacted Marquis Childs, who covered the Roosevelt administration for the *St. Louis Post-Dispatch*. Childs introduced her to Harry Hopkins, who recruited 16 writers, Lorena Hickok the first among them, to travel across the country to report on the conditions for the unemployed and their families under the auspices of FERA.

Gellhorn had no money to buy suitable travelling clothes in which to stomp about derelict towns, so she wore the Parisian couturier hand-me-downs she brought with her from her years abroad. Soon she became utterly absorbed in the work of meeting and listening to the destitute in the textile communities to which she was sent in the Carolinas and New England, barely concealing her fury about the treatment of the unemployed in her lengthy reports back to Harry Hopkins.

In an itinerary she made, outlining her whereabouts month by month from 1929 through 1945, Gellhorn noted that in November 1934 her first novel was published and she "met Roosevelts." Edna Gellhorn and Eleanor Roosevelt had known each other through the League of Women Voters, so Edna arranged an invitation to dinner at the White House for Martha, which she remembered attending in a black sweater and skirt, the only decent clothing she had.

Although Gellhorn had ended her affair with Bertrand de Jouvenel, they continued to correspond, confiding in each other about their loneliness and the work in which they were trying to find purpose. The reports she wrote for Harry Hopkins, he sent on to Mrs. Roosevelt. It was during November and December, reporting from the Carolinas and Massachusetts, that Gellhorn found her narrative voice, writing with outrage about the treatment of the nation's most disenfranchised citizens, the beginning of a lifelong determination to make her "little squeaking observation about the wrongness of things," and to work for change. She "was not the sort of person" who wrote about the big picture. She recorded what she saw and heard and how people lived. Writing would always be her "helpless small form of protest."

Bertrand de Jouvenel to MG

October 24, 1934
Paris

The fat morning-coated self-important ones meet in Bruxelles to squabble over the franc and they meet in London to squabble over cruisers. Farras, up in his cell on the hot hill of Monjuch, wonders whether next dawn they'll come and stick him against the wall that overlooks the sea and shoot him. In Paris, they're still waving—but now with some weariness—the overworked corpses of February—and I stand here in the sun out of it all thinking of us.

Thinking what bloody fools we've been—books! We want to write books and they won't be so damn good that we have to kick up such a fuss about them. Old gentlemen in wicker armchairs will read them and swear because their coffee isn't hot enough. We are not terribly good writers, you know. And as far as influencing the course of history, well all sorts of bums have done it. Having over us at least the advantage of being *sure* of their wisdom and capacity.

We were unique, we could be unique, in one thing only.

There was enough beauty, enough courage, or foolhardiness, enough will to stick to our own standards, in us, to make our love—may I call it that? Something that stood out, clear cut, something that could serve as an example...

Our couple—that was something—and now you've gone and told them all what they never should have known, what they—in the base part of themselves—wanted to know, that it wasn't as brave, as shining as it looks...

Of course it was imperfect—of course I was clumsy and you were nagging—and we didn't hit it off well in bed. Oh God, how unimportant it all is—like constipation and belching, who wants to hear about that—but it was a march all the same—we stepped together—we were contemptuous of everything and of ourselves—exacting. We stood for a way of living.

There's an image. That was our work. We should have put strong glass between it and the crowd—but no—we didn't wait for others to draw charcoal mustaches on our lips. We went and did it ourselves!

Well rabbit, that's all I have to say.

Always.
B.

       November 5, 1934
Charlotte

My dear Mr. Hopkins,

My original report on South Carolina covers 62 pages; it is a bare and not very sprightly statement of facts; record of interviews; descriptions of homes, mills, people. This will have to be a tablet-form version. What generalizations I make on South Carolina are based on those records. I visited eight towns, talking with everyone from mayors, mill owners, doctors, Federal Emergency Relief staff, to employed and unemployed workers.

To begin with: the relief load is going up everywhere. This is due in part to oncoming winter; and also to the fact that some mills have not reopened since the September strike, and that others have permanently discharged people involved in the strike. The general local criticism of relief here is that it is a "dole" and is "pauperizing" people: by which the local gentry imply that relief clients refuse jobs in private industry. The main factual attack is against the 30 cents hourly work relief pay: local private pay for manual labour is between 7 ½ cents to 10 cents an hour. County administrators, social workers advocate less pay and longer hours; so that the total relief would be the same (or preferably more) but that the relief clients would be occupied all week instead of a small fraction of a week.

As for the relief itself, all the authorities tell me that it is below subsistence level. The relief organization attempts to give some household equipment when it is absolutely necessary. This below subsistence relief is probably not responsible for, but it is continuing, a chronic health condition. There is much pellagra here: (I have seen it ranging from diseased skin to insanity). There is anemia (as well as rickets, worms, bronchitis, and other maladies due to lowered resistance) and all the doctors speak feelingly about the future of the children, from the health point of view.

The relief clients in South Carolina must be divided into three groups: first, unskilled negroes and border-line [sic] whites; second, industrial workers and tenant farmers; third, white collar. The white collar class is the hardest to study; if they are on work relief, they become broken and demoralized. Their pride is destroyed by the beggar-aspect of presenting charity orders. I have seen cases, where a nervous condition (produced by despair) which bordered on insanity was corrected practically overnight by giving the man, or woman, a job with some dignity and responsibility attached to it.

You suggested this question: "Is the sense of insecurity spreading?" It's here. In every shape and form; in every class. Take the low-class relief cases; their fear is that the government will stop feeding them, that the winter will be cold and no one will give them shoes and coats, coal or shelter. The industrial worker, employed, lives in a kind of feverish terror about his job. He is frightened that the mill will close; or run at such reduced time that his wage will not suffice for food. He is frightened of the winter; of having no clothes, of being unable to send his children to school. The white collar worker is in the same boat, though probably with less specialized or immediately material fears.

It goes from the bottom to the top; mill owners show me ledgers which are beautifully done in red ink; they all tell me (with one exception) that business is worse than last year; there is a lack of confidence, no demand, etc. etc. I have a feeling that people are good and panicked. As a footnote to this sense of insecurity; no employer has said that he would increase employment within the next three to six months. On the contrary, they have all said they expect to curtail. Naturally this gets around; and rumors are rife (and have been fostered in the press in a vague, whispering way) that the Federal Government is going to close up relief here in January. All this soothes no one.

But despite this sense of insecurity, I am astonished by the good humor, or faith, or apathy (or even good sense) of the unemployed; and the still (but not very happily) employed. There are no protest groups. There are no "dangerous reds." If anything, these people are a sad grey; waiting, hoping, trusting. They talk of the President very much as if he were Moses, and they are simply waiting to be led into the promised land. There is no revolutionary talk; and the mere suggestion of violence is rejected. The strikers are all proud of being "peace-loving" men and tell you with joy that "there wasn't even a fist-fight" and never will be.

I think the problem is not one of fighting off a "red menace" (those two goofy words make me mad every time I see them); but of fighting off hopelessness, despair, a dangerous feeling of helplessness and dependence. At the moment however "we're counting on the President; he's a man of his word and won't let us down."

The health problem is really terrific. Inadequate medical set-ups for the poor; and ignorance. Syphilis is uncured or unchecked; and to use the words of a doctor who runs a county v.d. clinic, "it is spreading like wildfire." Another fine problem is that of birth control. On the relief rolls it is an accepted fact that the more incapable and unequipped (physically, mentally, materially) the parents, the more offspring they produce; which offspring are in degeneration from their parents, and can merely swell the relief rolls. I can't see where or why this should stop; unless— in conjunction with relief—there are clinics; both to care for and improve present health, and to check the increase of unwanted, unprovided for and unequipped children.

I'm full of ideas which can't possibly interest you; you sent us out to do a reporting job which I hope will be satisfactorily done.

Bertrand de Jouvenel to MG

November 15, 1934
284 Boulevard St. Germain
Paris

My love,

Your letter from Charlotte [South Carolina] came this morning. It had to come: my need was so great. And now, now I am happy and proud and strong: not alone any more. You have gone among them. We will always give up the sun and sea and go among them: it is our appointed place. We will grow old and ugly. But not with the age and ugliness of pleasure seekers. There will be dignity in that age and ugliness: the marks of fights well fought, of angers kept alive, of visions remaining unblurred.

We will go on like this: if apart, spreading our common net further afield, fishing a double set of impressions, finding out twice as much about the wrongs of the world. If together.....

My beloved, will you not let us be together some time not too far away? Not to love. Let us not call it love, this strong link of exacting comradeship. But to feel the warmth of our alliance. It is an alliance, is it not, sworn on the roads of Italy, when the carnations, one by one, slipped from your hair.

My love. There are but two things strong and beautiful within me—it is that force of indignation and that force of love. Oh please let them be one. Let me love you with that same leap of the heart which the vileness of the world calls forth.

Je ne peux plus te parler anglais. Mon chéri, mon amour, mon petit, tu es tout ce que j'admire, tout le en quoi je crais, ne te refuses pas à moi. Je t'aime, je suis tout tendu vers toi. Laisse me te retrouver, tenir ta main, appuyer ma joue à la tienne. Laisse moi écouter ton recit furieux de tout ce que tu as vu et senti. [I cannot speak to you anymore in English. My sweet, my love, my little one, you are everything I admire, everything in which I believe, do not refuse me. I love you, I am completely tender towards you. Let me reclaim you, take your hand, press my cheek to yours. Let me listen to your furious tale of everything you have seen and felt.]

mon cher amour [my dear love]
B

MG to Harry Hopkins

November 26, 1934
Massachusetts

My dear Mr. Hopkins,

I want to deal with a subject which is not included in our instructions. The subject is the administration of relief. I would not hand on this information if I had only heard it, but it is impossible in travelling through the state and seeing our relief set-up, not to feel that here incompetence has become a menace; and that the unemployed are suffering for the inadequacy of the administration.

It seems that our administrative posts are frequently assigned on recommendations of the Mayor and town Board of Aldermen. The administrator is a nice inefficient guy who is being rewarded for being somebody's cousin...

I think this is a wretched job: wretched in every way. I have seen about four people who seemed both equipped and devoted, dealing with FERA work. Politics is bad enough in any shape; but it shouldn't get around to manhandling the destitute.

Now about the unemployed themselves: this picture is so grim that whatever words I use will seem hysterical and exaggerated. I have been doing more case visits here; about five families a day. And I find them all in the same shape—fear, fear driving them into a state of semi-collapse; cracking nerves; and an overpowering terror of the future. These people are probably (by and large) more intelligent and better educated than the unemployed I saw in the south—which isn't unfortunately saying much. The price of this intelligence is consciousness. They know what they're going through. I haven't been in one home that hasn't offered me the spectacle of a human being driven beyond his or her powers of endurance and sanity.

And they don't understand how this happened. There are some cases in every locality of unemployables; people who have lived for two or three generations on Welfare [sic]. (Why aren't there sterilization laws; all such cases are moronic, unequipped physically or mentally to face life—and they all have enormous families.) But the majority of the people are workers, who were competent to do their jobs and had been doing them over a period of years ranging from a dozen to twenty-five. Then a mill closes or curtails; a shoe factory shuts down or moves to another area. And there they are, for no reason they can understand, forced to be beggars asking for charity; subject to questions from strangers, and to all the miseries and indignities attached to destitution. Their pride is dying but not without due agony.

... I could go on and on. It is hard to believe that these conditions exist in a civilized country. I have been going into homes at meal time and have seen what they eat. It isn't possible: it isn't enough to begin with and then every article of food is calculated to destroy health. But how can they help that; if you're hungry, you eat "to fill up—but the kids ain't getting what's right for them; they're pale and thin. I can't do anything about it and sometimes I just wish we were all dead."

Health: the Welfare [sic] nurses, doctors, social workers, the whole band, tell me that t.b. is on the increase. Naturally; undernourishment is the best guarantee known for bum lungs. The children have impetigo—as far as I can make out dirt has a lot to do with this. Rickets, anemia, bad teeth, flabby muscles. Another bright thought: feeblemindedness is on the increase. Doctors speak of these people as being in direct degeneration from parent to child. My own limited experience is this: out of every three families I visited one had moronic children or one moronic parent. I don't mean merely stupid; I mean definitely below normal level intelligence, fit only for sanitariums.

Again, due to unemployment and also to prevalent low wages (all these mill hands and shoe workers are working part-time; and their wages are not more—and often less—than relief), families are evicted from their homes. So they double up, in already horribly overcrowded houses. The result (my sources are labor leaders, social workers, doctors, nurses) is increased nervous disorders; and the nurses who work in the schools speak feelingly of low scholarship; the nervous state of the children—involuntary nervous gestures, sex perversions, malnutrition, increased t.b.

Again I can only report that there are no organized protest groups: there is only decay. Each family in its own miserable home going to pieces. But I wonder if some day, crazed and despairing, they won't revolt without organization. It seems incredible to think that they will go on like this, patiently waiting for nothing.

… It fills both the workers and the unemployed in this area with astonishment that there is nothing for shoe factories to do; but none of them have shoes to put on their feet and are facing the winter with husks of shoes bound up in rags.

I'm not thrilled with Massachusetts.

Sorry about these reports, but it is impossible to gloss over conditions. I wish you could send somebody who could stay longer and do a more thorough job; but I honestly believe anyone would simply find the same and more of it.

My next report will cover New Hampshire.

Yours very sincerely,
Martha Gellhorn

MG to Bertrand de Jouvenel   December 2, 1934
                                                                    Providence

Smuf darling,

Today is low ebb. The kind of dark day one passes, lying fully clothed, on a bed, numb and doubting. Today I am hopeless about this country and other countries; about myself and find no suitable reason for going on, only an unlovely instinct called self-preservation, which has always seemed a footling [sic] reason for life.

I'm pretty dismayed about America. Just suffering, just misery wouldn't shock me. I've seen it before; it seems an integral part of our worlds of plenty; our luxurious Frigidaire-radio-automobiles-for-the-masses civilization. To see people living sub-marginally is no new horror; Hunger isn't new: I remember years ago seeing the freight cars lying on their sides with vegetables and fruit pouring into the sewer water of Mississippi; and knew that forty miles away people were eaten and destroyed by pellagra (which comes because vegetables curiously enough are not obtainable, costing too much money.) But what is new is the clear realization of this human material: and it's bad—it's underequipped and what will change that…

I think a lot about Lavandou; and our neighbours. They were a sorry lot God knows; those peasants in their filthy houses. But they were strong; and some instincts guided them; and the little Italian we had at the end was pretty on feast days, in white, and loved to dance, and ran a lovely home, and was clean…

Oh yes I suppose it's the same everywhere; horrible and hopeless. But what is the end, what is the answer. What world can be built on such foundations… Half of the people I see accept this relief querulously, their only complaint is that a neighbor is getting more. What neighbor I ask; where; how many in his family; have you ever stopped to think that he may have a larger family, sickness; have been out of work longer, have less resources. No, and what do they care: he's getting more—that's all that counts…

I'm all mixed up. And beginning to wonder this: is our disordered and hopeless world the final battle for the survival of the fittest. These people I am seeing—the unemployed—are (at least 50% of them) below normal intelligence; sick; unfit. We are keeping them; and they are reproducing. Their families mount more in these empty days than ever before; what is there for them to do…

I needn't worry; we'll have a war (how horrible and terrifying the papers are; what are these criminals who rule the world up to). And this war will leave behind only the incompetents; and civilization will be keyed to them. I thank God I have no children and I want none. This mess is unworthy of new life.

As for me: I am ill—principally from nerves, and because my brain is rushing in unhealthy circles… And very sick at heart; and very alone. Another myth: America is beautiful… every town and city I see is a fresh shock to accept. People are ugly too; ugly and vulgar… Poor the way I mean it; there are too few faces with warmth and intelligence, some harmony between experience and spirit.

I have only a week more of this may God be thanked. And don't much care what I do next…

Cam presents a very interesting problem; he has abandoned me. It is very strange; no doubt his wife doesn't like me (I'm sure she isn't jealous.) But I think she "disapproves." And it's very curious how Cam's withdrawal has startled me; how it's made me feel that this world is not mine; that I will find nothing here. At best one finds merry folk with whom to drink and dance; at worst one finds pompous ignorant bores. But how about friends, and lovers; how about all the ritual and tradition of living. What do these folk use for blood; how do the years go by. Gawd [sic], you can see I'm low; I warned you at the start. But if I write and send this, I shall be purged a bit. And I don't know anyone to whom I could send such a letter. I have no one here to talk to—think of it—120,000,000 people; and the rabbit hasn't found a pal. Well, well, no doubt there's something wrong with the rabbit.

Bertrand de Jouvenel to MG

December 8, 1934
284 Boulevard St. Germain
Paris

My dearly beloved,

I always admired your command of the language, your admirably accurate choice of words. You reach an almost surgical precision in your last letter. "If you can write to me without regret OR HOPE." "I don't want you to bank on me." And later on, the neat phrase about sleeping with gents, so rich a source of nightmares.

This admirable lack of humanity is combined with that everflowing deep rage against injustice, imbecility and weakness. It may please you to know that, here, we've won a very great victory, gotten an agreement with Germany over the Saar. I enclose an article wherein I sing a paen to Laval. Jules Remains was greatly instrumental in getting Laval to do the right thing. And Goy, a representative of the veterans. And maybe the *Petit Journal* played its part too. The interview I took of Goy was reproduced by 400 papers. That is one victory. Negative of course: the people are not more beautiful. They wont [sic] fight, that's all. I look upon the dwarfish, spitting me in the street, and say to myself: this man wont [sic] be filled and I've had some part in that.

Another victory half-won, of the same negative nature: fascists and antifascists may not fight after all. They may get to understand each other. I've interviewed successively the ringleaders, making it appear that they all wanted the same things. The dragon Philippe Henriot came out with a statement against the gunmakers which was a sensation. Then I've managed to squeeze in something about Bergery. I had to make it very colourless but its [sic] in anyhow. Preventing harm, that's all. It doesn't matter if one doesn't get paid which is unfortunately the case.

Through Roussi [sculptor married to José Maria Sert], Bettina [Bergery], Vera Lombardi, I see beautiful people all the time. Which forces me to wear tuxedo or dress-suit, and it's good for me. By the way, I wish you wouldn't allude to Simone Téry as my mistress. I have no mistress, doubt if I will ever take one.

And now that I've written as you want me to write, I'll spoil it all by telling you I cannot sleep, and am, quite without hysterics or nervosity, slowly shriveling up. I don't think anybody had heard any admission of sadness from me. I am not sad. I am very quietly, desperate. There is, will be, nothing else for me, in the way of private life, than you. Nothing else in the way of dreams, than you. I have gotten old enough and stiff enough not to blow up, ever. It just eats away inside. I don't know how long one can stand up, like this, looking just silent and not amused. But I warn you that someday, probably seen, I will arrive in Washington, ask you whether you can accept to have me be, in the background, undemandingly, a companion, the warrior's husband, someone to be talked to when one returns from the fray. Then, if you turn me away, I will know I've lost for good and all the only battle which holds a reward for me.

Always, alas.
B

THREE

The Trouble I've Seen

"I want to write great heavy swooping things,
to throw terror and glory into the mind."

—Martha Gellhorn, letter to Hortense Flexner

Gellhorn continued to work for FERA, with Washington, D.C. as her home base. She was "so angry about the treatment of the unemployed by the people who handled the dole" that she stormed back to Harry Hopkins' office and said, "I am going to leave and I am going to expose this." He said, "Don't do it until you've talked to Mrs. Roosevelt." So she went to the White House and "shouted to Mrs. Roosevelt about how terrible this was—the suffering of the people which was not only physical but also emotional," and Mrs. Roosevelt said, "You must talk to Franklin." Gellhorn was fired a couple of months later in August for inciting a riot among the unemployed in Idaho. She had suggested to the men to throw a brick through the window of the relief office at night in order to get attention. It worked. "The FBI thought revolution is starting. The FBI fellas said to these unemployed people, who is your leader? Who inspired you to this act? And, they said, the relief lady. Me."

Remarkably, the Roosevelts invited Gellhorn to move into the White House until she sorted herself out. There she met world-famous British writer and socialist H.G. Wells, who was invited to dinner by the Roosevelts while he was visiting Washington. He thought the president and first lady's home was "a queer ramshackle place like a nest of waiting rooms with hat stands everywhere." Wells became an important advocate for Gellhorn's writing, even personally negotiating her book deal for her Depression-era fiction collected in *The Trouble I've Seen*. He wrote many intimate letters to Martha throughout 1935–36 that she kept. Twenty years after his death, she wrote, "he was a dear; in some way I cannot explain I felt him to be vulnerable and solitary and disappointed. But I now think everyone ends disappointed. I find these letters very moving now, though I cannot remember thinking anything much about them when they arrived. Now they do make a picture of the inner solitude of a man who has won all his worldly battles and been acclaimed for his victories and still can't really understand why that isn't good enough." The letters from him "give the impression that a great passion was about to flower or be nurtured, and a lifelong union was being planned." However, Gellhorn insisted that Wells' *billet-doux* to her were "one of the purest examples of the imagination of a writer." Three decades after she received his letters, she regretted that she had been "so light-hearted and insensitive." At that time, in her early 20s, it did not occur to her "that anyone could be old, famous, rich, and working hard, and still be in trouble."

Throughout 1935, Martha also corresponded regularly with Bertrand, who clearly remained in love with her, insisting "that if there is some sort of Paradise (which I imagine as a place where one will be at one's best, than which there is no greater bliss), I'll be there at your side and no one else's." In August, he joined her at a friend's home in Connecticut where she was working feverishly on *The Trouble I've Seen*, the book that emerged out of her FERA work. Of all of the men in her life, he understood her best and loved her most fiercely.

Martha's father had cancer surgery at the beginning of 1936, but, although he believed it had been successful, he died unexpectedly in his sleep, his hand on an open book, on January 25th at the age of 65. Martha returned to the family home on McPherson Avenue in St. Louis for a few months to support her mother as she grieved. By June, however, she was using H.G. Wells "for bed and breakfast" at his new home at 13 Hanover Terrace, near Regent's Park in London—payback, she felt, for having been so annoyed by him the previous fall when he stayed with her in Connecticut. Then, he had bored her by talking about the Ice Age in the morning and finishing up with a treatise on Henry James by nightfall.

Throughout the summer of 1936, Gellhorn moved between France, Germany and Austria as she wrote her novel *Peace on Earth*, another book never submitted for publication because she judged it "worthless" after a year's work.[9] While in Germany she learned of the war in Spain and resolved to find a way to go there "as an act of solidarity" with Spanish citizens fighting for democracy.

She returned to St. Louis in November to be with her mother and her younger brother Alfred, then attending medical school, through the first Christmas without Dr. Gellhorn. The family decided to visit Florida, and when Miami bored them, Alfred suggested they take a bus ride to Key West.

1935

Eleanor Roosevelt to MG

February 6, 1935
The White House
Washington

Dear Martha,

I do not know when Hick [Lorena Hickok, fellow FERA investigator working for Harry Hopkins, but also intimate of Eleanor Roosevelt] is coming back, because it depends on when Mr. Hopkins has work for her.

I hope I will see you very soon and am glad you had a chance to see your brother.

Affectionately,
Eleanor Roosevelt

Bertrand de Jouvenel to MG

February 8, 1935
Paris

My dearly beloved child, your most welcome letter has so raised my spirits that I shall attempt to answer in English, knowing full well my incompetence. I'll flounder and then revert to French. It was very kind of you to let me know about your health and finances. They were a great source of worry to me. But, if you have Mrs. R [Eleanor Roosevelt] to give you your daily gymnastics, and the Secretary of the Treasury to hold the purse for you, all is well. Then you can be the Washington Traviata. Paint to your admirers the same picture of yourself that you painted to me, and fluttering hearts will be offered by the thousand.

I feel very light-minded because I've been so anxious about you and now all's well. I can form nothing but childish phrases. But I find even your style deteriorates. So why should I try?

I liked your story about my blondes. "Dealing with Blondes" might be a good title for a film, don't you think? As a matter of fact, any relations with women— what a coarse formula—are very strictly forbidden even by the more lenient doctors. I find it rather pleasant to be thus fenced in.

France, unlike America, is a poor country and gets tougher every day. So that making a living and paying off debts seems to be enough to fill up one's life, or what there is of it.

I see very lovely people that I enjoy. Rome was a discovery. I met people who are tall, scornful and sad. I like that. Their images remain in my mind, samples of a more romantic world. Occasional letters from that country which must have been rather marvelous before the vulgarity of Fascism came into being please me greatly.

I don't ask people to give me anything. I demand that they should be something. When they are, I am immensely thankful. For it is a very ugly world.

No, dear love, I have given no one a chance to make me unhappy. Or either to make me happy. I have given my love nor even my confidence to nobody. I stand quite alone. And there isn't overmuch "standing" about it either.

The curious selfishness of those who have a most earthly battle fighting itself out within themselves, has taken hold of me. I seek no other riches than sleep, of which I have little. And I manufacture for my very own use a sweet silent world wherein my most beloved child smiles all over a sunburned face.

B.

Percy Philip was one of the first people Gellhorn met when she arrived in Paris in 1930. Since he was the local bureau chief for the *New York Times*, she had hoped he would be able to provide her work as a foreign correspondent. Gellhorn was never a stringer on his staff, but he remained a cherished contact, someone who could provide her with news of personal interest from France while she worked and travelled elsewhere.

Percy Philip to MG   February 26, 1935
                                                     16 rue de la Paix
                                                     Paris

Now this is serious. That you should cable about the state of B's [Bertrand de Jouvenel] lungs after having received a sloppy letter from him is one thing. You should of course have known perfectly well that he was confusing his lungs with his emotions—but that can pass.

… You would have rejoiced in your young man going forth to battle—snorting. For he did snort. He was full of fight. It was the first time since you left that he had enjoyed anything. The de Js are like that. They waste their time in the conquest of women but their real instinct is for a fight. That is why they are pacifists and can't keep out of even the driveling politics of France.

… And so to you and your affairs. What a scrapper you are—to grudge a man a decent bout with a sword. Fighting is your life—sex duels social duels political duels. I wouldn't put you beyond having a hair pulling one of these days. Your health worries me—with sleeping pills and fainting fits. Of course I always knew that lovely body of yours would have finally to pay for the whirling speed of your mind and your emotions. When you got yourself involved with a lad who can go even faster than you without tiring then did I regret that it hadn't been some sluggish fellow like myself who had conquered you. Whats [sic] silliest is that you should worry about him. My darling—you are crazy to think that kind needs help. There's a hard core in him that will be untouched when you and all the others who have wasted themselves helping him have burnt out.

… Look at yourself—playing *femme fatale*—outwardly to your swains hard-boiled—and showing me that poached egg of a heart of yours. Let's laugh, my dear, I need someone to laugh with these days very badly. For things have hurt me and the joke I have made of living has turned against me. I shall out laugh and outjoke it and I aint [sic] asking for sympathy.

… The [French] don't even know when they are beaten and Hitler has them flat on their backs… I want to go to Algeria and write about the persecution of the Jews by the Arabs…

I shall like a Scotsman now save a Jews [sic] money by turning over the leaf and writing on the other side—as I should have done sooner if my instincts had been really those of my race.

All that I shall put here is that you are still very greatly loved around this town. You are quite right about B's need of women. But you will always be the only one.

… My Sweet you haven't a thing in the world to worry about—you are having a golden glorious life and if you leave the windmills alone you can be very happy. I hope you will—but do please give up fighting the windmills in your stormy head.

I put my arms respectfully around you and hug you.
Philip

Bertrand de Jouvenel to MG

March 18, 1935
Hotel Métropole
Bruxelles

This is the last spring, the last summer. In autumn, we shall wear the light blue, and in winter rot in the damp earth. Knowing full well the uselessness of it, we shall go, neither singing nor swearing. Nothing heroic about it. We shall file into the narrow trenches like quiet gentlefolk filing into a dining room. What is life worth anyhow in this bungling world? Let it be done in like. Well brought-up people who don't kick up a vulgar fuss about nothing.

The warm days and the slow fat waves. How we threw it all away. Oh my love and how richly we deserve the wrath of God.

B.

H.G. Wells to MG

April 6, 1935
47 Chiltern Court
London

Dearest Marte,

Just a line again. I'm hoping to get some letters from you soon. Answering mine.

I'm up to my ears in work & am bothered about my films. But did reread your letters several times. I *like* you—no end.

The essence of being in love I think is imaginative expectation.

Dear Mart

HG

Hortense Flexner was a poet and a beloved Bryn Mawr professor. Gellhorn wrote some of her most intimate, unguarded letters to her, a woman she affectionately nicknamed Teecher. Flexner was married to syndicated cartoonist Wyncie King, who often figures in the background of their correspondence. Several bespoke Wynice King illustrations remain in Gellhorn's Boston papers, including the personification of her novel *A Stricken Field*, and a globe, burning in flames of hate.

MG to Hortense Flexner

April 10, 1935
4366 McPherson Avenue
St. Louis

Teecher dearest,

It is very late and I am very tired: the house is empty with Mother and Alfred visiting in your Louisville over the weekend. I have been sitting on my bed reading a great batch of letters which I wrote Mother during college. My darling, *où sont les neiges d'antan* [where are the snows of yesteryear]… I must have a heavy dosage of semitic blood, and I do not doubt that somewhere an illegal ancestress was a sloe-eyed Russian. Melancholy comes to me more naturally than any other emotion.

Those amazing letters: in a handwriting that screams adolescence; using the English language thickly, as if it were marshmallow sauce. And such a capacity for absorption: everything I read, heard, saw, smelled, got its little note. And I think maybe one is not foolish to regret youth, which was evidently a painful and harrowed period. Because the mind, little pal, sleeps so quietly from twenty on…

I read the letter about my first solemn love affair (age 18 or 17, not sure). It is such a documented screed and fills me with terror. The seeds (coming from which direction, on what wind) were already sown: and ripened into Bertrand and an attitude of mind which is going to land me in some pub, some day, being generous and tearful over a stevedore. What makes people? I spent most of this afternoon discussing with a doctor what made hair, but when you consider it who gives a damn. Whereas people, now…

Teecher lamb, how are you? Being a good little hero I know, and lighting up the world around you better than any Mazda lamp. But your former pupil and permanent adorer is noddinks[sic]. Scared cutie, believe it or not. Terrified of this slime I use for brain: of the jobless future; of the fact that the shining adventure which was *Life* at twenty is now an endurance contest. There aren't even sentences. I have written nothing for months. A few days ago, in fury, I began taking my days apart and writing brittle little pieces called "Dirges," summarizing every hour, in as acrid prose as I could muster. But goddam it I want to write great heavy swooping things, to throw terror and glory into the mind.

Have you read Rebecca West's last. Such piffle: and so unreal. But it must be fun to handle words that surely, even if the very assurance and taste make the words die, like wired flowers.

Too weary. I love you. I wanted you to know at once… Today, for the first time, I went to a good [sic] Friday service in the Cathedral. The Bishop (who's a young man and a socialist and a pal) said these words, during one of the prayers: "Oh Lord, deliver us from a cheap melancholy." I find that a lovely combination: and it means something. But between the cup and the lip as they do say, there is only air.

Bless you and your man,
Gellhorn

H.G. Wells to MG

April 1935
Norddeutscher Lloyd
Bremen

Dearest Stooge,

You are good stuff. You stand the test of being absent & being read. *What Mad Pursuit* is a first rate book, a new story & all alive. I was afraid I'd find it amateurish & imitative. I had had a great impression of you, but one never knows. Are two things in it are a bit *young* and I think the turn of Michael from Charis to Judith might have been managed just a little better. (I'm not sure) All the rest is praise.

(Stooge I adore you.)

Here I am on a boat with dull people and nothing to distract me. So you are going to have a long indiscreet letter. It may be the only long intimate letter I shall write you.

I forget what I told you about Moura (not Maura). We have been lovers for years but I am afraid we have spoilt things by my desire. There's been flashes of bitterness & I guess things like that never get really repaired. Never. We shall ease off.

I am greedy about these few years left before I go flat & start dying. It's necessary for me to be loved closely by a woman of my own… make an "old fool" of myself? I don't know. There is one woman I could marry & I'm always happy with her when we are together. But what happens to all my women is that I suddenly begin to work… they go off and tangle their skeins or they get dull—and I emerge from the work to truth. Also I have an uncouth feminine disposition of not letting my lover know really what I think about her—being "charming" & all that—until a bump comes. It's an awful shock because before it comes the woman has been a goddess—just as you know how to make a man feel like a favoured god. Is usual crude deception. There is self-deception in it too. Aw, dear, I know, for you as for me, this bursting of the gas balloon unleashed tragedy in life for both lovers. You do all this so livingly in your book.

Dear Stooge I love you and it is more than apparent that I am absurdly desperate to fall in love with you.

I am much too excited by this mad idea of using you as a Major Domo or amanuensis… or what you will… the way my own imagination which has something of the same madness as yours, plays about with that idea… on an Atlantic crossing, is very symptomatic.

Dear Stooge, what *could* we do for each other? Something I can do for you is this. I can tell you that you are an Important Writer—Hollywood has unknown that important marveling. Your book *matters*. It is the *real* troof [sic] that you should get on with your next one, dealing with the strange new generation of the unemployed & underemployed young… You ought to do it. I do stand by you doing that…Combined be a sacrifice—an apprenticeship for you to become in some fashion my fag—mental secretary, an accessory conscience.

But you're restless. You'd make more disturbance than you'd be worth.

Stooge what are we going to do about it? What are we going to do with each other?

Dearest Stooge.
H.G.

And, he added.
Mark all your letters "personal & private." Not that I am secretive but I feel that things between us are between us. All my letters are opened in the office except the marked ones.

H.G. Wells to MG

April 1935
Norddeutscher Lloyd
Bremen

Dearest Stooge,

Here I am writing to you again. The most important thing that happened to me this time in America is certainly you.

And your book.

You are probably all sorts of weak things—vain, restless, troublesome—but you are fundamentally fine & healthy. You are INFECTIOUSLY fine & healthy in your mind. I've learnt something from you, caught something from you. You've *done me good*. You've reminded me of myself.

You are trying supposedly to get down tonality or as near to it as possible & to get hold of it & do something with it. So am I. Not many people are this way… They are swollen with self protection. We are not. That is where you get me.

That is why I keep thinking of you.

I waste people.

I think I wasted a good deal of Rebecca West and I don't want to bail & disengage you … your mentality is much closer to mine than hers was.

Stooge, dear, all this is ridiculous.

It's the Spring.

It's idleness.

I'm lonely & greedy & parasitic on the female of the species.

And you are about young enough to be my granddaughter!

Bless you.

Remember you are *important*. You count. You are responsible for yourself. You are one of US.

You are my utterly dear Stooge.
H.G.

Bertrand de Jouvenel to MG

April 23, 1935
Journal de la Semaine
Paris

Dearly beloved,

Your letter, coming with the "Portrait of an Earl" was very welcome. How welcome I shall not say, for I surely weary you with my flat-footed restatements. Write, dearest, for the world is empty when I do not hear from you.

Your setting forth, as a true knight-errent [sic] I admire enormously. When all is said and done, I admit I am no fit mate for you. The strength of your writing is something that leaves me gaping. That, and the ever resurgent impulse which now sends you upon your quest. There is nothing like it. You are peerless, my dear, I say it with a proud sadness, knowing full well thou hast escaped me forever. Yes, it was a presumptuous letter I wrote, asking you to "take it or leave it." A foolish letter. You have "left it" plenty, and I have done nothing splendid that might justify your "taking it" again.

… The "Portrait of an Earl" is litterature [sic], really, you know, not journalism. Not the sort of journalism one can print in this sort of paper. I speak just like any other editor. It takes genius to be as unprintable as you are, dear. I hope you wont [sic] lose what you write, when you write. You might send it to me for safe keeping. The only things I never lose are those which come from you. If you still have any ambition to be a writer, you may rest assured, that, should you ever stop writing now, you would some day achieve the reputation of Rimbaud. I say it not because I love you, darling. Rather, I love you because of it. I can be content with nothing tame and banal after you, and you make everything seem tame and banal.

I have an uncomfortable feeling this letter is incredibly tame and banal itself. I am certainly achieving a measure of journalistic success which is not a little disquieting when one knows what tosh people elect to admire.

When I was at school, teachers loved me. While my pals did not. That's a bad sign. Means one heads for the *Academie* from the age of bare knees.

I am bent upon making this letter quiet and chatty. And, as I have a tendency, as I sit there and blab to you, of conjuring your image, I have to combat a growing desire to shout and sob and laugh and kiss, a growing desire to push against you and be warm. And so I'd better stop.

B.

MG to Harry Hopkins

April 25, 1935
Camden

My dear Mr. Hopkins,

I have spent a week in Camden. It surprises me to find how radically attitudes can change within four or five months. When last I was in the field, the general attitude of the unemployed was one of hope. Times were of course lousy, but you had faith in the President and the New Deal and things would surely pick up. This, as I wrote you then, hung on an almost mystic belief in Mr. Roosevelt, a combination of wishful thinking and great personal loyalty.

In this town, the unemployed are as despairing a crew as I have ever seen. Young men say, "We'll never find work." Men over forty say, "Even if there was any work we wouldn't get it; we're too old." They have been on relief too long; this is like the third year of the war when everything peters out into gray resignation. Moreover, they are no longer sustained by confidence in the President. They say to you, quietly, like people who have been betrayed but are too tired to be angry, "How does he expect us to live on that; does he know what food costs, what rents are; how can we keep clothes on the children…"

Housing is unspeakable. No doubt the housing was never a thing of beauty and general admiration around here; but claptrap houses which have gone without repairs for upwards of five years are shameful places. There is marked ovecrowding. I have seen houses where the plaster has fallen through to the lathe, and the basement floated in water. One entire block of houses I visited is so infested with bedbugs that the only way to keep whole is to burn out the beds twice a week and paint the wood work with carbolic acid, and even so you can just sit around and watch the little creatures crawling all over and dropping from the ceiling…

Clothes nil. Really a terrible problem here; not only of protection against the elements (a lot of pneumonia among children: undernourishment plus exposure) but also the fact that having no clothes, these people are cut out of any social life. They don't dare go out, for shame.

T.B. is increasing: the hospitals for mental diseases (State and county) have over 1000 more patients than in 1932, epileptics and feeble-minded are increasing. Malnutrition seems prevalent among children but not among adults; and venereal disease is more or less static though an entirely different class is beginning to come to the free clinics.

It appears that the depression is resulting in a lot of amateur prostitution. This is commented upon by the people who have to deal with the courts and care for delinquent children. The age limit is going down and unmarried mothers are very young. I was talking to a girl about this: she said, "Well, the girls go out with anybody, you might say, just to have something to do and to forget this mess." (She herself was on relief, getting something like $2,00 [sic] a week to live on.) I remarked that it was understandable, considering that at least they got a good square meal. And she said, very calmly, "Meal? No, almost never. Sometimes they get a glass of beer."

The young are apathetic, sinking into a resigned bitterness. No good, most of them. Their schooling, such as it is, is a joke; and they have never had the opportunity to learn a trade. They don't believe in man or God, let alone private industry; the only thing that keeps them from suicide is this amazing loss of vitality; they exist. "I generally go to bed around seven at night, because that way you get the day over with quicker."

Yours sincerely,
Martha Gellhorn

H.G. Wells to MG

April 26, 1935
47 Chiltern Court
London

Darling Stooge,
(Though the name is all wrong)
(Is got on to you & so going to stay)
Dear Stooge.

I got your letter from Camden. I'm back among my stuff here & I'm not changed in the slightest. The most important thing in my personal life is to get clear with you. Are you clear with me.

Don't accumulate is my plea. And don't think you are going to do anything for human involvement by accumulating indignation…

I am unhappy & discontented & I have a superstition (is it?) that you can cure me…

… had two notes from your Bertrand. You have written to him about me. He wanted to see me… but he had to fly back to Paris for *Vu*. He saw you are his real wife…

I'm turning my flat & all my circumstances & I am buying a house close by [13 Hanover Terrace]… It's a quiet white house with a lot of green stuff & water before the windows. The only infringement against quiet is that sometimes you hear lions roaring because it is on Regent's Park half a mile from the zoo.

Love me please.
H.G.

Bertrand de Jouvenel to MG

May 14, 1935
Moscow

My dear love,

There was a cable that came in answer to mine. It said, "Will be on dock wearing my ten lira ring *mon amour cheri*." But that was a long time ago, and this time, is it "James, tell the gentleman there is no reply." Ah well! I am a gentleman in a dust-coat trying. Waiting for news is tiresomely alike, whether the town be Moscow or another and crowd endeavour is a sight doubtless inspiriting, but which ne'ertheless leaves me increasingly cold. No doubt this is the biggest airship in the word [sic], but that would gladden Mr. Hoover and I have nothing in common with Mr. Hoover. I am the ageing product of a civilized country and frankly I hate all this excitement about opening a new metro. Herein probably lies the future. Well to hell with the future. I'm all for Bonnie Prince Charlie and all that kind of thing—Dear heart, whatever your answer, whatever your silence, I shall come to America, if only for a few days. I have now undertaken to go and am bound to. It'll be a curious sensation to go there and not see you—rather verging on the suicidal mania.

I wonder whether you've found yourself at long last a fit mate, or what it is that prevented you from answering. All, I suppose, is thus for the best. There was a night on board an ugly little ship when a very tired, very thin, very young girl, slipped on my finger this ring, and saw that we were now bound forever. So I am, dear heart, and oh what jumps the poor old fish has made without freeing itself! Let me not hear of a different un-tender voice, let me not see a different, un-moved face.

For, oh my dearest love, all this is so near, so clear, such uncorruptible wealth.

Thank you, sweetheart, thank you for all my piled up memories.

Ever
B.

H.G. Wells to MG

May 25, 1935
47 Chiltern Court
London

Dearest Stooge,

First thing shifting addresses. I've written you one or two loving letters in the last few weeks & I don't want them to go astray. All to 1709 H. St. Washington D.C. Chase them.

I love your letters & your criticisms. The dreadful fact is that *limited* as the *area of free discussion* is in both America & Britain, it exists. It operates.

I don't think you've got much to teach me that I don't know about the lousiness and cruel mysteries of ordinary human life. I'm not a fool Stooge. I was born in a BUG INFESTED house.

At bottom I am grimmer than you, my dear. You are young and valiant and you still think that somewhere in this whole dark mess there is light and righteousness. Dearest it is nowhere but in our poor cramped little imaginations…

It is perfectly natural for the poor & sick to exasperate & hate each other. I don't deny that. But that isn't the class war. The class war is a cheap sloppy survivors doctrine invented to explain that natural reservoir of hate. The Dictatorship of the Proleteriat, American Democracy (Triumphant), Christianity are all in the descent for me.

I hold on to Stooge, some men of science, a curious dislike I fear in some people for things badly done, this sublimated fatuous cruelty that hates.

Dear Stooge I wish I had you about here with me.

Love,
H.G.

Late May 1935
Grosvenor House
London

My darling child,

If I were with you now, there would be nothing for me to do but move off and make room for that chaste solitary dry-eyed continuous session of suffering which is—though we do not realize it—one of the truest and best moments of our life.

Now the virtues of courage and patience and truth, the laughing childish goodness, come to your mind. Do you feel that you are the oldest son? What he did in one field, that plowing advance, you'll do it in another. I have the impression that, at such a death, the departed spirit enters in some slight measure, the true heir.

What is most alarming is of course your mother. Here is a responsibility for you. Probably you will move off, both of you, to Carmel or some such place for a time.

I lunched with Wells today, told him that I had the news yesterday. He was aware of the event. He told me Putnam was bringing out both your books here and was taking care of the new book in the U.S.

He is a wonderful man. You will, I think, marry him ultimately.

My dear love, I wish I could rub your cold cheek.
B.

Gellhorn's youngest brother Alfred was the sibling to whom she was closest. They were fiercely loyal to Edna (referred to as "Muddy" here) and shared a playful sense of humour. He was working his way through medical school in 1935 and would establish himself as a celebrated oncologist and become an attending physician to Eleanor Roosevelt in her final days.

Alfred Gellhorn to MG

July 1935
4366 McPherson Avenue
St. Louis

Sissy dearest,

It seems as though five dreary weeks have dragged their tiresome steps along since you left your ancestral home. We have tried to be cheerful and gay, but the effort has always fallen far short of any modicum of success. Even though you are five packs of bitches, you've got what it takes to make the world go 'round.

On the very day that you left, Muddy [Edna] brought your cigarette case from downtown. It is a thing of great beauty, sissy, and I love it very much. Thanks and thanks, and if you find that it would come in handy for some state occasion such as meeting King Edward the VII or is it VIII, I will gladly loan it to you—for a nominal rental.

... Mother really does miss you very much and she loves you so thoroughly that it makes me ache. She has more pride in your accomplishments than in any of the rest of us, and she is completely confident in your ultimate success. I think that you and I are agreed that this is just about the most important thing in the world. Your letters have cheered her no end.

I had a date with Olga Fredericks [later his wife] the other evening. She is, as you may remember, Lischer's finding, but I have his permission to exploit that sex problem just as far as I can. He is confident that I won't be able to accomplish a thing unless I dangle a ring before her eyes, but I think that she must be human and that if I don't make the grade somebody else will. I haven't had such lewd talk since you left, you bastard, and I miss it very much.

I have a very important examination in Obstetrics at the end of the week, and I do give a hell of a big damn about doing well in it.

My bed hour approaches. Goodnight Poops, and give all of those eastern slickers hell.

Ever,
Alf

George Gellhorn to MG

August 1, 1935
Saint Louis University School of Medicine
1402 South Grand Boulevard

You win, Dearest! I haven't even started on my book, though I know that eventually it will bring more money than yours. Years even after I am smoldering in

my grave a check for $3.15 will come to you every six months to remind you of
your Sire who lost out in the race for first place. But I *feel* the thing moving in my
womb—sometimes only very lightly like the fluttering of a very young bird, then
again with hard kicks like a young steer that strains against the ropes. I don't know
whether it's heat or old age or fear of bubbles or the aftermath of them that keeps
me away from work for which there is so little time left, every day less time left.

I have done the incredible, the unprecedented. I have—not given up smoking (I
shall leave that until I'll be flying about in heaven)—but I have actually reduced it to
reasonable limits. I now smoke from 1½ to 2½ of my small cigars a day, *never* more! It
seems to me that the last bubble was a little less severe and did not last quite as long.
I shall give it another trial for a month or so. But if the bubble takes no advantage
from my saintliness, then I shall run amok and go out in a blaze of glory and intem-
perance. I shall invite you to that spree and promise you entertainment.

… You know what continued darkness in the Arctic does to men cooped up
in a small hut. You now see what continuous heat will do to a man cooped up at
4366 [their family home on McPherson Avenue]. I won't read this over for typo-
graphical errors, lest I tear up the entire epistle, and it is too hot to write another,
more in the vein of the heavy father.

Anyhow, I like you pretty much. Major Seelig came into the Skin and Cancer
Hospital yesterday and made a playful pass at the stenographer in the crowded
front office, Miss Oechsle, who is six feet high and weighs 250 pounds, but she
said: It's too hot to love!

I haven't the faintest idea any more how I started out to end on a pessimistic
note. I believe I am merely giving me the luxury of throwing off all inhibitions
for one moment, a thing you are doing all the time and without any restraint. Else,
instead of bellyaching, you should be proud of the things the bringing forth of a
book is doing to you. Of course, you are nervous and panicky and doubtful. It is
the proper attitude for a creative mind that means to do its very best.

Did I tell you that it makes me rather boastful inside of me, though I never
mention it even to Mother, when I get a letter from you all to myself? Well,
anyhow, the old idiot [H.G. Wells] though he slumps more and more into senility,
is harmless—I can vouch for him to that effect. I hope, by the time you answer
this, if at all, my next bubble will be over.

Meantime lovingly,
Dad

Allen Grover worked for *TIME* and was an early reader of Gellhorn's fiction. They
had had an affair and remained friends. She valued his editorial comments and
also his directness with her about her personal life.

Allen Grover to MG

Listen my dear you give me a pain in a tender spot. Your-and-Wells' mixture of conceit and humility *is just too damn* bogus for a realist like me to get anything out of but a horse laugh. Let me articulate the *realist again* for all concerned. I am a critical capitalist (because I don't see any other workable system for this, my native land). I am also 34 yrs. old, 6'1" and weigh 170 lb. I am married, have 1⅔ children and a good job. This all pleases me.

… If you and Wells etc. all belong to each other that's just dandy. Such exclusiveness should make you happy if the monumental conceit of it isn't advanced paranoia.

… Now let's get another thing straight. You never saw anyone who less wanted a transient thrill or a goofy feeling of romance than I. And, Jesus, my dear, I loathe you or anyone else slathering love all over the place—to borrow a phrase. I like it in bed only. Maybe that's coarse or hard. I think of it as being economical.

… If we're in love with each other lets [sic] recognize it but lets [sic] also recognize its [sic] just too bad. If we want to sleep together, lets [sic] do. But lets [sic] recognize it as an outlet for passion. It would be a thrill all right. All right but romance, fictitious or otherwise—no.

… Just to finish an unhappy letter unhappily I didn't like *Jim* [in *The Trouble I've Seen*] nearly as well as *Ruby*. Only at the very end and the beginning (except for the silly episode with the girl in the roadster) did you seem to be going great guns. Those parts are fine and, through it all, there is plenty of evidence that you can *write*. But it's not lean and taut the way *Ruby* was. It's fulsome and overwritten. If anyone had puked once more I'd have been sick too.

… What it needs is cutting—pages and pages should come out. The end isn't real either. Jim *couldn't* be such a fool as to bury the clothes after a woman who knew them both had remarked on them. More likely… he would have slugged the janitor (maybe killed him) and returned the dress in the store. I'll read it again and mark it all up—God knows when.

… Take out your own anger—only the propagandist has a right to that—and tell the *story*, then I think it can be made as excellent as *Ruby*.

I could write all night about Jim, or us, but good night now. Darling, I'm not angry. But I'm bothered that we can't see what's what. I think I can and I can accept it. You must, too, or we had best be rid of each other because this sawing at each other just makes heartaches. You see my pride comes in, too… I didn't try to make you love me. I'm no thrill seeker. I don't ask you to give any of the things you crab about (I'm a young man in Manhattan) and I'll be damned if I'll be put on the defensive as a capitalist, a playboy, a satyr, a weakling, a coward, a moron, or the big bad wolf. I'm not perfect (even to myself) but I wouldn't change places with H.G. Wells or your pa (or mine either) or Henry R. Luce or B. de Jouvenel or Jim Barr. I like being what I am the way I am and your grieving about it seems to make me like it the more. The "I's" in this letter are disgusting, but you had them coming to you, my sweet.

A.

Allen Grover to MG   August 13, 1935
                                                                      New York City

Dear Marty,

    … This morning I got a cable signed Jouvenel which said, "Sailing *Normandie* tomorrow." How does that make you feel? There is something bizarre in the picture of my going to meet Bertrand though, of course, I will if the damn boat doesn't come in on Sunday.

H.G. Wells to MG   August 17, 1935
                                                               Digswell, Water Mill
                                                                          Welwyn

Dearest Stooge,

    My nerves are jangling today. Chastity. And bother with the construction of the new film treatment. I can't keep these things from ploughing deep & turning up the undersoil of life. I want to get together with someone I can go to & hold on to in these jangling distressful palesouled moods…

    Now I meant what I told you about Lou Pidou [his home in the south of France] & all you say about its unfurling fills me with delight & hopes. But before we can discuss much more of that I want to get together with you for a bit. I am coming to New York somewhen in October. I shall probably time my coming for the release of my film. Could we coincide some way? I'm free to go where I like & I don't see why I should have secretarial help. Then we could forward what is unbearable in each other.

    I'm in a queer position about my affairs. I'm taking certain risks. In a year I shall either be very well off & able to amble about or I shall be a defeated man. I tell you this so that there may be no surprises later. I *may* crumple up.

    Tell me how we can best fix up in New York. Is it hotels or is it apartments or what? I can do the essential business I have to do in N.Y. in three or four days. I have some idea of flying off to Hollywood for a few days there. I've got no reason for any dates after that.

All you say about being without a community is true of me. We are singular people you & I…

Bless you Stooge… I hadn't read your work. I didn't realize until afterwards how important you might be.

H.G.

H.G. Wells to MG   October 4, 1935
                                                47 Chiltern Court
                                                London

Darling,

Forgive me if I am presuming but this is your non-returnable advance fee as my general advisor about things American. I don't know when I shall get to America. I *can't* leave these people here to mess up my film… I may not get across the Atlantic before November. You finish on with your work. I shall look at this *ill* old thing!

H. loves you but, darling, I will never climb up mountains with you or swim by moonlight.

I've got Hamish Hamilton busy with your real book [*The Trouble I've Seen*] and Putnam of London is desperate to publish *What Mad Pursuit* in a new series of young American writers.

My film is in a hallowed mess. I don't know what to do about it.

I'm ill, worried & doing badly—but one has to go on.

Gods! What I would give to see you today & talk to you for half an hour.

Do you know Stooge darling that when one is 69 there is nothing in the world to whisper to…

So I conclude.

Yours devotedly
H.G.

Bertrand de Jouvenel to MG   October 12, 1935
                                                London

… *Je fais des interviews de Winston Churchill… c'est un succès.* [I interviewed Churchill… it was a success.]

… Allons, bonsoir, mon rabbit, j'ai encore un article à écrive et puis à six heures du matin je dois téléphoner à Paris Soir et puis à sept heures je pars à Canterbury [So, goodnight, my rabbit, I have another article to write and then at six in the morning I must telephone *Paris Soir* and then at seven o'clock I leave for Canterbury].

God bless you, Marty, remain brave and strong and alive… d'you [sic] remember that evening in Washington when you were so sick after we'd seen Mark Childs and I undressed you and made compresses and sat beside you. I felt very happy with my eyes upon you watching the colours flowing back into your face slowly. It seems far away.

… I have gone back, Wells told me, [Bertrand visited him at home in London.] to a life of leisure, success and luxury. Not me, rabbit…

I don't think you'll ever hold me again in those arms of yours, or bend upon me that laughing, indulgent face… But it was fine, darling, it was fine.

B.

H.G. Wells to MG

October 14, 1935
47 Chiltern Court
London

Stooge dearest,

I've lost your last letter.

Listen I sail from S'hampton [sic] on the *Washington* on Nov 7th. I shall be met effectively by G.P. Brett of Macmillan & Co—he *is* M&C—and taken to his home for a day or so. *Then I shall go where I like in N.Y.C. for a few days.* Then I shall set out to Hollywood by air where Charlie Chaplin, Anita Loos & others are prepping hospitalities. I shall have a great time & I shall not outstay my welcome. That takes me to Dec 1st say. Then I don't know. I just don't know.

Before I leave I shall pass on the contracts to make my new house here. It is the perfect older gentleman's home [13 Hanover Terrace, Regent's Park]. I shall move into it about April.

And I have been in bed three days—damn the climate—I feel all my 69 years. Wheezing.

Bertrand called yesterday. That young man has an insistence for political adventure. He may be shot or he be made be a dangerous politician in a few years [sic] time. He told me you are divorcing him. Darling how can you undo a knot when there was never a string?

Bless you.
H.G.

Fall 1935
                                                                                  New York City

Angel,

Your angry piece is lovely to read and nasty to think about. And it might do
some good. It's already done some, with me. You do this kind of thing beautifully. But I think *TIME's* non committal view of Hamms himself is sounder
than yours. And I'd hate the un-Americans in Russia as much as in Germany—
though I take it you wouldn't—quite. Anyway, here they stink—we can agree
on that.

  I'm glad you are happy, darling, I suppose I am too though Autumn is a sad
kind of time for me always and this weekend I could remember (too well) the
warm mist and the bright colors in New Hartford and H.G. Wells. If you come
here make loud noises and I'll do the same.

Love & a kiss,
A.

Fall 1935
                                                                                  New York City

Dollink (the old man's way),

  The solution for Lou sounds good. I've no kick about Jim—never did have.
Only I thought you should say Jim was different as well as make him so (or have
someone else say it). The reader will get it all right but his confidence in the
author is greater if he knows you know it, too. I've been expecting the ms again
eagerly—or has Wells taken you from your work… He was guest at a dinner Paul
West gave Monday night. I would love to see you in a degenerate mood. God
knows what Mr. Field would think of me. It's a pity he couldn't have caught the
white fire of social injustice I did. I just think that if you are consumed by it you
had best devote yourself to it. You know, Wells ought to do you a lot of good.
He has led a thinking, liberal life and yet never grew bitter or hysterical, if the
Experiment is honest. And in his plumpish years he manages to spend a week with
you on Mr. Field's hospitable hilltop *en route* to the Hollywood fleshpots! Sweet
and trusting may be your adjectives for him, my own would be adroit. Still you
need lots of the same and maybe it's communicable. Of course, I think you like
to dramatize your psychology. You aren't really afraid to face yourself. What you
haven't admitted successfully yet is that you are several different people. Gradually

one will crush the others. Then you'll be much happier and saner. Younger folk will then look at you and say you have compromised with life. Baloney. You will just be being yourself for the first time in your life. But before you can do that of course you have to have a self.

If I am cynical it is natural, accented perhaps by the hard week past & a harder one to come. (Also I tried to get $25,000 out of dad to buy a farm with but he wouldn't come through). Write me when you can. Your crabbing is sweeter than most people's singing. Bertrand, Wells, myself—and what others? I should one day publish your collected letters. They're magnificent prose.

Allen

Bertrand de Jouvenel to MG

October 31, 1935
194 rue de Rivoli
Paris

My dearest, for my birthday I am writing this letter which, I trust, you will receive on your birthday [November 8]. Or, maybe, on the eve of your birthday, when you sit down to write an ode to yourself. I want you to rejoice, on this, your twenty-seventh anniversary, for that year which has gone by is the very first you can be fully proud of. You have painstakingly reviewed the state of the nation [FERA work]. You have gone into the filthy miserable homes. You've smiled at the people, made them forget their slavery, you've taken stock of their needs, you've understood their joys and sorrows. You've written about it, chosing [sic] your words with care, moved by a slow patient anger. I wish I had fire enough in me to make you feel how grand you've been all this year—how happy I am to have found you competent, assured and strong, yea even tho' you want to deny it.

My dear love, I am writing in my home rue de Rivoli. From my window I see the well ordered Tuileries. There is no phone and it is very quiet here. I am going to work as I haven't done for years, not rushing at it but approaching it slowly, with the full appreciation of that privilege, with due respect for the work itself. Tis [sic] naught but articles as yet, but in them even I can infuse more thought than has been my want.

Did I tell you in a former letter that I was going to stand for Parliament in Corrège. Not thru any eagerness to "get in," but to continue a tradition to which I am deeply attached. I fear that I am really the direct product of my country and family. [His father Henri de Jouvenel served both as the French High Commissioner in Syria and Lebanon in 1925–26 and later as the French

Ambassador to Rome in 1933.] There is little in me that I can call my own. There was far more when we were together.

I see no one but Nelly. I practically do not move from here as I feel again quite weak. She has found a woman who "does" for me and she comes in every evening. I suppose I will have to do a financial alliance with Marcelle to get the castle out of hock. Roland [his son] is not all I want him to be. I'm going to take him to Castel Novel with me and he'll go to school there.

Darling, I answer letters, and within my means, I pay bills. Youth is over for me. By the way, go to Saint-Louis [sic] some time. In a very few years you may be sorry you saw too little of them [her parents].

My dear love, may God bless you.

Do not feel depressed on this your birthday. You are to some people—count me first among them—the proof and token that there can be a better world peopled by a prouder race. I love and respect you, my darling, and some day, there will be summer and maybe we'll laugh together.

B.

About Marcelle, divorce, and other such. She doesn't seem to be going to the U.S. but there seems no harm in you slipping a paragraph about Martha G, lately Mrs. de J, did this and so on.

> On her 27th birthday, November 8, 1935, Gellhorn wrote the following entry about loneliness on a single leaf in her personal journal: "I tell you loneliness is the thing to master. Courage and fear, love and death are only parts of it and can easily be ruled afterwards. If I can make myself master of my own loneliness there will be peace or safety: and perhaps these are the same."
>
> H.G. Wells had been staying with Gellhorn at her rich friend Freddy Field's Connecticut house. She was trying to finish the fiction based on her FERA experiences with the destitute, but Wells kept nattering at her, presumably importing his wisdom of the ages, and she was irritable. Bitter about the distraction of hosting him, she cabled Charlie Chaplin, begging him to invite Wells to visit Hollywood. He did, as Wells' letters to Gellhorn on Chaplin's personal stationery attest.

H.G. Wells to MG

November 27, 1935
Charles Chaplin
Los Angeles

Dearest Stooge,

    I had a rough air journey & after Kansas City the plane stopped & they put us on a train. But at Albuquerque… we flew over the Grand Canyon & all, to Los Angeles. I'm tired, but it's sunny thank god! I'm contented, but I'm restless & bothered. Why don't you make love with me & smooth me down & wake me altogether happy? Inconsiderate of you Stooge. You don't know your own mind about me.

    I've written to Sinclair Lewis about you. If he writes to you, good. If he doesn't—well, then he won't.

    I like CC more than ever & Pauline [Paulette] Goddard is a dear. I wish I was attractive to women. Why have I of all men to wander about the world without a responsive Stooge to talk to & sleep with & love?

    There ought to be a religious order of young women given to the service of Good, Deserving, Non Magnetic Great Men. You would given that nice body of yours just fritter it away.

Yours devotedly
but with infinite sadness

H.G.

H.G. Wells to MG

December 12, 1935
Charles Chaplin
Los Angeles

I'm just back from a visit to Hearst's fantastic palace at St. Simeon. It's beyond description. But the air is lovely… & I feel unusually my wounds… My dear, you're gnawing on that old situation. You are young. Why don't you cut your losses & love someone else? This business of (A) being oneself & (B) living, is just a doomed self-contradiction. Anyhow you are getting on with this book. Did Sinclair [Lewis] write you?

    To hell with Marcelle!

    Good luck & steadiness of mind to you.

H.G.

MG to Eleanor Roosevelt

1935 DEC 23 PM 1102
NA 1663 16 SCGTG 25= WATERBURY CONN=
MRS FRANKLIN D ROOSEVELT=
THE WHITE HOUSE WASH DC=
I WISH YOU THE HAPPIEST OF CHRISTMASES AND A GLAD NEW
YEAR WITH ADMIRATION AND DEVOTION=
MARTHA GELLHORN

Eleanor Roosevelt to MG

December 27, 1935
The White House
Washington

Dear Martha,

Many thanks for your telegram and for your holiday greeting. Every good wish for the New Year, and I hope you will soon be returning to Washington.

Affectionately,
Eleanor Roosevelt

1936

H.G. Wells to MG

January 5, 1936
On Board Cunard White Star
Majestic

Dearest Martha,

I've got a FRIGHTFUL cold. This is the important thing, this head—once full of opalescent active grey matter has become mud. I go about wanting to write a love letter to you and I can't even see the things I think I feel much less express them. 2nd of all I'm very concerned for you & your family. That matters enormously, your father's illness, your mother's distress because it fills your mind, which I love. I sent you a radiogram not too compromisingly express so as to sort of touch your hand for a moment. I am now very deeply in love with you, deeply & permanently. I cooled off a little in Connecticut because I couldn't see any hope of getting closer to you than I was. And love is an uncertain thing that has to be going on a needing. Darling, if I was sane I'd live hale & hearty twenty years & sure I'd be virile enough I'd cut my damn thing in the world that prevents us & try & get a firm permanent grip in your hair. But I'm not sure of either. I confess I am afraid of senility… it makes me delay. And that's that.

I found Hamish Hamilton, a London Publisher, on board. He works with Harper & Co. He is now reading your M.S. [sic] He knows you & he's read your last book [*What Mad Pursuit*]. He is approaching the syphilis part. I'll perhaps write again before we land if there's anything to report. If I don't get an offer from him I shall get his criticisms.

I love you because you are understanding, glamorous, more hardwilled than anyone I have ever met, with a lovely charm & movement of your mind— even when you are being a bit silly—& you are at times—it's as good as fresh violets—& you have a hundred bodily charms & lovelinesses & I like you when your chin is up & when it is down but most of all I love you when you whisper very close to me.

Damn it! This can't go on. Buck up H.G.

[Sketch, Martha on the floor, naked, reaching one arm up in supplication to standing, naked, pot-bellied Wells]

Surely like this please Martha
Dearest
HG

Bertrand de Jouvenel to MG
January 9, 1936
Garmish
Bavaria

My darling, our last letters were no good: my tone annoyed you and then your tone annoyed me….

I am wondering very much about you. Are you in a rough Lincolnian, Zolaesque, Walt Whitmanish mood, smelling stronger under the arms as you whack at your typewriter. I've loved you best that way…. Oh my little rabbit, I'm so fond of you.

… Possibly you will ultimately find the He-Man you have so longed for. I hope so.

B.

Bertrand de Jouvenel to MG

January 21, 1936
Garmish
Bavaria

My darling, you're just growing to be a bloody prophet, the thunder of God is in your throat like whooping cough. I think it's fine but don't overdo it. It harmed Tolstoi's [sic] writing as you'll remember. Also it alienated the best friend and the most understanding that he ever had, meaning Tourgeniev [sic].

I know solitude affects one that way. Nietzsche's megalomania was the direct result of Sils. And, but for it, we wouldn't have had Zarathustra. Still dearest, I think you shouldn't climb on top of Sinai to address those that love you. Do you mind my saying so? And do you mind my pointing out that literature demands "a sympathetic understanding of the ways of all men."

One of your letters says: "I've been trying to believe in men and ideas as long as I can remember. And slowly there is nothing or almost nothing that I can have faith in..." Darling have you ever been such a fool as to idolize that weak pitiful human animal and his queer little fancies! What a heathen you are! And as for ideas! Cloaks for interest and vanity, shadowy horses to be ridden by small men ambitions, to hoist themselves above the shoulders of others.

By all means, join with the workers. You shall certainly do some good and it will do you an enormous service. You'll learn the law of "little by little," you'll learn the law of "half a loaf," and I'm beginning to wonder whether you can achieve anything worthwhile, even in the realm of writing before you've been taught that lesson.

My darling, I'm not lecturing you from a sense of superiority. You know there's no human being I admire—yea, and envy—more than I do you.

I'll stop writing to you if you'd rather.

There is no sense in exchanging these letters if they are not a straightforward account of deeds and thoughts and if they are just a senseless and endless clash of standards.

Pour finis, I don't think it's friendly of you not to send me doubles of your chapters [*The Trouble I've Seen*].

Bless you darling—be a hero and don't be too much of a fool and remember: there's always Smuf to turn away from—which you couldn't do if he weren't turned towards you.

B.

January 28, 1936
47 Chiltern Court
London

Dearest Stooge,

How are your troubles? I get no letter from you… I am being a good Agent, which is all I can do for you just now. I have told Hamish Hamilton to wait for your book because his bid is not good enough & the M.S. is now with the firm of Putnam who wants to issue *What Mad Pursuit* & then follow with the real book.

I am flat & dismal. I am getting beaten by the dullness & obstinacy of these bloody film people & *Things to Come* & *The Man Who Could Work Miracles* will be at best only half good. They will carry something but they won't be strong & bright & lovely as they might have been. And the weather is inky wet & London is having an orgy of Royal Funeral. Anyhow Americans can jeer. Minor exasperation comes upon me. Some bloody photographers got at me through my own publicity people in N.Y., found me in a genial moment & persuaded me to be photographed "for their trade paper." It wasn't to go further. The bloody picture is all over… It is the most undignified thing I ever let myself in for. Why did I do it Stooge?

I have done the *Anatomy of Frustration*. It is as high & deep & clear & hard & plain & attractive as I can make it. And most of it reads like an old gentleman mumbling in his arm chair.

You are young, now & perfectly lovely, I have no delusions about you. You are *for me* the best thing alive. It has been exhausting but refreshing to write you this letter & I recall you by doing so.

Dear Stooge
H.G.

January 29, 1936
4366 McPherson Avenue
St. Louis

Teecher dear,

Thank you for your note. This is something I haven't found the words for. And as for feeling it is like being stunned and knowing you're hurt, but neither where nor how. Death I suppose is the last thing one learns about. Even now, after four days which have refused to end, lingered through many winters and been slower than prison, it still seems unreal. I find myself talking of Dad as if he had only gone on a journey and I could write him a letter any time and tell him about all five of us here missing him and wanting him to come back because it isn't good enough without him.

Mother is braver and finer than anyone has a right to be; always thinking of someone else, doing the superb and courageous thing without even having to make a choice. But she said to me, "I don't know how to be now, I keep wondering what there is to be." I never imagined anything about this. You see he had an emergency operation and miraculously got well. I went to NY on Tuesday, sure that he was allright [sic] and so everyone else thought and all their plans were made to go to Florida and get sunburned and have fun, every kind of plan, even long plans, for books to write… And Saturday I took the plane back because he'd died in his sleep, with his hand on an open book. His heart just stopped. It can't have hurt him, we all keep saying that to ourselves. And he must have known, during those three weeks after his operation, how much we loved him and how much all the other people cared and how glad they were for his being alive. Teecher, there aren't any more terrible words than "too late." I am beginning to be afraid of them.

I haven't any plans. My book [*The Trouble I've Seen*] is done and with the publisher. I haven't a job. I'm staying on to see what Mother wants though she simply refuses to want anything lest I feel she's a duty. There is very little money and so of course I'll go right on as I have, being a wage earner (it's the only way I want to be, ever). And I'll have to come east to be that; but not yet. It's very hard to think normally of tomorrow and Mother's face is enough to make me crazy with misery. They loved each other so entirely and so well, and for so long.

Kiss Wyncie for me. I hope you're better my little sweetie and that Wyncie's eyes continue to be shining brightly.

Always,
Gellhorn

January 30, 1936
4366 McPherson Avenue
St. Louis

My dear Mrs. Roosevelt,

I asked mother if I might not write you, knowing that she wanted to thank you for your helpfulness and thank Mr. Roosevelt for his splendid letter on Trained Government Personnel, but that she couldn't herself get around to writing immediately. My father died suddenly last Saturday. It has been very hard and Mother is deeply involved in personal obligations at this moment. The President's letter, she feels, was exactly what the League Campaign Committee wanted and needed and it has been of the utmost value to their program to have it. She is tremendously grateful to Mr. Roosevelt and she wanted to thank both of you at once. Of course, the Washington League will have sent their thanks already, but she wished to add hers. Will you please thank him?

I got a little note from you here. The incredible way you remember things— when you must have a trainload of identical telegrams on New Year's Day—is one of the wonders of the country. I am staying here now, though I don't know for how long. As long as Mother can use me anyway. We don't any of us know how to behave or be yet, but we will somehow, later.

Thank you and Mr. Roosevelt again, for Mother. The League is certainly on the right track, as no people know better than you.

Affectionately,
Martha Gellhorn

H.G. Wells to MG

January 31, 1936
47 Chiltern Court
London

Stooge darling,

Two letters from you. One says your father has turned the corner & that you are going strong; the other gives you cheerful in New York. Bless your vitality.

I've just sent you a cable letter telling you to accept an offer from Putnam £50 advance, 15% royalty to 25% & 10% on a subsequent cheap edition… I've asked Putnam [Hamish Hamilton] if he can fix an American publisher for me. He is urgent to publish. And that's that. Harpers may or may not write you on your side. Insist on an advance of $250 & 10% royalty & say I told you.

You are the most vivid thing in my imagination & I go endless places with you & do countless things. My mental camera was clicking & clicking all the time you were about. Even in the dark.

Bless you dear Stooge.

Good luck
H.G.

Eleanor Roosevelt to MG

February 4, 1936
The White House
Washington

Dear Martha,

I am so sorry to hear of your father's death. It must have been a great shock to both you and your mother and will you please tell her of my very real sympathy.

Hick tells me that you wanted a note of introduction to Mrs. Reed and I am wondering when you are going back to New York? Of course I will be glad to give it to you if you will let me know your plans.

With my deep sympathy to both of you, I am

Affectionately,
Eleanor Roosevelt

MG to Eleanor Roosevelt

February 7, 1936
4366 McPherson Avenue
St. Louis

Dear Mrs. Roosevelt,

Thank you so much for your note. You are grand to be willing to introduce me to Mrs. Reed. I wrote Hick very shyly, asking if I dared suggest such a thing to you, when I was in NY before my father died. It seems as if that were another life altogether. I have no idea what my plans will be; each day just gets lived through and we don't worry much about tomorrow. But this is a kind of comma which must pass. I'll have to be earning my living very soon again, and I suppose I'll have to do it in NY as Saint Louis is a town which has not yet realized that women can do more than sell dresses in smart shops.

I'm going to the hospital in a few days to have an ear tinkered with but as soon as I'm neatly remade and hearing things clearly—whether they're worth it or not—I shall be busy about jobs. May I write you then, and ask you—if it's not too great an imposition—to give me a letter to the omnipotent Mrs. Reed. I'd be vastly grateful. Though I'm pretty ashamed of myself to suggest such a thing. I got fairly anxious about even having a chance to get in to people's offices in NY.

My book on the unemployed is being brought out in England right off (three months I guess) with an introduction by Wells. It ought to get taken here some-time. Oddly, people don't enjoy nearly as much hearing about their own woes and therefore their own responsibilities as they enjoy hearing about strangers' messes.

Very normal. I'm currently grateful to the U.S. Government, collectively, and individually, for having had the opportunity to get the material for a book like this. If no one else learns anything, I certainly consider that my post-graduate course is now completed and I can start all over with the kindergarten work.

Thank you for many things. We admire you constantly in this house, and we are continually touched by your kindness.

Sincerely,
Martha Gellhorn

Bertrand de Jouvenel to MG   March 2, 1936
                                                     En route to London

My darling,

I write in the plane which carries me to London—maybe you heard about my interview with Hitler—Probably you don't know there was no French answer and though the sensation was enormous, the response of our press was miserable, petty, suspicious, bad-humoured. Now Hitler has gotten up in the Reichstag and said, "that interview was my last move for an understanding with France." The German troops are marching into the Rhineland. We brought it upon ourselves. But that's torn it. We've shown our stupidity by refusing to tread with Hitler. We cannot afford to demonstrate our cowardice by accepting his unilateral moves.

So darling, we'll fight.

It doesn't make sense but life never makes sense anyhow. When we parted, that didn't make sense. Man seeks his own destruction. *Pour moi, j'accept cette guerre d'un coeur resigne* [For me, I accept this war with a resigned heart].

B.

H.G. Wells to MG   April 20, 1936
                                                            London

Darling Stooge,

You're very good about Rebecca [West] and (with due excisions) I've sent your letter on to her. I agree. But I don't find her dialogue uncharacteristic. She doesn't give idioms but she gives the quality of their thought fairly well.

You idealize too much. You say you believe in simple people. Darling there are *no* simple people. The factory worker is just as intricate & intractable as a

Greek princess on the make. And there are no good (& probably no bad) people. The police bludgeon good & bad but perhaps bad more often. Every man in jail is a martyr. The *whole* system is bad… We shall get on better *as a whole* or not at all—or fail.

I'm moving home in England & when you come in May I shall have a house in Regent's Park close by here with a visitor's room & every accommodation.

Bless you,
H.G.

H.G. Wells to MG

May 2, 1936
47 Chiltern Court
London

Dear Stooge darling,

I've just got an advance of *The Trouble I've Seen*. It looks finally good to me & I guess he'll give it a respectable show.

… You're a dear unforgettable & how I wish we could trail about the world together. I came to America last time with that in my mind but somehow the tinder didn't catch.

I wish I wasn't seventy. If I was forty I would love you to be my wife & we would work out a lot of things together. I hate to be reminding you of a cancer… I try not to think to much about you.

Bless you dear Stooge. Someday—before very long I shall see you…

There are wordless things I'd like to talk over with you—but I can't get them into letters. I'm writing all day. Talking as we did in Connecticut is unpleasant but writing is work.

H.G.

H.G. Wells to MG

RCA Radiogram
May 9, 1936

W1024 LONDON 25 8 1230
GELLHORN CHEZ LEWISOHN
726 PARK AVENUE NEW YORK CITY
WRITE YOU MAY STARVE BUT YOU WILL KEEP SELF RESPECT BUT
TRY A FEW SHORT ARTICLES AND STORIES LOVE HG

Eleanor Roosevelt to MG

June 26, 1936
The White House
Washington

Dear Martha,

How very sweet of you to write me! I was very much pleased by your letter and your interest in continuing to do something along the lines which we discussed. When you get back we can talk again over what can be done.

I am very much more interested in possible far away developments and steady increase of women's influence, which, I feel, tends to ameliorate bad social conditions, than I am in any immediate political developments.

I loved your description of the landing at Cherbourg. I think you will probably have some interesting experiences during your trip which should make your book well worth while.

Hick is now in Michigan and, according to the most recent advice, intends to remain in the middle west until September, but, of course, her plans may change.

Every good wish to you.

Affectionately,
Eleanor Roosevelt

Eleanor Roosevelt to MG

July 7, 1936
The White House
Washington

Dear Martha,

Thank you so much for the book [*The Trouble I've Seen*] I more than enjoyed reading it and think you were sweet to send it to me. I shall look forward to the next one.

Affectionately,
Eleanor R.

Edna Gellhorn to H.G. Wells

July 12, 1936
The Lebanon
Chautauqua

My dear Mr. Wells,

You are a very kind person to take such very good care of my daughter! You have accomplished more than I have ever achieved—up at eight, and writing!

I'm glad you like her, so do I.

Yours sincerely,
Edna Gellhorn

Edna Gellhorn to MG

August 2, 1936
The Lebanon
Chautauqua

Marty beloved,

Your letter of July 23 has this moment been gobbled and regobbled by a starved mother bird. I'm so relieved to know that you are not in Spain. The reports from there are terrific and that you might have escaped the bullets flying in every direction I can't see how it would be possible if one were out to "get dope." Edna Ferber did an excellent article from the vantage point of some little Basque village. She told the story of booming guns and fleeing refugees, that were grimly reminiscent of 1914.

Your next objective is your own book. Nothing must be allowed to interfere with that. Do any of my letters reach you? I doubt it, as it seems each time that I have written, a letter comes from you within the very next day or two giving another address. This does not matter, except for the fact that I want you to know that I *do write*.

The list is now quite ready for Morrow [MG's publisher for *The Trouble I've Seen*]. It is impressive in length and is of such a nature that any business firm would pay money for it. If it serves our purpose of letting folks know about "Trouble," we'll be satisfied. I trust the publishers will use Mrs. Roosevelt's comments in some way.

I trust you are impressed with my typing. It has been a life-saver. The need for complete concentration while acquiring the "touch system" has made it possible to exclude other thoughts, and that is well.

Every word you write is appreciated by a most devoted and admiring, if rather useless Mate.

MG to Allen Grover

August 5, 1936
37 rue Caumartin
Paris

Allen my pet,

Are you prepared to read another book of mine in mss. Chapter One [*Peace on Earth*] is done. I wish I knew whether it was worth a dime or nothing. I am living in tongue-tied silence in Germany, unable to speak a word (or at least only those relating to food, mail and road directions.) It rains. But it is cheap and there are no fleas… I am slowly going out of my mind and losing my voice from never using it.

… I'm in love, this time not with you. It doesn't do me any good either; I seem to have a fatal capacity for choosing people who are not obtainable… If I weren't frightened of the future I think I'd settle down right now and never do another thing for the rest of my life except read other people's novels.

… I know exactly why Freud started on dreams. Sex, nothing: it's the bedclothes in these Germanic countries which make people so nervous in their sleep.

I dote on you, you monument to silence.
Marty

MG to Allen Grover

August 6, 1936
27 rue Caumartin
Paris

My little plum pudding,

I wrote you a *crotte* [dogshit] of a letter yesterday, in a sudden dislike of you, thinking what a grand hit and run drive that boy has turned out to be. You see, I never got any letter from you that I know of. You will admit it comes as rather a shock to be rewarded so largely with silence, considering the circumstances. Today there is a volume on orange toilet paper and here you are again, infuriatingly seductive, always the guy who makes me laugh; and I could go out and beat my head on the accursed cobblestones of this vile picture postcard town, for not being there to laugh with you.

Lamb: I haven't done any very concise thinking about you and I don't believe I will. If I do not mistake me, we have done a certain amount of talking and decided you and I were what is known as a vicious circle or something. There are no ideas to have about you, and no decisions to make… I think I can definitely consider you as the cream in my coffee, but not my breakfast. How do you like that for a change. And I am damn glad I didn't spend the summer, slowly blistering with you: because I'd be a very caught unhappy girl by now, and you wouldn't like me worth a dime. I simply won't get tied up with you: of that I am sure. Aside from that I could jump up and down and clap hands because of your letter; and I am moved in a way I won't bother to explain, that you have kept your memory of that one night clear.

Meantime: this next book is apparently going to be fiction to a degree [*Peace on Earth*, completed February 1937]. Because I don't know any facts for a change; and I am shaky all over, having to rely on my imagination (which is only good at twisting facts, not at inventing them). You'll like it: it's a love story and I, little waif lost in the inner depths of Deutschland—am in love with both the hero and the heroine.

Are you mad? I would collect garbage for $100 a month. Keep some job for me because I am rapidly getting so broke that it is only interesting not amusing. I have just done a fat article for the *London Times*. But the money is going straight to a little gal I love who needs a vacation and can buy herself a week with that. So I'm pretty low in ingots. Yes, do keep me a job.

I got my mail for the first time in two weeks today. There were two letters from Mother which break my heart. I had no right to leave and I am a swine. Now, unless she will join me here, I am going back to her fairly soon. In about a month. That comes first after all. My own life is not so important right now: I can write this book at home and I cannot bear to fail her the only time she needs me. So you may be seeing my ravishing round countenance almost before you expect. Besides, this European jaunt has already done me a lot of good: given me a chance to take a deep breath, relax, and start all over again. It's been good for my vanity which needs some encouragement from time to time, (I just swarmed with gents in London and got fine indecent propositions in Paris from what is known as the leading writers: all hunchbacks according to me.) I've seen some things and met some funny people and rushed about and re-learned French. That's all I need besides a little time in the *Bibliothèque Nationale* in Paris for this book. After which, it wouldn't hurt me at all to do something for someone else…

If my English lad can get a divorce I shall marry him. I think you'd hate him, but he's a kind of swell person and I am not bored with him. (Funny that in the end—I ought to know better after B. who wasn't boring but was everything else—I still want to be amused.) I doubt very much that he'll get a divorce. He is a Gentleman (vile thing to be) which means that unless his wife agrees he won't do anything. All this is about as secret as it comes. I should hate you if any word ever got out. I have a lot of funny standards about people I've discovered. For instance: I won't encourage that boy by promising to marry him. He's got to get himself free because he wants to finish one way of life; not because he wants merely to change women. I think that my reasoning is that I want to see what kind of guts and independence he has. (HATE people unless they are free of me. I have a real physical loathing of people who are morally weak. A man is no use to me, unless he can live without me. Odd, isn't it. Once I'm sure he can live without me, I'm perfectly willing to deliver myself tied hand and foot. Anyhow, there we are… But anyhow I'm pleased to note that I've gotten around to the point where I consider marriage with anyone as desirable and not a new form of water torture. I'm protecting myself as usual from a let down which is inevitable and from the very obvious future which is going to be a future quite alone, with a monkey and a Dachshund for company. That's all. And you're the only person who knows of this and I trust you to forget it.)

Please write again my darling. I make myself a feast of your letters. I will never change the way I feel for you. I still get quite crumbly with excitement thinking I shall see you sometime, before we are both too old or dead.

Your little pal,
Marty

P.S. Congratulations on the farm. You must learn to touch your hat the way English squires do, as they walk over their estates chatting aimiably with the tenants. I love the idea of you as a farmer: you with your face carved by a sharp knife out of stone, and hands that weren't meant to lift anything heavier than a pencil. My very darling.

MG to Allen Grover

September 7, 1936
Tutzing
Bavaria

I came to write a book and I have not done it, though later (in that sweet old world town, St. Louis) this summer may prove valuable because everything is sharp again in my mind, sharp and hurting, and I have lost my usual pity, lost it hard. For my fellow men (notably my own class) I now say happily: *merde*. Something has to happen to harden that book [*Peace on Earth*] into shape, into sentences. But I am going to get it down straight somehow, someday, and with plenty of cruelty.

And meantime, I have said goodbye. There is nothing to come back to in Europe. Nothing I love now so much that the Atlantic is worth crossing.

Allen, save me a lunch…

Always, you know
Marty

Edna Gellhorn to MG

September 12, 1936
On the B&O
En Route to St. Louis

Dearest Marty,

Your several letters written after your receipt of my cable were not quite as bad as I had feared they would be. Your disappointment that we should miss a delightful holiday together was no greater than mine...

... You say you can be on this side in time to see the election returns. I want to be home to cast my vote for Mr. Roosevelt, and then I want to come East and go with you to some place where we can be quite alone so that you can talk to me when you want, and work hours on end. I would like to be with you from November 17th or 18th until the 2nd or 3rd of January. All of us could spend some time in the Christmas holidays together in New York if you wished. Alfred has to come East at that time to take his tests for Mt. Sinai Hospital where he seems to feel he would like to start his interning.

Not for an instant do I wish to nail you to St. Louis. I know too well how unhappy you are there. But at any rate you have given St. Louis more times to prove its drawbacks and we *know* that that is no place for you to feel inspired to put forth your best creative efforts, and I am no less eager than you to see the book born [*Peace on Earth*].

... Yesterday from Washington I mailed you the *New York Times* clipping telling you of Mrs. Roosevelt's plan to read from your book [*The Trouble I've Seen*] at the Colony Club. You certainly have a good friend in that lady....

I might go on indefinitely, but someone has objected to my clicking typewriter so I'll close as I always do with my endless desire to see as much of you as is feasible from the point of view of your own need to live your life, and this letter can end on the happy note of expectation of a reunion in November which is only two months away.

Yours,
M.

COLUMN Eleanor Roosevelt

September 16, 1936
My Day
New York

At 6 o'clock, on Monday night I walked into the Colony Club in New York City with a sinking heart and that peculiar feeling one sometimes gets in the depths of one's anatomy when about to do something one dreads and wishes one had *never* promised to do. In a moment of enthusiasm my secretary told the publisher of Martha Gellhorn's book, *The Trouble I've Seen*, that when I read the first story aloud at my home the listeners wept. He jumped to the conclusion that this was a tribute to my reading whereas it was a tribute to a very remarkable piece of writing. He asked if I would read that story over again to some friends of his. I agreed with alacrity. For it was little enough for me to do not only for a friend but for a book which I feel on its own merits should be read by many people in the next few months...

The American edition of *The Trouble I've Seen* will come out on the 23rd of this month. I cannot tell you how Martha Gellhorn, young, pretty, college graduate, good home, more or less Junior League background, with a touch of exquisite Paris clothes and "esprit" thrown in, can write as she does. She has an understanding of many people and many situations and she can make them live for us. Let us be thankful she can, for we badly need her interpretation to help understand each other.

Alfred Gellhorn to MG

September 25, 1936
4366 McPherson Avenue
St. Louis

Dearest bitch–bitch,

Thanks for your letter of some little while ago. I have just reread it, and find that again you say the thing that I feel and can't say. Of course, I mean about Dad. For some reason, I think that you and I are the only children who feel just this way about Dad. I suppose George and Wally are blissfully happy at the moment, and physically unable to realize the void in Mud's [Edna] life or in their own.

I am overjoyed at the prospect of being with you this winter. I know I'll be a much better man for it. Mother and I are savoring the fun that your presence will bring already. Mud doesn't quite believe yet that you will come back to St. Louis so she says she is convinced that you won't come thereby trying to cut the edge of her disappointment. She is planning to meet your boat in NYC and tell you all the unpleasant things about St. Louis, but she is hoping with all her heart that you will discount them and come back. I think we could make it a pretty memorable time.

I have been reading reviews of your book [*The Trouble I've Seen*] avidly. From all accounts it should sell like hot cakes. However, I do wish to warn you of this point. Do not feel that the first ten thousand that you make is clear. You will find when you come to St. Louis that Mud is bankrupt and you will have to support her. The reason: she is buying your book by the dozens and giving it to friends and strangers. She feels that she must purchase from all of the bookstores in the city so that they will be convinced that the book is a national and world bestseller. We only eat one meal a day, and with the money that we save on the third, we buy yet another copy of your book.

I'll be waiting for you with open arms when and if you come, sweety,
alf [sic]

MG to Allen Grover

Octóber 4, 1936
Hotel Lincoln
Paris

Darling,

… This afternoon I am going to the riots. What I love about France is their sense of order inside a framework of anarchy. The Communists plan a manifestation at the *Parc des Princes*, the Fascists automatically arrange a counter-manifestation. All Paris knows. One puts on one's Sunday black and takes the kiddies along. It is sweet. They do not shoot, which makes it all gay but not nasty. At heart, they are not so serious— having marvelous good-sense and real humor—that they are prepared to die for anything. Except *la belle France*, in case strangers start walking over it.

I love this people: but Paris is rapidly getting as seedy and sad as Vienna. It does not pay to win wars. Everything is very damn bad. Everywhere. And Gellhorn personally envies the ostriches, and longs for a dash of blindness. I am, as usual, asking questions and reading. Tomorrow I see Delaisi (who is a partial French Keynes) who has asked me to come and talk about the world. Wait till he sees me. Right now he thinks I am a *cher collègue,* 50 years old, and spectacled. In fact I have reverted to Paris, with very long hair, vast very painted eyes, smart unbecoming clothes and fingernails like a mandarin. Just the old split personality.

We are in strikes again: the restaurants having closed because the waiters are sick of it all. In fact, one enters by back doors, eats behind closed shutters, fast, pushed; badly cooked and over-charged food. Poor waiters. Society gathers together, like a coiled snake, when anything *interrupts*. Last night I dined with Drieu la Rochelle, who used to be a fine writer and is now in love with war and sexy as a satyr. And we visited the Louvre (it is open at night, beautifully lighted) and the Tabarin, and discussed women's breasts. The result of all this is that I feel increasingly fey, fake and oppressed. I don't belong in an air so strange, so languid and so intense. What did I do here for five years? What incredible obstinacy or endurance held me amongst strangers for most of my adult life? They are now decided that I am a lesbian because no men mar the scenery, because I deny the gloating satisfaction in physical love whereof they all brag, and because I have explained icily that in an unhappy life we can at least be calm—alone.

I shall be ready for the long smoky, unexciting winter. And Europe is finished for me. A lot of things are finished. Which simply means growing up, growing old, growing soggy and discouraged.

Angel—
Marty

Eleanor Roosevelt to MG

October 9, 1936
On the President's Train

Dear Martha,

Your letter was very interesting and very sweet. I hear your book is going very well [*The Trouble I've Seen*], much to my joy.

I hope you will let me know where you are as soon as you land. We will be back in Hyde Park the night of the 17th and I will probably be in New York City for a day the following week. I hope very much to see you several times before I start for home.

Affectionately,
Eleanor Roosevelt

Alfred Gellhorn to MG

October 15, 1936
4366 McPherson Avenue
St. Louis

Sissy dearest,

Come two weeks from the receipt of this letter, and I shall be folding you to my expansive bosom. I'm looking forward to it with mixed feelings of joy and joyfulness. Needless to say, Mud [Edna] is a changed person. She is tremendously excited and happy.

There are a couple of things which I must needs tell you. What you seem to have forgotten is: (1) 4366 is usually draughty in the winter, and alternately like an ice box, and then a Bessemer furnace. It is almost always well covered with a one inch layer of soot. (2) St. Louis, like any metropolis of one million is noisy at all times and unbelievably ugly. In the winter you will wake to gray-yellow smoke that will make you gag. Within three minutes of getting out of the house, your schnozzle looks like the inside of a dark cave. (3) Need I really remind you of the people in St. Louis? Except for the W. Fischels, Grahams, Andersons and a very few others, they are a nauseating a group as there is in the world.

Anyhow, my large lump of suet, I'm happy beyond measure that you will be here, and I shall bask in your glory, insert myself into all of your private affairs, and get gloriously tipsy with you on occasion.

A thousand welcomes to the land of liberty.

More brotherly love than you are accustomed to.
alf

Gellhorn's book of fictional Depression-era portraits, *The Trouble I've Seen*, was published to great acclaim by William Morrow in NYC during fall 1936. Her publisher produced a pamphlet that included a blurb by Eleanor Roosevelt who not only supported the book because it was timely and important reading, but also because Gellhorn was a trusted friend. The Baltimore *American* kvelled that it was "startling… a volume every adult should read," and the *World-Telegram* noted that her "stories are question marks. Readers can't take them solely as entertainment. They have to say, 'Can't we do something about it?'" Even *The New Yorker* reviewer observed, "Martha Gellhorn writes truly and affectingly."

REVIEW

October 24, 1936
Globe-Democrat

BOOK REVIEW
Martha Gellhorn Gives "On Relief" a New Meaning

"The Trouble I've Seen," by Martha Gellhorn. (William Morrow & Co., New York.)
By Helen Long

AMERICA needs more writers like Martha Gellhorn. But why say America? The tragic problem of our country which she so cogently presents here is also a world problem, and the characters she depicts, although typically American, have their counterparts in misery and frustration all over the globe.

On relief: The term must have a new significance after reading these stories which are the result of the author's observations as a worker in the Federal Emergency Relief Administration. To consider the writer's technique seems oddly difficult after reading these terrible, convincing chronicles of the destitute. They are related without sentimentality, with vigor and precision, and with that life-saving perception without which no literature can be effective.

Here we meet those who have passed from simple security to want and bewildered distress. We observe in some the gradual deterioration of character; in others an amazing patience and pluck. We see the flushed face and high head of pride above ragged, cast-off garments and hear the faltering explanations. We see the stricken faces of mothers who, although they give all their strength and thought and time and thought, cannot save their children. We meet the sturdy worker confused by new conditions, the feeble, the incompetent, the predatory, the faithful—all comprising that stream of life upon which we are desperately drifting.

"I don't want nothing from relief," shouted Pete, "I can work, I can work." It required many humiliating experiences, days of standing in line at unemployment agencies and factories, of hunger, cold, miserable living conditions, of seeing his wife desperate and agonized, before he was reduced to terror and degeneration. There was Joe who organized the union among the factory workers, but somehow didn't understand very well why the strikers turned against him. There is the story of Ruby, the little girl who wanted something of her own, something pretty—a record of almost unbeatable horror. And there were Jim and Lou who wanted to marry.

And first of all, there is that delightful, unforgettable character, Mrs. Madison. This jolly, courageous, middle-aged woman worked unremittingly. She was always looking out for a bit of fun, wanting the young folks to have a chance, bouncing up under distressing circumstances, planting flowers around a wretched shack, and making pictures for herself in idle moments of a home, a reunited family, a garden, things on the shelves in jars, living like real people. She knew it couldn't come but it helped to dream about it.

We cannot quite forget that last glimpse of Mrs. Madison as she sat down to write Mr. Roosevelt a long letter, to thank him for his kindness, to explain about the children and why they could not keep the farm, assuring him she hoped to pay back the money they owed the government—only work was so hard to get.

Alfred Gellhorn to MG

November 6, 1936
4366 McPherson Avenue
St. Louis

Sissy dearest,

I'm glad you were born [Martha's birthday was November 8th] and I'm glad that we'll be together this winter. It's going to mean more to Mud than you can possibly realize...

Tomorrow will be the anniversary of the birth of one half of my religion. I miss Dad so damned much that some times I don't feel like going on with medicine.

My worth is greatly overrated by everyone because of Mud and Dad, but I personally know that I'm not worth a shit. [He became a revered oncologist.]

Well sweetheart anytime you need some more rays of sunshine cast upon your daily existence, look me up. I promise to be as bright as a penny when you come home. Now I shall get drunk by myself on good scotch which is intended for your sole use and I will drink many toasts to my favorite sister.

Alfred

Eleanor Roosevelt to MG

November 7, 1936
The White House
Washington

Dear Martha:

Thank you ever and ever so much for your letter. It is a great help and you have given me some of the best suggestions I have had.

No, I do not think much of myself as a writer, but I always hope to be better and am more than glad to make every effort.

It was grand to see you. Do not get discouraged, because you have the ability to write so that one sees what you are writing about, almost better than anyone I know.

Affectionately,
Eleanor Roosevelt

Someone sent me the article you wrote on the lynching. Hick & I thought it swell.

Bertrand de Jouvenel to MG

November 8, 1936
Paris

Take a lover, my darling, or rather take six since you seem to run to half-dozens…
This will sound bitter, angry, revolted. But it's not meant that way. Greenville, South Carolina, was the end of everything to me. The human animal is so built that the end of everything isn't much really. I mean when everything is broken to bits, such a lot remains, you wouldn't believe it possible. For five years, the thought of anyone caressing your body made me twitter with anguish.

In that loathsome apartment in New York, a line written on the first page of your book brought it violently back to me, when I joined you in Coeur d'Alène,

I discovered with wonder that it didn't matter. That all this happened, but that you were unaltered, stronger, more beautiful if anything. I write with clumsy words but you understand. And I felt too that no one in the future would "possess" you, that you would pick, choose, reject or accept, be a free agent and an aggressor.

Well, darling, of course it must happen, you must take a lover or rather lovers. Be nauseated by the absence of all that, to you, goes with making love, and gradually get used to it, till one day you'll find some tenderness and beauty where you bargained for none. And then you'll be grateful and held for a time. You'll grow to like the physical aspect of the business. It'll go by periods of greed and of disgust.

It doesn't really very much matter. Because you are a very great person, far greater than the woman Sand or than Colette. I know. Your letter about that short story you wrote gave me far more joy than the lover letter enclosed gave me pain. That letter written after a full night's work, was just heavy with sweat. My God how your room must have smelled! I love you that way. You're just a workingman, my dearest, the pen is as heavy in your hands as a hammer. And that is as it should be.

Probably, what you'll write will more and more lack taste, grace, discrimination. And I, growing more French by the minute, may come to turn up my nose. But I'll be wrong, and you'll be right. You exist, you are, you heavy, lumbering genius. Darling, let no one ever tell you you haven't the genius. It's there, and no force on earth can prevent you from howling what you have to say. There's no one in the world, man or woman, that I admire as I do you. As you well know, my dearest, there's nothing I wanted as much as to be caught in your powerful current, swung along by you. I think you made a mistake by severing our association. Because you do want companionship, love and understanding. And sometimes you faint, you know. And you like to kiss lips which are fresh from milk and lake-water and not heavy with whisky and cigars. And your letters wrap such a loving arm round me that I know you regret… sometimes. But that also doesn't matter. What matters is that you shall blunder into immortality.

The only thing that does worry me is your running entirely out of money. It's rather necessary to eat, you know. I have none at all, but if ever you cable (I keep two dollars for that purpose) I'll raise some in twelve hours.

You have formed a picture of me leading three Borzois thro' [sic] the Bois every morning, and riding to hounds. An enchanting image, however slightly untruthful. I am well dressed and clean, and my rooms are white and warm and I sleep eight hours a night and say shit to editors which [sic] don't offer me what I demand. But I've spent the last five or six days roaming thro' [sic] St. Denis preparing an article on unemployment. Privileges cum responsibilities, you know our old post-fevershamish slogan. By small installments, tho' for I am not strong the physicians are agreed on that point.

Today is the 8th of November, the second I spend without you. May God keep you, my little one. You are of his chosen people, meant to be mauled, and dragged in the dust, and finally exalted above all men.

Rest assured, Marty sweetheart, that no night goes without my dreaming of you, and that my hands hold you tight forever.

B.

"Justice at Night," the article about a lynching that Gellhorn wrote in the back garden of H.G. Wells's London house in June, was first published in *The Spectator* on August 21st, 1936. It was then regarded as straight reporting. However, "Justice at Night" was a fictional piece that emerged out of two facts. That her fiction read as nonfiction and her nonfiction read as fiction remained true of Gellhorn's writing for the rest of her life. She said, herself, "I swallowed the world around me whole and it came out in words." In the following letter to Mrs. Roosevelt, Gellhorn confessed that she would not be a suitable witness for an anti-lynching bill before the United States Senate, because she was only "a hack writer."

MG to Eleanor Roosevelt

November 11, 1936
4366 McPherson Avenue
St. Louis

Dear Mrs. Roosevelt,

Has Hick told you my latest bit of muddle-headedness. It's very funny; and I was going to appeal to you to extricate me, but that seems too much of a good thing and I am going to be a big brave girl and tidy it all up by myself. It concerns that lynching article which you said you liked (your last letter and thank you for it.) The *Living Age* pirated that—simply annexed without so much as a by-your-leave; and then sold it to Walter White who sent it to you and presumably a lot of other people. He likewise wrote me a long letter and asked me to appear before a Senate Committee on the anti-lynching bill, as a witness. Well. The point is that article was a story. I am getting a little mixed-up around now and apparently I am a very realistic writer (or liar), because everyone assumed I'd been an eye-witness to a lynching whereas I just made it up. I sent that story to my agent in London who sent it to Wilson Harris of the *Spectator* who published it. At which point Gellhorn, with $50 reward, ceased to remember the tale and went on to the next thing. It then appeared in German; was stolen by a thing called the *Magazine Digest* and published—very much shortened and confused—somewhere in the U.S.; and likewise was swiped and reprinted by the *Living Age*. Around now, I feel that I have attended twenty lynchings and I wish I'd never seen fit to while away a morning doing a piece of accurate guessing. The nearest I ever came to a lynching was being picked up late at night, somewhere in North Carolina, by a drunk truck driver, on his way home from a "necktie-party." He made me pretty sick and later I met a negro whose son had been lynched and I got a little sicker. Out of that, years later, appeared that piece. I have a feeling that I am on something of a spot but I can't see why exactly. Anyhow I shall write Walter White and tell him I'm only a hack writer, but not a suitable witness. Though God save and protect his cause on account of it's a good one.

How was the lecture trip and how are you? Are you rested a little? I don't see how you could be, but you must have magnificent powers of recuperation as well as endurance.

I got a little off my chest about democracy, at the Book Fair. Together with every other writer in the Greater New York area, I spoke at that shebang. I was scared and it was a funny night; jammed, with a thousand folk waiting, a bad room, a curious eager audience, and a pulpit affair that wobbled under one's hands… I sat and trembled all over with fear and nerves and wishing I were somewhere else. But the chance was seized to talk about dictatorships and democracies; and how we were responsible for democracy, if we wanted it we had to keep making it, and in this job writers had a part and readers an even bigger part, as they are the mass and therefore they are action… It seemed to make some sense to some people. And you do know, don't you, that though I'm more grateful than I can ever tell you for all you've done on my book [*The Trouble I've Seen*], that doesn't really count. What counts is that you're the kind of person you are, and that I love you for it. Now and always.

Marty

Eleanor Roosevelt to MG   November 30, 1936
                                                    The White House
                                                      Washington

Dear Marty,

That was funny about the lynching, but you had just enough actual fact to base it on for your rather remarkable imagination to do the trick and make it as realistic as possible! I do not think Walter White will care as long as you do not spread it around that you had not actually seen one.

The lecture trip seems to have gone pretty well.

As a matter of fact, I do not think Hick is at all frantic about the book. She grouses a great deal, but I think she really is much interested, and I am sure she will do a good job. George Bye told her she had done one-third already.

Of course, I do not do anything I don't want to do and I do want to help your book get all the circulation it possibly can.

Good luck to you on your next one.

Much love and admiration too.
Eleanor Roosevelt

Eleanor Roosevelt to MG

December 10, 1936
The White House
Washington

Dear Marty,

I have written the information you sent straight to Mr. Hopkins and we will see if anything can be done.

I am afraid a good deal of the cutting on W.P.A. which needed to be done to a certain extent is being stupidly done. I think the people in charge should always be good administrators and good people which would make life so much simpler!

I know that cartoon that Walter White sent you. It is a horrible cartoon. I saw him this week and will try to get an appointment with the President for him. I did not think he would be annoyed with you, for after all you accomplished what he wanted. I wish more people had the ability to visualize a lynching as you have done.

We did pretty well about not seeing people on the lecture trip though we did see a few. The book is progressing slowly. I expect Mr. Bye will close a deal this week.

Of course, I will forgive you for losing the notes. Perhaps it is just as well. We might do better later on as I am getting new ideas all the time.

Please go on writing just as you do, I should feel very badly if you should begin to be "respectful."

I feel about you and your attitude toward writing much as I do about Katherine Cornell and her attitude toward acting. Both of you have an attitude toward your job that makes you really top people where there is any appreciation of good workmanship.

Write to me at the White House and it will follow me anywhere I may happen to be. To be sure that your letter comes to me unopened when Mrs. Schneider is away, put your name in the left hand corner, otherwise it might be opened first though there is no chance that it would be one of those letters that you used to read!

I am finishing up my Christmas shopping and leading a rather busy life seeing people, etc., before going back on Sunday to meet the President when he returns. I dread their return without Gus as he meant so much to all of us. He was a loyal and devoted friend and in this life one never has too many of them.

Much love to you and a Merry Christmas.

Affectionately,
E.R.

FOUR

The Spanish Earth

"I didn't go to write. I just went to be there.
It was an act of solidarity."

—Martha Gellhorn, on Madrid, 1937

At the end of December 1936, Martha Gellhorn, her younger brother Alfred
and their mother Edna were vacationing in Key West, avoiding the empty first
Christmas at home in St. Louis without Dr. George Gellhorn, who had died earlier
that year. They met, by chance, at Sloppy Joe's bar its most famous patron: Ernest
Hemingway. Initially, he suspected Alfred was Martha's husband, but he soon
discovered the truth and offered the trio his services as local tour guide.

As Martha's intimate correspondence with Eleanor Roosevelt in January 1937
reveals, she was smitten from the outset with Hemingway's dedication to their
shared craft and what she might learn from him. At the same time, Gellhorn was
writing to Allen Grover, her friend who happened to be the Vice-President at *TIME*,
for feedback about the novel she was working on, which she called *Peace on
Earth*. Though never published, it's included in her papers in Boston with this note
in her handwriting: "I judged it worthless after a year's work." It is evocative, nevertheless, of Paris in the 1930s.

While in New York in January 1937, Hemingway suggested to Max Perkins,
his Scribner's editor, that he buy Gellhorn's story "Exile" for *Scribner's Magazine*.
Having admired her four novellas collected in *The Trouble I've Seen* (1936),
Perkins acquired it, and it was published in the September 1937 issue. Charles
Scribner himself wrote to Martha to say he'd buy the story, but it needed to
be cut. February 13, 1937, she replied: "I do not write so well that every word
is essential, but I hate having to change things when they have already been
done as carefully as I can do it... Books matter, but magazines are for people on

trains." According to biographer Caroline Moorehead, Gellhorn made Scribner's requested cuts to the story.[10]

At the same time, Hemingway signed a contract in New York with the North American Newspaper Alliance (NANA) to be their world-class war correspondent and travel to Spain to cover the Spanish Civil War. It had begun in July the previous year when General Franco attempted a *coup d'état* against the democratically elected coalition government.

On March 3rd, 1937, Kyle Crichton provided Gellhorn with a letter in NYC identifying her as a special correspondent for *Collier's*. That month, 28-year-old Martha pitched an article to *Vogue* with the working title "Beauty Problems of the Middle-Aged Woman." For research, she underwent an experimental chemical peel that ruined her skin, but the piece paid for her passage to France. On March 17th, the *St. Louis Post-Dispatch* reported she was *en route* to Europe with the hope of getting into war-torn Spain: "She has made arrangements to join Ernest Hemingway and other Americans seeking entrance into that country." That may well have been the first time their names were publicly mentioned together, though they were not yet a couple.

In her papers Martha notes: "March 30, 1937–Dec 2, 1938: Spain with Hemingway." Her journal entries were handwritten as she travelled, then typed once she had set up a base from which to work. In the early 1980s, Gellhorn mused, "There was plenty wrong with Hemingway, but nothing wrong with his honest commitment to the Republic of Spain… and nothing wrong with his respect for the Spanish people. He proved it by his actions."

In a late-in-life radio interview, she explained, "I didn't go [to Spain] to write. I just went to be there. It was an act of solidarity. I'd learned about the Spanish war in Germany. I was there in '36 when it began and read about it in the Nazi newspapers. And from reading about it in the Nazi newspapers I knew that the republic was the side to be on 'cause they referred to them as red swine dogs. And, if the Nazis said they were red swine dogs, then I knew they were the right people. And, I was an anti-fascist. And, I went there because those were the only people who were standing up to this horrible man via Franco. I mean, Franco wouldn't have won or existed if it weren't for the help of Mussolini or Hitler. I had no intention of writing and I hung around for quite a long time without writing. And then somebody said, you're a writer, why don't you write about it? So I wrote about the only thing I knew which was Madrid."

That piece about Madrid was published by *Collier's* on July 17, 1937, and called "Only the Shells Whine." Gellhorn preferred her title, "High Explosive for Everyone," which she'd use in her hand-picked selection of articles collected in *The Face of War* (1959). The "somebody" who encouraged her to write it was Hemingway.

In May, Hemingway's longtime friend Sylvia Beach, the warm-eyed, intelligent proprietor of the Paris bookshop Shakespeare and Company, convinced him to give a reading to help raise funds to save the store. She had been especially kind to him and his first wife Hadley when they arrived in the 1920s on a limited budget. Beach had allowed them to borrow as many books as they liked from the store's lending library and invited them to meals with her. It's largely due to Beach's extraordinary book collection that Hemingway read Henry James. Even baby Bumby, Hemingway's first-born son Jack, was a regular at the 12 rue de l'Odéon shop in those days.

On May 13th, 1937, Martha and Ernest dined with Beach and her longtime companion Adrienne Monnier a few doors down from the shop, in Adrienne's apartment at number 18, before the 9 p.m. event. Ernest was nervous about reading publicly, so drank steadily, switching between sips of White Horse whisky and quaffs of beer, his face growing ruddier and sweatier with each swallow.

According to Beach, "Hemingway promised to read a part of his novel [*To Have and Have Not*], and we wrote out a whole lot of invitations by hand and then twice a day he came in and said he could never read that novel—twasn't [sic] any good anyway and as for himself he just wanted to go back to the Spanish front and get killed right off."

The bookshop filled with enthusiastic supporters including James Joyce and his wife Nora Barnacle, French poet Paul Valéry and his family, philanthropist Natalie Barney, the United States Ambassador to France, and Ernest's friend Janet Flanner, Paris correspondent for *The New Yorker*. Hemingway mumbled his way through an introduction about writing and war, took a fortifying swig of foamy beer from the large mug on the narrow table behind which he'd tucked his bulk and read in a voice little more than a whisper from "Fathers and Sons." A woman in the audience implored him to speak louder, and, as the *International Herald Tribune* reported the next day, "he put expression in his clean, terse phrases, beginning to show grace under pressure."

The pale, lean English poet Stephen Spender, another fervent supporter of the socialist cause in Spain and a committed anti-fascist like Martha and Ernest, also read new work he'd recently written: "The guns spell money's ultimate reason/ In letters of lead on the spring hillside/ But the boy lying dead under the olive trees/ Was too young and too silly/ To have been notable to their important eye./ He was a better target for a kiss." When he finished reading five new poems, he gulped what remained of Ernest's beer and the two of them moved through the roar of chatter that trailed them out into the Paris night. A querulous Ernest muttered under his breath to Martha that he'd never again give a public reading from his work, not even for Sylvia Beach.

Back in New York at the end of May 1937, Gellhorn worked closely with documentary director Joris Ivens to forge connections to distribute *The Spanish Earth* and finish their film that chronicled the struggle against the scourge of fascism, expected to be ready for release in early July. She wrote to Eleanor Roosevelt asking if they could bring their film to the White House for a screening for her and the President, and it was arranged for July 7th.

By June 4th, Hemingway was also back in New York, where he delivered his "Fascism is a Lie" speech to 3,500 people gathered at Carnegie Hall for the Writers' Congress. He said, "There is only one form of government that cannot produce good writers and that system is fascism. A writer who will not lie cannot live and work under fascism." Martha was there in the wings, wearing her silver fox jacket that she bought in Madrid. The next night Martha spoke at The New School for Social Research, noting, "The writers who are now in Spain… were just brave, intelligent people doing an essential job in war… completely unaware of themselves… A man who has given a year of his life, without heroics or boastfulness, to the war in Spain, or who, in the same way, has given a year of his life to steel strikes, or to the unemployed, or to the problems of racial prejudice, has not lost or wasted time. He is a man who has known where he belonged." Thus began her much-lauded series of lectures across the United States in support of the citizens of Spain, a task which she loathed, but hoped would get the word out about what was happening in Europe.

On June 6th, while Gellhorn collaborated with the sound engineers at Columbia Broadcasting to do the post-production sound effects for *The Spanish Earth*, Orson Welles started to record the commentary that Hemingway had written for the documentary. He generously took a break from working on his landmark anti-fascist Mercury Theatre production of *Julius Caesar*, which opened later in the summer on West 41st, to lend his voice. Like the majority of those dedicated to the Spanish cause, Welles was willing to donate his time to help Ivens finish his vision of the film.

Welles wondered aloud if Hemingway's words were necessary, that maybe it would be better just to see the film without voice-over. Ernest growled in the darkened projection room, protesting, "Some damn faggot who runs an art theatre is not going to tell me how to write a narration." And Welles, player that he was, began to camp up his response: "Oh, Mr. Hemingway, you think that because you're so big and strong and have hair on your chest, you're going to bully me?" Then the two of them lunged at each other, two-hundred-pound Don Quixotes tilting at imagined windmills, their lumbering shadows thrown across the screen as the Spanish countryside rolled by, swinging in rage and missing most of the time. When the lights came up, everyone burst into laughter. Hemingway fired Welles because, as he told director John Huston later, he "sounded like a cocksucker swallowing." He then recorded the narration himself for the final cut.

Jack Hemingway, Ernest's eldest son, met Gellhorn for the first time at the New York screening of *The Spanish Earth* on July 5th. On weekend leave from boarding school to meet his father, Jack arrived at the off-Broadway theatre, and, when he alighted under the marquee, Martha rushed up to the 13-year-old and said, "You must be Bumby, I'm Marty." In his own memoir, Jack wrote, "I was overwhelmed by this marvelous creature who could say the F word so naturally that it didn't sound dirty, and otherwise talk like a trooper or a high-born lady, whichever suited the circumstances."

Two days later, Gellhorn, Hemingway and Ivens flew to Washington in order to show the documentary to President and Mrs. Roosevelt at the White House. In an August 2nd letter to his mother-in-law Mrs. Pfeiffer, Hemingway complained that they were fed "a rainwater soup followed by rubber squab, a nice wilted salad and a cake some admirer had sent in. An enthusiastic but unskilled admirer." He reported that the Roosevelts "both were very moved by *The Spanish Earth* picture but both said we should put more propaganda in it." And that "Martha Gellhorn, the girl who fixed it up for Joris Ivens and I to go there, ate three sandwiches in the Newark airport before we flew to Washington. We thought she was crazy at the time but she said the food was always uneatable [sic] and everybody ate before they went there to dinner. She has stayed there a lot. Me, I won't be staying there anymore."

By July 10th, Hemingway and Ivens were in Hollywood, hoping to obtain commercial distribution by one of the major film studios as well as trying to raise money for ambulances in Spain (at a cost of $1,000 each) by talking about their experiences there on the civil war front and screening the documentary at the house of Frederic March. There, Dorothy Parker was the first to pony up the full amount for a vehicle, having already donated $500 to help them finish the film. Scott Fitzgerald, then a script doctor for MGM, also attended and sent a congratulatory telegram to Ernest the next day. It read, "THE PICTURE WAS BEYOND PRAISE AND SO WAS YOUR ATTITUDE."

Gellhorn remained in New York and tried to finesse contacts there that would help to distribute the film to a wider audience, her frustration evident in her July 24th letter to Hemingway. By August, both of them had booked passage on separate ships to return to Madrid. Of that time Martha would later suggest, "in that prehistoric past we tried in vain to be discreet."

H.G. Wells to MG

December 17, 1936
13 Hanover Terrace
London

Dear Stooge,

I've had two nice letters from you—one very short & very sweet. I may be coming to America to lecture in October. I'm not sure.

Also I see your reading list in the *N. Y. Times Sunday Review*. Have you been reading me—NO! Bless you, all the same. I got a certain amount of work done in a better laborious way. Nobody takes much notice.

I have written a short story called *The Croquet Player* [novella, published in 1937 by Viking].

The abdication [of King Edward VIII, later Duke of Windsor, for the love of "that woman," American divorcée Wallis Simpson] was disgusting.

Bless you,
H.G.

Eleanor Roosevelt to MG

December 28, 1936
The White House
Washington

Dear Marty,

Thanks very much for your Christmas greeting. As you probably read in the papers, I spent Christmas with Franklin, Jr. What are you doing in Florida?

With every good wish for the New Year,

Affectionately,
ER

MG to Eleanor Roosevelt

January 8, 1937
Key West

Dear Mrs. Roosevelt,

I'm in Key West: to date it's the best thing I've found in America. It's hot and falling to pieces and people seem happy. Nothing much goes on, languidly a sponge or a turtle gets fished, people live on relief cosily, steal coconuts off the municipal streets, amble out and catch a foul local fish called grunt, gossip, maunder, sunburn and wait for the lazy easy years to pass. Me, I think all that is very fine indeed and if all the world were sunny I daresay there'd be much less trouble as well as much less of that deplorable thing called officially progress.

I came down with Mother and Alfred to escape a Saint Louis Xmas and they went back and I stayed on, praying to my own Gods (they both look like typewriters) for some wisdom. I have thrown everything I've written out again. It is getting me blue as daisies but there seems nothing else to do. Either this book [*Peace on Earth*] must be just right and as alive as five minutes ago, or it won't be a book and I'll sit and nurse a lost year as best I can. Anyhow, a week of steady mulling has produced a new and pretty good detailed plan for the book. The story itself is lovely and terrible and I know it's just right: but I lack the technical ability to make it come right. So I just fiddle along, writing and hoping and tearing things up and making myself a nuisance to my peers and betters. Life will be a fine thing when all this is finished.

I see Hemingway, who knows more about writing dialogue (I think) than anyone writing in English at this time. (In a writer this is imagination, in anyone else it's lying. That's where genius comes in.) So I sit about and have just read the mss of his new book and been very smart about it; it's easy to know about other books but such misery to know about one's own. So Hemingway tells me fine stories about Cuba and the hurricane and then I come home and somberly drearily try to make a solid plan for a book which seems to be a think-book in which everyone sits down all the time and talks and broods and nothing happens. It is enough to drive the strongest one quite bats.

Going home at the end of the week, prepared to sit there and first freeze and then broil until this thing gets done.

If the madman Hitler really sends two divisions to Spain my bet is that the war is nearer than even the pessimists thought. It is horrible to think of Germany just this side of food riots and that maniac—no longer apparently even caring about history or facts, stopped by nothing, and protected by terror— being able to lead a perfectly good nation into something which will finish them up nicely. If there is a war, then all the things most of us do won't matter any more. I have a feeling that one has to work all day and all night and live too, and swim and get the sun in one's hair and laugh and love as many people as one can find around and do all this terribly fast, because the time is getting shorter and shorter every day.

I love you very much indeed, and I am always glad to know you're alive.

Yours,
Marty

January 12, 1937
New York City

Dear Marty,

As you can gather, I have been busy or I would have fulfilled my promise to write about the manuscript before this…

Your letter this morning makes me disinclined to write you my criticisms of the manuscript [*Peace on Earth*] since you are going to finish one draft of it anyway. Still, if you want me to I will put down on paper what I think the trouble is, though I can't see that it will do much good until the first draft is completed. I can't resist this: basically, my friend, you're writing a political thesis and not a novel. There is no *story*. I say, if you want to write a thesis, do it for a doctorate at Columbia and let it be published in some foreign news journal, or if you want to write a novel, write a story of people. But you can't expect a guy shopping around a bookstore with $2.50 in his pocket to get much kick out of a work which is neither the one, nor the other.

Some people, like Shaw and Wells have been able to combine the two, but I think you are still too immature for so grand a design.

I am glad you got tired of Hemingway. The few times I've met him with Arch MacLeish, I have had just about enough of him in one lunch.

I think it's probably a good thing to go ahead and finish the book even if you know it isn't right. Then let the doctors have a clinical meeting and see if an oxygen tent is worth the expense. If not, you will at least have got something out of your system, and though the creative effort is a failure, it will not be a public failure. You are going to keep on being a good writer and it is not a little silly for you to be so distraught at the collapse of one idea—which even yet may not be so.

Give my love to your mother and much for yourself. If you acquire a batch of thirty or forty pages, send it along. I'd like to keep tabs on Nicky, though she is an irritating creature, and so far I can really discover no reason for her being in the book at all.

As ever yours,
A.

January 13, 1937
4366 McPherson Avenue
St. Louis

Dear Mrs. Roosevelt,

Nothing as pleasant as stopping off in Washington to see you is scheduled to happen right now. I have just returned from Key West. Saint Louis is torn between a nice flat rain, sleet storms, coal black snow and its usual carbon monoxide atmosphere. It is therefore even prettier and more livable than usual. I came home because that was what I intended to do with my winter originally, and here I shall continue to sit. Until spring. And then, *en route* for someplace else, may I come and use the lovely invitation you sent me.

The book is so horribly bad that I have adopted a new system in despair. I now write ten pages a day, whether I have anything to say, any ideas or enthusiasm, or not. I shall be finished in about a month and a half at this rate. Which means that I will have turned out a perfectly lifeless story in which all the details are accurate and who cares. My idea is then to do something hard for a bit, leaving the book which has become an obsession and therefore no good for me or anyone else. Then I'll return to it, or rather throw that version away and try again. I have to proceed at any cost. Rewriting the same chapter day after day finally makes you a little crazy.

I've had a wonderful time with Hemingway at Key West. He does know the craft beautifully and has a swell feeling for words and is very careful about them, working slowly and never using anything he doesn't think is accurate. He tells me what is wrong with me now is that I've worried too much and gotten the whole thing dark in my mind, and says the thing to do is simply write it and be brave enough to cancel it out if it's no good. We agreed that anyone writing ought to have time to fail and waste effort and not howl about it; but we also agreed that as the European war came nearer and nearer that there seemed terribly little time to do anything. I maunder on terribly don't I. It seems silly to be so frantic over one little idea, one little book, one little life, when things are blowing up so badly everywhere. I want to be in Spain desperately, because that's the Balkans of 1912. And if you're part of a big thing you feel safe; it's only waiting and looking on from the outside that makes one nervous and lost. For the first time in a long while I hate the way I live. But one has to stick by things until the end.

Thank you for your wire. You are pretty grand to me. I don't deserve anything right now except contempt. However. What is happening to your book and what is Lorena doing. She has become slightly more silent than the tomb, she must be working well.

Love,
Marty

> This letter to Pauline Pfeiffer, Hemingway's second wife, is one of only two found
> so far. In it, Gellhorn refers to two photos she enclosed of Bertrand de Jouvenel,
> her common-law spouse (his wife Marcelle refused to grant him a divorce)
> from 1930–34, imploring: "Send them back… I have no others." Those photos,
> depicting a sleek sunworshipper, are in her Boston papers, so Pauline did indeed
> return them to Martha as requested.

MG to Pauline Pfeiffer

January 14, 1937
4366 McPherson Avenue
St. Louis

Pauline cutie,

Being here is worse than I had remembered possible. It rains and freezes on its way down. You cut your way through the smoke with an acetylene torch. Everyone has flu and you wait your turn patiently. It is like living at the bottom of a particularly noisome well. I am not content. But it is going to be brief. My new system of the daily dozen (pages, by God), is going to finish this book in no time. Then I shall flush it down the churlit [sic] and be a free woman. I am going places. I find myself boring and all the usual life about me sinister. Perhaps I shall take a cutter (now would it be a cutter) and sail about the Horn. Or maybe the Himalayas are the place for an ambitious girl. Or something, anyhow.

Look. Here are two photographs of Bertrand, so you'd know. Aren't they fine. They were taken by me with my little Brownie three years ago, I think, at Arcachon. Arcachon was funny; as we waded in off a boat we had rented, Marcelle (B's wife) and her lover Byron, seeing us, waded out at a point farther down and quickly took a boat away. Like a bad farce on the Boulevards. It was sunny and as the naked eye can see Bertrand was brown and well. Now he looks shrunken and tired and pale green, but once he was a pleasure to see. Send them back; that is also an excuse to make you write me a letter. But really. I have no others.

I had a very fine time with Ernestino eating the most superb steak somewhere and then quietly and sleepily digesting and admiring the vast head of Mr. Heeney. That man—Ernestino not Heeney—is a lovely guy as you have no doubt guessed yourself, long before this. I have also been reading his collected works but I am afraid to, because the style is very taking and I do not want to take his style, no matter how fine it may be and superior to all the styles I've been trying on lately. A lousy thing, but my own is my literary motto. In passing perhaps it would be as well to tell you that his collected works are pretty hot stuff not to say tops.

I loved seeing you, I loved Key West because of you and him and the sun and we will not omit Masters Patrick and Gregory who are seductive. All my thwarted mother love received a rude jolt because I went up in the car of Mr. Van Hining to Miami and his eldest daughter Jean was along, a girl who brings out the paranoia (spelling) in anyone. I said to myself, hell no, I won't risk it. My brats would surely be like this and not little gentlemen like the Hemingway young. And I'd be the kind of mother who went in for drownings, too.

What I am trying to tell you in my halting way is that you are a fine girl and it was good of you not to mind my becoming a fixture, like a kudu head, in your home. It made me very happy and if I kept a diary it would be full of fine words about you. I'll just remember it instead.

Please give my respects to the lads [Patrick, 8; Gregory, 5], and to you *chère Madame*, my affectionate souvenirs.

Devotedly,
Marty

Eleanor Roosevelt to MG

January 16, 1937
The White House
Washington

Dear Martha,

Do not be so discouraged. I do think you ought to go right ahead and write the book without rehashing all the time. You do get yourself into a state of jitters. It is better to write it all down, and then go back. Mr. Hemingway is right. I think you lose the flow of thought by too much rewriting. It will not be a lifeless story if you feel it, although, it may need polishing.

Hick is on a regular job now and I think gets pretty tired. Also, she has had a guest steadily. She promises to go on with her book beginning next week when her guest leaves. Letter writing, I imagine, is a lost art for the moment with her.

My book is going along very slowly just now as life is entirely devoted to social duties—things which I like just about as well as you like St. Louis.

Of course, you may come here at any time you feel like it.

Much love,
Eleanor Roosevelt

At the end of January, Gellhorn provided a list of recommended reading to be published in the *New York Herald Tribune*. Knowing how close she was to H.G. Wells, it's not surprising to see one of his books included. Vincent Sheean would soon become known to her personally since he also covered the Spanish Civil War. Her comment on Lorant's book about Hitler is an example of her belief that writing truthfully could wake minds to what was actually happening in the world.

JOURNALISM

January 26, 1937
NY Herald Tribune

Good Reading

Martha Gellhorn, author of "The Trouble I've Seen," sends in a ruggedly individual list of books she's enjoyed reading lately.

"News From Tartary," by Peter Fleming (Scribner's).

"The War in Outline," by Liddell Hart (Random House).

"Experiment in Autobiography," by H.G. Wells (Macmillan). "This is the only book of his I've ever read but I thought it was magnificent. I'm pretty close to illiterate what with this and that."

"Personal History," by Vincent Sheean (Doubleday).

"Pylon," by William Faulkner (Random House).

"British Documents on the Origin of the World War," arranged by Goch and perhaps Temperley. "Required reading for people who like to be mad as hornets. I'd make every one read them if I could. Because the process of history repeating itself becomes pretty untenable when only men make history (and cretinous men at that)."

"The Economic Consequences of the Peace," by J.M. Keynes (Harcourt, Brace). "I just read this a few months ago and it couldn't be more timely."

"I Was Hitler's Prisoner," by Stefan Lorant (Putnam). "Terrifying reading. Healthy for the people who loved the Olympic games and know everything is roses in *Deutschland*."

January 30, 1937
4366 McPherson Avenue
St. Louis

Dear Mrs. Barnes,

You may as well begin all over and write another letter pretty quickly. I have rarely had a letter which left me so kind of dry in the palate and gasping for air. What do you mean?

Why are you going to Russia? For how long? Isn't it all too dandy. I am as excited as if I knew what it all meant.

Me, I am going to Spain with the boys. I don't know who the boys are, but I am going with them. I feel out of everything and would like to organize a column, called Martha Ellis column. I daresay one can't walk in Madrid for tripping over Great Writers, also debris.

Here [St. Louis] everything is simply wonderful. We take our actylene torches and pickaxes to cut our way through the coal smoke. The local gentry is as charming and wide awake as ever. I have renounced the society of my peers and live on the third floor like a Yogi. I work like hell, but it doesn't seem to jell. The book is half done [*Peace on Earth*] and will be finished in a month. Which is to say that it will be written, but it will not be a book. Then I am going to Paris to begin all over. Then I am going to rewrite it. I am almost mad with poopdom, and I cannot afford to think too much about the book. I just write it. Otherwise I get the shakes and view the entire cosmic scheme with grave doubt.

Mother is wonderful, so much better than anyone else that it is remarkable. She is in fine shape, gay and brave and busy. Alfred is superb, his blood pressure must be normal, he is so sane and collected. He knows a lot about medicine and will be a fine doctor. Mother took the car out yesterday and absent mindedly shifted gears without stepping on the gear pedal and would you believe it, the gear came off in her hand and they have left the car to die, lonesome-like, on a streetcar track in some desolate part of town. Our private organization has always been a trifle feeble and it is now going to hell.

I have nothing to say to anyone at any given moment, being a monomaniac, with a book eight months gone inside of me.

Mr. Hemingway telephoned me from New York at intervals of five minutes because he was a little lonely and very excited about ambulances for Spain. He said Mr. Barnes was wonderful, about the best new young man he met in New York. He said, judging by Mr. Barnes you have fine friends. I said yes indeed, you betcha [sic]. So that was allright. [sic]

My love to both of you little ducklets. I am thrilled about Moscow, but you ought to explain it to me. Here I sit in the wilderness and no one tells me anything. I hope to be in New York about March first, sailing at once, if possible. As I say I have no money, in the end that sort of thing might hamper me, but I doubt it.

Love and blessings, Marty

In an undated letter that sold at auction in 2008, written in early January 1937 from New York City, a few weeks after they met in Key West, Ernest praised Martha for discerning that he was not a character in *To Have and Have Not*, noting that she was "smart to see it." He was, moreover, grateful that she was "being awfully good damned good" to write him letters especially knowing he was "alone in this lousy town." He references an article written by French journalist Bertrand de Jouvenel—Martha's partner from 1930-1934—about the arms General Franco was amassing in Spain, noting he read it "with pleasure, on account of him being a friend of yours, *Notre Envoye Speciale*." For his part, Hemingway hopes that by going to Spain he will be able to describe the civil war accurately in order to "serve people here in the U.S. enough to keep us maybe out." He also does not judge Gellhorn for wanting "to be a man in this or the next world," insisting he'll swear she is one, "whenever it hits" because he is crazy enough himself "to understand a healthy streak of insanity in a pal." Martha responded to him in the following letter written from her family home in St. Louis.

MG to Ernest Hemingway

January 1937
4366 McPherson Avenue
St. Louis

Dear Hemingstein,

Please do not worry about my European projects. The Spanish war is an important part of my book so I have to find out about it, at least as much as I can. If it is anything like the floods, I will not find out much and will be very disappointed.

Your typing is lousy you ought to be like me, practically faultless. Come the Revolution I am going to be private secretary and pal to the Commissar for the Welfare of Teething Infants and Suckling Mothers. I have thought it all out with an eye to the future.

I am very unhappy, far too unhappy to write a good letter. This book is an obsession and it is no good and the coal smoke is really wreaking vengeance on me so I feel foul too. Then I have had all my Europeans all over the place discussing Situations and Conditions, but I like to read about those things or write about them or see them, but I do not like the talk much.

I don't like to talk really with anybody, not when I feel the way I do. My head is a gooey puddle of despairs and dissatisfactions and worries about being a stinking writer, and my insides are like the embers of yesterday's coke fire.

You and Pauline are grand fortunate people and it is a consoling thing to think that someone enjoys itself and I wish to hell I had gotten drunk too but I don't know how to do that either. I shall now walk out and find some ashes and buy two yards of sackcloth and give away my oddments to the poor. Everything stinks. I'm glad it's fine with both of you.

My respectful homage and affectionate souvenir,
Gellhauser
P.S. I loved your letter by the way. Did I thank you?

In her itinerary of these years, Gellhorn noted for February 1937, "St. Louis, in love with E." Hemingway wrote her a letter dated "February first," which is remarkable not only because it survived Gellhorn's fiery purge of his correspondence shortly before her death in 1998, but also because it praises her writing in her Depression-era book *The Trouble I've Seen* (1936). Hemingway was particularly impressed by "Ruby," the story about an eleven-year-old girl who "hadn't had a nickel as long as she could remember," a child who turns to prostitution as a source of income in order to have her own "luxury money" to buy a pair of roller skates.

His letter opens, "Christ, Marty, I didn't know you were that good a writer," insisting that "Ruby" was "as good or I guess better story than anybody ever wrote." Waxing rhetorical, he continues, "Who is your master, Mr. Hemingstein? Miss Gellhorn, the author of Ruby." He becomes political, suggesting that there is no government "you can honestly throw in with now. Only things you can be against," though he seemed to believe that individuals could try to relieve suffering when encountered. Gellhorn would do just that, making her "tiny squeaking noise about the wrongness of things" with regard to the most disenfranchised citizens for the rest of her life. Hemingway closes, "You're a great writer Marty. If you ever worked at it you'd be terrific." Those words clearly meant something to Gellhorn as that letter is one of only two that she kept from the hundreds that Hemingway wrote to her.

Attorney Cam Becket was a lifelong friend to Martha. He handled all of her business and legal correspondence. Later he would represent her in her divorce from Hemingway in December 1945.

MG to Cam Becket

February 8, 1937
4366 McPherson Avenue
St. Louis

Cam cutie,

I have a folder full of the goddamndest letters which are supposed to be answered. When I was young, my mail was fun. Now it is blah and has to be answered. It is all about the Spanish war, and lynchings and odd little people who think I am rich and successful and social workers who want me to make speeches. It is fine. There is neither amusement nor money in it. I don't write letters anymore, I write a foul book.

Have you seen Roussi Sert [sculptor who made a bust of Gellhorn circa 1933] and if so give her my love next time. I have heard weird tales about her, coming from Paris, and I am saddened. They cannot be true, but what really distressed me was a discussion of her jewels in a recent *Vogue*. The world is going to hell. I have no more friends. Except you.

Coming back, with the completed first draft of the most stinking book [*Peace on Earth*] ever seen, early in March. After that I don't know. I'm not very well and crazy with haste and distressed to find myself no writer at all. But New York, like the hanging gardens of Babylon, is full of music and hibiscus flowers…

Love,
Marty

MG to Ernest Hemingway and Pauline Pfeiffer

February 8, 1937
4366 McPherson Avenue
St. Louis

Sweeties,

God hates the middlewest (like me). It has been raining I couldn't tell you how hard, and thus the flood has gotten some more encouragement and now it is freezing which makes it easier for everyone. I wouldn't be surprised if God, somewhat tardily said, what the hell, I'm sick of it. Look at your gale, a careless effort to blow that part of the land into the sea. Look at the dust storms last summer and look at Hitler and Mussolini. I hope we get on the same ark when the real deluge begins. It would be just my luck to survive with the members of the St. Louis Wednesday Club.

I got a letter from my Union. They sure think I am somebody. They think I am rich. Everytime they need a list for getting money, they start off with Gellhorn. To date I have contributed piddling sums to everything because I want to be loved by them. I've never seen them but they must be hot stuff. They're the American Writer's League, or something very snotzy, by invitation, all of us bourgeois-proletarians are in it. Are you Ernestino? This time they wanted me to give an airplane. I have already given my all to a local unit that is buying an ambulance. There is a telegram quoted from your [sic], Ernestino. Maybe they want me to buy an anaesthetist's set, I am mixed up. Anyhow your telegram was wonderful, by Jesus. You have caught the spirit. It makes me tremble with excitement. I feel like the weak Rover boy, the one who never got into anything. I feel horribly out of it.

Now I am also doing book reviews to make money and if you ever want to do something that makes you throw up every inch of the way, then try that.

… I wanted to go to Hollywood and get a job as an extra in your film. I was sure there'd be a scene of Madrid Besieged.

… I don't even bother to think what I am writing. I just write it.

… All I want is a haircut and to get to New York. I am beginning to love all the gents I once thought were poops and look forward to renewing contact and being tight and happy.

… There is no reason to write you except that I miss you with such fervor and etc. Give my regards to the heirs.

Love,
Gellhorn

MG to Eleanor Roosevelt

February 9, 1937
4366 McPherson Avenue
St. Louis

Dear Mrs. Roosevelt,

I feel like one of Conan Doyle's best spirits. I follow your doing from a great distance *via* the daily press and have not written because—like other spirits—I have no life worth mentioning. But it's nice to write anyhow just to say greetings and renew expressions of devotion.

I'm coming east in three weeks and one would think I was terminating twenty years in Siberia or just about to be led into the Promised Land. I'm that excited. God, how I hate Saint Louis. My mother is still the most heavenly creature I know, and being comfortable and having three regular meals a day is not to be sniffed at. But the town. The ugliness of it, the bleak, dark gray, smoke sodden ugliness.

And the feeling that you have heard everything everyone says before, how many times before, and that it was never wise nor witty and usually not even kind. The thought of seeing my buddies in New York and finding out about the great world outside has me panting with joy.

The book [*Peace on Earth*] will be done, which is to say that I have written it almost and nothing more. There will be twelve chapters about 300 pages of typescript, a story which has a beginning, a middle and an end. And that is all. It could not be worse, it is far worse than the first novel I wrote when I was sixteen. Far worse. I am past caring, being too tired. It will be done and that has come to be the main thing in life. I shall consult with a few hard-hitting friends and literary advisers, and if they can see a glimmer in the gloom, I'll spend another year on it and make it right maybe. Or else burn it. I have no convictions about it anymore. Meantime I have to find work and I want like mad to get abroad once more. Working so hard on a European book has confused the things I once knew.

I can't write you a decent letter because I haven't done anything for weeks, perhaps forever, except sit on the third floor and write. Take a walk like an old man with rheumatism. Read the papers with a dim sense of wonder, not knowing what it is all about, the things that are happening in that distant world outside. And read books by the dozen and admire the people who practise my trade well. There are plenty of them and they are wonders. It is good to know someone can do it. This is not the material for a letter, it is all a crashing bore. But there is a lovely letter from you sitting in my desk drawer, which I have read several times, and at least I wanted to thank you for it and tell you again that I am yours, as fondly as possible,

Marty

Eleanor Roosevelt to MG

February 12, 1937
The White House
Washington

Dear Marty,

I was glad to get your letter and to know that the book was done. Revision will be easy after you have talked to some of your friends in New York. I am glad you are going on in two or three weeks and I know it will do you lots of good.

Hick is there now working hard, but you and she will certainly have some good times together.

Unfortunately, you are coming on apparently just when I start off on a lecture trip in the southwest. However, I do not leave until midnight the fourth of March.

If you should come east before that care to spend a few days in Washington, do drop in. I would love to see you.

Much love.
Affectionately,
Eleanor Roosevelt

This is an invitation to stay! I'll be back just before Easter if you care to come then.

MG to Ernest Hemingway

February 15, 1937
4366 McPherson Avenue
St. Louis

This is very private. We are conspirators and I have personally already gotten myself a beard and a pair of dark glasses. We will both say nothing and look strong. Angel, I have so much to tell you, but suddenly I find that there is no time even to think straight… please, please leave word in Paris. Give my love to Pauline.
… write if you can. Please don't disappear. Are we or are we not members of the same union? Hemingstein, I am very very fond of you.

Marty

On February 27th, as Max Perkins saw him off from the dock, Hemingway sailed on the *Paris* from New York and arrived at Le Hâvre on March 6th. A week later, he met with Joris Ivens at Les Deux Magots in Paris. Gellhorn followed a week or so after. She arrived in Paris on March 21st and took the train south and into Spain, alighting in Barcelona on the 24th, noting in her journal that she "slept like the dead."

Eleanor Roosevelt to MG

March 1, 1937
The White House
Washington

Dear Martha,
    I do not blame you about the way you feel about your book and I only hope some day you will make a play of it yourself. I think it would be very

good and I would make a play out of each story as I do not think plays should be crowded. If you try to put all of the characters in the book into one play, it would be cluttered.

I am terribly sorry not to see you before you sail. I am so glad you showed your book to Paul and he was so enthusiastic. All of you real writers need appreciation more than you do criticism for you are such hard critics on yourselves where your own work is concerned. I am not afraid you will do too little work on the book, but that you will do too much.

… Good luck to you, and, for heaven's sake, if you go to Spain, don't kill yourself, either physically or emotionally.

Affectionately,
Eleanor Roosevelt

MG to Ernest Hemingway
March 2, 1937
New York City

Darling,

No one cares about the war in Spain except you and me and Malraux. And then, I am neither of you, so no one cares about me. I have been running myself ragged; have seen two editors a day, telephoned two more, talked and talked, argued, explained…

… I am a little drunk from a large cocktail party in my honor which revolted me and all the men were sickening. You couldn't even face the theatre with them… I hope to God that I am not doomed to this, day after day, upper classes and too much liquor and men who fill you with doubt about men generally. I have everything except luck, to date.

If only I could get there. The barricades are my idea of where every man should be. And instead I have Park Avenue and a kind of terror that this is the end. I am not sober. I am very damn fond of you but respectably.

Marty

> This letter from her ship crossing to Paris, before taking the train to Spain, to her longtime friend and one-time lover Allen Grover, an old chum from her St. Louis days, is typical of the chatty, frank, amusing correspondence she would send him over many decades.

Early March 1937
Shipboard

Sir,

... You ought to see how I go up in the world like a skyrocket.

I have a first class cabin (the steward says the class here is '*mixte*'). It is enormous and cosy and hideous as is everything on every boat but notably on the French boats. There is a bath and a radiator which exploded once and was called for grumpily by two gents with cigarettes over their ears. There is a telephone which works on occasion and a bell which never works at all. The elevators are in a state of *arrêt momentané*, which means they won't work this crossing and probably not the next one either... I never get over the French, they're the nastiest people on earth and probably the best. They carry their pride around with them and no one ever treads on it really, and they're sly and greedy and prudent and scheming, and with something so wonderful, a warm tangible set of values which makes *crêpes suzettes* far more vital than the immortal soul, in the end. (Sir, you cannot eat immortal souls, not this year.)

I am eating partly in bed, since I sleep until two or three, and partly in first where the food is better. I am amused by the engraved invitations to cocktails and dinner (boats are getting sillier every season) and by two thugs in first and a theatrical troupe of three blank faced lovely tough kids in Tourist. Nobody else. Mainly I am amused by sleeping which is a treat let me tell you, and by languid reading, and by not having anything to do.

This trip ought to go all right; I am in no mood to get involved emotionally with strangers. I shall be rested when I arrive which is a guarantee of making some sense, shall leave if possible that same night for Marseille and the border. Only Spain worries me; I am nervous of not understanding anything, getting sidetracked somewhere and confused in my thinking. That would be pretty grim. No use worrying about it in advance.

... Anyhow lamb I still think you're more fun than all the other members of your deplorable sex, lined up one by one and stretching from here twice to Tokyo. I also think you're a relief to look at and you have a good mind which goes places easily and a helluva lot of other things, but I renounce you again as I renounce you every time I go or come, and every time I see you.

Love,
Marty

March 1937
37 rue Caumartin
Paris

Dearest old lawyer,

I hope you'll finish by thinking all my causes are right. I'd enjoy very much having you on the side of trouble and change and hope and infinite disappointments.

All I know now is this: (and I believe it's somewhere in the Bible in different words), *man scarcely lives by bread at all.* All the bread finally isn't worth a hoot in hell. What you live by is what you believe and what you are willing to sacrifice for, what you admire and love. And all money can buy is time. There is no security anywhere; only fools believe that God and man can be controlled into safety. But you can make a rich life out of trying, and that's what I mean to do. And you can learn, slowly and fairly miserably, to have respect for history and for your tiny anonymous place in the making of it. I know what I'm doing. I waste time and energy, and lavish my heartaches all over the place: but I still know what I am doing. I believe in man. I want to be with those who work to give man a chance.

Write to me, but remember I am in a country at war, where words are serious, and do not speak lightly of the cause because I should be in trouble. The difference between a democracy at war & a democracy at peace is that one has a censor.

And take care of yourself, and be happy, but don't forget how big the world is.

Love,
Marty

You wrote me a beautiful letter & bless you for it. You're about the lastingest friend I have.

DIARY   March 23–April 25, 1937, Spain

Gellhorn's diary from Spain reveals her journalist's eye for detail and her desire to record the facts as clearly as possible, regardless of how pleasing others might find them. She remained true to her prose throughout her life. The diary provides a real sense of how close she was to the front and how shelling affected her life daily. She is careful about referring to Hemingway once their affair begins, naming him vaguely as E. or H. As always, she's concerned with remembering the ordinary citizens in extraordinary circumstances exactly as they were in their frangible humanity. She refered to them as "the sufferers of history," those strangers who remain alive decades later through her words.

When she left on the Paris train early in the morning on March 23rd, 1937, she noted, "there were fruit trees in bloom, small pink ones, and larger round white ones. Little stony green fields." Within two hours, "the trees were of glass and the fields white and the snow blew straight over the land." When the train stopped at the Spanish border at Puigcerda, "the militia were friendly if somewhat baffled by my duffle-bag of canned goods, and my passport, the complexities of non-intervention, and my sex."

The train stopped many times *en route* to Barcelona, often at little villages where young men clambered aboard to head to the front. Gellhorn observed that they "laughed a great deal and were absolutely like boarding school boys on their way back to school after the Xmas vacation." They offered to share their limited food supply with her, and she noted that "it is always well to remember how *meagerly* workers eat, everywhere."

Her entry from Barcelona the next day reads simply: "Slept like the dead."

A few days later, she was in Madrid, walking "to the front as calmly as one would stroll through Central Park," noting that from one of the trenches, "with the Fascists within touching distance," you could "look up and see the posts of the trolley line." The trenches were "roofed over with branches" and "if you didn't hear the bullets it would be a new form of garden architecture."

She stayed at the Hotel Florida with many other foreign correspondents, where Hemingway and his minion Sidney Franklin had already set up shop in rooms 108 and 109 on the 3rd floor with balconies overlooking the street, stocking their rooms with booze and canned meat. On March 29th, she heard a shell fall at the corner as she was brushing her teeth. It "killed a little man who had been standing there, it took off his head, and wounded two others," while the women at the bread line did not move. That day Gellhorn, Hemingway and *New York Times* correspondent Herbert Matthews travelled by car out through the nearby town of Morata to the trenches being held by American volunteers. An Alabama schoolteacher, the battalion commander, told her that in the attack "he had men who did not know how to load a gun and he had to run from tree to tree telling them."

The next day Gellhorn visited the military hospital set up in the Palace Hotel which smelled "of ether and cabbage." The reading room had been turned into the operating theatre and the bookcases were full of bandages. She met a 23-year-old aviator "with a burnt face, thick brown scabs, his hands in two sacks, silent and patient and with tired eyes." And, yet, he said he would heal to fight fascism again. With a new friend she wandered to the Plaza de Espana, near the Casa de Campo, where she could "hear the guns as if they were in your pocket." And, although the entire section had been destroyed, there were people who remained in their basements among the ruins. They met one family in the frigid pitch black and "the wife was shaving her husband, with care and well."

There was the cognitive dissonance of citizens "anxiously, violently, constantly looking for food" and "a woman trying on high-heeled, pale fake lizard slippers" at the best shoe store in town. "Come what may, one washes one's hair, has one's nails tended, sends out the laundry, tidies one's room, and all the tiny details which are inevitable as tomorrow."

In spite of the struggle surrounding her, Gellhorn managed to retain her wry wit, noting an "influx of shits now that all is quiet." That influx included Josephine Herbst and "a nice handsome dumb named Errol Flynn who looks like white fire on the screen, but is only very very average off." She met a woman called Lolita, who was "a real born whore, with a basic respect for *ces messieurs*, which nothing can change. She is stupid but loyal and eager to seem something she isn't; a woman with interests wider than her hips."

On April 4th, she recorded only the following, "Sun like the thunder of God. H. [Hemingway] and I walked down to the Plaza Espana to see the new shell holes, and he explained the trench and street barricade system there, but I do not really understand. Gustav [Regler] not well. Myself jittery with a lack of tobacco and too many people and horribly worried about the writing." The next day she drove blood supplies with Canadian doctor Norman Bethune to the Jarama front, where she saw a young soldier with a huge bit dirtily sliced from his shoulder, who was getting peroxide put on it and "only his stomach shook and trembled." She was maddened by the nurses who seemed "all painted and useless and somehow lazy and inconsiderate." The hospital—a farmhouse—was filthy, everything a mess, and the men told her that the nurses "pay attention to the convalescents who can take them to the movies on their day off, but to no others."

Gellhorn was writing short news pieces to be broadcast on radio in America and was pleased when Hemingway approved, saying, "daughter, you're lovely, because he liked it," and then felt "so damned relieved" to find she "could write anything ever, no matter how poor." Buoyed by her little success, she treated herself to "an armful of mimosa, very yellow and soft smelling with the frail gray green leaves… really the most important item of the day."

She reflected on her weaknesses, for instance, on April 7th when she admitted, "Odd how really inwardly, almost all the time, unless I am seeing new things, looking at beautiful country or above all writing, I am bored. I have never yet really found the people who do not tire me in the end… I get homesick for places, for the way mountains look and for the color of the sky over Paris, and for the air in

New York, but I do not think I would get on a train and go anywhere to see anyone, except Edna [her mother]."

One morning in Madrid she called on the chief of prisons, an anarchist, whose offices were in an old convent. He drove her to the women's prison, which was the cleanest building she had seen in Spain. It was "glaring with sun and each cell a little different as each woman had the right to arrange her own." Throughout the day the women could "circulate and talk," take classes in stenography and dress cutting, but in "theory only because they have no cloth." There were 400 women imprisoned for political crimes, and Gellhorn visited the tribunal where a girl was "tried for passing as a nurse, though she was really a spy." That afternoon she walked back home along the trenches, occasionally peering over sandbags "to see how much land had been gained," her eyes stopping on "a corpse, like old laundry, lying alongside an abandoned stretcher."

On April 10th, she noted that novelist John Dos Passos arrived in Madrid, "stammering and without contributions to the liquor tobacco food fund," a fact that did not play well with the rest of them. The final line that day, "Note for H. I love you very much indeed," was proof that she left her personal writing for Ernest to read. There were no secrets between them there.

Two weeks after arriving in Madrid, Gellhorn was accustomed to listening carefully for the different noises of "trench mortars, machine guns, artillery and nine-inch shells. Lying there stiff but curious, just waiting and listening." She missed Ernest and got restless when he was gone all day, resorting to her daydream that ought to bore her, a home of her own, "books written, a regular job and finishing with a child." The only element that altered was "a slightly different décor for the apartment." Her commitment to writing was clear: "In the end it is the only thing which does not bore or dismay... or fill with doubt. It is the only thing... absolutely and irrevocably good in itself, no matter what the result." On April 15th, she wrote, "Had a late heavy fine breakfast with H. and then set out for the park. Lovely lovely lovely; forgot the war and the vague strange restlessness which is mixed up boredom and a kind of personal footlingness [sic], not knowing who I am, or what I love, or why I live."

One evening after visiting wounded at the military hospital in the Palace Hotel where a soldier, full of morphine, "had tears in his eyes from *attendrisement*" of the doctor who brought him a bouquet for his 26th birthday, she returned to the Hotel Florida where she "got a little tight talking with Hem and Dos and Bethune came in and had a bath (it is all very daffy) and grew pontifical about modern Spanish art."

Another night she travelled with brigade commander Randolfo Pacciardi down to the front, "crossing the river on two strips of steel which served as a sort of footpath under the high arched bridge," reminding her of "that viaduct of the

Romans near Avignon and the green warm country there." They stopped by the area where the soldiers lived, that "was exactly like the flea market outside Paris, little houses, with blankets instead of doors, bolstered with sandbags, on whose mud floors, men slept, picked lice, talked, smoked, played cards, cooked; and one boy was getting his hair cut. The soldiers all half rose and saluted with clenched fists and smiles" when Pacciardi passed.

At the front trench one of the soldiers said, "Look, there are some dead out there" and all Gellhorn could see were "two dirty bundles of grey laundry which may have been dead but when they are dead they are no longer men, only something finished and wasted and not good anymore and you have to think about it to feel anything, even pity."

The drive back was treacherous "as the car plunged in and out of shell holes, and the road was naked and glaring with moon." Yet, when "the chauffeur turned on the radio" and they drove "lightless towards town with the radio blaring American jazz sung in Spanish and the countryside like a dream, like an etching and a bad negative and too beautiful," Gellhorn was suddenly "desperately and unbearably sad… A feeling of the way things pass, before you can hold them, warm them, understand them, men and things: and of one's own phantom quality, of being without roots in a cyclone, and then the great aching sadness of not understanding, of not knowing at all why men live or die, or what this is about, or what the next thing will be about either."

By 6 a.m. on April 22nd at least ten shells fell on the corner of the Hotel Florida and Gellhorn felt the noise in her throat as the walls shook and she "had a feeling of being trapped. There was no place to go, nothing to do or say." One of her friends noted "the movement of the whores, all of them half clad and wide awake, running for the back" of the building, emerging "like beetles from every room." Antoine de Saint Exupéry stood in the hallway in a blue silk dressing gown, "handing out grapefruits," and Gellhorn snarked later, "It would take a bombardment to make a Frenchman give anything away—who said that."

The sounds of "terrible swift whistling" and the shells striking were "more horrible than anything" Gellhorn had dreamed of; "like an operation with anaesthetic, waiting, waiting, and not knowing what comes afterward." She tried to coach herself to focus on her writing, insisting, "if you write hard enough you can get yourself far away from anything, including panic, horror, and the something nameless and imaginable which is this haphazard shelling of a sunny city, on an afternoon in late April." She chastised herself for feeling safe when Hemingway returned, "as if nothing could hit" her and "not even the noise would be frightening."

This undated excerpt of a letter (likely early May, since she arrived in Paris on May 2nd) from Gellhorn to Hemingway evinces her lifelong insistence on paying her way. "Scrooby" was one of her many nicknames for him, which she claimed derived from "screwball" comedy. "Mr. Scrooby," however, was Hemingway's self-appointed moniker for his penis, a figure to which he referred playfully in his letters to her.

MG to Ernest Hemingway

Early May 1937
Paris

Scrooby,

This is a business letter; also the typewriter is French which adds to the charm as the damned or even fucking keys are thrust all over the place as they never were before.

Having received my royalty check [for *The Trouble I've Seen*], I find that it exactly corresponds to what I owe you, so I am leaving it here enclosed in dollars, and you may know that the book (which is the best thing I ever wrote) paid for Spain which is the best thing I ever did:

1) 2000 francs which remain from the money I carried in and out for you.

2) Valencia hotel—121
   Teruel trip—249
   Borrowed in cash—250
                    250
                    30

   _____

   900 pesetas (at 50 to dollar)
   –325 pesetas left for you in Barcelona

   _____

   575 pesetas or 11.50 dollars

3) Borrowed in cash--- 8000 pesetas at 58 to the dollar or 138 dollars

4) Half the expenses of the food which Tom brought in or 60 dollars:
   The sum total is: 2000 francs
                    209.50 dollars.

You will find same herein. If there's anything wrong with my arithmetic please let me know.

I leave also your play [*The Fifth Column*] with orders it is to be delivered only to you. I think I have done everybody's errands as desired. At the moment I am so angry at Joris I don't know what to do. I called Van Loon fifteen minutes after I arrived. Joris in Holland but returning to Hotel Lutetia Tuesday morning. I wired him there to call me immediately he got in. I've waited all morning and finally called his hotel only to find he had gone out without bothering to phone me. Now I shall miss the *Aquitania* and have to take the *Normandie* because I have to be sure he gets your messages. It is pretty sickening of him.

Aside from that nozzing. ["Nothing." They're beginning to use playful, idio-syncratic diction meant only for each other.] The peace is as I expected. I have decided to wear green mascara on my eyelashes as a disguise. I am bored and suddenly very tired. I am not at all hungry and the rich food makes me ill, and the steam heat cracks my face and there are too bloody many people whereas I would be very happy if I were alone.

As you can see this is a business letter. As you can also see I am working as hard as I know. I am your devoted henchman and war colleague,
Marty

MG to Ernest Hemingway

Late May 1937
New York City

Dear Ernest,

Joris let me see his letter. It doesn't tell you much. But of course it's almost impossible when he can't see you. I told him everything you said to. I must say I think the thing to do now is go away & write a hell of a book. The situation (so-called) is so complicated that it better just rot on the branch or something.

About Regler. He also isn't well & he has made no plans for in America. Nothing. Just thinks he'll get there. If it's a trip he needs, his wife could follow him on another boat. It would cause no trouble that way.

I just reread *Sun Also Rises* [sic]. Funniest damn book I ever read. Screamed with joy. You're such a wit, comrade. I always knew it. Feel sick, dead tired, hate boats. But working.

Yrs,
Marty

MG to Ernest Hemingway

Late May 1937
New York City

Hombre,

I am now Joris' finger woman, secretary and etc. I am ordered to communicate all the following dope to you:

Fine new material, very gut [sic], has come… Alta Voz, Madrid shelling (wonderful), the cement Factory and the Lincoln Battalion. The Lincoln Battalion is not so good.

… I kept the head of NBC waiting a half hour for me, so my reception there was cool. I've got them very excited about the film and RKO is a possible distributing agent if you want them. We'll have to do a small private prevue [sic] in New York with bigwigs of that nature on hand. It is all very shitty. I believe you told me to cut out the campaigning. Fat chance.

… Give humble respects please to Madame [Pauline] and *les jeunes messieurs* [Patrick and Gregory], or as we say in Spanish the *muchachos* or *muchaches* or even *ninos*. My Spanish is divine. I can discuss honor and patriotism easily with all comers.

Yours sincerely,
Gellhorn

Eleanor Roosevelt to MG

June 1, 1937
The White House
Washington

Dear Marty,

We will not be back in Washington until the evening of Monday, June 28. Do you think it would be possible for Mr. Hemingway and Mr. Ivens to come then? If this is not possible perhaps they could bring it here immediately after July 5, unless they will still be out in Hollywood. After that I will be gone to Hyde Park and I cannot say exactly when the President will be there.

Of course I want very much to see you in New York and will keep your telephone number and call you up.

I am very happy if I am any help. We would all of us like to help the people whom we know have the gift and sensitiveness to do really good work in the world, and you have both. You are right to be trying to make people realize that what is happening in Spain might happen anywhere. At the moment I am really more troubled by the German situation than I am by what is happening in Spain, because it may be the opening gun of a general involvement.

The air raid on Valencia is terrible, but it is exactly what war seems to do to people. It makes them senseless and cruel and needlessly destructive.

I loved seeing you and was only sorry that the President had to get much of what you told me second hand. Perhaps he will have a chance to see you before you flit back to Spain.

Affectionately,
Eleanor Roosevelt

MG to Eleanor Roosevelt

June 9, 1937
726 Park Avenue
New York City

Dearest Mrs. Roosevelt,

I'd have answered your fine letter sooner but we've been waiting to see how the film [*The Spanish Earth*] shapes up. I am so excited about that picture. Two nights ago we worked with three sound engineers in the lab of the Columbia Broadcasting, and we made the sound of incoming shells with a football bladder and an air hose and fingernails snapping against a screen, all tremendously magnified and it sounds so like a shell that we were scared out of our wits. That was lovely too, working there most of the night on sounds, with these men, everybody doing it for nothing, only because they love the work and care about the film and what it says, and everybody tired but not minding. This goes on every day and people spring from the ground who are eager to give their time and talent to a good cause. It makes me so proud of people that I now feel I am somehow mother of a million, and all of them doing well.

Meanwhile, I am a little dead with exhaustion because of the Bilbao refugees. Do you know about this? It seems that 500 kids (those tragic little dark ones I know so well) are waiting in Saint Jean de Luz to come to America. There is passage money for 100 of them, and countless offers of adoption. As you know, they are welcomed to England and France, the governments there actually do the reception work. Here, it appears, the Labor Department has decreed a $500 bond per child before they can get in, and also demanded the approval of Catholic Charities. I find it incomprehensible, a Catholic lobby no doubt, but incomprehensible anyhow. Those children are all Catholics, Basque children, but it is embarrassing to find that they were made homeless and orphaned by the people who wish to destroy the Godless Reds. That must be the root of it somewhere, but it is pretty terrible. I happen to know (so it hurts more and makes me guiltier) what those children come from, and it seems to me amazing that America should offer no sanctuary for them. I have been at this since dawn, trying to think of ways to make this clear to the Labor Department. It seems to me that it is two things, an injustice and a sort of backing down on what America likes to think it stands for: kindness to the weak. What do you think about it?

I saw Anna Louise Strong at the Writers' Congress, which was a wonderful show, Carnegie Hall jammed—3500 and more turned away at the door—only to hear writers. Ernest was astoundingly good and so simple and honest and Joris' slices from the film had a great effect. Anna Louise wandered up and we met later; she's a great admirer of yours so I forgive her for being the messiest white woman alive and so overworked that she doesn't make sense after four o'clock in the afternoon. It seems I gave you an erroneous impression: she challenged me on my facts. Apparently you thought I said there were 12-14,000 RUSSIAN troops in Spain, but I said there were 12-14,000 International troops in all. There are no Russian troops that any of us—the journalists—ever saw or heard about. I doubt if there are 500 Russians in Spain, not as many Russians as Americans. The Russians, like the Americans, come on private initiative as volunteers, and it's a hard journey. The ones whom I saw (I saw ten in all) are all technicians, engineers and aviators and munitions experts and writers. I didn't want you to think that I had been giving you the wrong dope, I talked so much that I probably didn't make myself come out straight. But that is the figure, and there is no reason to believe it inexact.

I'm going away in about ten days to Connecticut [to her friend Freddy Field's house] to write. Here they are eating me alive. I suppose it is very flattering and all the rest but it is killing me and I do not know how to work diffusely, I get addlebrained and upset and I want to do one thing until it gets finished and then another thing, and I hate to speak at meetings more than I can say. If I don't have to work here, could I come with Hemingway and Ivens on July sixth, if that's a good date: I'd love to have another visit and I'd love to see the first finished showing of the film.

… How I ramble on. I'm so glad I live in this day and age, aren't you, even if it gets you in the end, there is never a dull moment. Will you let me know if July sixth is okay. And please know how very much and how very admiringly I love you.

Marty

Eleanor Roosevelt to MG

June 14, 1937
The White House
Washington

Dear Marty,

It was grand to get your letter and of course the sixth of July will be perfectly possible and we look forward to having you and the two gentlemen for dinner and the night.

Now, as to what you have to say about the Spanish children, I think the group that has been trying to have them come over here has not been entirely wise and they have misrepresented the attitude of the Labor Department and of the State Department.

I think, without question, that the United States should bear as much of the expense as we possibly can, but it is against all modern ideas of what is good for children to uproot them and bring them to this country, where they are definitely cut off from all that they know and that would make them feel secure because of familiarity.

There is also quite an element in one group that has been agitating to bring them over which desires to have them brought up as Protestants; so, quite naturally, it has stirred the Catholic group into opposition…

Emotionally it is very easy to say that we should receive the children in this country, but it requires a little more than emotion sometimes to do the wise thing.

I will be in New York again around the 24th for a few days and will try to see you.

Affectionately,
Eleanor

I've just discovered the 7th is better, can they make it?

MG to Eleanor Roosevelt

Post-June 14, 1937
New York City

Dearest Mrs. Roosevelt,

You will be so wearied of me soon. I am covered with confusion but please do not think I am being unduly inefficient. The point now is that the Monday after July 4th is a holiday and apparently movie technicians have extra time off and cost a fortune to hire overtime. Joris needs the day of July 6th to finish the last printing of the film. Therefore, may we definitely make the date of showing the film to you,

July 8th. I hesitate to do this, but it will cost about $500 to get men to work on July 5th which $500 is hard to come by suddenly.

I see that you've been in New York so maybe you haven't had my other letter. If the 8th is okay, could Mrs. Schneider [Tommy] wire me: care F.V. Field New Hartford, Connecticut, just to say yes. And my oh my, I am sorry to be such a nuisance to you.

The film is very beautiful though, very very beautiful and Ernest has written fine words for it and I know when you see it, you will excuse me for writing you at intervals of two minutes to change dates.

I am at last dug into the country and hoping to get serious work done, and produce a book I needn't blush for. I loved what you wrote in your column a few days ago about Spain. I also wish more and more that I could get as much done in a day as you can.

Love,
Marty

MG to Ernest Hemingway

June 17, 1937
New York City

For Ernest Hemingway in Bimini
c/o Miami Aerial Corp
36th Street
Miami
Florida
(Please Forward)

[1st page missing]

So there it is, Ernest. I thought I knew everything about war now but what I didn't know was that your friends got killed. I am not thinking about Regler yet because I do not want to believe it. I only think about how Lucacs played such lovely music on a pencil, and his small moustache, and all the good humor of him. It is getting harder and harder to stay here. I do not know what one could do there, but surely that is the place to be. I wired [Herbert] Matthews for news of Regler, Joris has wired everyone, I also wired Ilsa [Kulscar, Madrid] and we have heard nothing yet. We are too far away and too lonely here [NYC] it seems to me. It is surprising that only six weeks should uproot one's lie [sic] that none of the old things are good, and none of the friends speak the old understandable language, and now life is just a painful wait between morning and evening newspapers, and a terror of what is happening to all of them there [Spain].

Bilbao will become a legend, the kind of thing people sing about. I can't even imagine how it is, those last stands; and yesterday, almost within the city, the Basques made a counterattack. I am so proud of them, and of man generally. Today the papers said Franco's bombers were dropping leaflets: "Death awaits you. Franco." His present to Bilbao. I am becoming very full of hate for the Fascists. I think even in time of peace they are people one would loathe always, without having to know anything specific about them.

All day Joris and I tried to reach each other, for comfort, and finally did so late in the night and I have never heard his voice anything but calm and merry and now he sounds lost and tired and said please he wanted to see me; and, he had forgotten the work and everything for right now. It is all right about the White House for July 6 [changed to July 8]. I am going away to the country tomorrow. I have to get back to some work and being quiet. This will never do. It doesn't help the troops any, and this kind of mixed-up life, sleepless and unhappy, is not getting me anywhere.

Well, *salud* pal. I would certainly rather be a *miliciano* than a writer right now. And tonight another great speech, but the last; and it is terribly hard to talk about Spain to those smooth uncomprehending faces. It is like giving away secrets.

If I can't work in the country, I shall go back to Spain sooner. I'm so worried about everyone, all the time.

Marty

MG to Hortense Flexner

Mid-June 1937
726 Park Avenue
New York City

Darling,

If it isn't the best news in a dark world I don't know what is: the beloved weakie has got her pins back. Not having had anything to contemplate with as much as a wry smile (since who knows when) I take this as one of the rare decencies of God. We will skip in bitter silence the fact that all doctors are evidently incompetent sons of bitches and that you could have been gamboling like a ewe lamb some time ago.

Darling, I am very happy. It makes me good and glad to think of Kingo [sic] too, and I am wondering what he will find now for his general anger to loose on.

Tell him for me that one can hate Fascism better even than doctors and if he needs instruction I will help him.

It also pleases me that my career as reported on page sixteen among the corset advertisements satisfies you. Me, it makes me sick. I do not write, I have long since ceased to write. I seem to have four articles currently in print and you better read the one in July 17 *Collier's*. But that is the sum total of my activity since who can say when and no one is going to sell me the idea that an article is anything but slop, whereas a book is like a tree, only somebody or other can make them. Instead of writing, I am winning the Spanish war. I think the war would do better if someone else took it on. I am up to my wrinkled neck in horror with it. Currently I am attempting to keep the correspondence and finance of the Emergency Ambulance Committee, which consists in Hemingway and me, from a confusion so great that jail will result. Likewise I am suddenly become a theatrical agent, attempting to thrust a fine film Joris Ivens made and Ernest wrote (on the War naturally, done in the war, done dangerously attacking with the infantry and tanks, during the shelling of Madrid and the bombing or Morata, and written with genius and so GODDAM [sic] good) off onto Broadway which has heard dimly that there is a country called Spain. As I do not know Broadway, I am a lamb amongst cigar-smoking wolves and am treated like a cuckoo idealist and given the worst run around you could hope to see, and lied to and generally cheated and I am so tired, and nervous like six cats not knowing—any of the six—which way to jump, and low in my mind and anything else you could name. I do not have time to write, even if I had the talent or the inner serenity which I haven't either. Another lovely thing is that everyone, even my darling Mother, has now taken to telling me that I write like Hemingway which is enough to turn me from my trade for life. God knows I think Mr. Hemingway writes like the heavenly host, but I prefer to write like mud, and have it be a poor thing but my own. I am accused of writing, thinking, talking like Mr. Hemingway and as yet people have only not told me that I had a black moustache, but that will come. It is my great misfortune to like and circulate with people who are not ciphers, and then all the other people immediately begin chatting. I am only retrospectively startled that no one bothered to suggest that I was going to marry Wells for his money, or that my poor little book [*The Trouble I've Seen*] was indistinguishable from the *Science of Life*. It is pretty goddam bloody awful, because for once I don't know what the hell I write like, if at all, and in fact do not write. The only hope for me is Spain, which I am waiting for with baited breath. Maybe I'll get myself back again in small pieces and be able to work on my own job again.

Well, pfui [sic].

There is a vague chance that I will have to run like the wind to Philadelphia on Monday to discuss contracts for this film with Ernest's lawyer who has seen fit to have lumbago in Philadelphia, and if so I shall whip out to Bryn Mawr faster than you can say Abracadabra, and see you, and then whip back. I sail August 18. Mother is here and I'm not seeing her enough because of all this Spain slime but she looks in fine shape and is as usual slightly more informed than God (you never have to tell her anything because she has it all guessed three weeks in advance) and lovely and kind and braver than they come.

I long to see your house and hope you will let me come there and lick my varying wounds at some time or other. I wrote a book [*Peace on Earth*], did I tell you, last winter but am not publishing it contrary to Morrow's announcements, because I don't like it. Next winter, beginning Jan third, I have to lecture the length and breadth of the accursed land for six weeks, an act of mental abberation I still do not understand. After that, I am free, though I may not be living and then I intend to settle somewhere and once more take the typewriter in hand and attempt to be a writer, or at least make a sound like one. The environs of Phila [sic] might be the place. Anyhow I must see you.

Kiss King warmly on the nose for me and tell him that I am sure your doctor is a Fascist. I adore you and am happier about you than about anything in a very gloomy world.

Love in terrific quantities,
Gellhorn

Eleanor Roosevelt to MG

June 24, 1937
The White House
Washington

Dear Marty,

How about you three coming to Hyde Park Monday the 5th of July and showing the film there? It would be much more satisfactory than having it down here, because I cannot be here on the night of the 6th or the night of the 8th, and both the President and I will be at Hyde Park on the 5th. However, if you cannot manage it, come down on the 8th. The President will see the film any way and I may be able to change and go on a night train.

I did not mean that one should not feel emotionally about things that are happening in Spain. I should think with your friends and your knowledge of what is going on, you would feel emotional. I simply meant that in our feelings toward the children we must not let our best judgment be warped by our emotions.

I think Allen Wardwell will be successful in raising the money and supplies for us to send to Spain and to the neighboring countries.

You will be interested to know that Mr. Melchor told me that you had made a perfectly remarkable address to the libraries and had stirred him very deeply. He thinks your book was a remarkable piece of writing... we never know where we may have sowed the seeds of our own enthusiasm or of our own knowledge. No individual ever feels really important, I don't suppose, but I am glad that you will have to go on because of the force of heredity, for I really feel that you are doing a good job.

Affectionately,
E.R.

Eleanor Roosevelt to MG

June 30, 1937
The White House
Washington

Eighth O.K. Will try to be here and perhaps take midnight to New York. Expecting all three [Gellhorn, Hemingway and Ivens] for dinner and the night.

Eleanor Roosevelt

MG to Eleanor Roosevelt

July 3–4, 1937
726 Park Avenue
New York City

Dearest Mrs. Roosevelt,

... I accept your comment on being emotional, and your explanation of the Bilbao children business holds. I still think it is not unsound to take children, briefly, as far away from the source of terror as possible: and from the beginning it was planned that five Catholic Basque priests were to travel with the children, so that religious objection would not be valid. But getting money to them is perhaps the most effective thing to do. It is a little harder to collect money than to obtain hospitality, however obviously it can and should be done. The next time I get sore about something I'll wait a week and see if I'm still sore. Emotional women are bad news. Reform will now set in. And thank you for taking the time to tell me the other side. It is hard nowadays not to get emotionally terribly involved in this whole business. The attack on Bilbao is one of the nastiest things I can remember having known about. And a great friend of mine was killed two days ago, a lovely humorous man, and a writer whom I admire is dying of a shell wound, and when I think of those people in Bilbao strafed by low-flying aeroplanes with machine guns, and think of thirty shells a minute landing in the streets of Madrid, it makes me sick with anger. Anger against two men whom I firmly believe to be dangerous criminals, Hitler and Mussolini, and against the international diplomacy which humbly begs for the continued 'co-operation' of the Fascists, who at once destroy Spain and are appointed to keep that destruction from spreading. This is emotional probably. But I don't know how else one can feel. You will agree with me that the role of the Fascists in Spain is something one cannot contemplate very calmly.

It is grand that Allen Wardwell is going to take on the co-ordination job which is so badly needed and I am especially glad that a man of that sort will be doing it. I can't bear having the Spanish war turned into a Left and Right argument, because it is so much more than that, and increasingly it seems to me the future of Europe is our future, no matter how much we want to be apart, man is one animal and our civilization is not divisible into water-tight compartments.

Right now, I feel personally terribly helpless about everything. I do not really know how one can serve. I know what I believe, and I would do anything for a certain number of ideals and hopes about the world, and how man can live in it, but I feel very useless and unable in any way to be of help to the people I know need help.

And if it is useless to work so hard at the different things which trouble me, then it is a poorish life. Because there isn't much time left for fun, for friends, for leisure, for enjoying what is lovely and can't be deformed. I've gone through this set of ideas until they sicken me, and come back to the conclusion that there is no choice; it is silly to talk of free will. We are what we are, by heredity and upbringing and because of the way life has hit us, and I suppose I will go on doing humbly and rather badly the kind of thing I do, whether it is purposeful or not, because I don't know what else to do, and because I can never forget about the other people, the people in Madrid or the unemployed or the seven dead strikers in Chicago or the woman who sells pencils in the subway. I wish I could forget, but I don't know the technique for that.

Always,
Marty

July 8, 1937
726 Park Avenue
New York City

Dearest Mrs. Roosevelt,

You did really like the film didn't you? Joris and Ernest were very happy about it. They were also impressed that you and Mr. Roosevelt said to make it stronger—that's what it amounted to—by underlining the causes of the conflict. I think Mr. Hopkins [Harry Hopkins, for whom Martha worked at FERA] was very moved by it. You were heavenly to us and I hope you like my two trench buddies, both of whom I adore. And I am so glad you let us come because I did want you to see that film. I can't look at it calmly, it makes it hard for me to breathe afterwards. Those shelling scenes in Madrid get me and the women choking and wiping their eyes with that dreadful look of helplessness, in the bombing of the village of Morata, and the grave waiting faces of the men walking slowly into the attack at Jarama: it's all very close. I think Joris did a magnificent job and it is a record of personal bravery that you'd get decorated for in any war but this one, which is a good one where they do not give decorations, and men do whatever they do for nothing. And I hope you liked the prose, the comment, despite that awful voice which mangles it. It is very beautiful: a good deal of it reads like poetry. Ernest has borrowed some money (he is now quite broke with paying for film and buying ambulances) and is going to pay to have that voice part done over with someone who knows how to talk and has enough imagination to feel. I think the film will gain enormously. They are out in Hollywood with it now and I am hoping it works well there.

I am the scribe for that group and so am delighted also to thank you for them, warmly. They were glad to be there, and both so happy to know you and Mr. Roosevelt, and we have seen so many people who had neither the understanding nor sympathy for Spain that it made them happy to see you. If I hadn't felt so like a mother with her two infant prodigies and been so nervous lest anything go wrong with the film, I'd have felt brighter. I was very nervous though, because I so wanted it to be good for you and so wanted you to like it.

Now it is just awful hot and kind of confusing here and I suddenly realize that I am not going to finish my book that I can't even do it properly because it is really too close to me and I feel it all too hard and can't get away from it to look at it clearly. I think that I must wait which distresses me and I have really wasted my two months since I left Spain. But I can't seem to get quiet enough to work properly, so I am going to Madrid, working for one of the big companies here [*Collier's*], and I am going to rework on the novel I did last winter [*Peace on Earth*]. But the Spain book will have to wait. I couldn't have written about the unemployed in a month [*The Trouble I've Seen* (1936)], after I'd only seen them for six weeks, so I comfort myself saying that later I'll do the book and not be too ashamed of it. Perhaps this is just rationalization.

What a poor letter. It's awful hard to thank you adequately for all the good things you do, only you know how grateful I am don't you! And how much I love seeing you and the President. I hope you're cool in Hyde Park and getting a rest and I hope I can see you again before I sail. Thank you again, endlessly.

Love,
Marty

MG to Ernest Hemingway

Late July 1937
New York City

Dear Sir,

I have so much to write to you that I don't see any sense in doing it at all.

There is nothing you can do, we are all beyond help it seems to me, and must wander dismally throughout little labyrinths alone. It would make Joris very cross, if he knew I were using this tone, which is known as defeatest, but I work hard all the time and never take no for an answer and have a hell life, so maybe I can indulge myself in a little gloom *via* the mails. Note: the gloom is only for you. I'm a mass of energy, plans, schemes and counter schemes with Joris, and just a sales-woman with everyone else.

First about the ambulances: the license has come. Shevlin and I have signed the Speiser power of attorney, so that's okay. However, one check for $1000 has returned from Hollywood for lack of endorsement…

About the film: it is abundantly clear that Morris will never do anything and we will still have that film on our hands ten years hence. To which end I set out on my own and sort of picked people from the blue. Tough Broadway Jews, who are known to be as honest as any Broadway people are. I've had Joris meet them, show them the film; have gotten propositions in writing which I am going to check with Maurice… you may know that this is the very best we can manage and that we cannot go on, being run around, stalled, lied to, generally humiliated, and with no results to show. If we take on this guy, and decide his schemes are okay, we will have the picture on Broadway in a week. That to me, plus road-showing it throughout the country, is the aim…

I wish to hell you were somewhere we could at least telephone you to get advice on these things. There is no one to ask about anything. Obviously no one gives a hoot in hell about Spain…Why should they. But it's hard to know what to do.

Everything goes very badly for me personally. My first appointment with Columbia was cancelled when I arrived…

Give my love to your folks. I have such fine books for you and Pauline that I started reading them, hope you don't mind. This is a splendid way to give a birthday present. I really will mail them any minute now. I send this to Key West but don't have the faintest idea where you are. Will see to it that Shevlin and Mr. Pfeiffer [Pauline's Uncle Gus] are asked to see the film Tuesday when your voice is in it…

As you can easily see, I am working like a witch woman. Awful.

Well, blessings,
Marty

FIVE

High Explosive for Everyone

"I wish I could forget,
but I don't know the technique for that."

—Martha Gellhorn, letter to Eleanor Roosevelt

Gellhorn's first piece as a war correspondent was written about the people of Madrid. Years later she'd recall of that time, "It was a feeling I cannot describe; a whole city was a battlefield, waiting in the dark. There was certainly fear in that feeling, and courage. It made you walk carefully and listen hard and it lifted the heart." After she submitted her next article, "The Besieged City," *Collier's* put her name on the masthead. Thanks to that magazine, she had "the chance to see the life of [her] time, which was war." Remarkably, unlike her earlier experience with *Scribner's Magazine*, she claimed that "they never cut or altered anything."

When she sailed back to Europe on August 18th, first to Paris, then to Madrid, Gellhorn met Dorothy Parker and her husband Alan Campbell and playwright Lillian Hellman aboard the *Normandie*. Hellman, Martha snarked, had no right "to inflict her misery simply because one man [Dashiell Hammett] left her." In Paris, they all met up with Hemingway at Robert Capa's favourite watering hole, the Hôtel Meurice, Parker pronouncing Martha "truly fine—even leaving aside her looks and her spirit and her courage and her decency—though I can't imagine why they should be shoved aside."

In addition to the intimacies recorded in her journal kept in Spain, Martha's correspondence with Eleanor Roosevelt revealed her outrage about the lack of support the orphaned Spanish children would receive from the West, explaining that it hurt her more and made her feel guiltier because she knew from experience how dire their circumstances were. Gellhorn could not understand why America would not offer political sanctuary to those vulnerable children. About those months in Spain shared with Hemingway, Gellhorn would tell biographer Bernice

Kert that she believed "it was the only time in his life when he was not the most important thing there was. He really cared about the Republic and he cared about that war," and she "never would've gotten hooked otherwise."

From September to December, Gellhorn filed stories from Madrid to *Collier's* about the ordinary Spanish citizens and their perseverance under extraordinarily stressful and vulnerable times. In her 80s, however, it was an evening that November that remained rich in her memory, when she and Hemingway had been invited by Mikhail Koltzov—"officially the *Pravda* correspondent in Madrid but really he was Stalin's man, Stalin's eyes and ears on the spot"—to drinks at the Russians's hotel, The Gaylord.

When they arrived, the Spanish general Juan Modesto was there. To Gellhorn he was "an intensely attractive man" and she was pleased that he had decided to speak with her, though she knew "that in Spain being a blonde was considered a sort of accomplishment." Within minutes "E. suddenly appeared beside us wearing an ugly shark smile" and insisted that he and Modesto play Russian roulette, which Gellhorn considered "a boor's joke… a double insult" to her "as a piece of female property" and to Modesto "as a thief on the prowl." Further, "it was too idiotic and shaming, a fine example of E.'s talent for making scenes."

After she and Hemingway divorced in 1945, Gellhorn wrote to a friend that those weeks in Spain she slept with him "as little as I could manage: my whole memory of sex with Ernest is the invention of excuses and failing that the hope that it would soon be over." Other than her post-war affair with James Gavin, which she regarded as the only true physical passion of her life, Gellhorn considered sexual intimacy something that the man in her life needed and she would participate in it with as little fuss as possible.

The October day that Gellhorn resumed her diary on the return visit to Madrid in 1937 was the day that Hemingway's *To Have and Have Not* was published by Scribner's back in New York. Her independence and determination are obvious throughout.

October 15

We started off in a fury. My voice rising, against the slammed doors: "All-right, I won't go, for God's sake." E. muttering to himself. Then he came into my room and said as long as you've started arranging the lunch you may as well go on with it. And there I sat at my typewriter, writing formally some unimportant letter, not hurrying, not willing to do anything, stiff with anger.

They were on their way in the direction of Morata with fellow correspondent Herbert Matthews through the Jarama valley past the "three black iron arches of the Armada bridge" that had figured in *The Spanish Earth*. They drove through Chinchon, "hardly talking all this way," she and Ernest, a tightness between them, "ready to say something cruel but not saying it." And yet, they stopped for fresh melon to add to a picnic lunch on the edge of the river, making "some kind of conversation without value."

Later in the day, back at the censor's office, they saw Lillian Hellman with her "expression of polite spite." Gellhorn admitted that she was "ready for anger" and that dinner "was a meal like scratching your fingernail over the blackboard," and Hemingway was spoiling for a fight, berating her for "money grubbing as lecturer," putting on "the kind of show usually reserved for enemies."

Recording his fury that night, she wrote, "It was very hyena indeed, with everything called out and spat on," the first round ending with a "swipe at the electric light which crashed beautifully all over the room," after which they both laughed and Ernest returned, "cutting his feet on the way." Gellhorn waxed philosophical, observing, "And then and then. Then one gets too tired to be anything and finally one can make love and no doubt forget everything except a feeling of loneliness. There is no right or wrong between two people and surely there is no guilt. There is only fear. Only a terror that things thought or spoken in anger must have had their beginnings somewhere, when the mind was calm and then the terror that if the beginnings can come, what is the end. To which question I have no answer. It is a good thing to write and a good thing to have the sun on your face, to sleep and to be warm. It is also a good thing to be happy but this is harder to come by."

By the end of October, Gellhorn lamented the start of the long winter, as "something to endure," observing "the face of that girl in the gutted house across the street, breaking the burnt wood that was once her furniture, her wainscoting [sic], her home, with a flatiron for kindling." Even though it was not possible for her to keep warm, "despite the pale blue woolen underwear, the woolen socks over the woolen stockings, the coats and jackets and the electric heater and plenty of food," she worried how much worse the cold must feel to others in Madrid who did not have those "blessings." She also fretted that she and Ernest would "wear each other out… chipping a little each day, with just a little dig or a minor scratch, until it ends in fatigue and disgust, and years later we will be able to think of all this as a brief infatuation," resolving to "make it work or make it end now."

On November 7, she noted her father's birthday, the second since his death, the birthday of Soviet Russia and "also the day they stopped the Fascists in the streets of Madrid." American poet Langston Hughes was now in Spain and stood in line with Gellhorn that afternoon for food, speaking "drearily of Soviet Russia, with a fairy accent and unable to link his ideas."

It was that night that Koltzov invited them to The Gaylord where Modesto and Hemingway "were like two not yet hostile dogs," Modesto making up verses to the tune of *la cucaracha*, including "my bones are melting, I am losing my conscious-ness upon the sight for you." By the time they got back to the Hotel Florida, "up to bed, getting Scrooby's boots off," it was already three o'clock in the morning and her 29th birthday.

Gellhorn worried about repeating her past involvement with a married man whose wife refused to grant a divorce, as she considered her current affair with Hemingway, who was still married to Pauline Pfeiffer. She contemplated "the cruelty and nastiness and talk and the suffering of a few good people involved," vowing that when she returned to New York City, she would do her best "to squelch it all." Still, over their remaining weeks together in Spain she recorded "fooling with Scrooby who has premonitions of death due to a hangover from three days' drinking and in this way two hours were wasted, which is very little considering" and how they "worried about the things that worry us both, now that they come closer" and the disappointing news of some bad reviews of *To Have and Have Not,* so they held each other through the nights, "Mister Scrooby… as friendly as a puppy and as warm as fur." On Armistice Day, Gellhorn reflected that she had grown tired in her mind from "worrying desperately about Scrooby"and her, not to mention "seeing the whole world reduced again to terms of who said what in spite and malice and what effect that would have on whom." And, yet, she wrote, "all the time, the feeling of going away, the fear of what comes next, and the rootlessness of this leaving."

Edna Gellhorn to Cam Becket

November 27, 1937
4366 McPherson Avenue
St. Louis

Dear Cam,

Ever since I wrote you about Martha's address, and some other things, I've been sort of unhappy over one sentence which as I remember sounded as if I thought Martha's article for *Collier's* was not good. Let me put my mind at rest by saying that that was not in the least what I wished to imply. I think the content and form extraordinarily fine—the point is that it seems so ridiculous to get one thousand dollars for the amount of work indicated by such an article, no matter how fine, and get practically nothing for a book, for instance *The Trouble I've Seen*, which is much more exacting. Now that clears that.

It is great fun getting all the "fan" comments on Martha's radio speech of last Sunday. Sometimes I am stopped at the opera, sometimes at the symphony, in an elevator, and within the last few minutes the little Russian who soles our shoes said, "Madam, I sure felt fine when I heard the man say 'Miss Gellhorn will now speak from Spain,' and I could tell my friends that I mended her shoes." It makes me furious to have missed it.

Goodbye till X'mas and much affection to the three of you,
Edna Gellhorn

> On December 15, Gellhorn sailed on the *Aquitania* from Paris to New York City where she arrived a few days before Christmas. The letter she wrote to Hemingway on board was all business about their fellow Spain enthusiasts, filmmaker Joris Ivens and political commissar of the XII International Brigade, Gustav Regler.

MG to Ernest Hemingway   December 19, 1937
                                                          Aquitania

Mister Hem,

I am now Joris' secretary again which is the good old days: he meantimes is writing masterpieces in Dutch, and very cute these days and I wish to hell I could make him take me to China *mit* [with him].

However: he has been thinking about Regler and this is the upshot of it.

Regler ought not to go to America to make a lecture tour now. He is not well, and he is a little crazy and he is not known there. But on the other hand, what he really wants himself is a rest, to get away, to be safe and quiet. So, if you wanted him to come and stay at the Hotel Concha (and have Anne Marie follow him on another boat and they'd have two rooms at the hotel and that would make it legally okay), then you could ask him for a month's visit. After that he would go up to New York alone and put himself in the hands of the Northamerican [sic] committee and that would fix everything. They could use him and the Spanish government would pay him while he lectures and pay his passage over in principle. (Never count on govts [sic] about finances I say: however.)… I think that is all. There is no reason he can't go and park on Mother (Regler, I mean) except it would drive him mad in Saint Louis, but he always can if he wants to.

… I had lots of cocktails and no lunch and have a foul cabin because Villars is on vacation, but the machine gunner barkeep is about and a great pal and perhaps all is for the best. I am stiff with tiredness but Joris is very fine. Also my luggage is temporarily lost, on the whole a blessing. I hope all is well with you and that the Yuletide Season is the yuletide season. See you sometime.

Greetings,
Marty

The enclosed is good, but we can beat it, eh comrade. What I am interested in is what you are going to write when you get good and ready about that very fine not to say perfect war. I've been seeing *Collier's*: they think my articles are the nuts and they cannot use them. On the other hand they want me to do one specially for them; they will have to pay through the nose for it if I can only keep my nerve with me. I got the whole bunch jumping with excitement about Spain. It seems they had already accepted a batch of articles and they are now sick with fury because they don't like what they've got, and they kept saying why didn't you get back sooner… Anyhow I am going to get them my stuff in four days and then sit on their laps and wait and wait and hope for more. Meantime trying to sell the other stuff elsewhere. Everybody very pleased and excited about the book on Spain which if things keep up as is, will never get going. I am supposedly and officially leaving town [New York] next week, though actually I shall only be hiding here in my gilded cage trying to get started.

I find now the *causa* is now my mother and father to say nothing of my children, and all my hope in life as well as interest. If only Joris isn't too busy to keep me straight on the party line… Thus far, humbly, I am doing my little best: and those radio folk are going to be handled somehow.

Anyhow they told me my broadcast was the nuts and just what they wanted and they could hear every word and so on, and I am to see them next week.

Thus we keep the old home fires burning or words to that effect. I dream of chassis now: and wake startled by backfiring in the street, wondering if the bullets are really explosive or if it's only hitting a rock or a tree.

Long live the republic, *salud* [to your health], and for good measure shall we just throw in *carga de mi padre* [burden of my father] or words in that vein.

How's fishing. If you write anything please let me see it.
Marty

1938

In January 1938, Gellhorn became a celebrated lecturer about the Spanish Civil War, touring the United States. The *St. Louis Post-Dispatch* reported on her: "voice, the culture, the art of pose, the poise, gesture, diction which succeed upon the stage at its best." Gellhorn, however, loathed the public speaking circuit; she felt that as a writer, she should be writing. Nevertheless, she believed fervently that the only way she could "pay back for what fate and society" had given her was "to try, in minor totally useless ways, to make an angry sound against injustice."

MG to Eleanor Roosevelt

January 24, 1938
4366 McPherson Avenue
St Louis

Dearest Mrs. R,

Haven't written because too frantic. Got back Dec 24 and then ran errands for Spain for 10 days & then started lecture tour. Most awful agony I ever went through, lecturing. Feel I *must* explain, comment etc in one hour (like Billy Sunday), so I've lost 12 lbs, have a fever & am ½ dead & the doctor says I'll have to call a lot of it off, which delights me. I want to write not talk. Tired of explaining to good admirable, ignorant semi-sleepy people about Fascism & democracy & war and peace. *Hate* being Moses with the tablets of stone.

Will you be in New York anytime from Feb 9 to Feb 15, could I see you? Want to find out about America. Hate our foreign policy, why is it like that? Please tell me.

Love,
Marty

Eleanor Roosevelt to MG

January 31, 1938
The White House
Washington

Dear Martha,

Can you come here for 12th or 13th? Am anxious to see you.

ER

February 1, 1938
4366 McPherson Avenue
St. Louis

Dearest Mrs. R,

I don't know what is happening. (Thank you for your wire, you're a darling.) It is like this. I have made some 22 lectures in less than a month, on Spain. I am not a lecturer and I don't know how to do it, reasonably, saving myself and not getting excited. I see these rows on rows of faces, often women and sometimes men, and think: I have one hour to tell them everything I have painfully learned and to shout at them that if they go on sleeping they are lost. I am shaking with exhaustion and perfectly ready to depart for a better and more restful world. (Cannot tell you how I loathe lecturing, the listening faces—I want people to talk back—the awful 'celebrity' angle which I have never met before and makes me sick—the flattery 'Miss Gellhorn you are an inspiration.' Good God, I have been a not always admirable character but nothing to justify being called an inspiration—and the horror of those frightened, lost uninformed, grateful, faintly slobbering people.)

So now my doctor says either stop it or you will crack up. So my agent says he will sue for damages. Blast him. I am really more busted than I have ever been. I've been tired before, but I was never a celebrity and celebrity I cannot and will not take. So now I am home and out of bed long enough to write you. Mother is horrified by the turn of events. We do not break contracts in our family but we are also not celebrities. She understands that and then I look so awful, so she thinks I must not go on. I wanted the money for Spain, but oh, what a mistake. So I don't know where I'll be, maybe in jail. It is all very difficult.

I want to go to Nassau and sleep and get out of this horrible cold, I had enough of that in Spain and am too tired to die. But I haven't an idea how it will all come out. If I'm not in Nassau maybe I'll be east but don't yet know, so will you give me a rain check. I want very much to see you, you know that, I always do. It's just complicated. I am not much these days. Thin and exhausted and worried for that people I seem to have adopted. Also for my own people. If one is a writer, one should be a writer, and not a lecturer. That's about all I do know now.

My respects to your husband. And to you my love and gratitude for your telegram.

Always,
Marty G.

Eleanor Roosevelt to MG

February 8, 1938
The White House
Washington

Dear Marty,

I am glad you are going away and whenever you want to come let me know. I will be gone from here on a lecture trip from March 5 to April 3.

I am glad you are going to write Spain out of your system. Writing is your best vehicle and you ought to do a good piece of work. Dorothy Parker, in the *New Yorker* this week, I think did a very arresting short piece.

No one can keep calm when they have seen the things you have seen and felt as you feel; but you know that you cannot do anything unless you are well, so, for Heaven's sake, get well and try to forget temporarily the woes of the world, because that is the only way in which you can go on.

Affectionately,
Eleanor Roosevelt

On March 23rd, Gellhorn and Hemingway sailed on the *RMS Queen Mary* to return to Spain *via* Paris. They arrived in Catalonia by the beginning of April and were in Barcelona during the bombing before the end of the month. In her letters to Eleanor Roosevelt, Gellhorn maps out the geography of the next few months and articulates her fear of the next world war, which she expected would "be the stupidest, lyingest, cruelest sell-out in our time."

MG to Eleanor Roosevelt

Post–March 23, 1938
RMS Queen Mary

Dearest Mrs. R,

I wanted to see you, and hoped all the time you'd be in Washington and that I'd get there. Then you were out west, and anyhow I decided on Sunday night in St. Louis to sail & sailed Wednesday [March 23] morning and there was no time for anything.

The news from Spain has been terrible, too terrible, and I felt I had to get back. It is all going to hell… I want to be there, somehow sticking with the people who fight against Fascism. If there are survivors, we can then all go to Czechoslovakia. A fine life. It makes me helpless and crazy with anger to watch the next Great War hurtling towards us, and I think the 3 democracies (ours too, as guilty as the others) have since 1918 consistently muffled their role in history. Lately the behaviour of the English govt [sic] surpasses anything one could imagine for criminal, hypo-critical [sic] incompetence, but am not dazzled either by us or France. It will work out the same way: the young men will die, the best ones will die first, and the old powerful men will survive to mishandle the peace. Everything in life I care about is nonsense in case of war. And all the people I love will finish up dead, before they can have done their work. I believe the people—in their ignorance, fear, supineness—are also responsible: but the original fault is not theirs. They control nothing: they react badly to misinformation & misdirection & later they can wipe out their mistake with their lives.

I do not manage to write anymore, except what I must to make money to go on living. I don't believe that anything any of us does now is useful. We just have to do it. Articles & speeches hoping someone will hear & understand. And if they do, then what. The whole world is accepting destruction from the author of *Mein Kampf*, a man who cannot think straight for half a page.

I wish I could see you. But you wouldn't like me much. I have gone angry to the bone, and hating what I see, and knowing how it is in Spain, I can see it so clearly everywhere else. I think now maybe the only place at all is in the front lines, where you don't have to think, and can simply (and uselessly) put your body up against what you hate. Not that this does any good either... The war in Spain was one kind of war, the next world war will be the stupidest, lyingest, cruelest sell-out in our time. Forgive the letter: I can't write any other kind.

love
Marty

Eleanor Roosevelt to MG

April 5, 1938
The White House
Washington

Dear Marty,

I was very sorry to hear you had gone back to Spain and yet I understand your feeling in a case where the Neutrality Act has not made us neutral. We are discovering, I think, that the Neutrality Act is not really a Neutrality Act, but very few people realize it. Of course the trouble is that most people in this country think that we can stay out of wars in other parts of the world. Even if we stay out of it and save our own skins, we cannot escape the conditions which will undoubtedly exist in other parts of the world and which will react against us. That is something which I have preached from coast to coast on deaf ears I fear. We are all of us selfish—note Mr. Hoover's statement on his return from Europe—and if we can save our own skins, the rest of the world can go. The best we can do is to realize nobody can save his own skin alone. We must all hang together.

Affectionately,
ER

MG to Eleanor Roosevelt

April 24 or 25, 1938
Barcelona

Dearest Mrs. Roosevelt,

Your letter made me very happy. It was a kind of *de coeur avec vous* [my heart goes out to you], and what you say about the Neutrality Act is what, for a year seeing it work one-sidedly in Spain, we have all thought here. Yesterday, the papers say, the Act was coming up for revision and we do not yet know what happened. We are asked by everyone and we ask each other, and we wait for the news. Right now, the Neutrality Act is of the greatest importance. Because the fight is far from lost here, but material is sadly needed. The much bragged of Italian advance to the sea was done with planes and artillery, against brave men who were inadequately armed. Whole divisions (amongst them the American Brigades) were surrounded and cut off, and fought their way through the Fascists, back to Government terri-tory, reformed their lines and fought again, again to be surrounded, again to fight their way through and reform…

There has been neither panic nor disorder, neither in the rear—Barcelona—nor at the front. A retreat before impossibly heavy armaments was carried out with order, and the line now holds. Even the refugees—and they leave home often with a small bundle wrapped in a handkerchief, abandoning everything to get out—are quiet and patient on the roads, neither hysterical nor dramatic, but only deter-mined not to live where the Fascists rule.

Just before the Fascists reached the sea, I was out on the road and watched for fifty minutes twelve black German planes, flying in a perfect circle, not varying their position, flying and bombing and diving to machine gun: and they were working on one company of Government soldiers, who had no planes or anti-air-craft to protect them but who were standing there, holding up the advance so as to permit an orderly retreat. That same day we watched thirty-three silver Italian bombers fly in wedges over the mountains across the hot clear sky to bomb Tortosa: and anywhere and everywhere is proof of the huge amount of new material sent in for this drive, and everywhere is proof of the unbending resistance of Loyalist Spain. But to penalize these people, who are our kind of people and

believe what we believe and want a kind of society we take for granted, seems
unheard of. I am again impressed by the unshakeably democratic quality of Loyalist
Spain, talking with del Vayo, reading their newspapers, seeing the troops and the
officers, watching life as it goes on here. And it goes on. It goes on in a way to
make you very proud of the human animal. Franco will have to do away with
about twenty million Spaniards before he could ever rule this country.

Now, for instance, plans are afoot for children's homes and hospitals, and no one
thinks in terms of time of war operations, but in terms of the future of Spain. The
air raids, lately only on the port, go on, and the siren whines over the city. We were
in a movie house Sunday morning seeing *The Spanish Earth* (remember?) It had
been running five minutes when it flickered to a stop. A man's voice announced
apologetically, "There's an air raid." There were about a thousand people there, and
bombs have fallen all over the city and you'd have to see what they can do within
a radius of five blocks to know what destruction is like. But no one in that theater
moved, or panicked. Presently the orchestra appeared and played the national
anthem and after that a selection of fine brassy romantic music that sounded
very funny indeed and everyone chatted and waited and after an hour the electricity went on again and so did the film. This morning at five there was another
siren rising and falling and wailing over the city, and then against the night sky
the searchlights climbing up and bending back against the clouds, and the tracer
bullets from the anti-aircraft slowly going up like hot red bars. And the searchlights
crawled against the clouds and the anti-aircraft pounded over the city and when
it was all over, I heard a man walking down the street, singing to himself, and city
was as quiet as a village before dawn.

I do not see how they can lose, unless the democracies allow Hitler and
Mussolini to continue sending unlimited supplies. Neither manpower nor ability
nor determination are lacking: but it is not a fight between Spaniards; it is a fight
between one democracy and three Fascisms. And so we sit here and hope to
heaven that sense of justice and a sense of self protections will guide the House
and Senate and that the government of Spain will be allowed to buy with good
gold those things its armies need to save its people, its land, and that droll thing,
the faith in a kind of freedom we still call democracy.

I am writing this by the light of two candles, uncertainly, after a day out at
a quiet part of the front. It has been one of the things to do lately, to go about
and find one's old friends. To find them so sure, so unchanging, so excellent and
humorous and simple and brave, is a good thing to have known in one's life. I
find myself foolishly patriotic about the Americans—about half of the Lincoln-
Washington Brigade is lost since this last push—I find that I love them immeasurably, am immeasurably proud of them, individually and collectively, and proud of
their record and proud of the reasons that brought them here and keep them here.

1916, 8-year-old Martha standing beside her mother at a League of Women Voters event in St. Louis.

May 1931

Dear;

I am home. The word as you know has always had merely dictionary
meaning for me. This is no longer true. I am home. It is like saying,
rest, peace, honorable things. I love my family; their love for me is
an unaccountable blessing. I feel protected from unnecessary ugliness
and I feel that there is after all some meaning to my breif transit
of this globe.

My fingernails are as beautiful as my toenails, and I have
bought an outfit of that new dead-white jewelry which deludes me into
beleiving myself sunburned. There are cornflowers in my study and
when I return from an insignificant but pooping shopping tour, I find
orangeade coolly on my desk. None of this implies vast histories to
you. I have travelled so much, lived so thoroughly alone, that these
piffling details of comfort and thoughtfulness come as a sweeping
surprise.

I would rather not go to Mexico but shall go -- in two
days time. Naturlally. One doesn't die on jobs; and besides I shall
doubtless be glad of it, as memory, if nothing else.

Your note has come. You are a very dear. Let us never
speak of the de Chambruns again. I should hate to feel myself growing
coarse-grained and vituperative inside; should hate to fester with
suspicion; should hate to change the tenor of uncalculated impulse
which is the scale and music of my life. I should hate moreover
to waste anything which is between us on the poor, soiled, obsession
of their thoughts. I should loathe having them occupy one of my
needed and ineffectual cerebral cells. Voila -- and , as the ~~ikkxi~~
Italians say so aptly, basta.

May 1931 letter from Martha to Cam Becket, a friendship that lasted more than 50 years.

A letter from Audrey delights my risible muscles; the girl belongs in Henry James novels, and in music by Couperin. Two letters from Bertrand are almost more than I can stand. I have been unable to cope with my own optimism; though I wrote him that we might as well abandon each other because of his wife, i hoped -- yes, hoped terribly .... And now with out meaning to he has so surely finished that hope, and his own blindness, his child-like refusal and inability to see what is what and what can be anything, merely adds to the piteousness and futility of it all. I have talked to Mother about this, and we have arrived at the conclusion -- she wisely, I bitterly -- that only work heals those stranger wounds, those sick deep wants that clamor in one's memory. I am not sure I shall do anything more about Russia next year; but probably try to get a job on a local paper; work, work, and home at night quietly. Some sort of anodyne; I have been counting my losses honestly and know that if I am to live with any joy or usefulness, without hideous waste of days and enthusiasm, I must forget all that B. means. Because he has meant too much. And I have spoiled months of my life already groping backwards, praying, weeping and wondering why I was doomed to this gi ignominious frustration. Enough about all this too. I am saying several "goodbyes to all that" in this letter.

Dearest thank you 1000 times for your sweetness in N.Y, And for giving Kitten a good time, and for being alive, and wise. I like Jean and Robin, and had not expected too, and find them pretty splendid news. As for you -- well, my old playmate, you will have to guess.

Write me here.

Yours, for probably always,

M.

1932, Bertrand de Jouvenel, a photo taken by Martha and later sent to Pauline Pfeiffer.

Marty - Do you know this
couple - I've known
Hadley Richardson always,
as you probably remember.
Florence Usher, Hadley's sister,
tells me that Mr. Mowrer is
great. What is your opinion?
Our U.S.A. world is so
thrilling that one wonders
how it can go on. We're
putting into the discard an
accepted law every other
moment. Scarcity supply & demand
no longer exist, only N.R.A.

Hadley Richardson Hemingway
and
Paul Scott Mowrer
announce their marriage
on July the third
nineteen hundred and thirty-three
London

93 Boulevard Auguste-Blanqui, Paris
after September First

1933, Hadley Richardson Hemingway, Ernest's first wife, was from St. Louis like Martha. In typical Gellhorn form, Edna has written a letter to Martha on the back of this found stationery, Hadley's 1933 wedding invitation.

RIGHT: Circa 1936, portrait used for book publicity.

March 1940 bespoke Wyncie King illustration to acknowledge Gellhorn's novel about the German-Jewish refugee crisis in Prague, *A Stricken Field*.

THE WHITE HOUSE
WASHINGTON

February 12, 1937

Dear Marty:

I was glad to get your letter and
to know that the book was done. Revision
will be easy after you have talked to
some of your friends in New York. I am
glad you are going on in two or three
weeks and I know it will do you lots of
good.

Hick is there now working hard, but
you and she will certainly have some good
times together.

Unfortunately, you are coming on
apparently just when I start off on a
lecture trip in the southwest. However,
I do not leave until midnight the fourth
of March. If you should come east before
that and care to spend a few days in
Washington, do drop in. I would love to
see you.

Much love.

Affectionately,

Eleanor Roosevelt

*This is an invitation to stay! I'll be
back just before Easter if you care
to come then —*

February 1937 letter from Eleanor Roosevelt with a rare sample of her handwriting since
most of her correspondence was dictated.

RIGHT: Spring 1937 in Spain with Hemingway, a silver flask out of reach on a fallen tree.

BELOW: June 1937, Martha wearing a silver fox fur purchased in Madrid, the night Hemingway delivered his "Fascism is a Lie" speech at the Writers' Congress at Carnegie Hall.

January 16, 1938, Hemingway uncredited in photo of a St. Louis newspaper. Martha's handwriting reads: "Just picked up the paper my dearest and there you are, stocking cap and all, listening so hard to the man. It will haunt me forever that I did not do Teruel with you. Send this back to me. For my war chest."

203

1939, Hemingway's passport photo that Martha carried with her for company while she reported on the war in Finland.

December 1939, Martha speaking with an officer on the front in Finland.

LEFT: May 1938, Martha in Prague, where she reported on the German-Jewish refugee crisis.

1939, standing at the edge of the finca pool, Cuba.

1939–1940, Martha and Ernest on his brother Leicester's boat in Havana Harbor, Cuba.

1940, Martha and Edna Gellhorn on the finca property, Cuba.

Mrs. George Gellhorn

has the honour of

announcing the marriage of her daughter

Martha

to

Mr. Ernest Hemingway

Thursday, the twenty-first of November

One thousand, nine hundred and forty

Cheyenne, Wyoming

November 1940 wedding invitation.

1940, with Hemingway, his sons Jack ("Bumby"), Patrick ("Mouse"), and Gregory ("Gigi"), and "Toby" Bruce at Sun Valley. Photo by Lloyd Arnold.

November 14,1940, pre-wedding party where Martha and Robert Capa are facing the camera at Cabin Creek. Photo by Lloyd Arnold.

I never saw better men in my life in any country, and what they are willing to die for if need be is what you—in your way and place—are willing to live for…

My plans are uncertain. I am staying to see what happens next. Things look fine now, the Fascists are directing their attack on the other half of Spain so it is very quiet here, for the moment. I have a huge job to do in Cheko-Slovakia [sic], England and France for *Collier's*, and my daily bread may drive me out for a while but then I'll come back. What goes on here seems to me very much the affair of all of us, who do not want a world whose bible is *Mein Kampf*. I believe now as much as ever that Spain is fighting our battle, and will not forget that night when we brought the film to the White House and the President said: Spain is a vicarious sacrifice for all of us… But I think Spain is maybe not a sacrifice, but a champion: and hope to God that America at least will not go on letting this country down.

And you know something else, this country is far too beautiful for the Fascists to have it. They have already made Germany and Italy and Austria so loathsome that even the scenery is inadequate, and every time I drive on the roads here and see the rock mountains and the tough terraced fields, and the umbrella pines above the beaches and the dust colored villages and the gravel river beds and the peasant's faces, I think: Save Spain for decent people, it's too beautiful to waste…

This is very hard work writing in this light, and I've written enough… words are going to do nothing: Fascism has the best technique of words, the daring sustained lie, and it works. Around now, the people of Spain need airplanes. What a world we live in after all: it seems such a ghastly mess that one cannot begin to place blame. I place blame very heavily right now on two men, and wish I knew more history. It is as horrible and senseless as earthquake and flood, and the faces of the people caught in the disaster—old women walking on the roads, with heavy bundles, walking away from their homes, and stretching out their opened hands, wearily and desperately, to all cars, wanting only a ride to go someplace else, away, though they do not know where and they do not care—well, one won't forget these faces, ever.

… There's a curious similarity between the endurance I saw in the unemployed—a kind of heroism in peacetime disaster—and this: and I want to write it. And this letter is now like a book and enough of it. I send you always my love and admiration, and please give my respects to Mr. Roosevelt.

Always,
Marty

DIARY

Tuesday, April 25, 1938

5 a.m. I woke up from the noise of the anti aircraft. From the balcony you could see the tracer shells like red bars, somehow the shape of toy airplanes, going slowly up the sky. The lights bent together over the port, five of them, very disorderly, and the low ceiling took the ends of the beams and smudged them and bent them back. More noise. To the right another raw [sic] of light began going flatly over the top of the sky until the lights were searching about us, but always stopped by the murky ceiling, and to the right, high and grey, the stars. And then an anti aircraft gun on the right opened up.

After it was quiet and the lights had gone off, lying in bed, I heard heel taps on the pavement, tough heel taps from cheap slippers and a hoarse woman's voice singing an Andalusian song down on the Pasea de Gracia. A little later still, there was a nightingale, a bird whose voice has been steadily overestimated. It was very cold, and one was far too sleepy to be really upset.

The letters written to her mother Edna in 1938 reveal Martha's preoccupations with the German-Jewish refugee crisis in Prague. In 1939, she wrote about the crisis in *A Stricken Field*, the novel in which she "wrote out the accumulated rage and grief," safe in the finca, her "beautiful bolt-hole" in Cuba.

Collier's asked Gellhorn to try to speak with Czech President Edvard Beneš, a liberal democrat to whom she refered as "a decent man in a wrong time." In Prague, Gellhorn found Mikhail Koltzov, the *Pravda* correspondent she'd met in Madrid, waiting to give Beneš a message from Stalin, that Russia would back Czechoslovakia in the event of war with Germany. That May, Koltzov sat alone on a bench in a long dark corridor of Prague's Hradcany Palace, and because he seemed to have no energy for talking, Gellhorn babbled "the nightmare news of Barcelona, a whole city, starving to death." She spoke to him in French, their only shared language, of the "beautiful small children wounded in the daily air raid," fed watery soup in the general hospital and "war bread, made of sawdust or sand."[12] The refugees were a new face of war, "tens of thousands of peasants, moving away from what they had always known to nowhere." Those refugees were in Prague when the Czech army mobilized, "like a fiesta," as it "rolled along the roads" to fortify the border, a nation united with "no panic about Hitler." And, of recognizing then the awful silence, "that was the sound of doom, and fear where there had been none."

She was back in Spain for a couple of weeks in November where she met photographer Robert Capa, who would become one of her finest friends. She called Capa "the best, the nearest in every way." He was her "real brother," a man whose attitude matched her own. Gellhorn scorned "objectivity shit," and Capa's corollary was "you must have a position or you cannot stand what goes on."

By the time Gellhorn left Europe in January 1939, she was sure that the countries she cared about were lost: "Czechoslovakia vanished into silence, occupied by the Nazis; Franco and Fascism won in Spain, taking terrible vengeance on the defeated; Hitler attacked Poland and finally, tardily, Britain and France declared war on Germany."

In November 1939, Gellhorn visited the Roosevelts in Washington and picked up a letter that the President had written to "All American Foreign Service Officers" on her behalf, to help finesse contacts in Finland, where she was being sent to report by *Collier's*, who paid her handsomely—$1,000 for each article they accepted for publication.

Eleanor Roosevelt to MG

May 23, 1938
The White House
Washington

Dear Marty,

I was very much interested in your letter. You can certainly write, my child, and give one a remarkable picture of what is going on around you.

Paul Willert lunched with me the other day and told me he expected to see you in Paris and that you were on your way to Prague. It seems to me that you have quite a large amount of work cut out for yourself.

Please do not get killed! I should like very much to have you come back, and as you found the White House rather a good place to work, perhaps you will plan to spend a little time with us and really do some of your work here.

I wish we did not live under the threat every minute of such senseless war, which seems to have no purpose in the world except to leave Germany stronger than she was before. All one can do is hope human beings will come to their senses. In the meantime, some of us concentrate more and more on the things that are around us. I rather think that is what people do in storm-tossed times everywhere.

My love to you and do take care of yourself.

Affectionately,
Eleanor Roosevelt

MG to Edna Gellhorn   May 26, 1938
                                                              Paris

Dearest,

… Ernest sailed yesterday and I am not exactly happy but am being what the French call 'reasonable.' There isn't anything left to be, I have tried everything else. I believe he loves me, and he believes he loves me, but I do not believe much in the way one's personal destiny works out, and I do not believe I can do anything about this. So I am hurrying, at last, on my *Collier's* job, and by tomorrow night will have finished collecting the material. I am allowing myself four days to write the piece. And then, by next Wednesday or Thursday, June 1 or 2, I hope to leave for London. With luck and concentration I can get the London job done in two weeks. I shall not take the car to Checko-S [sic], but shall fly to Prague and try to clean that all up in two weeks too. My only desire now is to get this job honorably and competently done, and then work on my own mind, which is in a sorry state of ignorance and disorganization. I want to read and write and be very quiet. Shall not come back to America this summer, it is somehow easier to be really far from all personal problems, than to be within telephoning distance of something you can't telephone to. Maybe, I say this very tentatively, you would come over here. I have entered into negotiations for a house near Lavandou [location of Bertrand's family home, Villa Noria] and maybe I'll get one. I would be happy to go back there with you.

Have to dress. Am, for my article, lunching with the Aga Khan who is eating a great deal these days because he is about to return to India where he gets his weight in gold from his poor misguided subjects who think he is a god. Then to the races, for the bright or social end of this article. Then a cocktail party, and then as a reward for a long bad day, dinner with Herbert [Matthews] and two soldiers who are friends of mine, one of them Freddy Keller—you remember his family— who is alive and out of Spain and only has two bullets in his leg to show for it. Tomorrow I lunch with Doriot, the Fascist leader and in the afternoon see Thorez, the Communist chief. That just about tidies up my work. I have quite a lot of stuff, if only my head will work well enough to allow me to put it into exciting shape. Dunno. Hope so.

My book [*The Trouble I've Seen*, aka *La Détresse Americaine*] will be out in French in two weeks and finally, with much effort, I succeeded in getting the translation done well, worked over every line of it with the translator and scotched the cheap and sickening publicity they were going to do. So that seems fairly tidy.

I love you.
Marty

MG to H.G. Wells

June 13, 1938
Hotel Ambassador
Prague

Wells darling,

Am coming to London next Sunday to sweat out my life's blood on behalf of *Collier's* for one week. I do not invite myself to stay with you, because do not think you like me anymore, but perhaps I could come to lunch in all cases, and see what we agree & disagree on. Shall call you up—hope you are in town.

This country is very interesting. If Hitler had stayed a housepainter, I think it might have become a model democracy. Anyhow they seem to have put the war off for a time & one must be grateful. Why don't you shoot Chamberlain, like a good citizen? What a man. With a face like a nutcracker and a soul like a weasel. How long are the English going to put up with these bastards who run the country?

I am *very* tired, and have a bad liver from too much war, and wish everything would become reasonable for once so that honest folk could get a sunburn and cultivate their gardens.

Love, as always
Stooge

MG to Eleanor Roosevelt

June 17, 1938
18 Square du Bois de Boulogne
Paris

Dear Mrs. Roosevelt,

I got your lovely letter, and meant to answer it at once, but between now and then I have flown in and out of Czechoslovakia and had an exhausting if very interesting time. I wanted to write you, straight off, about that France-is-helping-the-Loyalists story. It goes on here, in France, very violently. Doriot, the not very promising Fascist leader, told me most seriously that there were 35,000 troops, army equipped and officered, fighting with the Spanish government. I told him somewhat sourly that if that were true, the government would have won in Spain long ago. It makes me particularly angry in view of what is going on now: a massacre. I believe that some airplanes must have got in but obviously not too many, or else this heavy and general bombing by Franco would be stopped. I know the frontier well, having wasted two weeks of my time hanging about there at the end of the month of May. And I've asked journalists stationed in Perpignan and all along, and asked homing soldiers, and everyone

I can find, as well as authorities here: France is certainly not being the support it is supposed to be, and what does manage to get in is on largely private initiative. I only wish the stories were true, and would be the first to be noisily delighted. But there it is. Anyhow, they are now seriously considering sealing the frontier to what slight traffic crosses it, and in due time a blockade can win any war.

Czecho [sic] was amazing. The country is a fortress, and the atmosphere is of someone waiting in an operating room for a surgeon, who will come to work with a blunt knife and no anesthetic. I do not see how this armed peace can continue. Partly because of the disastrous economic burden and partly because of the wearing and abnormal psychological strain. And yet the Czechs seem to have called Hitler's bluff with as pretty a mobilization as was ever staged, and quiet now reigns. However it gives you a turn to see peasants working in the fields alongside black steel reinforced pillboxes, to pass a Slovak peasant girl with red skirt and high black boots, peddling along on her bicycle, with a gasmask [sic] slung over her shoulder, to see every road barricaded, guarded, and to know that all railway bridges are mined, and all the rest of it. People do not yet realize (because the mind isn't built that way) what war can be. They fear it but surely they fear it the way children fear nightmares, dimly, without definitive images in their heads of how it will all work out. Me, it makes me sick, the whole business. By now, Europe knows that the former housepainter [Hitler] holds the lightning in his hands and it is ghastly to think that this one mad man can plunge us all into it again.

Ah well, I think the summer's safe anyhow. Have to go to England next week and ask a lot of questions. I am so depressed and disgusted with English foreign policy that I am beginning (stupidly) to feel the whole nation is a mass of cotton wool. This business of being a hack is fine for finances and revolting from the point of view of serious accomplishment. I am beginning to think in paragraphs and pretty soon it will be headlines, and when the day comes I shall hire out as a scrubwoman, which will be more suitable and honorable.

My love to you always, and please give my respects to the President.
Devotedly,
Marty

Eleanor Roosevelt to MG

June 29, 1938
Hyde Park

Dear Marty,

You have no idea how happy I was to get your letter and to know that you are safe. This traipsing around Europe at the present time seems to me to a highly exciting but a very dangerous proceeding.

Of course, all you write makes me positively ill. Why everybody should want to kill everybody else is just beyond my comprehension. I rather gathered that the French assistance to the Spanish was not very great. And I gather that even our own State Department has people who are not very anxious to do much for the Loyalists. Strange how easily our pockets affect our feeling for democracy!

Let me know when you come home and come home soon. Corsica sounds perfectly lovely and I hope you do swim, lie in the sun and find time for work which you really feel proud of.

Affectionately,
Eleanor Roosevelt

MG to Edna Gellhorn   July 4, 1938
                                                        Paris

… I think that England is a kid glove fascism, worse because of its hypocrisy and the fact that all of the people are fooled all of the time… As Laski said, "The first economy an Englishman makes is on thought." There is no thought, nor is there information, nor is there any set of values a man can respect: there is the Empire and money and the two are perhaps synonymous… But day by day, the ten percent who rule that country are practising a cynical opportunism, which is certainly pushing off the chances of peace farther and farther, the while they deny with amusement the mere suggestion of war. I am sure the war will come, though I think there is a possible two year lull during which the English aid their future enemies to become strong, so that the war when it does come will last longer and be worse. Chamberlain is deeply committed to having Franco win… He is one of the most hateful figures in modern times, and his whole crowd is disgusting… You only hear what pays, and how all foreigners are muck anyhow and why bother.

MG to H.G. Wells   July 7, 1938
                                          18 Square du Bois de Boulogne
                                                        Paris

Wells darling,
    I didn't call you Friday because I was sure you would be quite as hectic as I was: and no good comes of bursting in and out, with one's breath gone and one's eyes wild. I'll hope to see you calmly someplace, but not in England. Gellhorn is renouncing England. It isn't enough to be beau-d about by bright but not

imposing young men. I detest your ruling class, really thoroughly and seriously. I despise them as mercenary and without any desires except those concerned with holding on to what they've got. I find them horrifyingly shrewd and horrifyingly empty: and the worst of it is that the People put up with them, tip their hats, grin all over their faces, and are delighted to be ruled, gypped, snubbed and lied to providing the gent who does it is a gentleman. Well, Christ. I prefer a lot of other countries: Spain is a paradise of reason and generosity and the finer things of the spirit compared to that green isle…

And as for a free press, mother of God. You don't need Goebbels.

In all cases, I left England Saturday as one escapes from jail and have been just breathing in Paris which is quiet and a little shabby. I've written my article on England (just whacking it out, and in such a hurry to be free) and shall soon be going somewhere to swim and sunburn and try to write a book. I won't move or earn money for at least six months, anyhow I hope so.

It was damned disappointing not to see more of you, but maybe you'll be coming in my direction sometime and maybe there'll be more leisure. I love you very much and find you always an enchanting guy. And I am your humble servant as you know.

Devotedly,
Stooge

MG to Eleanor Roosevelt

August 14, 1938
18 Square du Bois de Boulogne

Dearest Mrs. Roosevelt,

Too dull in the head to write a decent letter, but I wanted to thank you for your last note. I left Corsica which turned out to be a failure. My last day was spent trying to keep a semi-drowned man from suffocating (which he did, finally) and it was all a horrible inefficient mess and to me symbolic of the island. So it is lovely to be back in Paris which is like a village in August. It is cool and empty and quiet, and people seem kinder, and there are no more beautiful trees in the whole world, and if ever they bomb Paris, then I think man is worthy of doom.

Speaking of bombing, there is a very big war rumor going around: the German manoeuvres are the cause. People now say: War between August 15 and September 15. I have decided not to believe it, but it is very gloomy business altogether. Hitler is mad of course: he will lose in any case. But the longer he waits the quicker his defeat. And there almost never was a handsomer summer. If it's the last one before a war, it was very very beautiful.

I'm dull and tired and won't go on writing this dreary note. It was only to send greetings and love.

Marty

MG to Edna Gellhorn   August 25, 1938
                                                                    Paris

… It is so bad now that one cannot believe it. Edgar (Mowrer) called me up yesterday… He had come from the F.O. (Quai d'Orsay) where he had been told that his information from Fodor in Prague was exact. The Foreign Office expects war between the 15th and 18th of September and is acting accordingly. They went on to discuss the evacuation of Paris… The uncertainty of all this is enough to break your heart. All Europe suffers with it and the people in the know are going just a little mad… The Germans want war: Hitler's entourage that is. The Czechs are so terribly strained by these months of uncertainty and waiting and bullying that they do not much care… I believe that if Roosevelt could announce on the day war was declared America entered with France and England, there would be no war. But he can't do it. And so we'll just get into the war anyhow… Everything in Europe is now miserable guessing. Only Hitler knows whether eight million men are going to be dead within the next five years.

Marty

Eleanor Roosevelt to MG   August 31, 1938
                                                          The White House
                                                               Washington

Dear Marty,

It was very nice to get your note and I am glad that you are back in Paris and hope that means you are on your way back here. I somehow would like to get you out of the atmosphere of war for a little time. I know just how much of a war rumor there is at the present time, and, while I hope if you do stay nothing happens, I think it is just as well to get you away from such things for awhile. You are tired and dulled by too much emotion.

I hope when you do come home I shall be somewhere in these parts, for I am doing considerable traveling around this autumn, some lecturing and a week or so visiting the outlying children in Texas and Seattle and, of course, to Warm Springs at Thanksgiving, I count on you letting me know when you are to arrive and coming to us for a while at least. You found it a good place to write before—perhaps you will again.

Affectionately yours,
Eleanor Roosevelt

MG to Edna Gellhorn   October 7, 1938
                                                           Paris

I am flying to Prague tomorrow. I got a cable from *Collier's*: they want stuff from Beneš… Beneš is in retirement in the country, not talking. The only sensible thing he can do is get out… I can do a fine story called "Obituary of a Democracy." I am wild with anger and this is my chance. Democracy is dying. The disease is called cowardice… Everybody's in Prague, waiting for the end.

Marty

MG to Eleanor Roosevelt   October 19, 1938
                                                           Paris

Dearest Mrs. Roosevelt,

I am sending you this report that I just wrote. It isn't exactly a literary master-piece but it has all the facts. The press censorship (under German direction) is so strict in Prague that you can't get the story out and I could not cable you directly.

I've seen a number of catastrophes in my life, but nothing that could touch Mr. Chamberlain's Peace [sic]. For treachery and resultant human suffering, it beats all. And the record of the diplomatic demarches of that period (which I got from Prague) reads like third degree, like bad gangster blackmailing. Czechoslovakia will of course go Fascist, it has to and it is only a question of weeks. But I am not sure that Chamberlain has not so weakened democracy in Europe that democracy itself will perish here. And now he is starting on Spain. It has evidently been decided that if high explosive won't destroy the Republic, then hunger will. Chamberlain has clearly put class interest above the interests of democracy in particular and humanity in general; he has even forgotten about the British Empire in his determination to render under the dictators what is not theirs. I hope that if his government continues in power, if France continues to be ruled by cowards or crooks, America will build a Maginot Line around all its coasts and go into total isolationism. There may be no hope of saving Europe, but democracy must be kept alive somewhere. Because it is evident that war itself is better than Fascism, and this even for the simple people who do not care about politics or ideologies. Men just can't live under Fascism if they believe any of the decent words. The refugees are plain people—farmers, mechanics, shopkeepers, housewives—but they know for instance that there is a great difference between being a man and being an animal who may neither think nor talk nor feel as he desires.

I am so angry and so disgusted that I feel a little dazed. I hate cowardice and I hate brutality and I hate lies. And this is what we see, all the time, all over the place. And of these three, maybe the lies are worst. Now Hitler has set the standard for the world, and truth is rarer than radium.

Please give my respects to Mr. Roosevelt. Will you tell him that he is almost the only man who continues to be respected by honest people here. His name shines out of this corruption and disaster, and the helpless people of Czechoslovakia look to him to save the things they were not allowed to fight for. I was again proud to be American.

I send you my love and wish someday I could write you a letter not like this. But what is there to do, if you aren't blind, except burn with anger and disgust. I met a lot of people my own age in Prague, people like me, writers and architects, medical students, young lawyers. I asked them what they were going to do. They looked at me and everyone was quiet and then one of them said: "We have no money and if we had money, where could we go. We will wait here." And another said, "We will wait for the concentration camps." And of course, they were only saying what is true. Well, I can't bear it. I still believe in the fine words, too.

Always,
Marty

The report Gellhorn included with this letter to Eleanor Roosevelt is an example of her lifelong ambition to make a fuss about the wrongness of things, especially when it involved innocent, vulnerable citizens. She noted that the anti-Nazi refugees lived "in schools, factories, old age homes, private apartments, under conditions of great overcrowding, sleeping on straw, sometimes with blankets, sometimes without, eating when and as possible. They have left their homes in great haste, with empty hands." To the refugees, however, physical conditions were "of minor importance." The vital matter was safety. And, without money or passports, there was "no way for them to find another home." Rather than be

deported to the German-occupied regions from which they escaped, the refugees themselves stated a preference "to be shot in Czechoslovakia." Gellhorn
figured that there were about "ten thousand Austrian and Reich German exiles
in Czechoslovakia," who were "in immediate and grievous danger"—people who
lived "with the steady terror of being sent back to persecution."

Preferring to write about individuals rather than the big picture, she described
a four-room apartment she visited in Prague where 80 Germans ate and 30 slept,
most of them in their 20s or 30s, half of them women. She wrote about a stenographer from Berlin who had spent three years in a women's prison because she
"stated in her office, in some argument, that she believed in freedom," so it was
decided that she was a communist agitator. Having experienced "three years
(without trial) in this prison… famous because none of the women is allowed to
talk at any time and the punishment is solitary confinement in cellar cells," the
young woman "now faced deportation." Gellhorn insisted that there was not one
of the refugees she had met who did not have "some trade and good work habits."
Furthermore, their demand was simple: "they would like to live."

MG to Charles Colebaugh

October 22, 1938
4 Place de la Concorde
Paris

Dear Mr. Colebaugh,

About Beneš. I got in touch with Jan Masaryk as soon as you cabled me; we
talked a long time from here to London. It was pretty flat at the time that Beneš
would not write. Masaryk said he did not think I ought even try to get at him; he
said Beneš had not seen anyone, even intimate friends, since his resignation. For
political reasons, he could not talk or write. The political reasons are that Czecho
[sic] is now a Nazi vassal state and they dare not in any way offend Hitler. Beneš,
aside from being unable to speak about the really shocking diplomatic methods
that led up to the capitulation (an embargo which applies to all official Czechs),
also enjoys the personal hatred of Hitler. Therefore, he fears to compromise the
new dismembered Czecho-slovakia [sic] by pleading its cause. Jan Masaryk also
said: "The important thing now is whether he will get out of there alive."

So the minute I got to Prague I began on it. I saw Beneš' secretary, his *chef de
protocol* Mr. Smutny at the Palace, two great friends of his in the Foreign Office,
General Faucher and various others. The story is (it cannot be proved because by
now everybody in Czecho [sic] is afraid to talk about anything) that Beneš remains
a kind of prisoner at Cesimova Usti, because Hitler and Mussolini have made it
clear that they do not wish him to go about the world spreading "democratic

intrigues." That is probably in part true: another reason that he is in Czecho [sic] is that he doesn't want to give the impression of running away. No member of the Press had seen him since his resignation, no one could get near him, you couldn't even find out who—if anyone—did see him. I got a formal promise from Smutny to communicate your offer, explaining it to Smutny as Beneš' chance to win the public opinion of America etc. I did a very long and careful sales talk, but I am sure it did not come off. I would have heard from Smutny by now.

Then I hired a car and drove to his country house. The first thing that happened was the descent of the plain clothes police on me. I was well stopped at the gate of Beneš' house. I made a long sometimes indignant sometimes tearful speech (not wanting to get arrested for any of the odd things you can get arrested for in a troubled and distraught land) and at last they allowed me to send in my card. I made also speeches to the gate keeper and wrote on the card and waited. And waited.

At last a very nice little secretary-housekeeper kind of person appeared and told me in bad French that the President was desolated [sic] but he absolutely could not see anyone on any matter whatsoever. I had written on the card that I would not attempt to ask him any controversial political questions, but even that didn't help. The President, she said, knew I would understand that he was not seeing anyone at all; it had to be a blanket rule. I tried arguing but the police very politely and firmly saw me to my car and away.

I went back to Prague and tried it all over again and realised [sic] that I was up against something nobody could crack at this time. (If he actually does leave the country, as they say—they say he has accepted some post in the Univ [sic] of Chicago, but no date is set—then I am pretty sure you could get hold of him.) But as long as he is in the country, he must keep quiet: both for the sake of Czechoslovakia and for his own safety. In this connection, it is interesting to note that most of the men I knew there—Beneš men—in the Foreign office [sic], press etc.—are leaving the country as fast as they can. They know that concentration camps are the next step.

So, I know the story of those days diplomatically; I got them from the documents of the state department, translated from Czech for me by an official who cleared out almost at once afterwards. It is a story like a third rate police court grilling; nothing so shocking that I know about in history. But someone official would have to write it, to have it believed. I wonder if the British Government could sue for libel (of course it is all true, exactly what the British did) but I shouldn't think Chamberlain would care to have it known. Amongst other things, practically every note was presented either very late at night, having given the responsible Czech ministers just enough time to get home, go to bed, and go to sleep for about an hour—notes were held so that this could be done—or presented early in the morning from 6:30

to 7:30, after all-night cabinet meetings. It was a sort of third degree of fatigue and beats everything. Likewise it is clearly seen in this documentary evidence of the events, that England planned to sell out Czecho [sic] all along, and that the mobilization of France, the mobilization of the English fleet, the mobilization of the Czech army (which was ordered by England) were all part of a vast comedy to terrify the people of the world and make the Munich Pact seem a last minute rescue of peace, whereas it was a long planned betrayal.

I am not writing these things in my article. Perhaps I am wrong, but I have always tried to be as non-political and pictorial as possible for you, believing that was the way you wanted things done. The story of Czechoslovakia is, really and finally, the story of the dishonesty of the Chamberlain government and the cowardice of Daladier; but I am writing you a picture of a destroyed state, practically calling the lost sugar beet fields and coal mines and railroads by name, practically naming the refugees who are homeless and in desperate danger. It is the grimmest and most complicated story I ever saw: and worst of all, the war is now certain, and when it comes it will be a far worse war. And worse than that, Mussolini was at the end of his rope, and Hitler would have been finished after a few months of war, had it even come to that: but Chamberlain has given Europe to the dictators, and there seems very little hope that democracy will survive on the continent.

I am wiring you that I shall mail the story on the *Paris* instead of on the *Bremen*. I have been waiting to try to find out what Hungary was going to seize; in order to get the picture complete. Now I don't think that will be settled for sometime. Probably another Four Power Conference to divide up the southern part of the country. Hitler doesn't want Hungary to have a common frontier with Poland but it is difficult for him to say so, and so the negotiations drag and that part won't be possible to write now.

But already the Left and Liberal parties have been outlawed in Czecho [sic], and one "National" Party established. Nazism. They will be saying Heil Hitler in the streets of Prague sooner or later; and they will be saying it grimly.

I have noticed that you always use better pictures for my articles than the ones I provide, so I didn't spend any time on that end of it. I got you pictures of the Beneš country place; the Czechoslovakian Elba, just in case you didn't have any and would want them.

I am calling my article "Mr. Chamberlain's Peace." That seems to me a perfect description. But if you don't like that, I suggest as an alternative, "Obituary of a Democracy." Both are accurate.

Finally we come to the matter of my expense accounts. I have gathered that my expense accounts are locally regarded as little mysteries if not awful nuisances. The agreement with Mr. Davenport last spring was $500 for expenses per article and

$1000 per article. The expenses always come to just a little more, but as I wrote Mr. Chenery, that is my lookout. It is a great bother to try to figure them out in detail and as they only apparently baffle your accounting department, do you want me to go on doing it or do you simply want to handle it on that flat rate basis (which is the way it always works out anyhow.) Please let me know.

The next horrible story in Europe will no doubt be the blockade of Republican Spain, providing Chamberlain can work it, and I suppose he can work anything. If so, there will be starvation—which may be the worst thing there is—in Spain. As Italian and German high explosive is not working as well as could be expected, then try hunger. So Spain will be tragic news again too.

I am going to Morocco as soon as I get this story off. I want to see what is happening down there. It all sounds very curious and ominous. Maurice Hindus, whom I saw in Prague, announced one evening, "I am going back to America as soon as I can; believe me, in Europe even the roses stink." A very accurate statement, seems to me.

So you'll have the story on November 2. I trust you will like it. Czecho [sic] was much worse than war really, and the story is as moving as anything I ever saw. Evidently the four great "artisans of the peace" never met any little people in their lives: but I still have the nightmares over the old Czech of sixty-one who showed up at a frontier town with his front teeth knocked out and his ribs all but sticking through with the beating he got, and his hands black and swollen; and he was mussed up that way because he was a Czech and believed in having a president. He was only one of thousands on the march. It's some story.

This is a very long letter. There was quite a lot to say.

Sincerely,
Martha Gellhorn

Eleanor Roosevelt to MG

November 15, 1938
The White House
Washington

Dear Marty,

I not only read your report [on the anti-Nazi refugees in Prague] but I gave it to the President. I hope the day will come when you can write something that will not make one really feel ashamed to read it. The pity and horror of all these poor people—it is really appalling.

I rather think you should come home before long. You can't go on forever in the atmosphere you have been living in.

Hick is working very hard but I shall give her your report to read as I know she will be interested.

I am afraid we are a long way from any real security in the world but it is curious that, in spite of that, we all go on from year to year with the hope that some day things will improve.

Affectionately,
Eleanor Roosevelt

MG to Eleanor Roosevelt

December 3, 1938
Paris

Dearest Mrs. Roosevelt,

I got back from Barcelona this morning and found your letter. The report about the refugees in Czecholoslovakia was full of terrible things, and I could write you a long letter about the food situation in Spain, with special reference to children, that is quite as tragic. You and the President are much loved in that country. About 60,000 children are eating a half a pound of whole wheat bread, each day, for this month: so when I wander about schools seeing them they say to me (an American is a representative of yours in their eyes) "Many thanks, and many greetings for the President and the Senora Roosevelt." They also draw pictures, because with some food in them (they feel very lively and happy: so make wonderful pictures of the Quakers—who distribute this food—in their home, which is called the White House and the pictures are signed: *Para el Presidente Roosevelt, Juanito Menendes, 10 anos*). There is some confusion as to who is God, whether it is the Quakers, or the Red Cross, or the White House, or the Roosevelts. But all they know is that God sends them bread. The children eating these huge hunks of dry bread was about the only happy thing I saw. I was in various schools during airaids and the children waited patiently and sadly for it to finish. I shall never be a good writer, the human animal escapes me. Because evidently, the men in the planes have families too, and the men who sink the food ships have families, and the men who run a war have sons who also get killed, but none of this seems to have any serious effect upon behavior.

I shall be home December 20 and very glad of it. I am tired in the head. There is no escape from the world and how it runs. War itself, war in the trenches between armed men, is of course bad enough, but it is a circus compared to the helpless Jews living in ditches between Czecho and Germany, and the helpless solitary men caught up in the ghastly machinery of the concentration camp, and the seven month old babies with rickets or t.b. in Barcelona. I do not think danger is terrible and I am not sure I think sudden death is terrible—if at least you are fighting against something that makes living valueless—but lonely persecution and starvation and the fear of the women alone in their flimsy houses with the children, when the night bombers come over: well, those things are too bad.

If you have time to see me, I would love it, and perhaps you could send me a note to my brother's house at 440 Riverside Drive. And now in Europe, all the time, one is very proud to be American. I do hope I can see you. My plans are vague. What I hope for more than anything is to go back to Connecticut for six months and do a book. It would be wonderful to write again and to sit still, wonderful and fairly necessary. What do you suppose historians will make of this decade, one hundred years from now. I doubt if they will be able to reconstruct it or believe in it, it is too fantastic, and it goes too fast, but I should think the Dark Ages will seem neon-lighted by comparison.

I do look forward to seeing you, if you are not too busy.

Always devotedly,
Marty

MG to Charles Colebaugh

December 6, 1938
Paris

Dear Mr. Colebaugh,

The *Times* fell down very badly this time: possibly the General Strike was such an excitement to them that they forgot all about forwarding cables. So I got your cable about a Negrin article, when I returned from Barcelona. It is pretty maddening because I could easily have collected the material there and I would have liked to have done it. I cannot do it now, I don't myself know enough and there is no one here who is especially intimate with him and besides I wouldn't want to write it without having spent a certain amount of time talking to him and watching him work etc. I know him too slightly to feel competent, without special interviews, to light into such an article. And it's a damn shame too and makes me furious, but that's the way it has turned out.

I am returning on the *Champlain*, providing it runs, arriving December 30. I'll telephone you at once.

Meantime, the story that interested me in Barcelona is the one which will I believe ultimately decide the war: to wit, food. The army is okay and they are manufacturing munitions and light arms and the army seems astoundingly to get on somehow with a steady inferiority of heavy armaments and planes. The morale is fine and they have learned to dig: going along as is, without at least a Germany army corps and a few hundred more planes and countless extra artillery, it would take Franco forever to win the war and it is more than likely that he couldn't do it. This is politically tremendously important: being the first thing that has held up Fascism in Europe, since Fascism started. But the rub is food and the civil population. So I spent two very grim weeks going into vast detail on the life of the little man and his family and how they are facing the third cold hungry winter. It is a very moving story and of course, it is the real story about war. I took one typical Barcelona family and followed it through all the ramifications of a wartime daily life. So the story goes like a novel from a children's hospital where the seven month old kids have t.b. from undernourishment, to the front where the division commander is a fine 26 year old boy who was an electrician three years ago. I'm going to write it and will mail it, with luck, on the same boat as this letter, or if I can't manage that, I shall bring it along with me.

I do think the Beneš thing will work in due time, and it will be very interesting to know why he refused the offer of Russian aid and refused to fight. Even if he believed Hitler really would make war—which very few informed official people believed at the time, it now appears he still has never explained why he didn't chance it. He's the only one who will be able to tell and I hope he does.

If you are in town before Xmas, I shall look forward to seeing you, and if not, I'll come around right after Xmas. I plan to go to the country and work on a book [*A Stricken Field*], at the beginning of the New Year.

Yours,
Martha Gellhorn

1939

Gellhorn returned to the United States aboard the *Champlain*, docking in New York just before the new year. Early in January her beloved maternal grandmother died at the age of 88. Of her namesake, Martha Ellis Fischel, she wrote, "as she grew older she grew gentler and marvelously, I think, she seemed to laugh more easily and to become more accepting the way only excellent people can."

Her grandmother had a passion for community service that "came from an honest cheerful desire to have other people contented and safe and well as she was." The last time Gellhorn saw her grandmother they talked about the war in Spain and people Martha had known who had died there. Her grandmother admitted that was terrible, but "the dying was not the worst; it could happen any time to anybody." What was truly dreadful, she said, was "how people were forced to live, how little choice they had, between the life and the death."

January 1, 1939
Hotel Weylin
New York City

Dearest Mrs. Roosevelt,

The flowers were lovely. They decorated our first family Xmas for ten years. We all assembled, the army of brothers, their wives, one small child who equals a regiment, friends for good measure, and Mother.

It is very wonderful to be back. I also understand something that has been puzzling me for over a year. There was a great discrepancy between what seemed to me to be going on in Europe and the reaction to those events here. People here seemed shocked or angered or disgusted: but not afraid. In Europe, people are just afraid. And now I understand that too, all the salt water is a very blessed thing and it is at once absurd and delightful the way Europe melts once the huge lady with the torch is passed. I had a respectful and intimidated argument with my boss, during which he showed me up for a fool, a morose fool at that because after all he's an American who stays home, and I am a girl who had just gotten back, and suddenly I saw that it wasn't false optimism here, it was the physical inability to be panicked by something that is happening thousands of watery miles away. So you see, the answer to gloom is to come back to America. But—postscript—I still cannot forget how it is in Europe.

Will you have any time to see me. I do want to come down and call on you, for whatever moments you can spare. The rest of this winter is going to be a rest-and-cheer cure. Much world disaster is hard on the digestion of journalists; it would be nice if that was all it did, wouldn't it, and I want to get myself very hearty again and ready to go back when necessary. There is also writing to be done, stories not articles for a change, and sun to absorb and perspective, whatever that exactly means. If you could see me I'd like to stop off in Washington on the way to Florida. Would you let me know if that would be possible. I DO hope so.

Thank you again for the lovely flowers. You are a wonderful person. I don't see how you can remember to be so lovely, kind to so many people, and I am a very grateful and admiring recipient of that kindness.

Always devotedly,
Marty

MG to Eleanor Roosevelt

Post-January 8, 1939
4366 McPherson Avenue
St. Louis

Dearest Mrs. Roosevelt,

I did decide to come out and am very glad of it. Mother was more distressed than I had realized. Grandmother was 88 but Mother had grown to need the responsibility of her, as well as loving her, and besides that too many people die in our family of late years.

At the moment pretty disgusted with myself. I've done no proper work for my causes for a long time. Just been a hard-working journalist which, in the end, is to my own benefit. I still like to treat myself as if I were a respectable citizen who assumed some communal responsibilities and ever since I've been home I've been shrinking from the jobs—speeches, collecting money, etc—which I ought to do, well or badly, but still do them. And one of the things I always admire about you is your unwaveringness, the way you carry on all the time, without fatigue or doubt or discouragement. My mother has that same quality and I think perhaps women like you are just better quality than women like the rest of us.

Well. So this is enough of a rambling. If you aren't too tired of my changeful-ness about dates, I'll make myself a feast of seeing you.

Love,
Marty

Eleanor Roosevelt to MG

January 26, 1939
The White House
Washington

My dear Martha,

I don't wonder you feel as you do. Human beings have never been as fine as they should be except individually and in great crises.

I talked to the President last night as to what he thought the Congress would do about lifting the embargo, particularly in view of the Gallup poll. He said he felt that the majority of the Congressmen, because they were not sure that the people really understood what they were voting about, would try to delay any vote on changing the neutrality law or lifting the Spanish embargo, because they did not want to take the responsibility of the stand.

You might even say that Spain was fighting on the frontier of democracy, but I am terribly afraid that if you actually took a vote of the people they would be pretty confused as to how far they agreed with that conception of what is happening in Spain… People rise to great crises. That is what the Spanish people are doing too. That is what the Czechs would have done if they had been given a chance. But when people feel safe and comfortable they are apt to feel a way to go, as a good part of the United States feels. They don't even want to do much in the way of sacrificing to help the people who are suffering in other lands or to run the risk of any more suffering here by aiding the refugees from other lands.

Don't you and your mother want to spend Wednesday night here and start out from here on Thursday morning? I will be delighted to have you both.

Stop thinking for a little while. It is good for us all at times, and there will come a chance to do all the things for your country that you want to do. I have an idea that your younger generation is perhaps going to be willing to make some sacrifices which will really change much of today's picture.

Affectionately yours,
Eleanor Roosevelt

MG to Eleanor Roosevelt

February 5, 1939
Naples
Florida

Dearest Mrs. Roosevelt,

I see by this morning's paper (The *Tampa Morning Tribune*, a strange sheet mostly full of local gossip about oranges and grapefruits and their prices) that the Nazi press is calling the President, "Anti-Fascist Number One." As I can think of no greater term of honor, I am hurrying to write and congratulate him *via* you. I am also thrilled to see that the Italians are in a fury. In these days, unless the Berlin and Rome press are insulting, you cannot be sure where you stand.

… The thing about Barcelona is like having a death in the family, only worse. We have all been writing to each other, telephoning, thinking, and trying to understand it. I think the hunger had a lot to do with it. I hear now that the fine men, Lister, Paco Galan, Modesto and other divisional commanders, held where they had to, and the Catalans ran away on either side. When I first learned about cowards being shot at the front I was very, how shall I say, distressed maybe. Now I think that is okay. The cowards risk or sacrifice the lives of the brave ones. This time they seem to have lost everything. And I find myself thinking about Negrin [Loyalist prime minister of Spain, 1937–39] all the time. I suppose he will fly to

Madrid when it is ended in Catalonia and carry on there. Negrin is a really great man, I believe, and it's so strange and moving to think of that man who surely never wanted to be prime minister of anything being pushed by events and history into a position which he has heroically filled, doing better all the time…

There's one thing in your letter I don't agree with, and you don't practise it yourself. You say: 'Stop thinking for a little while.' You don't stop thinking. I'm no use of course, don't accomplish anything, but if I ran away from it, tried not to know or understand, stopped caring (or being hurt or angry at how the world goes), then I'd be guilty not only of ineffectuality but also of cowardice. I *hate* what happens in these times, but ignoring it won't change it. And someday if I go on trying to know and understand, I may at last get it all in some sort of shape or order, be able really to see how it all works together and why, and then maybe I could write something that would make just a few other people think too. If democracy is good, it must depend on the constant concern of the citizens.

Love,
Marty

MG to Eleanor Roosevelt

March 18, 1939
Finca Vigía
San Francisco de Paula

Dearest Mrs. Roosevelt,

… Everything that has happened these last six weeks has been so heartbreaking that I cannot endure to think about it. Perhaps because I try to be a writer, perhaps because I am a woman, I cannot avoid seeing history always in terms of people. And I see this disaster in terms of the plain soldiers I knew, and the others who were painters, musicians, dock workers or miners and became commanding officers, in terms of Negrin and the young man, a brilliant research scientist, who was his secretary. I keep thinking of Pasionaria, and the peasant women and the little old servant who took care of me in Madrid and walked to work through bombardments, sighing to herself 'for the poor people and the dead.' And seeing it this way, it is intolerable.… In Spain itself, as the final disaster has neared and overtaken them, the fools, hysterics, cowards and liars have gotten the upper hand. I suppose it is inevitable. It begins to seem to me that the rewards of the good and the brave must be in heaven, since they are surely not on this earth.

… I have taken possession of my finca. I had a moment of acute depression bordering on despair yesterday, which was produced by the protracted house-cleaning and shopping at the ten cent store for kitchenware. I'm not much of a house woman (*femme d'intérieure*, as the French so sweetly say) and the week's work of getting a place habitable seems to me far more trying than a week at the front line, or a week working myself to the bone getting an article in shape. I got very gloomy, thinking now I am caught, now at last I have possessions (and I have feared and fled them all my life), and what in God's name shall I do with this palace now that I have it. So I slept on it, and woke to look out my window at a saba [sic] tree, so beautiful that you can't believe it, and hear the palms rattling in the morning wind, and the sun streaking over the tiled floors, and the house itself, wide and bare and clean and empty, lying quiet all around me. And I am delighted, and feel almost ashamed to have all these wonders, and feel myself at last very serene and safe and I think maybe I'll get down to work at last and turn out the book that has been haunting me, but has never gotten written. It seems, somehow, shameful to be so well off in such a tragic world, but I console myself by saying that my money will run out in due course and I'll be back working hard for it.

When I was living in a $4 a week room in Albany, just after I left Bryn Mawr, working as a cub reporter on the *Times Union*, I never dreamed I would write myself into a grove of palms and bamboos and flamboyante trees, nor a terrace covered with bougainvillea, nor a swimming pool: and I can't believe it yet. I have a feeling I ought to put up a plaque to *Collier's* magazine.

Love,
Marty

MG to Eleanor Roosevelt

May 11, 1939
Finca Vigía
San Francisco de Paula

Dearest Mrs. Roosevelt,

... Here, on my hilltop (which is as remote as the moon) things go along very quietly from day to day. I am working with a sort of gloomy desperation on my book about refugees [*A Stricken Field*]. It is hard to write a novel that is not leaden with despair, about such a subject; and yet it must be interesting and exciting, and I won't fake any of it, so it goes very slowly, day by day, with endless, painful rewriting, and there will probably be a war long before I'm through and then good God, half the world will be refugees.

What beats me is that they still allow Mr. Chamberlain to show his nose in Europe and I suppose he will appease Poland okay too, and that leaves very little left, except France. I daresay he wouldn't mind carving France either. The one thing Marx certainly had absolutely straight was the whole business of the classes. (You are an exception; all truly good and brave and intelligent people are, but the basic idea holds.) And evidently those loathsome English upper classes can't even read, or they'd know that in destroying freedom they do not save their bank accounts, they only get robbed by their protégés, later. Ai [sic], it makes me sick, makes anybody sick, I daresay. I am opposed to this oncoming war. I do not give a hoot what happens to either England or France. In a truly belligerent mood, I wish they could all be wiped out at once, and leave Europe clean for a new sowing.

How are you? I saw some too heavenly pictures of you looking so resigned and patient, in some spring clothes, and by now you are having royalty on your hands [George VI & Queen Elizabeth]. I don't like kings either; I think Presidents are the best idea.

All love,
Marty

Eleanor Roosevelt to MG

May 17, 1939
The White House
Washington

Dear Martha,

I am passing that letter which you sent me on, at the President's direction, to both Farm Security and W.P.A., and I only hope that something may be done.

I do hope your book turns out to be not only all that you may wish, but that it will stir people on the refugee question the way Steinbeck's *Grapes of Wrath* seems to be doing on the migratory workers question.

The President was prevented by a bad cold from seeing Senor Negrin, and as this has to be done so secretly I do not know if he will have another opportunity. I hope very much to see him sometime in New York.

Much love.

Affectionately,
E.R.

MG to Eleanor Roosevelt

August 4, 1939
Finca Vigía
San Francisco de Paula

Dearest Mrs. Roosevelt,

I'm coming back before the end of this month, about the 25th I think, complete with the manuscript of my novel [*A Stricken Field*] which is within ten pages of being finished now. It's awful exciting to be nearly through. I never believed it, because somehow sitting down day after day to the white paper is unbearably like carrying water in a sieve, and now that it gets done, and has a shape, I begin to breathe lightly, and to float a few feet above the floor. With joy. I think it's a good book, but am not the one who will judge. (That's not true. When it is all done and gone over and over and over again, in its complete form, not just the endless piecemeal revisions, I will read it and decide and know.)

And then, I am going abroad again for *Collier's* but I hope they aren't in too much of a hurry so that I can have two weeks or so to loaf about in the east. And I do want to see you, if it's possible for you, before leaving again. Do you think I could? I'll be at the Hotel Weylin in New York, in case you could write me a note.

It is very hard to know what is going on in the world, from this distance, and working so hard on one thing, but doesn't it look as if we were in for another huge scare and crisis. If you get a certain number of miles away the whole thing seems too fantastic to be true, like the horror plays they put on at the *Grand Guignol* in Paris. You can't believe real men, millions and millions of them, and their women and children, are concerned in anything so mad. But when you see it in small (like in the waiting room of the U.S. Consulate here, with the people holding out their hands for visas), you can believe it, and fear it and hate it. What we seem to have plenty of in this world is fear and hate, for one thing or another.

I will hope hard to see you. Are you well and having some rest this summer?

Devotedly,
Marty

Eleanor Roosevelt to MG

August 8, 1939
Hyde Park

Dear Marty,

I will be right here in Hyde Park until September 10 and perfectly delighted if you can come up here for a night or so. If not, we will be in New York on the 23rd of August and I will certainly arrange to see you.

You are right I think in your analysis about a crisis coming on. I don't know what might happen now but it looks pretty hopeless to me and our hands, as far as prevention goes, are pretty well tied.

Affectionately,
Eleanor Roosevelt

MG to Eleanor Roosevelt

Late August 1939
The Weylin
New York City

Dearest Mrs. Roosevelt,

What a comic world it turns out to be. The next thing is to learn to say *Heil Hitler* in Russian.

I got here yesterday—and learned that *Collier's* wants me to go to Russia as soon as I can get a visa. It doesn't seem likely that I'll be able to sail before September 13 on the *Normandie* at the earliest. Will you have a moment that I could grab? Except for Labor Day weekend, will be here at the Weylin. Know how busy you are especially now. I would give ten years to know how this crisis is being reported in Europe. The President's message was magnificent.

Love,
Marty

MG to Eleanor Roosevelt

Fall 1939
c/o Guaranty Trust
New York City

Dear Mrs. Roosevelt,

I just got a wire from Bishop Scarlett, who is the Episcopal Bishop of Missouri, a fine and active and honorable man, and the person who can always be counted on to help those who need it. I wired him about the sharecroppers, because he's sort of handling it. He says: "Think most important move now is thorough investigation. Situation terribly confused by press. Knowledge of real facts now desperately needed." The WPA man is Matthew Murray in Jefferson City. I wonder if the investigatory agents would be WPA? They never were much good in Missouri, as bad in fact as any place I saw. Very limited political people. Anyhow I hope those wretched sharecroppers have tents and something to eat. Bishop Scarlett knows the facts and they're awful, naturally. The negro preacher who more or less started the movement said they had no program, they just went out on the road "because they'd rather die" than go on as they were.

I've been thinking about all the talks I had in Washington and it gets worse as I think about it. You'll perhaps excuse me of being impatient or unaware of political exigencies, and that's probably true, but there seem to me to be great things at stake and there's no room left in the world for patience or compromise. I wish I could write this properly and am afraid of being too "intense" (a repulsive word as its [sic] now used). But the thing that distresses me the most is this: do you think any people have a right to a moral attitude which they will not back with action, or have they a right to convictions without courage, or have they a right to speeches and writing and radio the while they complacently eat their national dinners and absolve their consciences with words. I do not believe that Fascism can destroy democracy, I think democracy can only destroy itself. It must have so weakened and cheapened and denied itself that it is no longer a moving or inspiring reality: at such a time, this colossal fake that is Fascism can masquerade itself into commanding an historical position. And I think democracy is talking itself off the map.

If one had the comfort of believing in God, one would begin to pray for miracles. Something has got to happen and happen quick. I myself don't give a hoot about empires, trade domination, or political forms. But I care desperately about the dignity of man. And it seems to me the world is almost too black to behold. Half of it is bullied and terrorized and debased by dictators and half of it is soppy with cowardice and sloth and selfishness. And then there's a tiny fighting percentage that is honestly willing to die for the decent words and what they mean.

If Spain goes, no one can yet know what kind of collective heartbreak and disillusion that is going to bring, or what bitterness or what hate. In our time, there has been no spectacle as tragic, in which the normal issues were clearer. (The last war being a blood bath of the most loathsome and cheap variety, in which everyone was almost equally guilty and equally undesirable in motives. Perhaps America was cleaner in point of view, but the whole thing was too alarmingly stupid to believe in.) But Spain was something else, and if there's anyone left to write history that will be proved. To see Spain go under, and with it those ideals, those few ideals that are worth living and dying for, seems to me a misery that we are not going to get over easily.

And then what will make us all wild with grief and fury is that though we were told it was nonsense to fight for Czechoslovakia, a decent democracy, or for Spain, and useless to help them, we will of course very shortly have to fight for the English trade routes.

The worst thing I ever saw was Czechoslovakia: and I suppose that worse than that will be Spain when Franco takes over, leading his allies in. When I think about Negrin sending the International Brigades home, when I think of the way he has run that country despite the war, and how the people have changed and grown and become free, and when I think of what they suffered for what they believed, the guilt of all of us, the three great democracies, is like a sense of personal sin.

I write you this way I suppose as one would weep aloud. There will be millions like me who will never know what to believe again, or what to do for their beliefs or whom to serve. It is impossible to tell people to believe in democracy when those who control democracies will not believe in it themselves. This is an accusing thing I am saying, not for you: I feel a condemnation of everyone, of all of us, the greatest to the smallest. The very smallest, though, can never be condemned: they are only led and later they pay with their lives for the errors of their ruling classes.

The people of Spain are a good people and they have proved during all this time that the spirit of man is very strong indeed. Now when one man, Mussolini, can simply cow the conscience and the decency of the whole world as he has been doing (backed by that other saver of civilization), and set about destroying a good people, and a way of life they worked towards for decades and fought for several times, then perhaps the individual democrat may justly feel that he is on a losing side. I wouldn't mind losing a war that we all fought because we had to, for what we believed in, honestly. Because the fighting would keep the belief alive somewhere. But to sell out, to give up, to play safe, to stand aside before such injustice is the worst defeat there is. I just don't think democracy can survive its own immoralities.

In the whole world there is only the President to lead the forces of democracy, and he's the President of the United States with an isolationist middle west and south and west behind him. But don't you think that in this tormented drifting frightened world, one man with honor and a fierce courage of his convictions could rally all the people behind him and make them loyal and brave, and make them know why they lived and what they had to pay to go on living. Don't you think maybe this people and the decent people in other countries are waiting for that? Or are people no good, is the human race not only muddled but cowardly, don't they want to be saved? I think (and I am nobody and what I think matters less than not at all) that the decent people of the world are desperate for leadership, crying out for courage and direction and something to believe. But they haven't any money or any newspapers or any lobbyists, and what are their names, and how is one to take a census. And besides, maybe I am too hopeful, and want to believe man is better than he is.

Thank you very much for letting me come down to see you. I love you very much and admire you. I'm picking Mother up in Washington Thursday morning and setting out with her in my car (somewhat dented from the time a train hit me in France) to the south. She sounds terribly tired and I want to see that she gets a rest. I can't do anything evidently for large causes and issues, can help no one, so at least I can be temporarily useful to my own. I try to absolve my conscience and keep from despair by giving my money to the boys of the Abraham Lincoln Battalion and helping them write articles, readjust to their parents, get married and find jobs. Small errands, of a service nature, to those people who did fight for what I care about. But I remember the dead all the time, all those I know who are dead, and it is horrible to think their own people let them down, democracy itself didn't want to be fought for, and their dying is made useless. It isn't that dying is so bad, but if you are young what is terrible is not to live. And not to live just because Mussolini and Hitler are willing to take chances and ship airplanes and artillery all over the place, is indeed tragic. Ah well.

Shall I see you again before returning to Europe? I hope so. Thank you again for letting me come down. I don't know how to tell you what I think of you but anyhow I think a great deal and much love.

Marty

President Franklin D. Roosevelt, on behalf of MG

September 11, 1939
The White House
Washington

To All American Foreign Service Officers:

The bearer of this note, Miss Martha Gellhorn, is an old friend of Mrs. Roosevelt's and mine. For a period of five months or so, Miss Gellhorn will visit Russia and various other countries. Her purpose is to secure material for publication for one of our weekly magazines.

I will appreciate it if you will kindly give her every assistance.

Very sincerely yours,
Franklin Delano Roosevelt

Eleanor Roosevelt to MG

September 27, 1939
The White House
Washington

Dear Marty,

I hope you are enjoying the sunshine and will not start your trek to Russia until you feel well and strong again. We can face anything if our physical condition is good, but that colors everything else.

I am glad that you had a good time with us and hope the next time it can be longer and you can have a little quiet in my cottage.

I am glad you stuck it out about your book. One cannot write only of pleasant things these days and one must tell the truth as one sees it.

I will be very happy to have your letter of people who might be helpful if I can ever get behind the powers that be with any real plan. Mr. Hoover turned us down, said he probably would be busy organizing a political campaign next year and did not feel he could support the setting up of anything else, but that he would be willing to give his help and advice to the Red Cross. He refused to call on the President.

I was very much afraid that the State Department information was not very good on the Spanish question. I do not happen to have very much confidence in our present Ambassador over there, though I do not say so out loud. It may be that I just do not have any confidence in his wife!

I hope you will be back if I can get off in March. I think the simplest way is to just go to Cuba without any fanfare beforehand and not try to hide. I would probably go ahead by myself and take whatever was coming and let the others follow when the disagreeable part was over. I think I could fly in quite easily.

Get well and let me know when you really go. I think the article which you enclosed does put what most of us are feeling very clearly.

Affectionately,
Eleanor Roosevelt

MG to Ernest Hemingway

October 16, 1939
The White House
Washington

My God it is almost winter & I'm still waiting.

Beloved, I saw Bobby & Jane [Joyce] yesterday. Both work in same bldg though Jane is file-girl in head man's office & Bobby is Balky [sic] specialist. Jane looks better than I ever saw her, good color, no lines, lovely. Due to quietly in one place 9 to 5 and home to bed. Bobby looks like death's head as usual, over-work (he has a huge conscience & much kindness: with those things you always overwork) But he's happy....

He'll be going away in about a month, to run an office, and will probably be seeing Herbert [Matthews]. I'll give him a letter of introduction.

Bobby insists that I see all the furrin [sic] big-shots so as to speed my work abroad. Of course, Colebaugh said don't bother, but one can't listen to them. They are deadly inefficient really: one has to do all one's own errands, planning, thinking. Even they forgot to arrange my G.B. visa, so I did. But imagine putting me through this typhoid-tetanus misery unnecessarily. Allen [Grover] tells me I ought to get at least some of my N.Y. expenses back from Charles [Colebaugh, *Collier's*]. It has been *very* expensive & I'd never have stayed so long in N.Y. on my own book.

Mrs. R [Roosevelt] is so lovely, lovely, lovely. She's giving a dinner tonight with everyone who could help me on transport.

Harry [Hopkins] said he was going to ask you if you wanted me to go, before he'd help. Had a very jolly meal last night with Harry & his wife & the Rs.

Can't sleep & have run out of sleeping pills, like you. Mrs. R. sleeps 3 hours a night only. I'm tired & slightly wore-out in head; and all the time grieving with homesickness. I miss my mon [sic] & my cotsies [sic]. And everything. Make my *hommages respecteux* [respects] to Mr. Scrooby [Hemingway's penis]. I love you my Bug.

Bongie

Late October 1939
4366 McPherson Avenue
St. Louis

Dear Mr. C,

You wrote me a very cute letter and thank you for that check and I shall obey and not try addition anymore and also obey about not thinking about the war. Seems like iron and overeating are the main prescriptions right now and I am busy on both. Was too proud to move on from here to the mountains but am leaving tomorrow as it is hot here and besides I think the whole state of Missouri gets run from this house and the telephone is enough to drive anyone bats in no time at all. Though on the other hand, the only place they really spoil you good is in your childhood home. Some hotel manager ought to work up that idea.

So until the next time and gratefully,
Martha Gellhorn

THE WHITE HOUSE
WASHINGTON

December 18, 1940.

To All American Foreign Service Officers:

The bearer of this note, Mrs. Martha Gellhorn Hemingway, is an old friend of Mrs. Roosevelt and mine. For a period of five months or so, Mrs. Hemingway will visit the Far East. Her purpose is to secure material for publication by one of our weekly magazines.

I will appreciate it if you will kindly give her every assistance.

Very sincerely yours,

Franklin D. Roosevelt

This letter from President Roosevelt was a personal favor to Gellhorn to help smooth the way with contacts in China in early 1941.

Early 1941, the newlyweds at the Stork Club in New York City before their trip to China.

Circa 1941, Martha steering Hemingway's boat *Pilar*.

Early 1941, arrival in Hawaii, *en route* to China.

Photograph of bearer

Martha G. Hemingway

PHOTOGRAPH ATTACHED
AMERICAN
CONSULAR SERVICE

4

This passport, properly visaed, is valid for travel in all countries unless otherwise restricted.

This passport, unless limited to a shorter period, is valid for two years from its date of issue and may be renewed upon payment of a fee of $5 but the final date of expiration shall not be more than four years from the original date of issue. See page 17
See page 16

American citizens traveling in disturbed areas of the world are requested to keep in touch with the nearest American diplomatic or consular officers.

American citizens making their homes or residing for a prolonged period abroad should register at the nearest American consulate.

SEE PAGES 6, 7, AND 8 FOR RENEWAL, EXTENSIONS, AMENDMENTS, LIMITATIONS, AND RESTRICTIONS.

5

I, the undersigned, Consul General of the United States of America, hereby request all whom it may concern to permit safely and freely to pass, and in case of need to give all lawful aid and protection to

Martha Gellhorn Hemingway

a citizen of the United States.

The bearer is accompanied by his

Wife,

Minor children,

Given under my hand and the seal of the Consulate General of the United States at Hong Kong, March 24, 1941.

mrs.
4366

Addison E. Southard

Description of bearer

Height 5 feet 7 inches.

Hair blonde

Eyes brown

Distinguishing marks or features:

Place of birth St. Louis, Missouri

Date of birth November 8, 1908

Occupation Writer

Martha Gellhorn Hemingway
Signature of bearer.

This passport is not valid unless signed by the person to whom it has been issued.

3

1941 passport.

One hundred thousand Chinese soldiers crushed gravel barefoot to build an airfield in 100 days in 1941. Gellhorn believed that the greatest weapon the Chinese possessed was resilience.

Alfresco with Madame Chiang in China, spring 1941. Of Madame Chiang's will to power Gellhorn wrote, "it was a thing like stone; it was a solid separate object which you felt."

1942, with ragtag Caribbean crew on a "horror journey."

1942, with U.S. airmen in Puerto Rico.

1942–1943, photo of Hemingway that Martha kept with her during war reporting from London. It may be seen tacked to the top left of her mirror in the Lee Miller photograph on page 249.

1944, in uniform in Italy.

In 1943, Gellhorn shadowed Royal Air Force pilots who flew Lancaster bombers and reported on their work for *Collier's Magazine*. From them she learned about "the point of no return," later the title of her novel about Dachau.

1943, part of a photoshoot for *Vogue* by Lee Miller in London in which Gellhorn wears the diamond and sapphire band from Hemingway.

1945, bespoke Wyncie King illustration, one of several Martha kept.

DACHAU CONCENTRATION CAMP
VISITORS PASS

The bearer ___Martha Gellhorn (civilian)___ ASN ___

is only allowed to enter the camp and compound during the hours

and on the date specified below.

Hour-from 16oo _____ to18oo _____

Date ___7 May 1945___

By order of Lt.Col. Martin W. Joyce

By: GEORGE E. BANG
1ST Lt M. A.C.
Adjutant

C.O./Adjutant

May 1945, of the two hours she spent at Dachau Martha would later say, "It was as if I fell over a cliff and never recovered."

1945–1946, a photo sent to Martha by James Gavin, showing him in animated conversation with their dear friend Robert Capa.

RECD SEP 11 46

Darling

How are you doing with getting my name legally changed to Martha Gellhorn? I am starting my travels again (briefly — to Paris + Nuremberg) — + the passport with Hemingway thereon is an infuriating nuisance.

Am doing short stories, pretty good ones, + hope to have a book of same by February.

And you?

love

Martha

Sept 7

September 7, 1946 letter to Cam Becket about reclaiming her name legally.

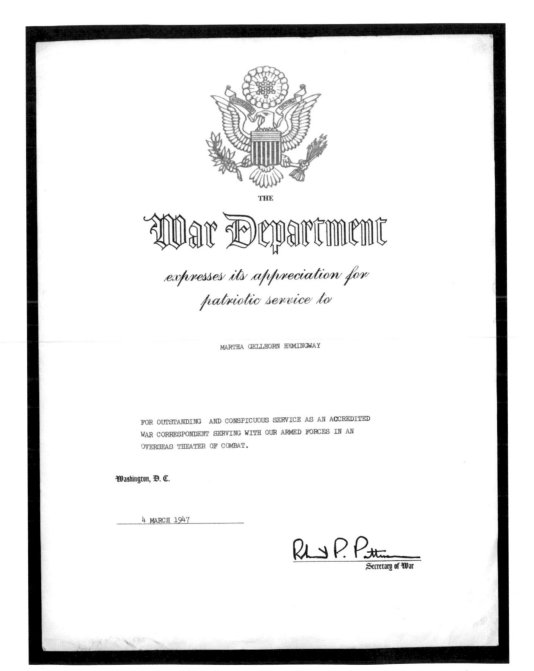

THE

War Department

expresses its appreciation for

patriotic service to

MARTHA GELLHORN HEMINGWAY

FOR OUTSTANDING AND CONSPICUOUS SERVICE AS AN ACCREDITED
WAR CORRESPONDENT SERVING WITH OUR ARMED FORCES IN AN
OVERSEAS THEATER OF COMBAT.

Washington, D. C.

4 MARCH 1947

Secretary of War

Though she would have chafed at the use of Hemingway in her name two years after she had divorced Ernest, Gellhorn selected this 1947 War Department citation for her personal papers at Boston University.

1948, fellow war correspondent and post-war paramour William Walton.

1949, bespoke Wyncie King illustration, celebrating the arrival of Martha's adopted son Sandy. On the reverse, his dedication reads, "for one of our girls who had a baby during the war."

Merry Xmas
Happy New Year
from
Sandy and Martha

Early 1950s, Sandy Gellhorn with Martha in Cuernavaca, Mexico.

1980s, the inveterate traveler, who continued to want to "go everywhere, see everything, and sometimes write about it."

SIX

Death in the Present Tense

"I haven't been in such a rage for a long time,
but where can one dump one's rage?"

—Martha Gellhorn, letter to Eleanor Roosevelt

Eager to travel to Finland where, as far as Gellhorn could determine, people "looked after each other's needs and rights, with justice: a good democracy," she noted that it "was unusual timing to arrive in a strange frozen country one dark afternoon and be waked the next morning at nine o'clock by the first bombs, the declaration of war," on November 30th. Her first piece for *Collier's* there, "Bombs on Helsinki," among many vignettes, showed a nine-year-old boy outside his home watching Russian bombers, holding himself "stiffly so as not to shrink from the noise. When the air was quiet again, he said, 'Little by little, I am getting really angry.'" Another, "Death in the Present Tense," had a 12-year-old bellhop who stood near the door of the Hotel Kamp "listening to the dreadful music; a long-drawn siren, the sharp, angry, too-close metallic pounding of the machine guns, the faint distant thud of the bombs." With shaking hands, the youngster closed faded brocade curtains over a rattling window, "waiting for death as those do who cannot understand it."

In Paris at the end of December, Martha would later recall that "Paris was the Sleeping Beauty. Blue dim-out lights shone on the snow in the empty Place de la Concorde… There were no crowds, few cars, no sense of haste or disaster. Paris had never been more at peace. I felt that I was looking at this grace for the last time." While she was in Paris, her mother was home in St. Louis, hosting lunch for Ernest's first wife Hadley and their son Jack. In a December 29th letter to Hemingway, Edna Gellhorn wrote that all three of them enjoyed the visit and when she asked Jack about where he planned to go to college, he told her that he "didn't know exactly, but wanted some place where he could fish."

Edna wrote several letters to her future son-in-law over the next two weeks as they both waited for accurate details about Martha's return from Europe, one reassuring him that Martha would "gallop through whatever needs doing in New York and speed her way to Cuba," and another insisting, "we make a very devoted threesome—a safe, dear, happy one." From Lisbon, Martha wired Ernest that she was delayed due to foul weather preventing the clipper's departure, and she was heartbroken. A telegram he sent on January 6th, 1940 became an affectionate testament to her imminent arrival, noting, "AT LAST SCHATZY."

When Martha arrived at her home in Cuba in mid-January 1940, she found herself playing stepmother to Ernest's sons. She was especially fond of Patrick, known mostly as Mouse, to whom she referred as "a wonder creature." She began working on stories to be collected in *The Heart of Another*, the title lifted from a phrase in a letter from Pauline Pfeiffer: "The heart of another is a dark forest." In March, her novel *A Stricken Field* was published, with one reviewer dubbing her "Walt Whitman in a woman's dress." Ernest wrote to Max Perkins in April, declaring that he was "so damned happy with Marty that it seems that made everything work better. Sort of as though there were a lot" of him that was never "really used before and that is all working now." He believed himself "a damned lucky bastard to be alive."

That fall, *For Whom the Bell Tolls* would sell out its initial print run of 75,000 copies by the time Hemingway arrived in New York in September. Early in November, Ernest's divorce from Pauline was finalized on the grounds of desertion, and he and Martha married on November 21st in Wyoming. Robert Capa was there to photograph the newlyweds for a spread in *Life*. Of their marriage, Scott Fitzgerald observed that Hemingway being married to a "really attractive woman… will be somewhat different than with his Pygmalion-like creations."

In December, the sale of film rights to David O. Selznick for *For Whom the Bell Tolls* for $100,000, an enormous amount of money in 1940, meant that Hemingway could buy the finca, for the princely sum of $12,500. Scott Fitzgerald died of a heart attack that month in Los Angeles. Gellhorn was fond of Fitzgerald and blamed his death on his script doctor work for the studios, writing later to Max Perkins, "Hollywood ruined Scott, unless he was terribly dead before."

MG to Allen Grover

Pre–November 19, 1939
S.S. Westenland

Darling and sweetie and comrade,

You made this sailing a good thing when it could have been a very bad thing indeed and am now just as happy as if drunk with friends. The cabin is like a little Frigidaire but the steward has my best interests at heart and the ladies poo-poo is definitely mid-Victorian and weak on water but the shower baths are fresh. Otherwise all fine here and me all fine too, and with my wind back again and prepared to laugh my head off and never worry.

They are carrying a cargo for the Belgian government (very ominous, see E. Phillips Oppenheim) and 45 passengers with a capacity normally of 544 so expect to be inty [sic] with all before you can say Dale Carnegie.

I love all my gifts and presents and also love you and miss you all the time and if you want me for anything write or cable the Grand Hotel Stockholm and be good and have fun and will see you very soon. My war aim is: come home quick. Or, alternately, New York or bust.

So long,
Marty

MG to Allen Grover

November 19, 1939
S.S. Westenland

Darling,

We are anchored in the Channel as it is too dangerous to cross the minefields at night (I imagine them as something strange, like a spiky wilderness, or rather black mounds bobbing on the surface of a troubled sea.) Up to now this trip has taken the cake for longevity. I would be able to tell you how long ten days at sea on a small, bored, waiting and uncertain boat can be. Sleep is a figment of the imagination, as that berth you sat on is made for pigmies and the mattress is full of nails.

Needless to say I know everyone on the boat and am the local toots. The people are quite funny, if you see things as a writer (I am very busy seeing things as a writer. As a woman, I would have stayed at home.) Now the situation is tense again. Simply we are at last approaching danger, that dull and repulsive and violent danger of accident and error, the mine that was not intended for you, the bumbling into something that might just as well float harmlessly for years until it was washed up on the shore of Holland and used by the thrifty Dutch as a flower pot. The radio announced early in the a.m. that a Dutch boat, one day ahead of us, bound for the West Indies and carrying 600 passengers, hit three mines in the channel and blew up with a loss of 150 lives... Now the crew, stewards and passengers *chez nous* have sunk into a marked but inarticulate unease. I am so stupefied with boredom and liver and insomnia that I feel nothing except a vague resentment against the idiocy of fate and all wars. Still, we have to go through that mess these next days and you can feel the change in the people. As a writer (note) I am interested. I am getting a story out of this trip. I think it's a fair sample of a war of nerves, and I know what the phrase means. It means that you go stark dingo with *ennui* and any little noise at all would be welcome.

I still think I will be home early in January. We will become like Neolithic man again. We will seek our caves and our own fires and our women (or our men). We will listen to nothing and we will not care. I am feeling, in myself, the beginning of one of those chins that Wells uses to illustrate pictures of his prehistoric men. I feel a very great indifference seeping over me. It is impossible to believe in anything much any longer. Did you know that a torpedo could weigh 1500 kilos and travel five or six miles. Men are too clever. It has really gone too far.

Goodnight sweetie. We'll have a wonderful drunk celebration when I get back. But let's be gentlemen farmers or publishers or something. Let's get off by ourselves and be kind to everyone we see. But let's not worry too much about those large issues which apparently are the meat of the supermen who rule us, those shitlike creatures who can talk faster than we can.

I am your devoted colleague,
Marty

MG to Ernest Hemingway

November 30, 1939
Hotel KAMP
Finland

Rabby,

I love you that's the main thing. That's what I want you to know.

… At 9:15 I was dressed and ready to go downstairs to breakfast and I heard the siren and I thought, simply, well, I'm damned. I went downstairs and there was nothing to see. The people were behaving wonderfully in the streets, getting into airraid shelters but not panicky and it was a beautiful morning, and I stood in the street and watched. Then I saw a huge trimotor bomber go over at about 500 metres. Low and slow, just wandering around. It had dropped propaganda leaflets, it appeared later, which said "You know we have bread, why do you starve?" Honest to God. They bombed the airport this morning.

The clouds settled down by midday, Helsinki weather is an almost permanent natural fog like in London. Everybody felt very cheerful saying: now they can't come over. I didn't feel cheerful at all, as—flying in—I had decided that curtain of fog was God's gift to the Russians. They could stay above it and either bomb on instruments or dive suddenly; you would never see them. They have an airbase at Talinn which is 15 flying minutes away. At three o'clock, getting a belated lunch, they did just that; came in unseen, dived to 200 metres and dumped the stuff. From the sound and the results they must have been 500 kilo bombs and they dumped thermite as well. I never felt such explosions; the whole damn place rocked. Must have been like March in Barcelona. I went out and there was a huge curtain of smoke rolling down the street and people were saying: Gas—gas... That was pretty awful I may tell you. I left my mask in NY and it would have been unmanageable anyhow and I really thought okay we are lost. Then as nobody seemed to be choking, I went out with two Italian Fascist journalists and we followed the smoke. There were three colossal fires, four big apartment houses—just plain people's homes—burning like tissue paper. Glass was shattered for six and seven blocks around those places. One house, by a gas station, had a vast hole blown in its side, a burning bus lying beside it, and a man shapeless and headless and dead the way our little man was on the corner of the Florida [in Madrid] that morning. The raid took less than a minute; the siren began blowing as it was over...

It is going to be very terrible Rabby. They are about as well off as Spain from the point of view of material. Nothing is to prevent the Russkis [sic] doing this three and four times a day. The people are marvelous, with a kind of pale, frozen fortitude. They do not cry and they do not run; they watch with loathing and without fear this nasty sudden business which they did nothing to bring on themselves.

... I have your little passport picture in my purse and I hope it will protect me. I am very alone here. I have bought books and hope to be able to weather this very calmly but it is bad. I know how bad, because I have standards of comparison. Apparently there are no more planes out and the Russian fleet has moved from Kronstadt so that I suppose the sea will become unsafe. I don't know either when or how I can leave. I cannot wire you because there is no cable communication. I am trying to get through to our old pal Peters who is now in Copenhagen and asking him to wire for me. Oh Rabby, what a stinking mess. We should never have left Cuba.

Marty

MG to Ernest Hemingway
December 4, 1939
Hotel Kaalp
Helsinki

Beloved,

I got your two lovely cables today (December four) and am so happy you are proud of me—though what for? I'm just surviving—and you are my own and beloved and I knew you'd want to come but don't. The book [*For Whom the Bell Tolls*] is what we have to base our lives on, the book is what lasts after us and makes all this war intelligible. Without the book our work is wasted altogether.

And as I love you I love your work and as you are me your work is mine. I could not have you maul that about and mess it up. We will come back later maybe, but now you must go on and finish this.

Besides that, if *Collier's* is willing (and perhaps if they are not) I am leaving next week. I have wonderful material, the best war stuff of this year—and no competitors in the field by Golly [sic]—and tomorrow at six in the night that never seems to end (six in the morning and six in the night are indistinguishable but this time the morning and Christ have I been getting up early and boy do I hate it) I am leaving for the front. No other journalist has this privilege but due to R's [FDR's] letter I am on my way. I think it will be quite something. War in the arctic is very remarkable business. The climate is the best protection as are the forests and it is curious the way in the end the only way to fight man's inventions is with these uncontrollables. It snows and we are not bombed. The Finnish mist sets in and we are safe. The night begins at four in the afternoon and ends at eight in the morning, so we take to the woods at eight. I find the cold absolute torture and love the snow because it is warmer then as well as safer. Anyhow, I shall have been here a week tomorrow and plan to be here a week more or almost that long and I will have—from Helsinki, environs, front, enough for three bangup articles if they want that many and will have stuff no one else has. Then one week each in Norway and Sweden and home. So you see, it is not even worthwhile joining me. You open our home in Cuba, as a Xmas present for me, and I shall return and wallow in sun and quiet and above all my *Schatzy* [sweetheart] I shall be glad to be home with you where I belong.

There was one hell of an airraid which I wired you. I was in a sort of pocket which they bombed, the three main messes all within three blocks. It was a terrific job though they didn't use as heavy bombs as Barcelona. I judged by the damage about 100-150 kilo bombs. But they used thermite and burned the places to bits. There was no time for an airraid warning. This was the first day, the first taste of war and you should have seen the Finns. They took it as if they had been seeing this every day for ten years; there was no sign of any panic. They stood and watched; they walked about; I never saw such control and discipline. It is like iron. I think it can be a very long war and I think it is possible that—unless Russia sends an army of four million against these people—that the Finns will win. They have been steadily successful to date and their pilots are wonderful. And they can't be starved like our beloved Spaniards; they already produce 90% of their own food. Petrol is going to be the problem, and planes and munitions. I'll put my money on 3 million Finns against 180 million Russkis [sic]. After all, they are fighting for their lives and their homes and God alone knows why the Russians are fighting.

So. Now I must go to bed. I have had a hard day. It has been quite alarming to see the panic amongst the diplomatic corps and the journalists notably American and English. Last night a real panic set in started by the English who began to evacuate their nationals (they have done it twice already) at 2 a.m. saying that gas would be used this morning. Geoffrey Cox waked [sic] me and told me to beat it and I told him what the hell and went back to sleep. I had arranged with an Italian journalist (it is too funny being such pals with them, a story in itself) to go in his Legation's car out to the country at seven thirty to escape the probably eight thirty bombing which the Russkis [sic] must do one of these days in revenge for having had 16 planes shot down…

I have the curse and am somewhat wore out but I got exercise and I needed air and a change of scene and talk. I have been sleeping in town every night, while the English speaking contingent pulls out and am feeling very snotty and superior. But Rabby, my God, if they begin being scared pissless of probable dangers now, what are they going to be later when it really breaks loose on them. I am scared when it is three minutes off and am scared blind three minutes after, but would be sick by now if I thought about it all the safe time. Besides that, the Finns give a very good example of taking it and keeping the trap shut and I learned from you not to have the vanity to think the planes were looking for me and all bullets had my name on them.

I am tired Bongie and wish I were with you. When I get back I shall go to Washington briefly to talk to R [President Roosevelt] about this and then hurry to you. That will delay me one day; it is my sort of repayment to these people for their goodness to me and their elegance and courage in undertaking this war rather than be kicked around. The little nations are rather more first class than the big ones I think, these days. I have a steady pain in my head from thinking about the folly of mankind. I love you so much that it is almost hurting to think about it and I try to behave as you would want me to, and hope I am not mean to anybody though you know people sometimes think you are being snotty when you are only in a hurry, but I try to be good and I try to be very serene and I do my work hard and as well as I can and hope I am a credit to you and a sound workman. And soon I will be with you and where I want to be, and Bongie let's never never leave each other again. Or rather, I'll never leave you and you can go anywhere you want and do anything you like, only please, I'll come too.

Goodnight my dearest love. Sleep well. And take care of Mother for me. I cannot write and write to you both so hand everything in the way of news to her and keep in touch with her and keep her unworried and all right. This is the biggest thing to do for me. Because she is ours too, like the book [*For Whom the Bell Tolls*], something we have to take care of together.

I love you.
Bongie

MG to Ernest Hemingway

BKC9/31ˢᵀ/RA
LISBOA 18 31 1815 –VIA IMPERIAL—

LC HEMINGWAY
    HOTEL AMBOS MUNDOS HABANA CUBA.

WEATHER UPHOLDING CLIPPER HEARTBROKEN TELL MOVER [sic]
LOVINGLY BONGIE
HOTEL VICTORIA LISBON

1940

MG for Ernest Hemingway

GUARANTY

To whom it may concern (I guess it concerns Mr. Warp Dimpy Gellhorn Bongie
Hemmy)

I, the undersigned, (Mrs. Martha Warp Fathouse Pig D. Bongie Hemingstein)
hereby guaranty and promise never to brutalize my present and future husband in
any way whatsoever, neither with weapons nor pointed instruments, nor words,
nor uncalculated sudden phrases nor looks. I guarantee (providing my future
and present husband does not wake me from a sound slumber when I am not in
control of all or even half of my faculties) always to express the appreciation I truly
feel for everything he does for me, gives to me and means to me. I promise equally
to cherish him so that he knows I am cherishing him, and not only to cherish him
so that I know it. I also state for witness that far from putting him out of business,
he and his business are what matter to me in this life, and that also I recognize that
a very fine and sensitive writer cannot be left alone for two months and sixteen
days, during which time many trying and unlikely things are put upon him, volun-
tarily and involuntarily, and that said fine and very fine and very beloved writer
should immediately be in a state of perfect calm and confidence and that, in so
much as I, involuntarily, was a great cause for his uneasiness of mind during this
long period of solitude, I am deeply sorry therefore and shall attempt (with a few
relapses due to general stupidity and personal lack of intelligence) to make up to
him for the wretchedness he has gone through, and shall also attempt to protect

him against same wretchedness in future. This statement is given of my own free will and in my rightest mind and with love.

Signed:
Martha Gellhorn Hemingway

Witnesses:
Judge R.R. Rabbit
Judge P.P. Pig

Done at San Francisco de Paula
this 19 day of January, 1940.

SECOND GUARANTY

I, the undersigned, guaranty also that after marriage I will not leave my present and future husband not for nothing no matter what or anything.

Love,
Martha Gellhorn Hemingway

THIRD GUARANTY

I, the undersigned, further guaranty not to divorce my husband (previously named, see other page) not for nobody, only he has to be a good boy too and not love nobody but me. But he will not love nobody but me. This is an unnecessary guaranty.

Love,
Martha Gellhorn Hemingway

MG to Eleanor Roosevelt

January 31, 1940
Finca Vigía
San Francisco de Paula

Dearest Mrs. Roosevelt,

If you had time could you write me a little note to tell me what is going to be done for Finland, or what *seems* to be what is going to be done for Finland? I have never read nor heard such unanimous loud enthusiasm for anything or cause, as is being generally manifested through America for Finland and Finland's war. But then there comes a full pause, after the words, deep silence. It would not be necessary to make such a vast prayerful noise, if nothing is going to happen. What is up? Could you tell me? Am beginning to feel very ashamed. I was so sort of sturdy and reassuring in Finland, because thought I foresaw our national sympathy.

… Here it is awful cold, same as there. We are anxiously awaiting a return to normal and the Cubans have a general feeling that this is all the fault of the people in the north who started the storms.

When are you coming south? Hope you wait for the sun, and hope hard that I see you.

Love,
Marty

Hemingway was fond of Edna Gellhorn, Martha's mother, the person Martha regarded as her "true north." He wrote many intimate and affectionate letters to Edna beginning in the early days of his courtship of her only daughter and continuing long past their divorce at the end of 1945. He respected and admired Edna and sought her approval always. Martha admitted that she believed he truly loved her mother.

When Gellhorn returned in January 1940 from reporting on the Russian invasion of Finland, Hemingway wrote to Edna thanking her for sacrificing her own time with her only daughter in order to speed Martha's return to him in Cuba. Such a selfless gesture was typical of Edna but it is important to recognize that Ernest did not take her kindnesses for granted, noting that she was taking care of him, "and no one could ever do more."

Being physically fit mattered to both Martha and Ernest and in many of their letters to each other they report on their weight or their exercise routines, so it is unsurprising that Ernest comments on Martha's weight gain of "thirteen pounds that brought her home healthy instead of broken down and a wreck," claiming that he was "fond of every one of them." He realized that Martha had had "to eat and drink plenty to survive that cold" in Helsinki and he was proud of her and her work as a war correspondent. That Ernest missed Martha while she was away gathering first hand material for her *Collier's* pieces is incontestable. And, he confides to Edna, "All the good part I would never think about while Marty was away because it made me too lonely to live." With Martha back home he felt as if his soul had returned to his body, the two of them "awfully good for each other in every way." He recalls, "it was a great and lucky thing" that Edna, Martha, and her brother Alfred "came into Mr. Josie's that time," when they met in December 1936 in Key West. Hemingway closes the letter in gratitude, writing, "Almost no one gets what they should have and I have… thank you again for sending Marty."

Eleanor Roosevelt to MG

February 9, 1940
The White House
Washington

Dear Marty,

I cannot tell you a thing about Finland except that I think the general feeling in Congress is that we were able to lend to China and sell to China because there was no declared war between China and Japan and we sold to both sides. They are desperately afraid if we make a loan to Finland it is going to be called an unneutral act and may, therefore, lead to difficulties. I believe personally that if we simply asked the people of the United States to subscribe personally to a loan without any strings attached we could get it over. However, that is something no one knows. I do not know what will happen in the end as the President still seems to have some idea about the way this loan could be made and still not be unneutral.

I have been so busy that I haven't had time to think about anything else but appointments. However, I do expect to get to a house on Golden Beach just above Miami Beach somewhere around the 19th of February until March 3. I would love to have you come over for a day and do hope you can manage it. I should like to come over to you but I am told that it is not too safe.

Affectionately,
Eleanor R.

In March, Hemingway's play *The Fifth Column* (written in Spain, with Gellhorn as the surrogate for his main character Dorothy Bridges) opened on Broadway to tepid reviews, running only a few weeks. The same month Gellhorn's novel about the German-Jewish refugee crisis in Czechoslovakia was published to mostly hearty reviews. *A Stricken Field* had the dedication "for Ernest Hemingway" just as *For Whom the Bell Tolls* in October would have the dedication "for Martha Gellhorn."

268

COLUMN   Eleanor Roosevelt's "My Day" about *A Stricken Field*   March 7, 1940
My Day
New York

I must tell you about a book which I finished on the plane last Sunday. The book is called *A Stricken Field* by Martha Gellhorn. Here is a foreign correspondent's story which could not perhaps be written for the daily newspapers, for the reason that the correspondent writing it would be thrown out of the foreign country and would cease to have a job. This is a picture of stark tragedy painted by the use of simple events in ordinary lives which are important to the individuals concerned, but which count for little in history. This book is a masterpiece as a vivid picture.

MG to Allen Grover   March 8, 1940
Finca Vigía
San Francisco de Paula

Allen petsky:

It was lovely seeing you. The pelotaris are still talking about your tennis, as they never saw any like it before. The only tennis they know is mine and Ernest's and though his is strong (the greatest compliment) it lacks the expensive shine of yours. As for mine, their theory is that if I eat a great deal I will become big and powerful and play with more endurance. Endurance is the keynote. I hope you liked them.

I was very ashamed after you left, and went about whining and beating my breast and making vows, and woke up ashamed for three mornings, because I bragged so much over the house… please apologize to B. for me.

Have you ever gotten my book [*A Stricken Field*]. I sent a copy to you myself with a compliments-of-the-author card in it. I am not sure any of those get sent out. It appears publicly today and yesterday Max Perkins sent an advance copy of a review in the *Herald Trib* which seemed pretty good to me but God knows wouldn't sell a copy. Though, anyhow, why people should read in order to twist and suffer I would not know; and I have no feeling that people should read my depressing works, and if they do, it is certainly a favor. God knows I would not read any such book myself.

E's play [*The Fifth Column*] it seems also opened with a bang in NY and that is fine, though they must have improved it a lot from the Glaser version we read. I would like to know what you think of it.

E. thinks you are very splendidly constructed and we spoke of this at great length and with some admiration; also that you are very nice and good and that I have fine friends.

Nothing to say. All fine here, Mother a darling and I think having a good rest, and me just sort of contented and slow in the head and gathering myself up to start writing again and E. writing like mad and very beautifully, and the war as far away as you can imagine.

I LOVED seeing you.

Always,
Marty

Hortense Flexner to MG
March 10, 1940
Bryn Mawr
Pennsylvania

Dear Menace to my Peace of Mind,

Yes, I am much obliged for a book that makes me feel like a piece of useless lumber in the world. Yes, darling, I am very grateful for being haunted by horror that makes E.A. Poe seem a silly little boy, and I do most deeply appreciate your sending us not only a story, but a state of mind, a terrifying emotion, a sense of rage to keep handy on the bed table or the window seat in the living room.

It was dear of you, Gellhorn, to send us your book. Reading it again, I stand by my first opinion. It is remarkable in what it conveys about the uprooted people— not just the physical cruelty, but the inner side of the picture from their point of view. Knowing this time about Rita and what would happen, I could give more attention to the backdrop and see how fully it is put in. Just the best kind of work! I think you have done something very hard to do, and very necessary to this world. If we can still have breakfast in bed after your book, why we can also expect to roast in Hell a thousand years. And I think we should. Between you and Mrs. Roosevelt, I am just about to go out and enlist in an army. It would be one way of getting out of this house.

I am afraid, between you and King, unless dying is very simple and pleasant, I shall be just a little sorry I came to this star.

News in the backwoods is all about the upspringing daffodils, crocuses and returning birds. I haven't been to Phila. [sic] since I saw *Fifth Column*. I am at work on my final volume of poems to be called "Archaic Warrior." Good or bad?

… Goodbye and thanks again. It makes old teacher's heart throb a bit, remembering so much good work that shaped up to this—lots and lots of blue and yellow sheets of paper. Every now and then, things do happen as they should. A big hug and a kiss for having done your part in the meanest fight.

As ever,
Hortense F.K.

P.S. Yes—I saw you didn't change that part you said you were going to change. I'll bet the publishers wouldn't let you. And it's allright [sic] anyhow. Be sure to let us know what things happen and how it goes. Remember when we thought Czecho [sic] would be an "old story" at the time of publication? We didn't guess about Poland and Finland. H.

The review of *A Stricken Field* that was printed in the March 18th issue of *TIME* caused tremendous distress for both Gellhorn and Hemingway as their names appeared together in print while he was still married to Pauline Pfeiffer. Martha's rage was incandescent because she had believed that her close friend Allen Grover, then Vice-President at *TIME*, who had visited Ernest and Martha in Cuba a couple of weeks before, would have literally stopped the press rather than print such gossipy and potentially damaging words.

The book review titled "Glamor Girl" focused on examining Gellhorn and her relationships rather than her work. The opening sentence was enough to make both Martha and Ernest apoplectic: "Like her great & good friend Ernest Hemingway, Martha Gellhorn is a novelist with a legend." The reviewer went on to namedrop Harry Hopkins and Mrs. Roosevelt and "French Journalist Count Bertrand de Jouvenel."

Finally quoting *A Stricken Field* in the penultimate paragraph by referring to protagonist Mary Douglas' "wry view of her own radicalism," a foreign correspondent who "knew she would always say yes, when she was asked for help, because she did not feel she had a right to her privileges: passport, job, love," the reviewer snarked that "as a character Martha is still miles ahead of Mary."

In the series of correspondence that follows, Gellhorn spilled out her hurt and indignation in a logorrheic fury.

Allen Grover to MG

March 11, 1940
9 Rockefeller Plaza
New York City

Dear Marty,

Thanks for the two letters. Even if one was a squawk. What happened to me was precisely this: Ernest's publishers refused to give the *TIME* researcher his address except to say that he was in Cuba. However, she (the researcher) is an old schoolmate of yours and has followed your career with interest. She also follows the local literary gossip, as her job is researching for *TIME*'s Book Department. So she simply said to the AP man in Havana: "Try to find Hemingway through Martha Gellhorn, whose address is San Francisco de Paula."

How she knew *your* address I don't know and I do not mean to ask, either. The pursuit of facts is the business of these magazines and while I would not personally contribute any information which might make life uncomfortable for you, I also would not thwart anyone here in their efforts. Nor would you want me to. (As a matter of fact the *Tribune* review of your book, which was in the researcher's hands on Saturday, goes out of its way to mention that *A Stricken Field* is dedicated to your friend, Ernest Hemingway.)

Nobody here that I know of has any ulterior motives in this matter at all, other than curiosity which is part of our business. But I would warn you that you and Ernest are both newsworthy because of your achievements and there is no use your trying to dodge it. It is also unrealistic of you to think that San Francisco de Paula can long remain a secret. So far as I know, secrets can be kept by no more than three people. However, I have told *TIME*'s Book Department that Ernest's address is as you gave it to me and that in future they can find him there. But, of course, having found him at San Francisco de Paula, this draws anything except polite stares.

As to the Finca Vigía, we found it the nicest place in Cuba and occupied by much the nicest people. I really loved that afternoon and was just sorry you and Ernest weren't with us at the Jai Alai, where we had such excellent care from Paz and Hemingway, Jr [Bumby]. We wanted them to go with us to the Casino, but Paz said he had to go to bed (because of the training) and Mr. Hemingway had neglected to wear a tie so did not think he was properly equipped. But what a place Havana is and how I am going to go back there in the days to come is nobody's business!

As to your friend, Mr. Hemingway, I found him completely charming. That's the wrong word, but you get the idea. He and I can have fun together if we ever get the chance. You will have to be there as a sort of referee, because he has to listen to me for about five minutes and then I will listen to him. Then we can all three talk at once.

Tell your sainted mother to call me, please, when she next comes through New York and Bea joins me in most profound regards to you all. Bea did not think for a minute that you were boastful about the house and if you had been, her idea is you had damn well a right to be!

A.

Eleanor Roosevelt to MG

March 12, 1940
The White House
Washington

Dear Marty,

I finished your book [*A Stricken Field*] several days ago and wrote about it in the column. I have been slow in writing you, not because the impression the book made was not vivid, but perhaps because it was a little too vivid.

It is one of those books you put down every now and then because you cannot bear to go on reading. And so, my dear, I think you did what you wanted to do. It is beautifully written, and put in novel form, it was possible for you to say certain things that you could not have said if you were simply reporting what you had seen and heard. I hope many people will read it, for we need to realize the fear of the little people all over the world. It will make us more understanding in our attitude toward them and perhaps will save us from bringing about the same condition in our own country.

It must have been hard to write this book and I now see why when you were through with it, you were completely exhausted physically.

I hope you had a wonderful week with your mother and that you could induce her to neglect some of her many duties and stay on with you a little longer. Let me know when you are coming north as I should like to see both you and Ernest.

With my love and congratulations,
Affectionately,
Eleanor Roosevelt

MG to Charles Colebaugh

March 13, 1940
Finca Vigía
San Francisco de Paula

Dear Charles,

It doesn't look as if there would be any Finland to go back to. We have seen a lot in our lives, haven't we? (I am beginning to wish I had never learned to read.) That revolting offer of Chamberlain and Daladier, to send 50,000 troops, now, after three months and more than three months, when Finland is I imagine too tired and too wounded and Chamberlain and Daladier know it… I cannot put down the disgust I feel about all this. We have seen too bloody much. Hitler is what he is: a monster who happened in our time and was produced by it. But let us never forget those two—that ignorant Englishman with the complacent lips, and that smeared Frenchman who could never make up his mind except for the destruction of others. I hope they go down in history, together with the men who accept them and work with them, as great traitors and as murderous liars. The Finns have gone through enough and they are not fools. It is horrible to think that after all this, they are offered 50,000 men. The Swedes are not too dopey either: and have watched Austria, Czecho [sic], Spain and Poland. The Swedes are absolutely right in saying: you can either send enough to save Finland or you can send nothing. The technique of the false promise, the lying hypocritical offer of hope, is something that is enough to drive one mad. And after this, those horrors, those second rate cheats, expect us to espouse their cause. (I am now referring in my fury, to the French and English governments.) I only wish to live long enough to see the men who have ruled Europe in the last six years destroyed. A firing squad is too good for any of them. When you think of the people anywhere, who have paid with their lives, and have paid with their living, for the stupidity and treachery and brutality of the bastards who govern, you could go out with hand bombs yourself, and do something about it.

Anyhow, I suppose Finland will accept the peace terms because there is nothing else to do. It has been abundantly clear that France and England, so governed, have not even wit enough to save themselves in saving Finland. This makes the fourth actual count in my immediate memory: Spain, Czecho [sic] and Poland, establishing the beautiful precedent. Any nation which expected anything from France and England as they now are, would be a nation of illiterates without newspapers.

The story in Finland will be months from now, if one can get in: the same story there is today in Poland and Czecho [sic], the same ugly miserable heartbreaking story. But the Finns fought superbly: and even that cannot help them, or change the shape of the next story. (I wish again that I couldn't read.)

As for us: if I believed in prayer, I would be making same at ten minute intervals. I hope we acquire an isolationism so great that the wall which once served China will seem by comparison a single strand of barbed wire. Anything we could believe in, in Europe, is gone. Let them ruin each other. They have produced leaders so despicably, and they follow them or are forced to follow them so totally, that we cannot help or save. We have only one job as Americans: and that is to cultivate our own garden. It looks to me as if it needed some cultivating too. There are plenty of odd things going on. But here, anyhow, there is hope and something to hang on to.

Well. I am almost too mad to write a letter. I think there is quite a good deal to be said for political assassination: the only trouble being that the assassins usually get the wrong guy. They ought to let us all ballott [sic] amongst ourselves, for the victim, and then they ought to hire competents, not excitables, to do the work.

… I sent you my book [*A Stricken Field*] to Florida. It is getting very bad reviews. Have just seen Poore and Gannett, both very friendly so maybe it is only women who don't like the book. I don't understand any of it but would certainly would not buy the book, reading even the good reviews. It seems that I am a wonderful journalist and ought to stick to it. I am advised to write my experiences as autobiography, and not stuff them into a novel. Had I written said experiences as autobiography I would just be a damn liar. Perhaps I should be very cheerful about it, thinking how well I have fooled the reviewers: what I make up looks so true that they think I am only reporting what I have seen. Maybe I ought to write some eyewitness stories of Finland, from here (which I could do) and then that would make me a fine novelist, and a lying journalist. It is certainly hard to please folks. I have also been told that the character of Mary, in my book, is so definitely me that the thin disguise seems unnecessary. Well. If I ever write about myself (a subject that has not seemed interesting or vital) I would take a swing at it: no decent, simple honest, confused young American type of stuff. I could invent a really startling character and call it myself: and how would they know the difference? Meantime I shall just go on being a writer and a journalist: and it can be described by any third party in any way that seems suitable at the time.

Am in a foul and furious humor today, not yet having accepted the day's newspaper. But the thing to do probably is to accept without surprise all the filth that happens: but it is impossible and unbearably painful to think what the Finns are feeling.

Greetings to all of you. I'll be up in May probably and we can talk it all over then. We always know that when I have to go some place, I can go fast. But now is not yet the time, for me.

I hope you are in grand shape and had a lovely time. We can also talk about bills, sometime. I guess the bills in Florida have the bills in Cuba beat. But if we live in Hoovervilles, when we are old, we will at any rate recognize that there are some blessings.

Yours,
Martha

—————————————

MG to Eleanor Roosevelt

March 17, 1940
Finca Vigía
San Francisco de Paula

Dearest Mrs. Roosevelt,

Mother has sent me the clippings where you spoke of my book; aren't you kind and good and generous and I am very happy that you think it is an okay book. (You are almost the only one who does, except Mother and E., and that's quite enough for me, I want no finer judges and no bigger world.)

You will have seen the *TIME* write-up of my book I suppose, mainly because it is so spacious and showy that it would be hard to miss. It is a very dirty job indeed and I most deeply regret that you were brought into it (I hate them for that, with passion) and I do not know how to tell you what I feel about it. If you are going to be mentioned from every time from now on that people take cracks at me, I will be sorry you ever had to know me. I would not want any trouble ever to come through me, and I am very ashamed about it all.

They certainly did a fine job of destroying everybody in sight, didn't they? One wonders where the malice comes from, and why, but there it is. I am sorry because it is causing a lot of trouble to E., in personal matters. He has been wanting to write you, but wants to wait until all this nastiness simmers down, because he too doesn't want to spread it anywhere. *TIME* did a very neat job of ruining me professionally as a writer, but I intend to outlast *TIME*, and far outlast it, so that is not so bad.

You must know that everything in that little article is from their own little hearts and heads: none of it came from me, and almost none of it is true. Harry Hopkins knows perfectly well I was no Parisian-looking doll, and if you see him will you tell him I am also sorry his name had to be in such a skunking piece of work. There is nothing I can do about it, though I would have given anything to keep anyone else's name out. I do not give a damn what people say of me or think of me, and my work will stand by itself in the long run no matter what is said about it: but I hate (and suffer from) the thought of causing trouble to anyone else, my friends, or anyone who has been good to me and should not be rewarded in this way.

I can't write you very much about this, but I could weep about it as it affects anyone else, and please know that. I have been more careful and more successfully careful than anyone could be, for three years, and the real horror of this is that the *TIME* story stems directly from a man [Allen Grover] who has professed to be one of my great friends for years, and who—apparently without a backward glance— felt perfectly allright [sic] about selling me out and the people I care about, so that it could hurt me, in order to get a little circulation for his foolish, inaccurate paper.

I love you very much and thank you for everything.

And now the Finns are gone too. Who will England and France manage to abandon next, do you think? If I were a Turk, I would be very scared.

Goodbye and love always,
Marty

Hortense Flexner to MG

Mid-March 1940
Bryn Mawr
Pennsylvania

Dearest Gellhorn,

I have just read "Death in the Present Tense." Thanks for telling me not to get excited about Finland. Hmmmm. And if I do, kindly tell me who is to blame. Well, I won't kid you, as it is really such fine work. That one little paragraph about the lady who leaned her bicycle among the columns, and didn't talk and then, did talk about the dead. "There is always one child, one old woman etc. to fasten on." Not your words exactly, but the idea being and truly, that the brain has to pick out its tragedy in digestible portions. That was why everyone went mad after the big war—1914. They couldn't get it down to man-size. I do feel good at the writing and the amount packed into that article, Gellhorn. You know if *Collier's* made a reprint of that and distributed it, it would get lots of money for Finland, which (I hope you'll bear with me) I still want to see raised.

I am excited about your Scrooby's play [*The Fifth Column*]. Think only two things will count against it; it makes sense and it is full of hope for the human race. At first, I thought [Franchot] Tone was going to spoil it. His back-talk to his officer looked more like a movie star in the tantrums than a big he-man having a nervous breakdown. But that is the actor. Of course, to me it is Max's play [role played by Lee J. Cobb]. I would run off tomorrow with Max, scars and all. Why, I thought that kind of man had died out entirely. He is magnificent. The whole audience broke into spontaneous applause in the middle of the act, after he told the girl why Philip could not go with her. To read that passage, without seeing this man say it, would not give you half an idea of how splendid it is—although I know he had to have the lines to do his stuff. The combination is superb. To me it is Max's show. He is what will save the world. And the peculiar way he was made to be subordinate—not prince Hamlet—just a cog, giving the quality of the whole wheel was a great piece of writing. There were fine passages for the girl, who is not a good enough actress for the part, but maybe that was because I had such definite ideas of the real woman reporter, whose brown legs against white leather might very well have been responsible for such a passage.

I do like the way Hemingway makes war come first—even the symbolism of the man who tried to be playful and got killed for it. The Spaniard's speech in the last act… about hovels at the foot of the great cathedrals the hungry people who had made the fight for all the rich people against Fascism, was just perfect—and the actor is perfect. It is because these scenes, saying at last what we all want to hear, are so powerful that the old business of love is quite second place in the play, whether or not it was meant. I think it was meant, in fact I know it was, in the play anyhow, the meaning of the whole seeming to centre about the dislocation of everything, where such a slow murder as that of Spain was happening. Well, tell me if I'm wrong-and I think I can count on you to do it. Anyhow, at the end of it, I wanted to enlist in the Loyalist army—not in the Finnish. It is a play like Yeats's poem Easter 1916, with that refrain "A terrible beauty is born." –Well. Gellhorn, I think you have seen something and been somewhere to have been part of that fight, and I think Hemingway is going to keep it alive. My vote—but as Wyncie says, "too bad it makes sense for this world."

Best love,
Teacher

MG to Allen Grover

March 19, 1940
Finca Vigía
San Francisco de Paula

Dear Allen,

As a suite and finale to our telephone conversation:

I saw the query the AP man brought here to the house; it came from NY, from *TIME*. It said: Reach Ernest Hemingway at San Francisco de Paula… The AP man thought E was living at Varadero. He did not see E, who was, at the time, talking with his publisher, and who left after that visit. (E. has been around a long time and he knows how things develop, and develop they certainly did.)

Therefore *TIME* did not get such ideas from the AP, the AP got them from *TIME*. I would like to know how. There were two things in that incredible page about me which were damaging: the first was the opening sentence (*TIME*'s new trademark: I should think it would make you very unhappy to see your magazine slyly, with its own little phrases, entering it the field of competing and defeating Hearstlike press with its brand of phrases). The second was the statement: MG returned to SF de Paula where EH is wintering. That is of course a libelous statement, and I would like to know who dared dish it, and with what knowledge. It *cannot* have come from the Havana AP. So where did it come from?

I will not insist on the damage, it is plenty, and you know that. I will not even insist, full of outrage and contempt, on the shamefulness of having a Book Review department which has so little understanding of respect for books that they can handle books, by making a *succès de scandale* of the author. (This, in fact, is what really revolts me the most: not only because I am the writer in question. I love books and I have a passionate respect for writing, and I think it is absolutely horrible that cheap, small people, who could never work through the hardship of writing, can destroy the goodness and the effort of writing, by reporting personal problems of the author. I do not know anything about the personal lives of those who discovered ether, the circulation of the blood, the spirochete: the work of a writer is a thing as apart from himself as the work of a man in science: I think it is barbarous, and the mark of microscopic minds, to confuse the man and his work: as long as the man, in his own life, is not the enemy of the commonwealth (but only a man, with a man's troubles and failings) and his work is definitely done for the common good, the common knowledge, the common progress.

The damage is all done and I will get through it allright [sic] because there is no damage anyone can do to me which will be permanent. I have lived my life exactly as I thought best and it is a perfectly good life and I don't give a goddam what anyone, who could be influenced by *TIME*, thinks about it. But, because I have work to do, I would like if possible to have as little interruption, as little useless messiness as possible. I am not a menace to society, and what I am asking for now is a certain amount of co-operation from you, and I am asking it not only as a friend (because I have always thought you were my friend), but also because I am a serious writer, and we are much more important, and our working each one on his own screnely is much more important, than any pages or paragraphs *TIME* may want to print about us.

So what I ask is this: that you issue a blanket order that when I am to be mentioned in *TIME*, the copy be submitted to you first. I do not wish to jeopardize your job, or ask you to do things which are impossible for you. But I do wish to be warned in advance, so that I can take my dispositions before the next little vile story appears. Also, all queries, emanating from *TIME* and going to their UP or AP agents, could be reported to you, and you could report them personally in advance and by cable to me. If this is against your principles of journalism, you will not do it: but I have asked for it.

I am not important myself and have never had any positions of power: but have observed that it was possible to get people out of jail, to get them in safe countries, to help them with their lives, to get their books published. I do not think it is so desperately hard to help people. I do not understand the mentality of people who want to ruin other people, unless the people they want to ruin are themselves destroyers. I do not know what I could have done, ever, to be considered by *TIME* as a public enemy and therefore fair game. And as I told you, I am a writer: they can perfectly well decide that I am not a good writer nor a valuable writer, and if so, they have only to ignore my writing. That is their privilege and no one would have a word to say. But they can only report me as a writer, because that is all I do that is "newsworthy." And as such, I feel it is quite reasonable to expect them to treat my writing as their material: or else to keep quiet. I have not been in the papers to date (my name has *nowhere* been mentioned) as anything but a writer.

I do not like to write you about E. because for E's sake I would like to keep him well separated from that horrible whorish photograph of me and that horrible whorish write-up. E. is in Camaguey, where I hope he is peaceful and undisturbed to do his writing. (Allen, it is absolutely horrible that that man, who is one of the best writers in the world, and writes as he does because he has a very delicate instrument for a brain, should have been so hounded—because everything comes back, you know, with interest, on the personal angle: use your imagination—that is his writing, the finest and most large and rich book of his career, should be jeopardized: especially as he is ending the book, was writing smoothly, with ease and magic and like an angel. I *love* writing. I think to do that to someone like E. is a stinking crime. E., you know, can take anything that comes his way, quite as easily as I can: and laugh at it and laugh at the tadpoles who do the damage. But at the end of a book, after a year and three weeks of unremitting work, he is open to all comers. You can lose a book, if people make you enough trouble. He will not lose that book, but the times are being made as tough as possible.) (And I was never in the papers before. There is that to remember.) However, going on about E., I ask for myself—I do not think he would ask any favors—that the same business apply to him and that I be warned when next they start to get their hooks into him. I ask this also for myself only: and it can also be refused.

Well, it is the first lousy luck I have had for some time: that Tom Matthews [later Gellhorn's husband, 1954–63] was away and you did not see the copy.

The thing is all over now and we don't have to write about it or talk about it again. I don't believe in dwelling tightly with the disasters that can come. But I would like, if possible, to be a little less startled the next time....

I am sort of sorry I will not be seeing E.'s kids: because I like what they say too. Anyhow, I can write fine about kids (no one noticed that in my book, but that is what is best in it), and I can have a fine time writing. Best to you, and good luck.

Marty

P.S. E. had to come in from Camaguey to file his income tax return. Before he went back he explained to me how *TIME* makes news, working through the press associations; tipping off the press assoc [sic] on suspicion to stuff they would never touch themselves: getting the assoc to ask the questions and at the same time putting the chance of getting something, into the hands of the press assoc [sic], which they would never have known about themselves. He said he admired the skill of it very much: because the *TIME* man never asks the questions, and nobody would ever hit a working newspaper man who is only doing his job, even if his job is being corrupted for him. But he was very bitter about the sliminess about this particular thing, and what it had done to him now and in November of 1938. He was bitter about that, but really sore about the review of my book. He thinks it a very good book and feels that, if I invent so well that it seems fact, it is pretty stiff going to be damned for having the invention look true. He said that, actually and in the end, the only thing that remained of the *TIME* review was the damage done to my professional career by the flippant, unjust cheapness of the review. But I think my writing will go on a long time, and stand up okay, and I can live down any rotten lousy confusion. Only it's hard to have nine months of stiff work, and what you most believe in, made so cheap: when it isn't cheap.

M.

Charles Colebaugh to MG

March 21, 1940
New York City

Dear Martha,

Thanks for your letter and also for the book which I received in Clearwater.

You are quite right about the trip. There isn't anything in Finland now, and I say it very sadly. And, of course, it is a good thing that you did not get into Russia. It is difficult now to make plans that have any sense to them, and it may be that the time you have set for your return here will be all right.

I read your book coming up on the train and, fortunately, I have seen no reviews so I think it's very good. Of course, I did identify you with Mary and that is inevitable. You are billed on the jacket as being the only woman war correspondent who still gallops madly to fires, and since Mary is of the same breed and looks not unlike you it is only natural that the boys should think the book more than slightly autobiographical. There is a young lady bullfighter in Mexico City who is doing very well for herself these days I am told, and if she were to write a novel about bullfighting in which a lady bullfighter figures, I am sure everyone would think she was telling her own story. But that I hold to be a very small matter. More important to me is that your book is compassionate and warm and moving and that the people in it come alive and their misery and sorrows are my misery and sorrow and I wish I could do something about it.

I do believe not too complacently that we have done some little about it. We have tried to lambaste tyranny and greed and cruelty as they have shown themselves in Europe. The trouble is that these vile attributes are not confined to one side and that hypocrisy, which is at least as hateful as all the others combined, is being cheered here as well as abroad.

I see that Monsieur Daladier is out this afternoon but I suppose he will be back again by nightfall and choosing another Cabinet indistinguishable from the one which just went out of office. Mr. Chamberlain is still afloat and his sanctimonious burblings still get respectful attention.

Anyway, we are probably in for an interesting Spring and Summer, although I have no high hopes that justice or mercy or freedom will be greatly served by anything which now seems imminent.

I did have a good vacation. The sunshine was warm and Spring had happened all over the place before I left. I shall see another one here in a few weeks, and I find that at my time of life it is an excellent thing to crowd two Springs into one year. It gives you something of a feeling of omnipotence, illusory though it may be.

Ever yours,
Charles Colebaugh

Eleanor Roosevelt to MG

March 22, 1940
The White House
Washington

Dear Marty,

I did read the article in *TIME* and I do not think the man meant to be so disagreeable to you but was just trying to hit at me as a critic, and in doing so he was rather hard on you. As a matter of fact, I haven't heard anything very disagreeable and am sorry it has upset you so much. If you had as many cracks made at you as we do, you would soon get so that they made no difference to you.

You have not caused me any trouble and I only hope that nothing in it is making things harder for you. If the article was written by someone who was your friend I can understand your feeling pretty badly about it, but you know sometimes even friends think they are not doing anything very bad and do not realize how much they hurt.

I too would be a little scared if I were a Turk these days. I wish peace could come to the whole continent and perhaps everyone could sit around the table and be sensible.

Much love, my dear, and do not worry about what anyone may say about me.

Affectionately,
Eleanor R.

MG to Allen Grover

March 23, 1940
Finca Vigía
San Francisco de Paula

Allen my sweetie,

Let this be the last letter on this bloody subject. I don't believe in making it all worse, indefinitely… besides the fury at the *TIME* job there was the hurt of your having pulled out on me, when I actually needed you, would have done for you anything under the same circumstances and it's there that *my* hurt comes in.

Ernest is another problem (and you can easily see that, put yourself in his shoes, he is the one who has to pay for this personally and it might very damn easily have ruined us, just us, in our lives). The wickedness and bad taste of the *TIME* book review department has very effectively bitched what might have been a good and valuable and satisfactory relationship between the two of you. You will never be exactly easy with each other again. E. loves me and believed you loved me as a friend. He simply could not understand your letter, your first one (because it sounded like a flat denial of any willingness to behave as friends do), and when *TIME* came out with that thing (which he saw as very damaging to me professionally and personally), he felt you had valued me very lightly.

I am now living in a hotel in town, E. has returned for the moment because if you remember the children were to come to us, but now I can't be with them or see them or live in my own house. (P [Pauline] read the *TIME* article and felt VERY strongly about it) and there has been a lot of wear and tear resulting in my getting such a bloody nervous disorder of the intestinal tract. Because of that *TIME* article

I am, for the first time in my whole life, put in the ghastly position of being around the corner, or in the alley, or wherever people live who can't show their faces.

I would appreciate your not speaking of this to anyone, nor mentioning me, and also you can forget it.

I think it is immoral, that's all. Aside from being sick in the body and sort of gloomy in the mind, I am not going to be done in by any such nonsense. The public doesn't matter, but we all live in tiny private worlds, with about ten other people at the most who can be permanently hurt and particularly if they are children. Those ten other lives are our only final responsibility. And if you have done a bang-up job on them, and kept them all serene and understanding and dignified and proud and unhurt, it is pretty grievous to see all that risked.

Anyhow, I am through with it now. I will also get over my colic and I hope to Christ I can get back to work. I am sort of tired and whether people like my writing or not, writing is what I have to do.

The Cuban hotel is my idea of a death trap; if you lived in one long enough no prison would seem dour.

Have you read my book; it is getting good reviews from the provinces where people have time to read and do not know anything about my personal life. I think a few people will read it. I think it is an okay book; and now I have to do a far better one.

I am, you know, your friend,
Marty

Please *burn* this letter and all others dealing with this matter.

Hortense Flexner to MG

March 26, 1940
Bryn Mawr
Pennsylvania

Dearest Gellhorn,

I think I am like old Momma RipVanWinkle—just out of the world too long to interpret happenings in the correct way. You should be a little comforted by my assumption that only books of importance get so much real attention, and my ability to salvage from so much print, the kind of appreciation, I did find in much of it. All of my experience has been with authors who can't get a review to save their lives, who go about agonizing, not at what critics say, but at what they *do not* say.

But if the people who confuse your exciting life with your exciting book are making trouble for you, why I can be furious at them too. As to the pictures of your Scroob [Hemingway] drinking from a bottle, they were most enlightening to me. Please ask him, if putting the mouth of the bottle to the corner of his mouth, is the proper and only technique? You know the world does think of him as a great he-man, rushing from bull-fight to war fronts, so that a bottle or two lifted skillfully, does no real damage. And he hasn't got crepey throat. No, a good firm column of a neck. I think you are getting sensitive.

What you must practice is a bit of healthy obscurity that the rest of us can't avoid to save our lives. Why, I sat for 2 hours on a sofa last night with Robert Frost, trying to "draw him out." Well, that old buzzard had never so much as heard of a thing in the world that I have written. But your old teacher who has sweated and died for poetry, and kept on trying to write it no matter what, was just a little squinched up school marm to that old bastard, not even worth a look. You try that dose for a while and the pleasant thought that the world has to take notice of what you do, will not seem quite so hard—or maybe it will. Neither case is truly desirable.

… No, darling, the love story in your book [*A Stricken Field*] is beautifully done, and the writing about the refugees is an all time record. I saw a number of reviews that did make this point—and some day I think you will admit it, after you have swept out the drivel that such as *TIME* lets fly.

… Wyncie is going to write you. He volunteered this, but he may never do it. Still, we both talk and think of you so much, and would hate to go to far parts without seeing you again before we do.

As ever,
Teecher

P.S. If I am dumb about understanding how things are with you and the press, it is because I know you are happy anyhow in your own life and because I don't know much about the press. But there is nobody like you—that I do know—and I believe in your star & love you. H.F.

MG to Hortense Flexner and Wyncie King

March 29, 1940
Finca Vigía
San Francisco de Paula

Dear Weakies,

I love you very much and I can easily see that my last letter was very bullying, by the humble tone of Teecher's reply. When I bully, the thing to do is send me a telegram, of one four letter word, or one four letter word with 'you' added on to it.

Then I will know I have been a bully and will be more respectful next time. I have the soul of a Hun and need to be stepped on.

(If the Pig [Ernest] knew I was writing a letter this morning he would come in and hit me with a shoe. I am supposed to be writing. People are disgusted with me because I lack discipline, am wasteful, lazy and complaining. I have started to write again. Am doing five finger exercises. That is what we call them and they are very good. If you see something, you write it, to give the exact emotion to someone who did not see it. You can concentrate on your failings: with me for instance, I cannot write dialogue, nor can I write anything funny, nor can I write about sex. So now for two weeks I write these things, practicing dialogue, sex or humor as the case may be. They do not have to be stories (no plot), just a complete picture of something.)

I am now suddenly a mother of three and I must say I love it. It is certainly a lot more fun to be a mother of three (without ever having to lose your shape) than being a mother of one, your own, and not know how the brat will turn out. E.'s three sons have turned out very very good. They are all just as funny as their papa, which is saying something. The littlest is eight, and dark and with a wonderful smile and bright black eyes, and you ought to see him shoot craps. He is called Giggy, but known as the Jew due to his great respect for money (the whole family is just waiting for him to grow up and support them he has such an acute sense of silver. His brother Patrick, aged eleven, says, with admiration, 'I never saw a man more careful of his pennies.') Giggy knows all the dice language, never bets more than a nickel, consistently wins, refuses to play when he doesn't feel 'hot,' and addresses the dice with friendship, saying, 'snake eyes,' 'little fever,' 'Richard,' according to the points, and also sits there mumbling to himself, 'Seven, Seven, treat me good, dice, and I'll do the same by you.' He is very funny. He told me that Patrick read aloud to him, but that it bored Patrick because he could go faster reading to himself. He said, 'Mousie (that's Patrick) is about the biggest reader anywhere. He can read a book as fat as the *Green Hills of Africa* in one morning.' The way you describe all books is whether they are fatter or skinnier than the *Green Hills*. Patrick read aloud, with emotion, (we overheard this) parts of E's new book to Giggy, and they told Ernest they thought it was 'terrific' and very interesting and would sell a lot.

Patrick is the jewel of them, a beautiful little boy, with such a good swift mind and such delicacy and so funny I almost never saw. He is a great gambler too, and a fine shot, and we all have taken up tennis together, which is almost too exciting to bear. And the oldest, Bumby, who is sixteen and taller than Ernest and has a body like something the Greeks wished for, and to make you cry is so lovely, is a boy who concentrates on one thing at a time, and just quietly thinks it through, and never has any problems because he never thinks about himself, but only about trout fishing, tennis, fencing, and sometimes he thinks about the one act play he is going to be in at school. So that, riding in the rumble of the car, you will hear the Bumby reciting, in different voices and with feeling, all the parts in his play. We are very good friends and have long interesting talks on a variety of subjects. They all think I am a sort of colossal joke and one of the boys; and refer to me as 'The Marty,' and I think it all goes very fine. Anyhow I am nuts for them, which is a grand thing, and they are no strain, each one having a very full and busy life of his own; and they love the house and the life here, and I am hoping they will be around a good part of the time.

As for [Robert] Frost, Teecher, he is a relic, and I would certainly not worry about an eldery relic who was satisfied with New England all his life. You are a damn fine poet, as far as that goes, and you have the great thing of the professional which is discipline and persistence and passion. You have another thing which you probably don't give a damn about, but in that entire ivy covered ruin of a college, you are about the only one who can make the youthful mind come alive. I regard that as a great talent, not as a teacher, but a talent as a human being.

Now I have to do some work myself, to justify my existence. Such as it is. Tell King I challenge him to write me a letter. I do not believe he can write. I know he can read because I have seen him reading the papers, but I am not sure at all he can write. I bet he has to print. I will give him a quarter if he writes me. You two beloved darlings. I love you very much indeed, always. I love you for having all the guts and all the laughter.

Your devoted dopey old pal,
Gellhorn

MG to Charles Colebaugh

April 3, 1940
Finca Vigía
San Francisco de Paula

Dear Charles,

I have been thinking a lot about the next job, and what would be good for the magazine, and I want to talk this over with you when I come up.

As a writer, I am pretty much getting branded as a disaster-girl. This has certainly not been my fault, because nobody lurking around Europe these last years could have arrived at any very happy conclusions, and one would have to be blind not to see the sorrow and despair and cruelty which I have seen. I do not know of any place that would have given me a chance to write happily about happy people, because though in Spain (and only in Spain) people were often wonderfully gay and loved life while they had it, the first fact was that life was more than hard and life was ominously brief. In articles, it is not possible to delve into every variation of feeling and one must honestly record whatever is the predominant atmosphere.

… But if you only see disaster, and write only disaster, there is the danger of being regarded as one who is blind to everything else, or even an inventor of catastrophe (in order to suit one's special talents) and finally people will say: she always says things are terrible, they can't be as terrible as she says, it's just her racket—or her style of writing—or her own psychological approach. Then the force of the facts is weakened by the personal brand one has as a writer.

This is very damn bad. I can't change Europe, and I can never write with hearty optimism about events which I find blacker than night: but I can look at some things which are fine, entertaining, good and pleasing. As I myself always have a fine time.

So I would like to do some writing about America, because I have a lot of confidence in America and enjoy the country and the life very much indeed. America is far from being entirely bad, and is not without hope, and a lot of the people are pretty happy a good deal of the time: and I would like to write about success, for a change, rather than about failure and defeat.

Also, I think such articles would make good, lively, entertaining reading. For instance: I want to drive west this summer, taking a lot of time, and stopping in tourist camps and small towns. It is not at all hard, in any place, to pick up pals and see what goes on, to see how people amuse themselves, what the country is like, to join the local rabbit hunts and swimming parties and Lodge dances.

Anyhow, you see what I mean. I see about three bang-up American articles, which are cheerful because the subject matter is cheerful, and full of odd enlivening information, and written gaily and happily.

There are two kinds of articles about America, both valid. One is to show what is wrong, in warning, because we cannot afford to have things wrong, as we are the last large so-called civilized country on earth with a lot to save and a lot to lose. And there is the other kind of article, which shows how America is good, and what there is to love and be happy about, and what is worth all the effort of keeping.

I'd like to do the latter.

Will you think about this? How's everything up there? Here it is getting lovely and hot, and I am writing short stories with great pleasure, and playing bum tennis, and going to the pelota games on Saturday night and being indecently happy.

Yours,
Marty

288

MG to Hortense Flexner and Wyncie King

May 17, 1940
Finca Vigía
San Francisco de Paula

Darlings,

...... E bought a very costly radio a few days ago so that we could get our disaster shrieked at us, fresh and on the minute, whereas previously we got it four days late on the mail boats. Still, I am very calm, brooding over maps and watching this disaster with a feeling that I have met it all before. To me, truly, the battle was lost in Spain and in Czecho [sic]. I do not think any nation can countenance the steady betrayal of all others, and remain unbetrayed. In the end, England is weakened with the treachery of its leaders, accepted by all Englishmen. It had to be something like this.

I suppose we will get in the war because we are fools like everybody else and man seems to carry the seeds of his own undoing in his pockets, generation after generation. Yes, I daresay we will be in the war and the movie house will ring with the loud courageous voices of the three minute speakers and women will walk the streets selling Liberty Bonds. As soon as we get in the war I am lighting out for France, where I shall get myself (God willing, though it is going to be a serious drawback to be a woman, it always has been but probably worse now than ever) attached in a journalistic capacity to the armies of the Third Republic. I do not mind the French, in action, because they are sane tough people who do not sing hymns and every *poilu* [infantryman] is given two or three litres of red wine a day as his human due. I would enjoy very much being a journalist as near the armies as they will let me go, when said armies are marching into either Italy or Spain. The country is beautiful in either case and I would take an unholy pleasure in doing great damage to Franco's Falange and as for Italy, with Ernest, I believe that on the whole one has less chance of being killed when around Italians. But I am going to avoid both my country and countrymen because I can still remember as a small child how awful it all sounded and even now, ahead of time, I feel a definite nausea at the sound of all the words. Patriotism is surely the most revolting emotion people go in for, and as a nation we can do it as well as the English when we get started.

I read the last parts of E's book [*For Whom the Bell Tolls*] last night. He is like an animal with his writing; he keeps it all in one drawer, close to him, and hides it under other papers, and never willingly shows it and cannot bear to talk about it. It is of course an absolute marvel, far and away the finest thing he has done and probably one of the greatest war books of always. It is so exact that it becomes truer than life, and yet it is all invented. And in places it is so funny that you scream with laughter and E screams with laughter and embroiders from the book, telling you all the other things they said that he didn't write, and it is breathlessly exciting. I think he may have it finished in a few weeks, though we have been living with it for so long that I consider it as the basis of our life and I do not really believe it can be finished any more than one believes breathing can be finished.

Crandall [Bryn Mawr colleague to Flexner who started their writing program] delights me. I never knew the old crow was a Catholic but in fact that explains many things about her. So women shouldn't go to a war because they get in the way and *Wind Sand and Stars* [by Antoine de Saint Exupéry] is the nuts. She should have seen us taking care of the author of W.S. and S in Madrid, where he spent one day and night and then beat it. He is, so some French aviators I know tell me, a very swell guy, but he is not used to ground artillery and when the hotel was shelled at six one morning, as on many other mornings and was hit five times, he stood in his doorway, an inner room (I lived across the hall and patio facing the street and did not know how dangerous my room was until it got blown up one time when I was away from Madrid) and handed out grapefruit, in an intense state of nervousness. He had a lot of grapefruit and he evidently thought it was the end so he was sharing his wealth. She also should have seen me cooking for the menfolks and taking care of a typhoid patient, when of course I do not know how to read a thermometer but someone had to take care of him. You might tell her that under menace of death, chivalry is a very outdated idea, and though men put themselves out for the woman they love (which is normal in peace or war) no strangers spend their time throwing their cloaks over the mud. The only place a woman is not welcome for reasons of her sex is in the lines immediately before a morning attack is going to begin, because the men are going to the bathroom (in agony of spirit) in all the trenches up and down the countryside and supposedly it would embarrass the woman. I can't say it does. It is a damn sight more trying to have a company of infantry come on you, in a similar position.

I have two stories I am mad to do if I can ever finish this bloody one. I want to do a story about Finland, about an aviator I met there and a woman who should be modeled on Clare Boothe Luce whom I have never met. I want it to be a story of pure sex (because I am so bad at handling that), with the man full of a bitter and hurried contempt, and the woman trying to understand life by handling the body of a man who deals exclusively with death. I write it horribly now but it is some story as I see it. The aviator was a wonder. It gave me cold shivers to look at him. I suppose he is dead now. And then I want to do one about the first day of the war in Finland when I ran through the burning streets with an Italian who had bombed the niggers in Ethiopia and flown in Spain but never seen what a bombing was like on the ground. That is quite a story too, and I liked that man better than anyone in Finland which goes to show that we never know what we are talking about.

Oh hell. I wish I were at the war this minute and didn't have to write and work and learn to think and learn to read and discipline myself and lead a decent life. I wish E and I were roistering and running about with all the other overexcited loonies who live in the moment. But maybe there are no more wars like the ones I have attended. Maybe they talk at these wars now, and there is nothing to do at them except die.

Give my love to King. Tell him to cheer up. There is *much* worse to come. Tell him to drink more. No one can even guess what a difference scotch can make to the world situation.

I love you *very* much.
Gellhorn

MG to Eleanor Roosevelt

MA New York NY 120 pm
June 7, 1940

Dearest Mrs. Roosevelt;

E. gave me a letter for you. He said he has too much emotion about you, and your letter to him, to write properly. I will have to ask you many questions about the raising and care of children, you ought to see me with my young ones [Jack, Patrick, Gregory]. They think I am pleasantly insane and they regard me as a wonderful new addition to their lives, an official grown-up who has no authority at all and can be counted on to agree with all their plans.

I foresee that the next thing is that they will decide I am a dope and they will bring me up.

Marty

MG to Hortense Flexner and Wyncie King

June 8, 1940
Finca Vigía
San Francisco de Paula

Sweeties,

Have just finished my day's work, five typed pages, about 1250 words, and am both exhausted and in a state of deep doubt and soul searchings. Soul searchings are not indicated for the novelist at work; what you need is a blind and bubbly confidence. So. I have been thinking about writing until I am dizzy and a little ill. And have decided that what I have is patience, care, honor, detail, endurance and subject matter, And what I do not have is majic [sic]. But majic [sic] is all that counts. Or do you spell it magic. I am a little mixed up due to Czech street names. And so I am feeling fairly gloomy. Because, with magic, I have here a little tale to break the heart. And without magic I have here a set of facts, damning and terrible facts, but without magic who will weep and who will protest? Oh hell.

Tomorrow we lay off and go on a boating peekneek [sic]. It is with the pelota players, eleven Basques and us. They bring the food: Ernest and I are being invited. We go on Ernest's boat to a cove and drop them and they make a fire under the trees and cook a chicken-with-rice which is made in a dish two feet across and has everything in the world in it, as well as chicken and rice, and we wash this down with wine from gallow straw-covered jugs and later we all get blotto drunk and they sing Basque songs, which are like hymns, except gay and fighting.

Then someday, when I am surer of myself (because either I am going to learn to write or by God I am not going to write at all), I shall try to put down on paper what it means to have lost the war in Spain. Not being a Spaniard nor a lover of war and hating Fascism only very specifically for what it does to human life, I find it rare that I should every day of my life, in my heart and mind, hurt because that war is gone. Nothing in my life has so affected my thinking as the losing of that war. It is, very banally, like the death of all loved things and it is as if a country that you had worshipped was suddenly blackened with fire and later swallowed in an earthquake. I think this feeling must be carried by all of them, somewhere, in their minds, or wherever feeling rests: and I know it because I have it every day. Czecho [sic] made me fighting mad and sick with rage: but Spain has really broken my heart. I haven't the faith of a flea left and am acquiring that detachment which Wordsworth, the old bastard, preached: due to the indifference resulting from having lost what I cared about. Also, I wonder if this can be true, can you love land that is not your own, more than any other land. Spain of course looks like the west, only eaten with history and used with all the life and blood and cruelty and gentleness and hope of a complicated, childlike people. But there come days when it seems to be utterly unbearable to have lost that land, those bald, always moving, forever hills, the claw sharp mountains, the green plains that go down to Aranjeuz where they grow strawberries and asparagus. I don't know. Maybe that is not a book but a poem. A lament.

I am reading with interest about the Napoleonic wars. And living here, like the gent who loved Thais, stuck up on a pillar in the desert. And writing. And torn with doubt about the writing and wanting so fiercely to have it right. But where is the magic? You can't breed it into people and you can't learn it. Ernest has it. He doesn't know how it comes or how to make it, but when I read his book I see it, clear as water and carrying like the music of a flute and it is not separate from what he writes, but running all through it. I fear I am German. Well. Goddam.

Kisses to you both. I have been reading about the Writers' Congress, and suffering that such worthy ideas and such hardworking people should appear such poops, in print. For folk with dirty minds (like me) there was plenty to laugh at in the reported speech of President Donald Ogden Stewart who is not so much a comic as an ass.

I dote on you,
Gellhorn

MG to Charles Scribner

July 7, 1940
Finca Vigía
San Francisco de Paula

Charlie my dear (that's how you start letters),

Your letter had our household in what is called gales of laughter. You are very cute and far too jolly to be an English country gent. This is not a letter as I have nothing to say. Only that I am not coming to New York, so you won't need to build up health for future destruction. E. is coming alone as soon as the book is done, sometime between the 15th and 30th of July, and going to do his business quickly and return. You and Max however take good care of him and see that he doesn't get in the papers. The bridge is blown, or did I tell you, and is *very* exciting and worth waiting for.

I have been writing about the local Nazis and now that is finished and I am not pleased with the article but relieved not to have to go to town every day and return with my clothes sticking to me and the general feeling of having crossed the Sahara on foot. We had a good hot time at the pelota the last night of the season due to one of the big Nazis getting above himself, with their defeat of France, and talking too much and too loud. But he wouldn't fight. He sounded awfully big until E called him and then he evaporated, but it was good while it lasted. I think a war against those guys will be a necessity someday and something of a pleasure, but I do not think we ought to bother with having France and England for allies: we stand a better chance to win doing it on our own, and on our own territory. I must say, though, that Nazis individually or *en masse* call out to be shot at. It is curious that people can be as unattractive as their philosophy.

You will be impressed to hear that our mango and alligator pear crop are record breaking, that arsenic judiciously sprayed has liquidated the caterpillars that were eating the bougainvillea, and that the pigeons are doing very well except there are too few females and so life in the coo factory is kind of like a dance at Yale, with far too much courting and rushing around. We are going to buy some new ladies and put an end to the belle system: those lady coos have to settle down, marry and reproduce, like in the novels you appreciate.

Don't know when I will see you but sometime. Perhaps we will come to NY in the fall. I don't imagine we'll meet you riding over a mountain in Idaho?

Always,
Marty

MG to Eleanor Roosevelt

July 20, 1940
Finca Vigía
San Francisco de Paula

Dearest Mrs. Roosevelt,

I hope the next four years will not be the hardest ones yet, and I suppose one ought to pray for miracles for the sake of the country, and all of us, and especially for you and the President who will have the toughest job of all. When will either of you get a real rest, or even a good breathing spell? It doesn't look as if you would at all, but I hope you do.

Mother is here now and has been telling me of seeing you. She is another of your great admirers (our family is full of same.) We are trying to give her a good rest, which she needs. We have been out fishing in the Gulf and yesterday had a terrific day, seeing a whale shark—which is very rare—that swam right by the boat. It was as big as the boat, and you can't believe anything so big is true, it is as if something from the Smithsonian woke up and began plodding around the ocean. Said monster had a mouth twelve feet wide and all it likes to eat is sardines. We also saw a pair of marlin playing in the water, playing as fast as pursuit planes, and diving and racing after the light blue flying fish. We clambered up and down the side of the boat and swam miles in clear green water near shore, and Mother had already turned a nice salmon color from the sun, and looks very cute and fresh and gay. She's a wonderful woman, wonderful company always, and loves to laugh, and right now I am glad of the unreal calm and the great beauty of this place, because she can't think much about the war here. In a way I think this time of history is worse for people who remember the last war clearly: she of course remembers it all (and you know my father was a German, and there was always that delightful angle, of having people be dreadful to him, because of where he was born). I think you can feel as protective about your parents as they felt about you, when you were a child. The only thing is that you can't really take care of anyone, though I wish I could sort of develop great solid wide wings, and keep them around Mother. She however would enjoy being protected as little as I would only

I am glad I can persuade her to take two weeks off from time to time and at least see that she gets rested and sunburned and takes exercise.

Yesterday we ran into one of the local Gestapo in a bar which we frequent. We've known this man for a long time: he is a German and a Nazi and a pretty good example of what they are like. He doesn't surprise either E or me, who know the type, but Mother curiously enough has never met a real Nazi. She has only seen the people who were victims of the Nazis. It was very strange and interesting, because the Nazi gave Mother the horrors. I've never seen her so uncomfortable with anyone: it was the same sort of reaction people have to seeing repellent sights, buzzards eating, or mashed bodies. It proved to me again the difference between seeing with your own eyes, and reading: and it occurs to me that the mentality of the English, up to the war, may also be explained by the fact that they were stay-at-homes by and large, and reading about the Nazis is not the same thing as seeing them.

This Fifth Column stuff is a red herring. When you look at France, Norway, Spain, you can see that the real destroyers of a country are natives of that country. I only hope Americans will realize this in time, and recognize their enemies. No redheaded hairdresser on the Bremen ruins any country: it takes Quislings, Lavals, Juan Marches and people like that to do the trick. The established and respected traitors, who belong to the best clubs, are the ones to fear.

Greetings to Tommy [Malvina Thompson, Eleanor Roosevelt's personal secretary], and Hick [Lorena Hickok] if she is still there. If Hitler would only die from being hit by a thunderbolt, the next four years would be easier, wouldn't they?

Love,
Marty

MG to Ernest Hemingway

July 24, 1940
Finca Vigía
San Francisco de Paula

My dearest Peeby,

Your wire came this morning. Yesterday afternoon Mother and I were talking about your book [*For Whom The Bell Tolls*] The Maria Robert part at the end. Mother cried just thinking about it: "We won't be going to Madrid now." We talked all about it. She said you didn't read it, it was if you saw it, the bridge and all, she said, and you were so frightened that he wouldn't be able to get the wire clear and blow it in time. She said, "There's a piece of description that's just like holding some beautiful jewel in your hands." She thinks you're wonderful. By the time you get this, Max and the others will be telling you too. It is a great book, my little Buggy. We talked of you a long time with love; we talk of little else.

… I have a hangover (from a total of 4 highballs) and feel awful and furious with myself and bad tempered. Mother was cross last night too, because she didn't like the English and the Basque fiesta was dreadful and it was agony-hot. She was tired and we didn't get home until two and so she isn't in good shape today either. We'll have to sleep and walk it off, and get to bed early and avoid city life. Even in Havana, I find I detest city-life, and certainly the minute you are away my cobra raises his head and howls.

… Today you are on the train going over your book and tomorrow you will be in NY and I guess you will find it very hot and I only hope you have a fine time with the boys and don't get depressed. Maybe by now we are just like two peas in a pod and if separated it gets sort of lonely and chilly in the world. I love you very much always my dearest Bongie.

Chickie

MG to Hortense Flexner

Late July 1940
Finca Vigía
San Francisco de Paula

Another letter, try again, or turn around as Dr. Lippmann used to say when Mrs. Lippmann swam out to sea in Lake Michigan.

Yesterday Pig found the title for his book so we went in town and got drunk last night. He got drunk but I ate too much dinner to risk it and anyhow I stayed up with him until two and feel today like a washrag that has been lying damply in the corner of some basement for twenty years. The title is a wonder. It comes from John Donne. Who is a wonder too. (Pig said, happily, "Donnie's got the brains, Hemingstein makes the money.") It is "FOR WHOM THE BELL TOLLS." It comes from a very superb passage: I don't remember it all but it begins: "No man is an ilande [sic]—"and it goes on to say "any man's death diminishes me because I am involved in Mankinde [sic]; And therefore never send to know for whom the bell tolls: It tolls for thee." Read it all in *Oxford Book of English Prose*, called "The Bell."

We know it is good because it gives us the shivers. Then where we ate, in a café that the barkeeps and the waiters own and all are great friends of ours, we tried it out on Firpo the Barman. They all follow E's book with the greatest interest: he tells them the story as it goes along. We translated it into Spanish for him: "*Para Quien Suenan las Campanas*." He said it over several times and then shook hands with E. Man, he said, you have something serious there. He called the cook and said, "Ernesto's title is" and told the cook and asked the cook, "What thinkest thou." The cook reflected and said, "I see it very clearly, it is that all men must die, a bell rings for all men today or tomorrow." You know, they are the *goddamdest* people.

At this point there has been a slight interruption. Ten Basques have arrived, drunk as goats, having been up all night (a Basque will never sleep if possible) and they have been to Mass, drunk, and brought the Priest with them. The Priest is an old friend of ours, a former Machine gunner during the Civil War (with a Communist outfit) and the Basques who don't give a hoot for church but love the singing, go to Mass to sing in the choir especially when they are drunk. So here they are and it is almost lunch time and I daresay someone will have to cope with this, but not me. Ernest just burst in, roaring with laughter, saying, "Drunk, drunk, everyone's drunk *still*" and I suppose he will find food for them. I am feeling to [sic] weak to take this on.

We had the *Oxford Book* with us last night at the Jai-Alai and tried the title on all our friends. There was Ben Finney who is in town on a mammoth yacht (you remember that yacht story of last year: same yacht) and with him Mike Tarafa who owns all the sugar in Cuba, and we stood at the bar between matches and they were wildly excited about the title, and Ben has been out here for two days, shut in Ernest's room, with his shoes off, reading the manuscript. For a living, Ben shoots in the live pigeon tournaments where you bet $2000 on a bird. He is a gambler and a fine man. I think literature, in this atmosphere, cannot fail to be real. If you get barkeeps and pelota players and Ben Finney and Mike Tarafa all madly excited about what you write and crazy for a title out of John Donne, you cannot lose.

So now I guess I will have to put on some pants and go out and handle the boys. I do have a really wild life. I never seem to move with less than fourteen men in tow (there are no other women who have the stamina), and the boys just regard me as one of the bunch, a slightly younger less competent member of the gang, and my language is so obscene from long association with men who do not notice me as being different, that I cannot talk to women any more at all. My talk makes women pale and ill, and I can do it in Spanish as easily as in English. Ernest, who loves me very dearly and will not do anything without me will get very tight in a bar as last night for instance and at two in the morning remember I am there and I am his Bongie, and not just a blonde boy who happens to be drinking with the group, and he will put his arm around me, like a friendly but destructive bear, and say, "Well, men, we've got a good Marty anyhow haven't we? We're sure lucky to have a good Marty like that." And then he will say dimly, "Maybe you want to go home sometime, Schatzy?" And I will say, "*Que va*, home. I am growing here." And he will say proudly, "Look at that Marty, never says a mumbling word." But today I feel a little shattered. And then there are those Basques. Now they are singing Latin in the living room. I will have to take care of them.

So long darlings. Come down and see us sometime if you think you can survive. Maybe I better come up and rest a bit. I'll be there in June by the way, and CRAZY to see you.

All love to you sweetmeats.
Marty

Eleanor Roosevelt to MG

August 2, 1940
The White House
Washington

Dear Marty,

… I am so glad your mother has been with you and you were able to give her a good rest and a holiday. Life sounds perfectly delightful and it may not be four years before I join you as one of your acres! I think you feel protective about me just as you do about your mother. As you know the President has been nominated but he hasn't been elected yet and Mr. Wilkie has all the best publicity firms in the country working for him and it seems that they are doing a pretty good job.

I agree with you that our fifth column is in the people of one's own country. The English are appeasing on the Burma Road question but the President says that it is only for three months and he hopes and prays by that time something will happen to prevent its closing. Our people are as slow to awaken as the English but they will wake up. They do not clamor yet to aid any other nation but they do begin to think and to say that we cannot live alone in the world.

I haven't any plans yet for going out to see Anna [daughter]. If you will let me know when you are going to be in Sun Valley and how long, I will let you know if anything takes me out that way. I would love to see that particular spot.

Hick is just moving up to New York for the campaign and I think that will be grand for her as it will give her a chance to use her little house in the country more often.

Good luck and much love to you.

Affectionately,
Eleanor R.

MG to Charles Scribner

August 23, 1940
Finca Vigía
San Francisco de Paula

Charlie darling,

I am not near married at all, and even if I were that is scarcely a reason to become formal with me. I find the prospect of matrimony frightening enough without your doing that.

We have been working very hard here. Duran's corrections of Spanish came yesterday and so everything will be perfectly tidied up and ready for you on the date you named.

Now about your suggestion. E talked to me about it, and I thought it was a very sweet picture, the two of you sitting there making up plans for Marty, and thinking of good things for me. I do appreciate it, darling, very much indeed. I don't see how I could do it though. Perhaps I can explain, perhaps not. You see, I write with a great deal of difficulty, partly because I am lazy and partly because it is hard to write. The only way I write well at all is to be very excited about what I am writing. The *Collier's* articles are always easy because I go to a brand new country which is usually in the midst of some stupendous trouble and I am excited by everything, from the food to the disaster. I go around for two or three weeks all day and most of the night, collecting every known kind of information and putting it in notebooks. Then I sit for two days and try to bring order out of the notebooks and then for two or three days more I write. By that time, the excitement is pretty well gone, but the article is done, and it is only hard work, but always it is sustained by the pressure of the newness and if there is any danger then I am really lucky because I function well under such conditions and feel lively in the head.

I have published three books and written four (one huge one still in my drawer, not good enough: it took a year of study and one year to write and I nearly died over it, but I lost the excitement almost before I began and just plodded on and it was a poop.) I have never been not writing, since I can remember, something or other, but there is very little to show for it because most of it is not good enough. I could not do a book (a book, Charlie, think of the high pile of bare white paper that you have in front of you before there is even the beginning of a book), unless I believed awfully hard in it. Unless I wanted to do it so much that I could sweat through the dissatisfaction and weariness and failure and all the rest you have to sweat through. I really and truly could not write a book to order. And also, I really don't want to.

You see, if I had to for money, I would do anything from scrub floors to write corset advertising and I would never think that was hard or remarkable or anything: only doing whatever anybody has to do to eat and have a roof. I used to do that when I had to, I wrote fashion articles and I wrote about face-lifting and I wrote about the festivals of Jeanne d'Arc in France and about the Dolly sisters and anything else you can name. I wrote nothing but corset advertising really, because I had to. It was okay and I did not mind. Only now I am older and I have worked through that. It took me almost ten years. I was lucky to get it done that fast. I don't need to do for money anything except articles for *Collier's*, or for somebody else, but that same kind of article, what is called foreign correspondence, and if lucky war correspondence. I like that work very much, and am of course delighted that I can earn my living doing a sort of hack writing that interests me.

The books I do are what I earn my living for. Very odd sentence. I mean it would depress me a great deal to earn my living just to eat: I earn it very well and as fast as possible so as to have time to do the kind of writing I want to do. This writing so far does not pay too much ($1500 advance on the last novel: that is what I get for one *Collier's* article). But it is what I want to do, and all the time I try to learn so I can do it better, whether it pays or not. I simply could not write a book for any motive more serious than that I wanted terribly to write the book. I am a writer of very serious books, because it is so hard for me to write at all that I can't waste my juice on anything that isn't very very important to me. Do you see?

That is not to say that I do not appreciate very much what you suggest. It might be that one day E and I made some kind of odd and rare travelling and then I would want to write about it. But Cuba is not odd and rare to me, it is lovely and interesting and where I live: and I could not set out cold to work up a book from it. (That is to say, within the limits of the gravity, that of course I could and would if I had to. But I don't. And *Collier's* being after me all the time to set out for the wars again, I don't imagine I will have to.)

We were talking the other day about you and publishing, and me and my next book. Now you have up and offered yourself as my publisher. Do you remember the things you said against publishing two people in the same family? Another thing makes me feel shy about talking publishing with you. It is that we are pals, and I would not want to be published because you liked me. I think Charles Duell very probably hates my guts, but he thinks I am a good writer. (I do not think he necessarily knows, but that is his impression.) So it is just professional and non-feminine. I am somewhat the enemy of feminine, you know, except in a strictly limited field of personal relations. Oh well, this has been a very long letter indeed and it begins to meander and go nowhere.

… We have been very gay here, with that letter. Duran said (to compress it), that the book was a Spanish book, and he Duran recognized the place and the people, the voices of all the men and their way of thinking (the obscure manner of thinking of my people, he said) and the road to the attack and the place where Robert Jordan was wounded, and the look of the early morning coming through the pines in the Sierram and said Duran, I felt as if Robert Jordan were me, and Maria is a girl I only had once in my life and long ago. He said "the situation is authentic and the scene exact." Oh he said a lot, and all good. You see Duran commanded that attack (which E did not see) and being himself a Lieutenant General of the Republic and a Spaniard, what he says is the real and important thing to have said. If to him everyone is real, everyone is someone he has known, the war part is so true it is as if he had lived it, then there is nothing more to say about it. You will be glad to know this. I myself never doubted it for a minute and did not need Duran nor anybody else to affirm it.

It really is a whiz of a book.

The third of September will be the beginning of vacation. I think it is needed.

E is working beautifully and easily.

Always,

Marty

MG to Hortense Flexner and Wyncie King   August 25, 1940
Finca Vigía
San Francisco de Paula

Teecher sweetelpipes [sic],

Are you interested in dreams? Normally I am not so crazy about dreams myself but we have been having a lot of spirited dreams around this house, whose symbolic meaning is indeed dark and various. Perhaps the best one was had by Scrooby who dreamed that he saw a large picture in *P.M.* on the front page. It was a picture of all his friends and hear friends: there was Waldo Pierce and Max Perkins and Bayard Swope and Gene Tunney and other citizens. They had their arms around each others shoulders and a look of pure delight on their faces, and they were singing. Underneath it was printed what they were singing. They were singing happily together:

"Hark the herald angels sing
Ernie doesn't get a goddam thing."

I think that's a pretty nice one. Scroob says he was terribly hurt to see all his good old friends singing so happily about him in this manner.

I, on the other hand, had a very trying dream, from which I woke, twisting and straining and muttering with rage. I don't know what happened exactly and I was quite alone. But what had happened was that I was wedged tight, up to my neck, in a huge tub of lard, which was studded on the outside with precious jewels. Now, Teecher, what do you think?

Aside from dreams though, nothing much is happening down here.

Right now it is pouring rain, and the sky is winter grey and there is a wind beating the leaves off the trees and a steady stage rumble of thunder. It is winter already and I feel it coming and I hope the fall is lovely enough, out west, to make up for the always yearly despair of having the summer end. I wait every year for summer, and it is usually good, but it is never as good as that summer I am always waiting for.

Mother was here for five weeks which was the longest vacation she has taken since she left college. She got so pretty that it was like watching your own child come out from long legs and a sort of crane-awkwardness into something smooth and finished and beautiful. She got younger right in front of us, and she slept well and long and was jolly and contented and relaxed. She said it was the first time she had been really happy for years (since when Dad died, she meant) and that she didn't know she could be so happy.

So that way, it has been a good summer. I love her very much, and I feel older than she, and tougher. I know I am not, not in any real way, the way of enduring and believing and patience and wiseness. But I am certainly less startled by evil than she is, and not being a very good person myself I can take a lot of non-good. I always want to protect her, which goes to show that life is surely some kind of goofy circle: and in one way or another, we have all the emotions before we are through.

Meantime Scrooby's book [*For Whom the Bell Tolls*] is nearly finished: that is to say really finished, as Scribner's set it up in type the minute they got their hands on it. We have been reading and correcting galleys and as it is about 200,000 words long that is no joke for anyone. But it goes off in the mails in a few days and appears in hard covers on October 10 and then we are, at last, out of jail. I hope to holy heaven that we do not have to write another very soon and I am just as exhausted with it as if I were the doctor at the birth.

But it is very very fine indeed, oh my what a book. It is all alive, all exciting, all true, and with many discoveries about life and living and death and dying: which in the end is all there is to write about. I am proud of it and so is Scrooby and maybe we can rest easy for a bit.

We are going west now. (I know just how that lard-rub idea started: I feel almost unbelievably safe and I am not a one who is nuts for this safety racket. We will have to get into some sort of serious trouble next winter or I will curl up and melt. I like my catastrophes; I like to feel myself a small blown and harried part of great havoc. The times being havoc, I have no desire to live in a sort of superb cotton wool, all the year round. At least four months of something tough, says [sic] I, so that I don't choke on the ice cream.)

I have done no work since I can't think when; yet I am working all the time at something or other.

… We'll be in Sun Valley as of September 8 or so, and through to the end of October. Address simply: Sun Valley, Idaho. There is also much divorce talk going on, and probably it will actually materialize in due course and I will be made an honest woman. I feel so honest as is I am a little tetchy about this legalizing stuff, though of course it won't change anything and everyone seems agreed it is more sensible. Well, hell.

Gellhorn, the first of her class to sin, the last to legalise. They ought to put it in the yearbook. I am engaged right this minute which I enjoy like mad; being married for three years it is very nice to be engaged simultaneously. It gives you an impression of permanent youth. I have a ring that is all bright with dimons [sic] and sapphires and snappy as hell and the only problem is not to wash my hands with it on and get it all mushed up with soap, but accustomed as I am to jewels I can scarcely remember and my day is partly given over to picking at my bauble with a safety pin to get the Lux off it. I love the ring but mainly I love the idea of being engaged and we both think that people who get engaged when they aren't married are chumps and Scroob says, you might almost say that people who haven't at least started a baby before they're married are slackers. (Don't get ideas. I want to go to the wars.)

Have you noticed the way our friend Archie MacFlees [MacLeish, Librarian of Congress] is going in for vulgarizing patriotism. Get a can of MacFlees patriotism, good for everything that ails you, only fifteen cents at the nearest *TIME* vendors. Myself, I cannot bear patriotism and feel certain that if we are going in for that (and evidently we are) I am going someplace else. War is not the worst thing that can happen: but by God war on the home front is worse than whatever could happen anywhere.

Oh hell. If there is a war anywhere I want to be at it.

Since my book [*A Stricken Field*] came out, I have been asked by two Councils of Jewish Women to make speeches. I am flattered and tell them I would rather be shot at five paces than make any more speeches. But that is what I got from my book. I better do another. The *Trouble* netted me invitations from Social Workers. Maybe on the third book I will get invited by the League to Protect our Feathered Friends.

How are you guys? I hope you are okay. It has been a long time since I engaged you in conversation via the mails. You are pretty tight, though, you never write unless I do. How's for cracking, and telling me what goes on. Please Teechie, little Teechie. I get nervous if I don't know about you and Wyncie for too long at a time. Kiss that Wyncie for me, leaving if possible a big smear of lipstick on him. Kiss him twice. I hope everything is dandy in your woods.

Love
Gellhorn

MG to Allen Grover

September 6, 1940
4366 McPherson Avenue
St. Louis

Allen darling,

I have been missing you now for quite a long time, in a ruminative way, like a cow, chewing on the missing of you and thinking maybe that is how things are or get to be, but I do not like it. I do not think we had better lose each other, no matter what, because there is always so little time and nobody ever comes along who is the same thing, and then it is very lonely to have once been really at home with someone, and then not have them anymore...

It's a little complicated even to write these things. I would not want to seem a critical and disloyal bitch. You can tear letters up, can't you, quickly, and not remember anything except what they told you? E wants me for himself, altogether. He has me too, and need not worry. But you know, you do know, how people get hurt when you don't mean to hurt them, and think things are rivalry, when in fact it is two different and uncompetitive kettles of fish. You do know. I don't have very much privacy. I don't really have any right now. It isn't worth while to write me a very good letter, because you can sort of figure that it will be shared. (Do you suppose I would be that way if E had a woman who was Allen to him).

... I'm leaving by plane tomorrow for Sun Valley. I had planned to stay here longer and wanted to. I am very tired. E's book has been an agony, like having children without interruption for months and months. I am tired in my head with it. I don't think anyone can be a great writer and do great books without pulling down the pillars of the temple all over the place. But I have to hurry out because he is lonely, he feels abandoned (I have not seen him for a week), and besides I evidently have to read the proofs again. In principle we are marrying this summer. In principle. I have a quiet horror of marriage. I have seen the women getting their divorces and if that business is linked to marriage, boy I can do very well without marriage. I would rather sin respectably, any day of the week. E thinks of course that marriage saves you a lot of trouble and he is all for it, and practically he is right. But Allen, it is awful isn't it, the way you can make someone pay you in stocks and bonds and furniture and Christ knows what all, for not loving you. I thought if people stopped loving you, you went in a corner like a sick animal and held yourself very tight, so as not to break. But on the contrary, it seems you get the best possible advice and see how you can ruin the son of a bitch who no longer feels the sun shining inside him, when you enter the room. This is all deadly private and to be torn up. I count on you. I do not and cannot speak of it with anyone. Myself, whatever grand things I have gotten from men, I did not consider that you could deposit any of it in a bank: equally with the bad things you can get from men, but since when can pain be paid for in dollars? Or then, what class of pain is it that it can be bought off? Anyhow, I like it better clean: I think sin is very clean. There are no strings attached to it. There is all the deadly intense obligation of one human being to another, but there is no insurance. You are probably less free, socially, but anyhow you feel awful simple and straight in your heart.

The book [*For Whom the Bell Tolls*] will be out in November and then, having done what I could to be helpful during all these months, I want to get back into the life I care about, seeing how the world works, and how the people in it behave with their disasters. I am really more interested in seeing France than anything else. The cradle of civilization, as I recall. Well, I believe in the French, and I want to see whether that is true or a mistake, and whether a people can remain despite their government, and their defeat. I want to see whether all the minds stay good, no matter how they issue official proclamations of idiocy from Vichy. For the sake of history, it is more important to know whether the Nazis can conquer the minds of the French, than to know whether they can take any amount of ground, or any set of fortifications. I am crazy to go: all this time I have been wanting to, but we have our small personal jobs and must stick with them. Mine will be done when that book comes out. I wish I felt in myself a more valuable and necessary person: then I would be able to think that I had a duty to society, and that I was anointed of God to keep the record straight, to the best of my ability.

…What are you doing? Are you very thin and brown and are you interested and happy: and what do you think we should be doing about this war and what do you think about strange Mr. Willkie [presidential Republican nominee] with his honest homespun hair and that complicated cruel mouth, and those odd flowing utterances, as if he did not know himself, when he said something fine and when he said something that made him sound like the Burns Detective Agency, strikebreakers on the side…

I love you. I love you a great deal and always. And I have to known you are there and sticking with me, and that we have each other in our good way, our being at home over lunch in the Gotham way.

Take care of yourself,
Marty

Although Hemingway had been negotiating with his second wife, Pauline Pfeiffer, about their terms of divorce and believed that it would be granted so he would be free to marry Martha, letters that he wrote to her and to Edna Gellhorn in September 1940 reveal he was unsure of Martha's certainty. Gellhorn had no intention of forfeiting any assignments as a *Collier's* correspondent and was at the time planning to travel to China as soon as her accreditation papers came through. Ernest told Martha that her work plans gave him "a fine roaring headache and a good sound busted heart," in spite of the fact, he admitted, that he had been as she suggested, "no gift for a big part of the time," while he was writing *For Whom the Bell Tolls*. However, he insisted that there was only "one important thing" she had to know other than he loved her truly and "never will love anyone else." He did not want to hold her to any promises that she did not want to keep. Yet, if Martha intended to marry him, he would feel "cockeyed delighted," and he would try to amuse her more than anyone else she'd ever marry.

To Edna, to whom he wrote two long letters on September 28th, Ernest confided, "I would rather be dead than live without Marty," insisting that was "not rhetoric" because he could not live alone—self-awareness that had the ring of emotional truth. He wondered, "how can you tell someone that the most exciting adventures come in the head and in two people loving each other... and not seem selfish saying it?" He thought that the answer to his distress was to go along with Martha to China, which is what he ended up doing, but in the meantime he asked Edna to keep all of her old booze bottles in case one of them had his "soul in it right now." He reminded her that *For Whom the Bell Tolls* was dedicated to Martha and that he ought to wire Scribner's and get them "to add If I Can Find Her" to it.

Hemingway's divorce from Pauline Pfeiffer came through on November 4th, and he wed Martha two weeks later in Cheyenne, Wyoming, a celebration photographed by Robert Capa for *LIFE* magazine.

Hortense Flexner to MG

Post–October 21, 1940
Bryn Mawr
Pennsylvania

Dearest Gellhorn,

In a minute I am going to sit down and write to Ernest, which will probably be a horrible letter saying none of the things I would like to say, out of sheer inability to cope with or reply to such a completely charming inscription/ Gellhorn you are a lamb. I am writing you first because (a) I must limber up my brain and (b) I want to say what a perfect moment it was for us when we saw the printed dedication. "This Book [*For Whom the Bell Tolls*] is For"—a man's dedication. So glad there was nothing about inspiration and devotion. Just that little preposition "for." Well, the Kinglets got out the finding list of your year in college and just went over it, girl by girl, thinking what they would say to THAT. Judging by our reaction, the campus will be breathless, even these later generations and what your own will feel, will be pleasant food for thought for us for many a day. Well, Mr. Hemingway didn't give you any disciplinary flunk.

So far I have just read the opening chapters. But as I was pulling up the reading lamp and getting started last night, Wyncie sat down on the little stool by the big chair, gently removed the book from my hand and said: "Let me see about my Martha once more." So, beginning with John Donne, we read all those preliminary pages, and then talked about you and your thirty or 29 years and made it fit very nicely with what we knew about you when you were a freshman. We also reviewed your recent letter, with its discontent about the story that would not come right, and decided that, even if the story never does, you are a bit hard to please. (Especially when I glance at the photograph on the jacket of the book.) By now however, the story is probably going better—but anyhow, you should be having a marvelous time, which may be why you can't.

This is just a letter about the book, so I will not go into the matter of our house and staying here. We both hate it, but will get some work done.

You know we did not realize the book had been printed and finished. So you can add surprise to all the other pleasant feelings. But you know that is a lovely inscription—lovely for us to be so placed with him in our affection for you.

The book begins beautifully. I am going to leave all the critics' words for the critics—just tell you, that after the good letters you have sent us about the writing of it, and after what I expected in interest and reality, I am not a bit disappointed—in fact, the opposite. As you know old Crandall isn't a meaner reader than I am, but I am just carried along and feel that I have seen that country and known those people.

Goodbye and thanks. I am going to write your Mother a little note now. Did you see our inscription? "To Mr. and Mrs. Wyncie King from somebody who loves Marty too—Ernest Hemingway." How is that, Miss Gellhorn?

Love,
Teechie

October 24, 1940
Sun Valley
Idaho

Dearest Mrs. Roosevelt,

Is there any way for the citizenry or even the single citizen to protest this loan to Franco, actual or proposed, of one hundred million dollars? I cannot believe such a thing can happen, it is at once too evidently scandalous and too apparently an idiocy. But it is written of and talked of, as if it were truly going to happen.

Is there no place to say something very loud and angry against such a deal?

Today Franco met Hitler, or yesterday, not that it was necessary for them to meet to prove what we have all known since 1936; to wit, that the small fat-faced Spaniard is a pal if not a servant to the not very big man with the moustache. So are we going to give Franco, as a *cadeau d'amour* [love token] (in recognition of his services in destroying democracy, as a token of appreciation for the amount of civilian death he accomplished) one hundred million dollars? He will find a very good use for it: it will pay for the material with which to take Gibraltar.

My God, how can such a thing be? Hasn't there been enough appeasing to prove to everyone, everyone that appeasing will not work. Haven't they done enough futile buying off? And don't they know at last the that Republican Spaniards fought 38 months because they had something to believe in, and the French did not fight at all because their rulers had destroyed all faith, with this same system of appeasing. What are we supposed to believe in, after a deal like that? We never helped the republic of Spain, but now we will help the open ally of Hitler. We never did one damn thing to spare the people of Spain their misery, to help them save their lives: but we will give money to a man who is still executing republicans at the rate of 30 a day...

I never thought awfully much of being as repellent as one's enemies, because finally there is so little to choose that the great mass of simple people grow confused. That's a bad, bitter sentence but you see what I mean. But aside from being loathsome and crooked, why also be stupid? Why *give* weapons? Who is responsible for this suggested, proposed, or consummated deal? Can't we, all of us, furiously protest?

And good Lord, think of the people of Spain, the hungry and driven, who are still getting shot for their beliefs, and are still believing. What a fine thing for them to read in the papers that their tyrant receives from that last great democracy one hundred million dollars.

I hope it isn't true. It's too damnable to be true. It just can't be true. How is it that practically any royalty can get into this country, and that visas for Anti-Fascist refugees, who have proved their good faith in the prison camps of two or three countries, cannot be obtained? What is happening, when such things go on? Who decides it? Who runs such a show? Doesn't it look pretty grim and godawful to you? It scares me. There is a horrid upper-class tone about such reasoning and goings on, perhaps we need some plain people in the state department for a change.

I haven't been in such a rage for a long time, but where can one dump one's rage? What can the citizen do about such matters? It's something I've never clearly understood: what citizens can do.

Things are quiet here. E's book [*For Whom the Bell Tolls*] is being a vast success every way. The movies have just bought it which is nice for him because that way he has financial security for quite a piece. The reviewers know what a fine book it is, which gives me great pleasure. I've been having flu and am trying to finish a book of short stories. When that's done I expect to get started again for *Collier's*. With luck (saying prayers and doing hex magic), perhaps I could get myself shipped to the Burma Road. If not, something, I don't much care: I want to get back into seeing what goes on. It is always easier to see what is going on in a foreign country: one doesn't feel so bitter and so helpless (because you aren't expected to do anything about foreign countries) and one doesn't feel so personally ashamed. If we lend one hundred million to Franco, I bet there are at least one million people who will feel deadly ashamed, and for a long time: and later one hundred million will be able to regret it, the way the English can regret both Spain and Czecho [sic] to their hearts content all during the wakeful bomb-loud nights.

Do you see Edgar Mowrer at all in Washington? He's an absolute wonder, if he turns up and you should see him. He's one of the very best people there is anywhere, with his head screwed on right and his heart clean.

Give greetings to the President and to Tommy, please.

Love always,
Marty

MG to H.G. Wells

October 26, 1940
Sun Valley
Idaho

Wells sweetie,

Where are you? I read your piece in *Colliers* [sic]. It was good. It was full of faith which is a fine way to be and the only happy way I wish you'd be somewhere within reach sometime.

Now a thing has just come up, and maybe you could do something about it. I just heard last night (and don't know how far it has gone) that the U.S.A.

sometimes referred to as the greatest democracy in the world, is planning to lend one hundred million dollars to Franco. It takes one's breath away. It is a neat pile of cash and would, I should think, buy all material necessary to attack and take Gibraltar, and would also be useful in buying those easily shippable light armaments which would fit out the German-organized and efficient Falange Espanol throughout central and south America. You will also recall how little money, late and grudgingly, we have given to China which is fighting a battle of ours (Great Britain's and ours). Aside from the evident point, that such a loan to Franco is deadly dangerous to our two countries, there is another moral point, not to be spat on either. If the US wants to pick up where Chamberlain stopped, appeasing, how is it going to be possible to raise a thrill of honest passion in the hearts of the people, saying: defend democracy boys, but kindly overlook the fact that we are financing a dictatorship which is executing an average of thirty people a day, people who believe in democracy. By God it smells too bad. And speaking of smells, our state department appears to have a faint odor like that delicious scent given off by Chamberlain-Hoare-Laval, the smell-kings of this era.

If there is one hundred million dollars lying around loose why not buy airplanes and send them to England?

Wells, this is really terribly bad: it's the path of evil and whoever is behind this loan ought not to be allowed to get away with it. Can you prod a few people in high places, with warnings and prophesies? If you're in New York, could you telephone Jay Allen at once, or see Edgar Mowrer if you're in Washington. They'd give you any further dope. But it seems to me now is the time for everyone to ask questions, loudly, saying: what are you boys proving, with this money to Franco, and how many examples of the idiocy of appeasing do you need to have, before you stop being crooked and fools?

I'm finishing a book of short stories (with difficulty) and then going to NY on Nov 15. After that thank God I shall start working again, rushing off somewhere for *Colliers* [sic]. But oh my and oh man, there is work to do in this country: we've got plenty of worms in the core right at home. Only they don't get noticed.

Otherwise, everything is the same as when I last saw you. I thought you [sic] all the time and wondered about your house and if it would be standing and hoping you were okay and imagining you would be, on account of I do not think you would ever be very impressed by danger and your country is showing up wonderfully now, the best it has in ten years. If they blow up the houses, worse things have happened.

How's Moura? Where and when will I see you, do you suppose?

Much love as always from your devoted henchman,

Stooge

October 29 or 30, 1940
Sun Valley
Idaho

Dear Charlie,

Do you want to publish me or was that talk. The reason is I have decided (in any case) to tell Charles Duell farewell. I have no contract with him, and after much discussion E and I decided that one couldn't go on publishing with a guy just because you didn't want to hurt his feelings by leaving. I think Charles did whatever he could, but it doesn't seem to work for me anyhow and it is pretty bloody awful damn gloomy to work so hard on writing and then when a book is published it is more like putting the book in a vault than putting it on sale. It isn't money either (he gave me a very decent advance): it is the depressingness [sic] of writing into a void. I feel anyhow so sort of shaky and uncertain that the prospect of putting one more book in a vault (my fourth) is really a little more than I can bear.

The book I am doing now is short stories and short stories are note very sale-able [sic], as I have heard. But (this sounds very pitiful) what I would like is to go into a bookstore anywhere and actually be able to buy one of my own books, if I ever wanted to. They always had very good reviews, and specially so for the second book, but you could literally never find a copy in a store, which—you will admit—is sort of unhappy for an author. Possibly this is too much to expect, and I should gladly wait until I have written ten books before I can reasonably hope to find any of my works for sale, but right now I am a little weary of the slowness of time.

Anyhow the present opus is ten stories of which four long ones are new. One of the new ones is almost a novelette in length. E says they are good stories. I think they are. They aren't scrapings off a bottom desk drawer anyhow: they're the best short stories I could do.

If you are interested I can send you the contents and later the mss. I am working on the last story, but expect to be finished in ten days or so.

I cannot go to the Burma Road because *Colliers* [sic] has already sent someone else. If one is never around and never ready to go anywhere, one must expect to lose the goodest [sic] jobs. It has been a very bad disappointment as I have been wanting to go for months and dreaming of it and planning it in my mind and looking forward to it with joy and a great deal of hope, and now that is out, so I will take anything they give me and be very grateful to have work.

E is out duck shooting and the weather has changed and become clear and cold and good, after a long raininess [sic]. The duck shooting is apparently very good.

I think he is rested and well and happy. The children are absolutely lovely, and I think Mousie (the 12 year old) is about the best company in the world. There is no other news from here. We will be in NY by Nov 20 surely. It will be lovely to see you Charlie.

Always,
Martha

MG to Hortense Flexner   October 30, 1940
Sun Valley
Idaho

Hello Teechie darling,

I have just been out riding, for the first time since the flu started almost two weeks ago. I feel pink and shaken up and fine. The high hills are covered with a grey frozen snow, very thin and cold looking and the sky is made permanently of asbestos roofing.

Then I came home and found your letter and I love your letters Teechie and maybe you don't know what you and Wyncie are to me. I could tell you all right but I am always a little scared of telling. You're *my* friends. It is very lovely to have had you all my life for myself, for no reason I could ever see and not because I deserved it you were my friends, just like that, for me. It has always been good and happy and safe for me, and as I have been and often am and probably always will be quite lonely a great deal of the time, the knowledge of having you, and getting the letters, is something I very much count on. That's the selfish part. The other part is that I admire both of you, what you are, what you stand for and the way you never give up goodness for any cheap rewards. I admire also what you have made together, the thing that is the two of you (that's the loveliest finest and last thing people can be and few can ever get there, but you have. My mother and father too. It takes great class and very clean hearts to do something like that.) I hope I never lose you…

I am going to break with Dull, Slum and Pus (Ernest's name for Duell, Sloan and Pearce), because they depress me and I am tired of putting my books in a vault instead of putting them on sale. I believe Charlie Scribner will publish me, anyhow he has said so often enough, so I think I can guarantee that the book [*The Heart of Another*] will appear. Those two ifs being settled I would like to dedicate it to you and Wyncie, if okay with you.

The little girls on the campus who think it is wonderful to have a fine book dedicated to you (and it is wonderful) should however realize that like everything else in life you do not get it for nothing, and tell them to try sticking around with a very fine writer during the two years he is doing a difficult book and then after that they can decide how often they want books dedicated to them. I myself will settle for once, in that I am still a little shattered from the books and there are moments when I find Bug just as goofy now, when it is all over, as he more than frequently was during the writing of it. In any case, it is not an exact bed of thornless roses either to write or to watch writing, and I am always amused at folks's idea that whatever good happens to you in this life is just that much gravy. I never saw anything that came as a gift, except trouble, which one rarely has to work for. Bug is perfectly unaware that he is probably the talk of the town; he is deeply engrossed with duck shooting. We never heard anything about Dotty [Dorothy Parker] writing the movie and she will not do so, or anyhow over Bug's dead body, as he has less feeling for her writing than you have. [Ingrid] Bergman is taller than I am, I crossed on a boat with her. In all cases the movie won't be made until next spring or fall and I hope to Christ that I for one have nothing to do with it. It was mad-making enough just to listen to the deal being settled and gave me nervous indigestion for days. If Greta [Garbo] were a braver actress I think she might do Pilar, without eyelashes, but with all the strength there is in her, unused and never to be used. Averell Harriman who owns this five million dollar dump is asking for a job as assistant cameraman and if we are all going to get sucked into the making of this movie, maybe they will let me take care of the horses…

All the sudden money is just figures on paper, I want nothing really and Bug wants such sunny small things, like a rifle and a pair of binoculars and a new sleeping bag, and thinking very hard I have decided I would like an ice box for the Cuba house, but beyond that we don't want anything really. It will be nice to give hunks of it away and Bug does that better than anyone I know…

Teechie we live in cheap times, that is the worst of them: the dignity of man is getting smeared out. I want to be back with the plain people, who never heard of publicity and are not so busy buttering their bread that they have no time to believe in anything.

Now I have to write to three papers to send subscriptions to a guy I never saw who is in a Canadian concentration camp and also send him some dough, and then a few more letters of that general nature and then it will be time to bathe and drink whiskey.

I love you both dearly.
Gellhorn

Eleanor Roosevelt to MG

November 8, 1940
The White House
Washington

Marty dear,

There is no discussion whatsoever of any loan or the extension of credit to Franco. There was discussion of Red Cross aid—impartially to starving people—but even this has not been carried through because of Franco's present position in the war.

I am glad this campaign is over. I have never known such a vicious one nor such a bitter one. I am not too excited at the thought of four more years of this existence, but I feel that what I want isn't important.

I am going away tomorrow on a lecture trip and will not be back until early December. I will then try to see Mr. Mowrer.

I have just started to read Ernest's book [*For Whom the Bell Tolls*] and I find it fascinating. I am glad to hear the movies have bought it and glad to see the divorce [from Pauline] was granted and nothing harmful was said.

I hope your book of short stories [*The Heart of Another*] comes on well. I am looking forward to it.

I am distressed that you are planning to go off to some other end of the world [China]. Somehow I think it is time for you to think a little of what you mean to other people and how important it is to have you safe.

Affectionately,
Eleanor Roosevelt

MG to Eleanor Roosevelt

November 9, 1940
Sun Valley
Idaho

Dearest Mrs. Roosevelt,

I didn't know how to write you after the election. It seems so odd to send congratulations. Congratulations are for people who win tennis tournaments or something like that. It does not seem right to congratulate you for doing what you have to do and what you can do best; it is like congratulating you for doing your duty, which is surely a curious idea. So maybe the thing to do is say: thank you, the two of you. So then I guess I will just say that. I'll write it all the time, maybe once a month. I think it is going to be a tough four years. Only take care of yourself, somehow, won't you....

This is not my typewriter and I have not dominated it. E is divorced now and we will be getting married very soon. I think Mother will send out those engraved announcement things (such a cute idea after all) and so I will send one to you and I trust you will be very impressed by all the formality. Have you read E's book? [*FWTBT*] It is good. A lot of people say so, in reviews, without knowing why: but it is a fine book anyhow, despite their dopey sort of praise.

I love you very much and thank you very much for being where you are and I hope the four years are not going to be as terrible as they probably are going to be.

Love again,
Marty

November 9, 1940
RKO Radio Pictures, Inc.
Los Angeles

Dear Marty,

Getting back here depressed us so that I haven't been able to write… we had a swell time with you two [at Sun Valley] and it did us worlds of good. (I often make up little phrases like "worlds of good" I think they make my speech more colorful.)

Nothing much has happened here except that everybody is talking about *For Whom The Bell Tolls*, and the Paramount Deal. [$100k—Hemingway bought the finca, December 1940, for $12,500.]

Scott ([in MG's handwriting] Fitzgerald, writer) called up yesterday to say that he was writing to Ernest about it (a long critique, I gathered) and wanted to know Ernest's address. I told him Sun Valley Lodge…

The tennis raquets are a present for you kiddies, for any occasion that might be suitable…

We worked very hard on the election (and isn't it wonderful and how about brave little Idaho) and spoke over the radio—Dotty beautifully, me in a kind of snarl (I heard a re-broadcast the next day) which appalled me, but which I was assured sounded 'just the way' I always sound. It probably does, too.

We were delighted to hear from you, and we miss you both terribly. Will you give our best to all the pals at Sun Valley ([Lloyd] Arnold sent us some swell pictures of the cabin creek party) and there is much love for both of you from both of us.

MG to Eleanor Roosevelt

December 5, 1940
The Lombardy
New York City

Dearest Mrs. Roosevelt,

I have been wanting to write to you ever since last Thursday's luncheon to tell you how much we both love you (which is nothing newsworthy but just an old settled fact) and to thank you for having given us such a grand time. However, since last Thursday I have scarcely had time to bathe and even now I am dictating a letter, which seems a very odd thing to do to you. As honeymoons go, this one seems to me to have been on the hectic side.

I am going to China, the Phillipines, the Burma Road and surrounding parts for *Collier's*. Ernest will catch up with me in a month or so. We are both very pleased with this assignment. I have never been to the East and since the age of sixteen always hoped I would be able to earn my way there and finally, knowing that I am going to, I have a happy feeling of being a successful earner.

I will be coming down to Washington to get my papers in order about the end of next week or beginning of the week after. Are you going to be there any of that time or is there any other place I could see you?

We saw Harry Hopkins over the weekend at the Harrimans'. (The weekend was something of an experience for a country girl like myself, being as there were 50 house guests and I had the frightened impression of having landed in a handsome railway station where everybody else knew everybody else!) Harry, I thought, looked much better than last summer in Washington and he was, as he always is, perfectly grand and he and Ernest are great buddies which makes me very happy.

We also saw young Franklin at lunch last week and were unable to have dinner one night when he and Ethel very sweetly invited us. He seemed in awfully good shape, entrancing, jolly, and bursting with his usual confidence. I think he has a talent for being happy, which is a very great talent indeed.

Haven't seen Hick, but mean to as soon as things get a little quieter here.

Regards to Tommy.
Love always,
Marty

What a *horrible* letter.
Love, M.

President Franklin D. Roosevelt, on behalf of MG   December 18, 1940
The White House
Washington

To All American Foreign Service Officers,

The bearer of this note, Mrs. Martha Gellhorn Hemingway, is an old friend of Mrs. Roosevelt and mine. For a period of five months or so, Mrs. Hemingway will visit the Far East. Her purpose is to secure material for publication by one of our weekly magazines.

I will appreciate it if you will kindly give her every assistance.

Very sincerely yours,
Franklin Delano Roosevelt

MG to Eleanor Roosevelt   December 27, 1940
Finca Vigía
San Francisco de Paula

Dearest Mrs. R,

Will you give this letter to the President. I still don't know how you address an envelope to him. It is a bum little letter but I don't know how to thank either of you for all the good and wonderful things you do for me. I am very conscious of not deserving anything, and then I stand around and receive such blessings. Maybe if one is just not too lousy a citizen it is the only thing one can do for either of you. That and love you.

It is heaven to be home. I had of course forgotten, as I always do, how lovely and fine and solid it is to be in your own house, and I had forgotten also what a dream house it is and how handsome the land is. So I came home as if I were coming for the first time, and I am homesick for this place already and wishing that I was staying here to watch the trees grow, instead of jaunting off to the Orient, to see what the Japanese are up to. The children are here and I love them very much and it makes me happy and humble to see that they love me too: and they think of this house as their home and they own Cuba and we are all together as comfortable and safe and happy as if we had lived together all our lives. What is wrong with New York is that there are too many people and too little time, but here that is not true. There is no one and the days are long and Ernest and I belong very tightly to each other and we are a good pair and the only thing that mixes us up is rushing around and having engagements. So now we settle down, for this one short week and do not speak of its only being a week, and are having a proper honeymoon here at home.

He is absolutely angelic saying "Mrs. Hemingway" at every opportunity, and we are both crazy about being married and we will have a fine time in the East, but we will be glad to come back her [sic] and handle the momentous problems of the roof and the water pump and the vegetable garden and the pigeons. We are careful not to be bad, having so much luck and happiness and now even money: but I think that if we always take care of the people we know, and get jobs for them and give away the money, then it is allright [sic]. Allright for a while anyhow, because life is not forever and one should not be ungrateful to the Lord either, and if you get a lot of blessings you should take time to enjoy them while you have them.

I am writing Mrs. Rawlings now (she wrote *The Yearling*) and asking her to write Tommy about good places for you in Florida. She ought to know: she is a great Florida specialist, and she herself has the loveliest beach place I have seen in this country. She'd give it to you like a shot, but it is too small for four, only really comfortable for two to live in, but maybe she can find you a good one nearby.

We are buying this house on Saturday, and so, after 1944 [the presumed end of FDR's administration and therefore Eleanor's duties as First Lady], you can have it, and by then everything will work like a clock. It is awful to have to wait until 1944 before I can offer you anything.

All love, as you know. Take care of yourself *please*. I can't bear to think of you working at your desk until three in the morning.

And good luck, all the luck there is.

Always,
Marty

Charles Colebaugh, on behalf of MG

December 30, 1940
New York City

To whom it may concern,

The bearer of this letter, Miss Martha Gellhorn, is a member of the writing staff of *Collier's*, The National Weekly. She is engaged in collecting material for a series of articles to be printed by *Collier's* and any courtesies extended to her will be greatly appreciated.

Yours very truly,
Charles Colebaugh
Managing Editor

CC;dw

SEVEN

Mr. Ma's Tigers

"I would really have been a very something man,
and as a woman I am truly only a nuisance…
and will never be really satisfied or really used up."

—Martha Gellhorn, letter to Hortense Flexner

In early January 1941, Gellhorn and Hemingway set out for Hawaii by ship after meeting with Ingrid Bergman in San Francisco to gauge her interest in playing Maria in *For Whom the Bell Tolls* (the highest grossing film of 1943), opposite Gary Cooper as Robert Jordan. Their sea voyage aboard the *Matsonia* "lasted roughly forever." In a letter to Edna in February, Martha wrote of their reception in Honolulu, "There were finally eighteen leis on each of our necks," provoking Hemingway's ire. He said, "I never had no filthy Christed flowers around my neck before and the next son of a bitch who touches me I am going to cool him and what a dung heap we came to and by Christ if anybody else says aloha to me I am going to spit back in his mouth."

They flew from Honolulu to Hong Kong, where Ernest snarked to the local cronies, "M. is going off to take the pulse of the nation." She traveled without him along the Burma Road but he joined her other excursions led by their enthusiastic, but rather inept, guide Mr. Ma, who insisted the scorched hills they saw were "burned to clear out tigers. Tigers eat a certain sort of tender roots." With him they visited a remote Chinese airfield built by hand by 100,000 soldiers in only 100 days, wiry men who stomped the gravel barefoot. On that same excursion on March 30th, Gellhorn recorded in her tiny reporter's notebook "E. took picture of old man covered in raffia cloak—appears he was secret agent returning from front. E's horse fell on him." Those prompts became an amusing anecdote fleshed into an engaging narrative in "Mr. Ma's Tigers," one of the chapters of the "horror journeys" Gellhorn wrote about in *Travels with Myself and Another*.

Hemingway traveled back to their home in Cuba by clipper, a long-range flying boat, a couple of weeks ahead of Martha, leaving her letters along the way in Manila and Honolulu. Many of those letters reveal how much he missed her, being "so homesick lonesome for you that it is like being dead and in limbo" and insisting, "it is lovely fun with you. Even in the worst circystances [sic]." On May 2nd, he recounted one horrible flight from Kunming where, because of storms, passengers vomited, most of them never bothering "to fool with the paper sack but just let everything go." He was glad "poor Bongie [Martha] wasn't there," because it would have been too much for her to stomach. From Manila on May 7th Hemingway mentioned the jade gifts he bought to send to Edna and to Eleanor Roosevelt, as well as some writing he did in Hong Kong and brought out in his shoe because he did not "want to bother with a censor."

He also bellyached about the fame attached to him as a result of the meteoric success of *For Whom the Bell Tolls*, that had sold half a million copies in the first six months: "if anybody ever speaks to me about that book again (It's a poem. It's like Walt Whitman. It belongs to the Ages.) or even mentions that book I will go nuts." Riled up in early May, he insisted that Gellhorn never wish that any of her books would have similar success because "the government takes the money and you get the shit." He closed, "I would tell you how much and how I love you my beautiful chickley [sic] but do not wish to have censor impound letter as a human document."

Leaving the island of Midway on May 17th he wrote in solidarity, "I dont [sic] drink to try to make it up to you for not smokeing [sic]." By her own account Gellhorn enjoyed cigarettes as much as a restorative sleep. Ernest bought his "beloved Pickly" a gift of little lapis lazuli animals and left them for her in Hawaii to take with her as good luck charms to chaperone her home to him "across the Pacific safely." He wrote from Honolulu on May 18th the imperative that "you and I must *not* get fucked up with this present *goofy* war set up… we owe it to each other and our childies [sic] and Mother [Edna] and the Holy Ghost to A. get in shape and B. do some sound refresher work at our trades of writing." After five months away from her "beautiful bolt hole" that the Finca Vigía was, it is easy to see that Gellhorn would welcome time there to rest, recover and write and be with her love. In his final letter *en route*, a whopping 13 pages long, Hemingway enumerated some of the ways he loved Gellhorn: "like Mr. Roosevelt loves his place in history… like Giggy [son Gregory] loves to win; like Mouse [son Patrick] loves me… like Mrs. Chiang Kai Chek loves being Mrs. Chiang Kai Chek… like the sea loves the beach and rolls on it all the time."

Decades later Gellhorn would write that she had known how dangerous plane jaunts in China were, "how ice looked as it formed on the wings and the way the plane swayed and sideslipped over the unseen mountains, and dawn when the mountains showed themselves like teeth, and roaring down between the walls of the gorge to land on a narrow strip beside the river at Chunking." Those tired planes seemed "like people themselves, so battered, so separate, so depended on and cherished," spaces where she met passengers "who had so little hope and so much fear that they seemed not like people, but like painted or written symbols of how humanity can be reduced." With regret she admitted that her China articles had not been entirely candid: "They did not say all I thought, and nothing of what I felt... I had been included, twice, in luncheon parties given by the Chiangs. They struck me as the two most determined people I had met in my life. Their will to power was a thing like stone; it was a solid separate object which you felt in the room. They were also immensely intelligent, gracious and I thought inhuman." As a result, she "never again accepted hampering hospitality." Despite the hardships and danger, after her return stateside Gellhorn wrote to a friend, "I love the life of the wandering journalist very much."

That fall, Scribner's published her book of stories, *The Heart of Another*. Hemingway snapped the photograph that appeared on the book's dust jacket, which Gellhorn told editor Max Perkins made her look "Isadora Duncanish... with masses of wild hair and an expression of combined bewilderment and sunstroke."

1941

Eleanor Roosevelt to MG

January 6, 1941
The White House
Washington

Dear Marty,

I think of you now with your mother getting ready to leave, and I am glad you had the time in Cuba and that all was so perfect. I hope you will find when you get started that you will be happy in your work and get through it so that you will be very glad to have Ernest join you when he can. I confess I think of you with a great many prayers and a good deal of trepidation and will welcome you back with open arms.

I hope the letters will be useful and every best wish of mine will be with you on the way.

Affectionately,
Eleanor R

Eleanor Roosevelt to MG

January 24, 1941
The White House
Washington

Marty dear,

There are some slight complications about getting an agreement in exchange for food. I have no idea that anything was being given to Spain except milk for babies and mothers and vitamins and medical supplies, just as is being sent to unoccupied France.

We cannot bring any people out on the ships that take over Red Cross supplies without legislation to permit it and there seems to be doubt that we can get that legislation out of Congress.

We are making representations on the subject of prisoners do not think any loans are being made to Franco. At least any time I ask about it, I am assured that nothing is being done, nor do I understand that wheat is being sent.

Your mother wrote me a sweet letter about the two perfect weeks she had had with you in St. Louis. I am so glad that you and Ernest are going together [to China]. I would have worried about your going alone.

Best of luck to you both and may you have a happy and safe trip.

Much love,
Eleanor R.

Charles Colebaugh was Gellhorn's longtime editor at *Collier's*, who would betray her in a way when he accepted Hemingway's offer to become the magazine's foreign correspondent in May 1944, when he decided that he would report on the war, something that Gellhorn had encouraged him to do and something that she had been doing herself since *Collier's* sent her to Finland in November 1939.

MG to Charles Colebaugh

March 1, 1941
Hong Kong

Dear Charles,

Hongkong [sic] is the busiest place I have ever been in. So now I will write you very quickly in order to get this off on the Mar 2 Clipper, and tell you about my works and acts.

1. I returned yesterday from Lashio. Lashio is at the Burma end of the Burma Road. It takes about seven days in a passenger car if all goes well to drive from

Kunming to Lashio, and the plane trip is three hours… We came into Kunming as soon as possible after the Japs left and the town was burning and we flew over it and saw the smash-up. Our pilot, an ex Indiana boy, was the personal pilot of the Generalissimo and Madame [Chiang] and flew them out of Siam when the Generalissimo was kidnapped. He is a very nice boy who makes puns all the time; he is the damndest aviator I ever saw. Point is: I am doing a story on this line [China National Aviation Corporation], how it works, who flies it, what it means and it is such color as I have not seen for sometime. I think you will like this story very much. I am getting pictures. There is a famous citizen named Newsreel Wong and I have bought three pictures from him.

2. Remember Press Wireless, which I used from Amsterdam? They function out of Manila and their rates are 4 and ½ cents a word which is nice. When I wire stories will try to use them, but you remember you have to keep in touch with them in New York because they have a tendency to hold copy in NY and not let you know at once.

3. We have been keeping very close tabs on the Singapore end… the local authorities, both US and GB feel nothing is apt to happen for four to six weeks. They think the Japs will want to wait until they see how things go with the Germans. On the other hand, everyone agrees that the Japs are not reasonable therefore not predictable.

4. There is a very good story right here. It is Hongkong [sic]. I don't know quite how to describe it to you, though you will see when it is an article. The city is jammed, half a million extra Chinese refugees. It is rich, and rare and startling and complicated.

5. With our military attaché, E and I are arranging to get front passes to the Chinese war… This is a non-Communist front. It will be very remarkable to get there and some trip I fancy, from the slight bit of travelling I have done. The Japs very evidently hoped that there would be a civil war in these parts between Chiang and the Communists, but the civil war did not come off…

So, if nothing blows up sooner to the south, we will be here for 2-3 weeks, then the front in China for 2 weeks if passes come through as planned, then we will head out in the direction of Indo China and Singapore.

Hope all of this letter meets with your approval. Have never been happier in my life (aside from the fact that I picked up some kind of a throat and can't swallow but what the hell.)

Hope all is well with you. Love and kisses,
Martha

Gellhorn met drama critic and Algonquin Round Table member Alexander
Woollcott at the White House in 1935 where they both stayed for a time, Woollcott
recovering from abdominal surgery, but witty company nonetheless.

MG to Alexander Woollcott   March 8, 1941
                                                            Hong Kong

Mr. Woollcott darling,

I would do almost anything to oblige you, but please do not make me return
at once from China… I wonder why you are not here. I thought you were going
to pop up from behind a malarial bush on the Burma Road? And where are you?
Rotting in America when you could be out here, racketing about like a loony.

… Life is awful jolly and I have never been happier, only a little weary. Ernest
goes about really learning something about the country, and I go about dazed
and open-mouthed, just seeing things and not having an idea what anything
means or might prove. He has a good friend named General Cohen, who used
to be Mr. Sun Yat Sen's bodyguard and who looks like a gentle retired thug.
He was born on the wrong side of the tracks in London, and addresses me as
Moddom [sic] and I love him. Ernest also drank snake wine (with a snake right
there in the bottom of the jug) while out on the town with a policeman. I have
done nothing so drastic. I am just trying to keep some pieces of my liver, for
future use. Whiskey is so cheap here that we do not see how they can afford to
sell it, they ought to give it away.

I wish you were here. You would like it very much indeed. Nothing is at all
like anything else. Everything smells terrific. Someone once described the citizens
of this country (in a moment of genius) as China's teeming millions. My theory
is that they have children every six months, being smarter than other people, and
liking to keep up the population. I have not yet seen anything at all like any of the
books I ever read…

I miss you anyhow. Take care of yourself. Are you back in residence at the
White House. They will have to put up another plaque in the Proclamation of
Emancipation room, saying: Alexander Woollcott gives breakfast parties here, when
in residence. What do you want me to bring you back from here. Just name it.

Much love from your old White House classmate,
Gellhorn

MG to Allen Grover

June 2, 1941
Finca Vigía
San Francisco de Paula

Allen petsy,

You wanted a jade ring and you are getting one. Ernest found it. I looked at jade all over Hong Kong and was absolutely revolted by the going modern bright green rings which looked as though they had been made for export to Woolworth's. This ring is several thousand years old, the only kind of jade the Chinese themselves will even bother to spit on, having turned brown due to being buried.

It must have been stolen from some working man's tomb. What it actually is is an archer's ring. They wore them over the thumb and used the ring itself to pluck the bowstring. It occurs to me that times were better when the infantry went out armed with bow and arrow and arrows and a jade ring. I hope you will like it.

… I am not nuts for the spectacle of this country marching as to war, without the faintest idea of what it takes to make war or what war means. As this dreary realistic approach is extremely unfashionable I am glad to be leaving. Having now attended my fourth war briefly, I am god-damned [sic] sick of it just when the whole subject is becoming frightfully popular.

Anyhow, I hope you can use your influence and the influence of your publications to see that when we do get into this war our army, navy and airforce will be commanded by our own people and not by those shockingly incompetent Limeys.

Love,
Marty

MG to Eleanor Roosevelt

June 3, 1941
Finca Vigía
San Francisco de Paula

Dear Mrs. Roosevelt,

I am sending you a souvenir from China. Ernest found it, having made friends with a jade collector like the smart boy he is. It is a piece of very old buried jade (that's why it looks as if it were stained with tobacco juice) thousands of years old and the only color the Chinese take seriously. I haven't the faintest idea what you can do with it, but it is lovely to look at and feels fine in the hand and in all cases it comes with our love.

I will write you a long letter once I get back to Cuba and catch my breath. *There is really too much to talk about, though, for letters.*

Always devotedly,
Martha

Eleanor Roosevelt to MG

June 10, 1941
The White House
Washington

Dear Marty,

It was good of you and Ernest to send me that lovely piece of old Chinese jade and to say that I am delighted with it is putting it mildly. I am grateful to you both.

I am so disappointed to have missed you this trip. I am very anxious to see and talk with you and I hope your next visit will not be long delayed.

Affectionately,
Eleanor Roosevelt

MG to Hortense Flexner

June 18 or 19 probably, 1941
Finca Vigía
San Francisco de Paula

Teechie dearest,

I hope you and Wyncie will like the title of your book. I have just now found it. It is *The Heart of Another*. From your pal Dostoyevsky, you know, "The heart of another is a dark forest." [Also in a letter from Pauline Pfeiffer] I feel at once exultant and ashamed, since nothing I could write would ever be as good as that, and still that is what all the stories are about. Coming back after four months, and never having thought of them all this time, I began to reread the stories. You know I am never confident or happy about anything I write. And suddenly there they were, and I found them better than I knew how to write, and good, good, good, and not dull (which is what I always fear), and lean, and full of things that I did not know I knew. It is really better written than *A Stricken Field* and so I have that happiness of *seeing* it get better. I shall go over it, as soon as I finish this last article, the Singapore one, and eliminate the commas which I throw around as if they were seeds.

I am full of brag this evening. I never reread *A Stricken Field*, either. Last night I began to look at it. I saw everything wrong with it, in sentence forms, and construction of plot, and still damn all it is solid Teechie and that is what we are working for. So maybe I can write ten solid books, which no one will ever read, and then I will always have that to keep me warm during the winters.

I have been working terrible hard. The trip was no lark in itself, and writing the four articles was a something. Then I came back (with the children here too) and had an awful lot of house horror and still have gotten out the Netherlands Indies article, which is the best of the trip, and now am doing my daily seven hours at the last article. If my head weren't so tired, I think it would feel quite nice and lean and muscular. But as it is, I am a little punch drunk and longing for some kind of rest. Then we never have a dreary minute anyhow, what with E's pals. We have had an invasion of drunks. The one now remaining, Mr. Josie who owns Sloppy Joe's Bar in Key West and is an old toothless darling, completed seven days of non-eating and steady brandy drinking by getting hauled to the hospital and having a gangrenous hemorrhoid removed. So today, between writing the article, I have seen the doctor and called on Josie, as Ernest was not home. I had to convince Josie that something had not been put over on him, and get them to give him some extra morphine for his pain.

I hope you are better; I hope you are well. Do you know that Alfie [brother Alfred Gellhorn] works with a Dr. Flexner who is maybe your nephew or something. Isn't it sweet, like a full circle. And also little Alfie has a baby named Martha, thus beating me to the draw. No reason for me to bother now. Easier to be an aunt than a mother, any day of the week.

At this point, they are getting the Louis-Conn fight on the new Capeheart. So I have to go and listen not that I give a damn. The children are staying up for the occasion; the night is hotter than can be believed; they have been out spear fishing on a reef in the ocean and really should sleep; I am so tired I feel as if my feet were heavy enough to anchor the *Normandie* and my back is made of a rusty iron fence: but we will all be excited about the Louis-Conn fight anyhow.

I hope you will like your book when it is all done. I am feeling very happy about it. It will be out in October.

All my love little monster.

Always,
Gellhorn

MG to Charles Scribner

June 21, 1941
Finca Vigía
San Francisco de Paula

Dear Charlie,

We are in such a sad and unhappy state here that I really do not know what to do. Mr. Josie died of a stroke yesterday afternoon, and he came for his vacation. It was such a pitifully useless death (and maybe every death is, except when people are so old that they have died already). It is unbearable to think about it. It is worse than anything anyone could have written. It does not even seem real. No, that is not true. It is real. That is why it cannot be thought about, and why now—since there is nothing to do today—I am just wandering about looking for some way of keeping busy.

So as I must write you anyhow a business letter perhaps the thing to do is concentrate and write it. I sent in the title for my book by wire to Max. He has probably told you of it. It is an awful good title I think (not being any great champ of titles myself, this one seems a pure Act of God).

Now the business part. Maybe if I number everything I will remember it better.

1. Please Charlie, when doing advertising, keep the journalist business out of it. That cooked my last book. They said, ah-ha, it isn't fiction because after all she is a journalist. So please skip that journalist business *entirely* and simply say that I have written two other books. This is very important. Also Ernest wants to see and approve the blurb and initial advertising, so please send it on. The reason is this journalist business. It would be an awful thing to go through life as *Collier's* "Blue Eyed Blonde from Missouri."

2. Please use a normal size type for the dedication. I loved that Neon sign you put in Ernest's book, but don't want it in this one.

3. About money, the $1000 advance and 15% royalty and whatever else you and Ernest discussed is fine and if you send a contract will send it back right away signed.

4. If you want a picture, do you want that one of me at the edge of the pool, looking healthy with a tennis racket. If so, have you a copy. If not, will get you one. Or do you want a more solemn picture.

5. Please send me the galleys bound, the way you sent Ernest's last set. Much less pooping to go over.

6. I will return the manuscript this week, but want to ask Ernest's advice about the table of contents and now is no time to ask.

Can't think of any more business. Wish I could. Will now work over manuscript again. That keeps people very busy.

How are you Charlie. Max said you had neuralgia or something. I hope you are okay. You've probably been drinking too much haven't you? Seems everyone does. Hope not. Do be sensible. It is a fairly hard thing to be sensible, I guess, living in such an unsensible world as we do.

Was going to write you a jolly long letter about everything here but don't feel like it. We were very happy until yesterday. It was so lovely to be home and finished with that filthy Orient. The house and the place are beautiful and the children are a delight. Can stand anything about living but cannot bear death, and am so sorry for Mr. Josie who was really crazy about being alive.

Well that is all for now. Will write again some other day. I hope you are getting good and well, and have no pain of any kind. Please take care of yourself.

Always,
Martha

MG to Allen Grover

July 1941
Finca Vigía
San Francisco de Paula

Allen darling,

I dictated a letter to you when I was in New York, at the beginning of June. I was there for two days, submerged by suitcases and conversations of a business nature with *Collier's*. I did not even try to call you because there was no time, and besides I was too gloomy to be any gift. Am still gloomy.

So. And how are you? China was awful in case you want to know. So was the whole Orient. I do not feel cosy in places where the poor literally never straighten their backs, and seem to be born, live and die in the mud. The wage scales sadden me… Then too I don't like the English. If you are not nuts for the English in England, you are close to vomiting over the English in the Orient. Also there is so much shit written in our business that finally you feel very ashamed: you cannot write the straight truth because people resent it, and are conditioned not to believe it. So, finally, you write a certain amount of evasion yourself, carefully skirting the definitely dung features of journalism. You know how it goes. Madame Chiang that great woman and savior of China. Well, balls. Madame Chiang is the Clare Boothe of Cathay, different coloring, different set of circumstances. Perhaps more health and energy. But far far far from Joan of Arc.

I cannot write you about the war. Maybe you know what you think. I certainly don't. But it is far worse not to know what to believe. It only seems to me that this war to save democracy (this second war) is going to finish democracy for good and all, win lose or draw. I can only see that as usual the innocent and ignorant get it in the neck. I definitely do *not* believe that England is the perfect standard bearer, any more than I believe that the Nazis are human beings and capable of living in a world of men. You might tell me what you are tying on to, in these so-called troubled times, so as not to have such a disgust in your heart that you can scarcely bear to think or read…

Do write me.
Love,
M

Eleanor Roosevelt to MG

September 15, 1941
The White House
Washington

Marty dear,

I was glad to get your letter of August 20 and would have written sooner except life has been busier than usual…

As you probably know, the President's mother died September 7th, very peacefully and suddenly. She had not been very well all summer and I think we all feel she would have hated to go on living as an invalid.

At the moment my brother [Hall, died September 25th] is really seriously ill and I am staying in Washington until I know the outcome.

Three of my boys have all been off on more or less hazardous trips and Johnny is about to leave for San Diego for his Navy duty. At the moment they are all safely in the United States…

I am going to work regularly with the Volunteer Service in National Defense that was appointed by Mayor LaGuardia. I have been in touch with what is being done and I hope I can give the program a push, as it is not moving very fast and a lot of people are getting impatient.

When are you coming up here? Do let me know ahead, as I surely want to see you.

My kindest regards to Ernest and much love to you.

Affectionately,
Eleanor Roosevelt

MG to Hortense Flexner

September 22, 1941
Finca Vigía
San Francisco de Paula

Teechie dearest,

I forgot to write or wire the President about his mother's death and I will have to do something now, too late, and it is very grim and I cannot yet face it. So will write to you. As I have a honey of a HANGover [sic], one of the real ones, with burning stomach, the shakes and all, I think I may wait a bit before writing to the President expressing sympathy over the death of that old lady who he must have loved since she was his mother, but surely there was not a goddam [sic] thing about her that any outsider would work himself up into a frenzy about.

I am living here in bachelor splendor and though it sounds very disloyal, I was a bachelor for a hell of a long time and it is a thing that I understand and no one on earth appreciates it more fully, my Christ how I enjoy myself. So lately I have been out on the town with the boys, drunk as a goat I may say in passing and dancing until six in the morning. When you are married you do not do such things because you can never stay awake and maybe you don't both like to dance. I go out only with the Basque pelotaris, who combine—to me—those beauties which the Greeks wrote about, with a simple direct and comic mentality that keeps me absolutely shaken with mirth. They have no shame, which is the first sign of honest people, and their language is at once so clear and so brutal that anything you say in it gives you an electric shock.

... I know what I want: I want a life with people that is almost explosive in its excitement, fierce and hard and laughing and loud and gay as all hell let loose, and the rest of the time, I want them bloody damn well not to get any place near me, I want to be alone and do my work and my thinking by myself and let them kindly not come to call.

It is, Teecher, a grave but not important error that I happen to be a woman. I do not think that history will, shall we say, suffer: that mass destinies will be altered and blackened because of this. But, on the other hand, what a waste. I would really have been a very something man, and as a woman I am truly only a nuisance, only a problem, only something that most definitely does not belong anywhere and will never be really satisfied or really used up.

So, to my permanent disgust, I am not a man, and if I am a woman I am going to make the most of it and not let this biological accident hamper me any more than is necessary. I can resign myself to anything on earth except dullness, and I do not want to be good. Good is my idea of what very measly people are, since they cannot be anything better. I wish to be hell on wheels, or dead. And the only serious complaint I have about matrimony is that it brings out the faint goodness in me, and has a tendency to soften and quiet the hell on wheels aspect, and finally I become bored with myself. Only a fool would prefer to be actively, achingly, dangerously unhappy, rather than bored: and I am that class of fool.

This is ever more odd because my man is another hell on wheels character, and what is so christed odd is that two people cannot live together, with any order or health, if they are both hell on wheels, so for the mutual good, and the sake of the party, they must both calm themselves. And that is a loss, but I have not yet found out what to do about it. Ernest and I, really are afraid of each other, each one knowing that the other is the most violent person either one knows, and knowing something about violence we are always mutually alarmed at the potentialities of the other. So, we are together we take it fairly easy, so as not to see the other burst into loud furious flame.

The other night, before I started on this wonderful epock [sic] of drunkenness, laughter and dancing, I was home here being decent and elegant and all the rest. So that night, the quiet night, impressed by Brahms which was playing on the Capeheart, I started to write memoirs, addressing them to you, since I can always talk to you. (And, in fact, what do you know of these things: and in fact, what is so wonderful is that you do not need to know, and I think that is the greatest talent of all.) But the memoirs cooled off, because I knew what I was doing; and if there are any rests left, on paper, of my life, they will have to be like this, disjointed and uncertain, done for no reason, and put in an envelope to mail. I cannot do the other.

E is at Sun Valley and I will leave here October 2 and spend about 10 days in St Louis seeing Mother and doing dentistry and then I will go there too. I hate it like holy hell. It is the west in an ornamental sanitary package. But maybe by that time I will need sanitation and anyhow I am going, because that is my job. I am an old woman now (33 in November) and unregenerate and in my heart still as curious and generally angry and anxious for trouble as when I was young. But I will have to get over that. There is no sense in allowing one's own arrested adolescence to become a problem for the general public.

I love you. Have a hell of a good time. I don't really know what else is worth having.

Always,
Gellhorn

MG to Eleanor Roosevelt

September 23, 1941
Finca Vigía
San Francisco de Paula

Dearest Mrs. R,

I have been thinking all the time how to write the President and I can't do it. It is an impertinence anyhow to write to somebody when their mother or father dies, because there isn't anything you can say that will be comforting and you haven't a right anyhow to try to be comforting. So I don't know, will you just please tell him I am sorry for him and I can imagine how awful it is and I hope he can get a little rest. And give him my love, please.

You never really believe anyone you love will die. It is a strange thing, considering how long it has been going on, that no one can ever get used to it. I know when my father died, I thought it surely could not be true *ever*, and I didn't want anybody to talk to me about it.

And you, poor darling, you must be very tired and I wish there were something I could do for you, except love you, which I do, steadily, at this great distance.

Always,
Marty

Eleanor Roosevelt to MG

October 1, 1941
The White House
Washington

Dear Marty,

I gave your letter to the President and he asked me to tell you how much he appreciated your thinking of him.

We are all constituted differently, and kind messages help some of us bear sorrow. I think I agree with you that nothing helps in real sorrow except time and pleasant memories.

My brother Hall died last Thursday after a painful three weeks, so we have had an upsetting month. My mother-in-law was eighty-seven and she had a grand life, full of rich experiences. Hall was just fifty-one and could have had much more out of life.

I am starting as Assistant Director for Volunteer Services in Civilian Defense under Mayor LaGuardia. I am to do my best at organizing all the men, women and children who want to volunteer. It is under the federal government and the machinery needs speeding up. I expect to have a good time, although a busy one.

If you love me and think of me at any distance I will be happy. Do let me know when you are coming to the United States.

Much love,
Eleanor R.

Mrs. Ernest Hemingway
San Francisco de Paula, Cuba

The Heart of Another, Gellhorn's collection of nine stories, was the first of three books of hers edited by the legendary Maxwell Perkins. The review in the *Chicago Tribune* noted that each tale was "vibrant with a deep and intense emotion," and that Gellhorn was incisive and shied away "from anything remotely connected with sentiment." The next two books, her novels *Liana* and *The Wine of Astonishment*, would surely have been followed by others in his care had Perkins not died unexpectedly in June 1947.[13]

MG to Maxwell Perkins

October 17, 1941
Sun Valley Lodge
Idaho

Dear Max,

I think the book [*The Heart of Another*] is *beautiful*. I never saw one that looked so fine, and we are all enchanted with it, and I treat it as if it were some marvelous piece of decoration, a thing to stand on a table and look at. The cover is far better than any of the books I have seen recently and the book itself, the cloth cover and the print, is a joy. Ernest thinks so too and so does everyone who has seen it.

Now maybe some critics will like it and maybe they won't... I always envied Ernest when a book came in, because it made him so happy, and when mine came in I just generally felt sick, and always disappointed and sort of scared inside and usually regretting the whole thing. But this one, no. I know it is more grown-up than anything I have done before, and I am very surprised to do anything grown up, and therefore full of hope. The weak story is "Slow Train to Garmisch," which brings back that old familiar sick feeling. But I can read the others and could never before read anything of mine in print, could only sort of look at it, and then tell myself I would do better next time. Still, don't get the idea I am just wallowing in smuggery and thinking all is for the best. There is still everything to learn, and everything to do sharper and tighter...

I would rather be a writer than anything else on earth, but I am lazy and there are communal demands on time, and then besides, I feel very troubled in the head and heart. It is as if all the time one was boiling inside with some kind of help-less indignation, enraged to see such a good-looking and possibly decent world always going to hell, and going to hell with such cruelty and waste... I must say I was very disgusted to see that Dos [Passos], at the P.E.N. Congress in London, said that writers should not write now. If a writer has any guts he should write all the time, and the lousier the world the harder a writer should work. For if he can do nothing positive, to make the world more livable or less cruel or stupid, he can at least record truly, and that is something no one else will do, and it is a job that must be done. It is the only revenge that all the bastardized people will ever get: that someone writes down clearly what happened to them...

That *Oxford Companion to American Literature* is a bunch of dung, frankly. Have you seen it? I think it is the Oxford Companion to American Literature for Rotary Clubs who want to know about books without reading. I think it is a shame. There is a whole thing about Ernest in it which is as silly as anything I ever saw, and looks as if it were taken from the blurbs of books or cheap book reviews. And the way he retells the *Bells* in one half paragraph is a marvel of bad writing and taste. This awful condensed culture is one of the horrors of our time, surely...

I must stop maundering on.

Thank you very much for all the trouble you have taken with my book. Please tell Charlie [Scribner] how happy I am about its looks.

Always,
Martha

MG to Eleanor Roosevelt

October 17, 1941
Sun Valley
Idaho

Dearest Mrs. R,

I just got your letter, darling, and I have been thinking about you and thinking what a terrible time you have been having these last months. I suppose you must bury yourself in work and not have much time for yourself, ever, and then anyhow you do not think about yourself hardly at all, so you will get through it. But I wish there was something I could do for you, besides just write you letters and love you.

... I am sending you today the first copy I have of my new book [*The Heart of Another*]. Will you like the book, I wonder? It is the first time I am happy about one of my own books, and that makes me nervous because perhaps if I am happy about it, it is punk. But I never could read what I had written and this time I can, without that awful sick gloom of someone knowing they did not carry it off as intended. I think it is getting more like an iceberg (which is the aim of all good writing): one ninth of it shows, but there truly is eight ninths submerged and you can feel it there. But maybe this is just idiot optimism on my part.

And, you know, it is just a book. It is a book of stories about people. It is for no purpose. And for the first time I feel I did say what I meant, just writing about people, without any special point of view, only wanting to understand them and tell about them as truly as I saw them. So finally, it occurs to me that the human heart is what lasts and what always did and always will last; and maybe the human heart is the proper field of study and the only undeniable concern of writers. Now, with this war, we must all be expedient, as the thing to do is to win. But the war will not matter in the end any more than all the other wars, but what happens to human beings, before during and afterwards, is all that matters. And it is by God not a question of democracy, nor of nations, or of any of those abstract words: it is a question of human lives, and they have names and places where they were born, and jokes and sicknesses and despair and jobs and children and taxes and hopes, and they die: and they are all that matters. Life must be *for* them and *about* them. I think our time is so unspeakably lousy because human beings seem so completely forgotten, and the rules do not consider them, nor the rulers, and the human race seems to be living on sufferance, whereas it should live in full possession of the earth.

That's my politics. I wish I knew who my co-religionaries were, and I wish we could organize. I wish people could stick up for themselves, for the absolutely real and concrete dignity of human life, and nothing else. I am sick to the nausea point of all the idiot things men have been shouting about in their ignorance, one way or the other. The British Empire seems to me as foolish as Nazism is horrible. A country is only good, where life is an honorable, decent, kindly and even exciting experience: where men have dignity, where each man has his dignity and need not scratch or kick people around, to live. The only real reason for this war is to remove, if possible, terribly and finally, a system which makes life as bad as life can possibly be. But that does not mean anything positive; it does not mean life has been made good. It is like cutting out a cancer and leaving a tuberculosis, which need not be fatal and is surely not painful. Still the tuberculosis is there. There will have to be a great deal of work after the war. I am afraid all the good people will be either dead or tired, the way they were after the last war.

Well, here is a very long letter and you cannot have time for very long letters. I love you dearly as always. I wish I could hug you and tell you so.

Always,
Marty

Eleanor Roosevelt to MG

November 10, 1941
The White House
Washington

Dear Marty,

Many thanks for your book [*The Heart of Another*]. I have read it and enjoyed it. One of the stories is perhaps reminiscent of Ernest's style, but three of them are exactly like reading some of your letters. I think perhaps the first one is the one I like the best as far as the writing and depicting what happens inside human beings goes.

I have had so much to put in my column I could not mention the book, but will do so. I hope it is going well.

Anna writes me that they have loved being in Sun Valley with you and that you have been so good to them. They are both very nice people, so I am sure you all had a good time together.

I do not feel as though I would ever be doing anything which is not in some way tied up with work. I am planning in January to spend two days with Anna in Seattle, but I will have to do a certain amount of work at the same time for Civilian Defense. I am ridiculously busy and life certainly was never meant to be lived in this way, but then life was never meant to be lived as it is in the world today.

I do not know whether our way of living has made this world situation inevitable or not. Perhaps what we need to do is to scrap all of our new inventions and settle back into a nice old-fashioned way of living, and then the world would settle down.

If you do come into this part of the world, let me know because I want to see you very much indeed.

Much love,
Eleanor R

MG to Eleanor Roosevelt

November 17, 1941
Sun Valley
Idaho

Dearest Mrs. R,

Your letter came and this morning Anna gave me a copy of your column mentioning *The Heart of Another*. Darling, I am very happy if you liked the book and you did pick out the best story in it to like the most. But *gosh* don't ever get the idea ever ever ever that you have to write about a book of mine in your column. I send it to you because a book's the only real thing of my own that I have to give away, and because I hope you'll read it and like it: but not for any other reason. I'm not a responsibility or an obligation, darling, I'm just your friend who loves you.

But you know, you better not work so much. Nobody can work at the pace you do, all the time. In the end it would just wear you out and it isn't the soundest way to be useful. You aren't made of steel and anyhow even steel has to be cared for. I hate to think of you sitting at your desk there in the White House until those ungodly hours in the morning with your mail, and then getting up at dawn and all the time giving out. You *must* give yourself some time to take in, and absorb rest. It sounds very bossy to be lecturing you this way, but even if you won't consider yourself (which apparently you never do or will), you can just consider objectively that your work will suffer from overwork.

I think this war is going to go on for so long that sooner or later it will seem that it is going on forever.... I would like to kidnap you and take you to the unreal but very lovely peace and quiet of Cuba. You'd have to go slow there. There is no other gait in the whole country.

It seems to me that our own propaganda ought to be definitely oriented into the anti-Nazi rather than pro-British groove. There's too much wrong with the British, before and during the war to make them a wholeproof sales basis. The Nazis on the other hand stink one hundred percent, and a true understanding (not either an hysterical or exaggerated one) of the danger they represent is surely required now. It is curious how little people really know about them: perhaps because everything said about this is said in headlines, not in clear continuous and concentrated form.

If we get into this war, I hope I can get a good outdoor job, with a sane and unconceited outfit, the nearer the war the better. It gives me gooseflesh even to consider what they call the "home front." The home front is evidently very necessary but I'd rather be loading trucks somewhere with the boys, where there is no talk and never any of the big words. Also, do you imagine the world will ever be free of war? I was wondering bitterly the other day what nation would rise up, after the Germans, to spoil the earth?

I love you. I wish you'd take a rest.

Always,
Marty

EIGHT

Messing About in Boats

"There is little enough that one can do to help,
but it makes me sad when it is so hard even to do that little."

—Martha Gellhorn, letter to Eleanor Roosevelt

Gellhorn spent much of 1942 at home in Cuba, living "in the sun, safe and comfortable and hating it." But she had come to know "the changes in the sky, and what the hot rain and the hot drought did to the land, and to one's own mind and body and what they seemed to do to other people." In March, *A Stricken Field* was published to appreciative reviews in England that noted how she brought the refugee problem "vividly to life," one review declaring it "a fine novel and finer propaganda." Another insisted it was a "faithful survey of Nazi-occupied Czechoslovakia" and made "tragic reading."

When she traveled in May and June with Edna for several weeks by car throughout the United States, she wrote long, loving letters to Ernest. America had entered the war after the attack at Pearl Harbor on December 7th, 1941, and there were news broadcasts "of German submarines sinking ships along the eastern seaboard." She decided to report "on this sideshow" for *Collier's.* From mid-July through the end of September, she was on a three-month-long journey in the Caribbean that was "part so-so, part horror, and part magic." She visited interned Nazis in Haiti, the huge American naval and air base in Puerto Rico and the surviving sailors from torpedoed merchant ships, 251 of which had been sunk in the Caribbean alone during 1942. In St. Thomas, she hired a sloop with a motley crew of locals to carry her to other tiny islands, "small green jewels, pinheads," including Tortola, St. Martin and Anguilla. Anguilla was "as far out of the world as you could get," but surviving sailors who had drifted on the sea for three weeks in an open lifeboat had "washed up on shore," and the effect was "dreamlike, fantastic, incredible, as if the sky had rained rocks." Gellhorn later recalled how her "heart rose like a bird at once. It always did incurably, except in rain, as soon as I felt I had fallen off the map."

Back at the Finca Vigía she worked on *Liana*, originally titled *Share of Night, Share of Morning*, lifted from an Emily Dickinson poem. That fall she was in New York to help get 13-year-old Patrick Hemingway ready for school, but she was already impatient to be covering the war in Europe for *Collier's*. It would be almost a year before she was sent to London, holed up with the other foreign correspondents at the Dorchester Hotel in Park Lane in November 1943. While waiting for her travel papers in New York from June through October, her letters to Hemingway are both affectionate and rife with her anticipation of doing real journalism again. She always lived best by Mauriac's maxim, *travail: opium unique*. Work was Gellhorn's opiate.

1942

MG to Alexander Woollcott

January 22, 1942
Finca Vigía
San Francisco de Paula

Dearest Woolkie,

Having a bad pain this morning and I think I will write you for a little while. Is it true you have been ill? I do hope not.

I am not very well myself but that is due to the fact that I got all mixed up and hurried yesterday and forgot to eat after breakfast but on the other hand went to a cocktail party (a feast here that begins at 6:30 p.m. and ends at 4 a.m.) and drank a certain amount. This is my second big party here in five years, and perhaps the fifth party in all. I think I would like to be a philosopher, being as I think such deep thoughts after parties and in fact any time my stomach is distressed.

However, as a philosopher I think parties are really the last refuge of the empty and shriveled brain, and are more destructive to the body than cocaine and more destructive to the spirit than jail…

I went to this party with Bumbi [sic], Ernest's eldest boy who is four days this side of the army. Bumbi is blonde [sic] and very good to look at and 18 and sweet and six feet and one inch tall. (Ernest, canny to the last, put himself to bed before the party with a sore throat; he seems fine today)…

… now I feel hungover and sick in my soul: think of the wasted time of these parties, think of the wasted money; think of people meeting each other day after day, drowned in flowers and martinis, with nothing to say to each other but all talking like parrot cages. I shall not go again anywhere for a year and the horrid effects will wear off.

… I am still writing my story and still happy with it; but this hangover is no condition in which to produce that pure and gemlike literature we like to see. Why don't you ever write to me? You are a sloth not to. Or don't you love me anymore? Have you taken up with a new bride? Please answer.

Ernest sends you regards. I guess you got his story all right for your toilet paper anthology. I wish I saw you sometime. Give Mrs. R [Eleanor Roosevelt] my best love when you see her again.

Always,
Gellhorn

MG to Charles Colebaugh

February 3, 1942
Finca Vigía
San Francisco de Paula

Dear Charles,

As you say, it is really too late to do anything about my sex. That is a handicap I have been struggling under since I was five years old, and I shall just forge ahead, bravely, despite the army. Probably, when anything happens, and we want very very badly (both of us) for me to get there, maybe I can arrange it. No sense fretting in advance, though. I do not observe any note of frenzied haste in your letter: and do not feel any special violent urge to move right now myself. This is going to be a nice long war, and sooner or later they are going to want to make it popular, and then folks like us can work.

Meanwhile, I do my homework, like a little boy getting ready to take West Point entrance exams. It is very instructive. I split the rest of my time between trying to write (which is the soundest occupation I know) and trying to shoot 20 out of 20 live pigeons, flying like hell bats.

I shall be right here and you can reach me any time you want me.

Your devoted servant,
Martha Gellhorn

March 8, 1942
Finca Vigía
San Francisco de Paula

Teecher darling,

Mother is here, very cute and lovely to look at and Scroob says; hell I'd marry Mother any day, she's the finest thing in the family. We have a good time, the three of us, and thus far nothing has broken in the house, neither the electricity nor the plumbing nor nothing. I am holding my breath. It all looks very fine too.

However due to the war and what not a great many people are coming to Cuba this winter which is a fate far worse than death. I certainly hope there develops either malaria or a revolution or something in order to spare us our visitors. I am buying a big chain and padlock to put on the lower gate, and shall also go sentry—go with my shotgun on the front porch. I am myself the enemy of the casual person who drops in. Life is far too short for all that stuff. Alternately I have decided to live in the pump house, or else dig a tunnel from my room so that I can leave quickly as soon as I hear a car coming up the drive. E. is always very nice and civil with people, and he drinks to take the edge off his dismay, and when he has had a certain amount to drink he becomes recklessly friendly and suggests seeing them again. Then I make a cold hating face and begin to whisper, saying: Not me, not me anyhow, I'd rather die. I drink too but it only makes me sad and the whole horror shows up in a dreary alcoholic clarity, and I think of how little time I have left to live and maybe seeing these people again will bring me a bad luck stretch of boredom, and so I sit and smile if anyone speaks to me, with a false dropping smile, and do not hear; unless I hear Ernest saying, well, on Friday we might…

All this is very secret and I would get hell for writing it but it is very funny too, so I shall tell you but burn my letters. The Scribners (publisher and wife) came and of course had to come to dinner. I told them to come at six thirty for drinks because we were going in town afterwards to the pelota. At six twenty-five, we were all out behind the farm running up the hills after the band of wild guinea which we had just spotted. I also ran home and found two little men with their mouths full of pins changing the chair covers in the living room. I took off my shoes since they were covered with dung from the farmyard and was out in the kitchen trying to stimulate my black boy to make some appetizers. The black boy was at the time wearing a pale pink silk shirt and a pair of rather bright blue serge trousers and he said he was tired. I walked out of the kitchen, sweaty and soiled and found Mr. Scribner in the dining room. So I said cordially do come in, where's Mrs. Scribner. She was in the car; she is not terribly young but very pretty and southern and one of the most outstanding asses I have seen for years. She tells you right away that she cannot stand spiders but is not afraid of snakes, cannot drink whisky but grows orchids, and she talks steadily about fox hunting. Mother was in her room, and to get a bath, which she needed after hunting guineas, she had to cross through the living room wearing a bath towel. Mrs. Scribner even wore gloves and a hat. I rushed them outdoors, thus giving Mother a chance and also allowing the small men with their mouths full of pins to complete their work. Ernest was still out with the guineas. I love to entertain. Later, before dinner, I saw Mother getting the most awful giggles and had to take her into the bathroom so she could laugh. It seems she had just told Mrs. Scribner that she loved to fox hunt. Mrs. Scribner said her daughter was staying with the Rawlings (that happens to be the *Yearling* woman) and Mother said, quick as a flash, "The Florida Rawlings, I suppose?" and then Mother got red in the face with laughter. During dinner Mother kept calling Mrs. Scribner, "Mrs. Stribling." The Striblings are some insane people in Saint Louis, with two or three members of their family in the loony house. It was a very fine meal indeed; the pelota was a serious strain too, and afterwards it was worse. We got home at one thirty and I just thought: dear God, let me die. But we have not seen them again. They were coming out to tennis today, but Mother and I were going to take a picnic across the island and thus escape; but now it is raining and we are spared. I naturally would make a fine wife for a man who had to be nice to his business acquaintances, as you can easily see. Ernest says I ought to get a cobra for a secretary.

How do you like my book; I told them to send it to you. It is better in this version. I think it is very prettily gotten up.

We were all fools not to live in tents and eat nuts and roots and talk only in sign language. That is the mistake we made. Why we tried so hard to come up from the ape beats me.

(Now it seems the Scribners are coming out even with the rain, so Mother and I are leaving in a hurry.) You two have NO TROUBLES AT ALL.

Love always,
Gellhorn

Allen Grover to MG   April 30, 1942
                                                      Hawaii

Dear Martha,

I miss you greatly and I would like to know why you choose to sit out this war in Cuba. Perhaps you don't like Madame Chiang, or the English who floated out of Singapore on a wave of gin slings, but good God woman, there's work to be done for the country. What occupies you from morning until night?

I have thought about you and Ernest often since I have been here (Pearl Harbor) and others have asked, too, where you were.

I'm being Arch's [Archie MacLeish] Associate Director of the O.F.F. It is the central governmental proaganda agency considerably bound about by steel cords of red tape and overlapping authority.

Still, I'm proud of what we have been able to accomplish in four months… Hopefully, along come June sometime I can go back to Time, Inc. where I belong, and where I think I will be of equal or greater value.

If we don't lose the war by this autumn, we may be able to win it in a couple of years…

How about writing me a good pre-war, introverted letter full of evil four-letter words? I could use one in my business.

Regards to Mr. H.

Ever yours,
Allen

While Gellhorn holidayed with her mother in May, she and Hemingway wrote letters to each other in place of conversation that they both missed, letters rife with love and light and daily life, hers in Florida, his in Cuba with his young sons. He wondered, "who wakes you up in the morning when there isn't either Dillinger [a cat] nor your Bongie [EH] to wake you? I'll bet I know. You sleep." By all accounts, Gellhorn loved to sleep. Edna Gellhorn wrote to her son-in-law as well, assuring him how much Martha missed him and how grateful Edna was for these precious weeks with her only daughter.

Gellhorn's previous publisher, Duell, Sloan and Pearce (nicknamed by Ernest as "Dull, Slum and old Cap Pus"), brought out a novel that copied "whole sections" from *For Whom the Bell Tolls*, substituting Maine for Montana. There were "solid pages re-written slightly." Hemingway figured "they will copy that book now until people will finally think they are sick of it."

Their ever-increasing feline menagerie figured frequently in their correspondence as they both adored their cats, with Hemingway using them often as surrogates for his own wishes. When he asked Dingie if he "had any message to send," all he could send was "a purr-purr." He closed that letter, "The cats all send their varying loves and I send a big early morning worst part of chins hug-a-lug." Throughout their shared life Gellhorn and Hemingway created and used idiosyncratic diction that revealed a cherished intimacy between just the two of them.

Hemingway doled out advice to Gellhorn, especially when she worried that her writing would never go well again. He reminded her that she had "started with the wonderful standard of [H.G.] Wells" who could produce a book every year, that only "Dumas Pere [sic] and Simenon ever wrote more than three good books," and "Flaubert wrote all his life and only wrote one really good one." He insisted that "these are bahd [sic] years for writing. If can get a good one out very lucky Miss Martha very lucky." He projected that some time in the future people would "run excursions to ruined temples of San Francisco de Paula and guys in foot thick lenses" would "dig around for bits of your old pottery and thousands write theses on whether you were as good as you were beautiful."

MG to Ernest Hemingway

May 22, 1942
Hotel Bellerive
Kansas City

My dearest Buggy,

… Mother is very good and jolly and lovely and looking tired to death.

Am having fine time being with her, but will be very happy to return to Cuba to see you and all our quiet little friends. Think it was very wise of you to decide to stay and not interrupt your writing as I think you would have found the atmosphere rather difficult for writing and thinking. Of course the war effort is wonderful and so inspiring to see.

… Mother loves you very much and sends you a big kiss. She is the best woman I know and for me, as a woman, the best company, and her head is screwed on okay too.

I love you Ichabod Pickle. Give my best love to Dingie and Winkie. Give them a big kiss from their mamma. Tell Best I will love her if she will love me. My regards to your pigeons.

Mrs. Bongie

MG to Ernest Hemingway

May 23, 1942
Hotel Bellerive
Kansas City

My beloved Pickly,

There is going to be an end to private pleasure travel, of course quite rightly because regular military need the space. So planes are not going to be wasted just on civilians; and trains too…

Her [Edna] idea of only staying a week was because she thought I'd have to get back to you but I told her you were a good and generous Bug who has me, for better or worse, always and that you know I ought to see more of her and want it…

I know you will be sad being alone so long; but I think you will agree that I am doing the right thing. Be sure you get the children's passage arranged quick (get them over as soon as you can Bug), because we must see our families now.

I love you & love you.
Mrs. Big Drum

Edna Gellhorn to Ernest Hemingway

May 25, 1942
Bacon's on the Sea
Fort Walton

Dearest Ernest,

Yesterday Martha was so homesick for you all day long that I went to the door of her bedroom this morning, half suspecting that she would have flown. Fortunately for me she is still here. At the moment she is sitting not far from me, crosslegged (good legs?) yellow sweatered (it is deliciously coral)… reading a Wodehouse. Maybe she will be just as homesick today. No she will be for she is missing you I know. You are the refrain or the backlog or the texting far opinions as well as the fun of living. Do I sound jealous? I should hope not. All this means happiness and to know of your happiness and Martha's equals mine.

It is perfectly beautiful here. We are near the white beach, the sea filled with exciting life, the delicious air and the newest addition a twelve year old jalopy [sic]—I'm sure Martha will tell you of our first ride in our ridiculous vehicle.

I feel a selfish somebody having all this but my enjoyment of it is none the less—the ten days with Martha in Lavandou had for years been my highwater mark of sheer pleasure. George Gellhorn [her husband] gave me those days to visit my daughter. You have given me these—they will become my second reaching of the mark, so I am grateful to you always. Shall be your very happy and truly loving M.

MG to Ernest Hemingway

May 26, 1942
Bacon's on the Sea
Fort Walton

Pussy dearest,

Since there is no letter from you yet (have been gone a week) this morning I began to reread old letters you had written me last fall from Sun Valley when I was in St. Louis. The letters were in with the clothes Mother sent me this time to Miami; so I have been sitting reading them all over and am awful homesick.

There isn't much to write about, my pickly pot. I don't hear from you so I can't carry on a conversation; and our life here is as uneventful as you can imagine. We just chat and sit in the sun, and probably grow a little stouter. I love you very much and only hope it is the bad mail system and not any sickness which keeps you silent. You aren't going to shoot the cats etc. the way you said? You're not in a gloomy mood are you, it isn't that which keeps you silent?

All love and a big hugalug kiss,
Mrs. Bingo

MG to Ernest Hemingway

May 29, 1942
Bacon's on the Sea
Fort Walton

Dearly Bug,

I got such a sweet letter from you about the kotsis [sic] and their love lives. But I am astounded at Best calling again so soon. She must be over-sexed I think maybe. I do not believe that tiny little baby Dingie could be a father do you; anyhow I sure hopes [sic] not as I do not think Best is old enough yet and anyhow I do not think she should begin Motherhood by producing black and white Persians. It might be a shock to her and throw her off the idea for good.

I am so homesickly for you.

Will buy you magazines and all.

Would you write Mr. Robert Blake at the Guaranty in New York and deposit $150 to my account there. It is almost dry. I went off like an ass without my American check book, on the Bank of Boston, so had nothing but the Guaranty with $200 or so in it. I have kept accounts of every penny spent and have spent several pennies. I will pay you back the $150 when I return to Cuba. Please do this right off darling as do not wish to be overdrawn or run out. Thank you very much indeed.

Have got to get all this in the mail. Wrote you earlier today. Do so love you. Take good cares of yourself and keep the mails rolling. Always devotedly your loving wife,

Muki

MG to Ernest Hemingway

May 30, 1942
Bacon's on the Sea
Fort Walton

Dear Isaacson, Pup-Pup,

I think next year when we make out your who's who thing we might say, "also known as Isaacson, Pup-Pup." If Best has a son we must name him that with a Jr. attached. How are the kotsies and their love pobblems [sic]…

I used to be a believing and faithful person, and thought mankind was good more than anything else and that's how I wrote. But of late I write about nasty people and mainly with malice and maybe that is the way I am now, too. What do you think? I think *Bells* is so fine because you were fine (the way *To Have and to Hold* [sic], you remember that book, is your least good because you were your least good, you were at your thinnest). What do you think of this? Of course it varies; sometimes one is a better person than other times… But I do believe that it is the love that is inside the writer which makes a fine book. And without the love it is no good really; not lasting good…

Now my typewriter ribbon mechanism is breaking so I better stop.

Hell.

I love you so much my dearest darlingest Pup Pup. Better than nobody at all anywheres any time. I got faith in you and love for you anyhow, so maybe I better just write a book about you, eh.

A big kiss, also for kotsies.
Muki

MG to Ernest Hemingway

June 1, 1942
Bacon's on the Sea
Fort Walton

Dearest Wooster,

I got your cable yesterday saying you'd sent 11 letters. I'll leave my forwarding address and they'll give me pleaser [sic] to read beckfiss [sic] at the finca. I've had three and loved them. If none of them got lost you'd have 12 letters in all from me, and a big letter with enclosures. Tomorrow I have been away from you for two weeks. It seems verra verra verra [sic] long to me.

… I love you very much indeed and hope you are getting on allright [sic] and are not too mizable [sic] and that your kotsies [sic] keep you company when you're asleep and I love you like nothing on earth.

Always,
Marty Bingo

MG to H.G. Wells

June 14, 1942
Finca Vigía
San Francisco de Paula

Darling,

I always feel like writing but you know how it is: I must have got some sort of quirk through living in Europe which makes me rather rat-eyed and glum when I think the people at the next table are listening, and I do not like to have letters read (even the most innocent, honorable: anything that does not begin Dear Sir is private) and besides I know so little. My world is really small: part of the time it is an island thirty by eighteen miles, which I invented *(thus horning in on God),* and the rest of the time it is ten or eight acres, I forget which, of this finca. I concern myself in the way the bougainvillea is cut and look with dismay at the rain washing the new whitewash like milk from the house. And answering all our business mail and lately I have had Paramount with me, via the cable and the long distance, since they are such people, Paramount with organ voices intoning the splendors of the unseen film FWTB [*For Whom the Bell Tolls*]. They want us to come to NY all at their expense, to be present at what is called the woild [sic] preemeer [sic], on Basteele [sic] Day (no less), but of course we cannot and really we would not if we could.

The writers I now admire are Koestler, Nelson Algren, Nicholas Aldanov and Ira Wolfert: I think they are full of juice, with good sharp new eyes, and not enough comfort in their bellies to make their minds boring. I recognize them too: they are part of a lovely lost life, when everything was at once harder and easier.

One thing time has not removed from me, the last toughness of my youth, and that is to live alone. I am glad of that; I would be scared to death if I found I was really needing people, needing the comfort and the reassurance, since one's own society though varied is not exactly soothing. And I read so badly. Do you read well? It was a talent I always coveted and thought I could acquire but apparently no. I wish my memory were better and my brains less languid; I would like to read fiercely and learn from it and remember. There's so much to know. But it leaks away, or else the cutting edges of my brain are blotting paper.

Perhaps we'll be in England together now that spring is passed. That would be very rare.

Goodnight,
Marty

> On June 24th, Hemingway wrote that he was "a lonely mon [sic]" without his "sweet," and that he was "disgusted with many things," but would not write them. None of them was Gellhorn, he insisted. She was his "hero and always would be" and he was grateful that she had come to Key West and married him.
>
> Gellhorn returned to the Finca Vigía at the end of June and alighted for a few weeks, working on her novel *Liana* while she waited for her accreditation papers that would allow her to travel throughout the Caribbean reporting for *Collier's*.[14] While she moved among the Dominican Republic, Haiti and Puerto Rico, Hemingway took frequent excursions on his boat the *Pilar* with his "crook factory" of ragtag shipmen, looking for German submarines off the coast of Cuba. The postal system must have been more obliging then as Martha and Ernest managed to send and receive correspondence shuttling from place to place.

MG to Ernest Hemingway

June 29, 1942
Bacon's on the Sea
Fort Walton

My beloved Binglie,

… Yesterday we drove over to a town called Crestview in the afternoon. There's a field and you pick up soldiers and give them lifts. On the way home we picked up two boys from Brooklyn. I asked him if they talked much about the war in their mess, what it was about and so on and he said you never heard anyone mention it, they just all hoped it would be over as soon as possible. I thought it was gruesome and very interesting. I am very sad most of the time.

… We saw Garbo's latest, *Two-Faced Woman*. It was tragic; I hope she never makes another. Or at least that they don't have her doing comedy anymore. She looks as if she were in terrible pain when she smiles; her laugh sounds like a sob… It is enough to break your heart. The most beautiful woman of our time just hideous and ruined; with nothing left. She is about ripe to play Queen Victoria or

Eliz. of England now; those seem to be the two roles which remain. The camera is a cruel thing.

The week ahead seems to me the longest unit of time yet invented. What are you doing? Oh please write me? I need a big hugalug.

Always your mopey wife
Marty

Eleanor Roosevelt to MG

June 29, 1942
The White House
Washington

Dearest Marty,

... If you come up to Washington and I am here and you do not come to stay with me at the White House I shall be very annoyed with you. That is the only way I get a chance to see anyone. If you come to New York City, I can come down from Hyde Park, as I do want to see you.

I am glad you are going to do some work in the Caribbean. It does not seem to be the safest spot, particularly if you travel on boats. I hope you do most of your travelling by air.

You are right about the hate that is being built up in the world, but I am afraid it cannot be bred out on the scale you are thinking of, but I think there are lots of things that can be done but whether we have the courage and the perseverance to do them, I do not know. Anna seems to be fine and not the least worried by the Aleutian Islands.

Affectionately, always,
E.R.

MG to Eleanor Roosevelt

July 10, 1942
Finca Vigía
San Francisco de Paula

Dearest Mrs. R,

I got your letter yesterday... I think your generation and Mother's is a far far nobler thing than mine. This immense ability to welcome people, and have them with you is what I admire! It's a very special kind of unselfishness. I am willing to do almost anything for people except live with them: so you can see at once that nobility is not inherited in our family.

My passport has been validated. I wasn't going to bother anybody in a simple minded way, because there are no rules against a journalist (even a female one, that type of outcast) travelling in war zones, in the line of duty. But I found out that I could not get a visa to Martinique, unless there was some kind of intercessions. That is to say, the French authorities needed a little extra recommending before they'd grant one…

I do not understand this at all. If they (State Department, I suppose) are afraid that I might write something factless, they need not worry: since every line will be submitted to U.S. censorship obviously. Further, I happen to speak French about as well as English, and have known the French well for a long time and gotten on well with them and have what they call good contacts with all kinds and shades of thought. I should think that it would be useful to have an unsuspicious looking journalist who speaks French, make a tour of those territories. I should think that things that I could see and learn would be useful in reports to the State Department itself and to our intelligence…

There is little enough that one can do to help, but it makes me sad when it is so hard even to do that little.

Meantime, I am in a joy to be going. I love the work, really love it. I would rather be a journalist than anything except a first-rate writer. The writing of books is hard and lonely work and you are never sure for a minute that you have done the thing you planned and hoped to do. Journalism is hard and exhausting and marvelously exciting and always rewarding and you know exactly what kind of job you are doing, every minute. If you are lucky, you get to places where the trouble is. I adore to travel too and life with one suitcase is my idea of life with exactly enough possessions. And now, the thought of seeing places whose names I have always known and loved, but never seen, is enough to make me spin like a top with happiness.

Everything is fine with my family here. The children love this place and Ernest is a wonderful father, teaching them everything from how to read (so that they read with taste and remember their reading) to how to shoot, steer a boat by compass and splice ropes. He is with them all the time and they are very lovely to see together: two small boys roaring with laughter at Papa's jokes and following him around like puppies…

I get wonderful letters from people I used to know in Spain; most of the American boys are now in our army. When the war is over, and if he's still alive, I'd like you to meet a young Jew named Jack Friedman born on a farm in New York state, one of the purest spirits I ever had anything to do with. The first time I saw him he was filthy and trying to get something fairly cold to drink in a Valencia Café. He ran an ammunition truck at the front, and was on two days leave. He recognized

Ernest and all he wanted to talk about was: is James Joyce really a great writer. He had never been beyond high school, of course, but he read anything he could find and had found an Everyman's edition of *The Portrait of the Artist as a Young Man* in Valencia. He came to lunch one day in New York with me and H.G. Wells, and Wells was so happy, after the horrors of a lecture tour, to meet an absolutely simple and honest man with such a good eager mind and such a really generous spirit. We were terribly lucky to have Spain in our lives: I have a sort of capital of fine people whom I rarely see, though they do write (those who are alive, those who are not in concentration camps) and having known them, I can always believe in the dignity of man and have hope for the future no matter how much lousiness I see besides.

This is a very long letter. I'll send you postcards of the beautiful Caribbean. I wish you were going along.

Love,
Marty

Edna Gellhorn to Ernest Hemingway

July 15, 1942
4366 McPherson Avenue
St. Louis

Ernest dear,

Whether this note won't reach you on your birthday or later it carries my birthday greeting and happiest wishes. Were I to be with you this year I'd be gay with the others—we'd be having a fiesta perhaps or maybe just a family party with the boys—we'd be celebrating in some way the glad tidings that Ernest was here to make me and millions of others glad. The Walter Fischels and I have arranged a tiny birthday party for you "*in absentia*"—we'll drink to your health, wealth and happiness in old fashions [sic] scotch and martinis. Kitty sent the clipping "Ernest Hemingway has started to work on an assignment similar to John Steinbeck's job for the U.S. Army Air Corps. Hemingway is writing a book and motion picture story, for the Engineer Corps. The movie rights will be sold for $250,000, which will go to Army Relief… [sic] Robert E. Sherwood is borrowing Harry Hopkins' Baedecker… [sic] Warner Bros. plan to send a film…" —How about it?

It would be necessary to carry a notebook in which to make constant entries were I to try to keep up with the references to you which come via radio, news columns or conversation—It would be fun to do it, but I'm not methodical so I shall not—But I am emotional all right and so swell with pride as if I had "born you myself." (just an innocent pleasure you afford your old ma)

Olga and Martha *tertia* [Alfred's daughter] are now... with Mrs. Frederick. I drove them there Sunday. Martha is very cunning. She finally liked St. Louis. Give my love to your Martha and to you I send happy days & devotion.

M—

MG to Charles Colebaugh

July 16, 1942
Finca Vigía
San Francisco de Paula

Dear Charles,

The letter of credentials and radio card have come. Thank you. I am now all set. I am just holding my breath until the Saturday plane and the joy of working again. The radio card is made out to Martha Hemingway. That is okay. But don't get mixed up; my articles are always to be signed Martha Gellhorn, always. That is what I always was, and am and will be: you can't grow a name onto yourself.

Always,
Marty Gellhorn

Gellhorn began her Caribbean tour on July 17th, 1942, and it lasted through the end of September. Among the pieces from those weeks that she submitted to *Collier's* Martha reported on a U.S. airbase in Puerto Rico where she "flew on a patrol in a Flying Fortress which seemed as large as the Queen Mary," and from other smaller islands where she found sailors who had survived the sinking of Allied supply ships by German submarines. She wrote about those weeks memorably in "Messing about in Boats," one of the "horror journeys" she included in *Travels with Myself and Another*. At about the same time Hemingway had assembled a crew of Cuban locals to join him on the *Pilar*, which had been outfitted with gear by the U.S. government to hunt German subs. He nicknamed the endeavor the "crook factory" and referred to their work obliquely in correspondence as for the "Museum." On August 6th, 1942, he said he'd received a congratulatory wire from "Department of Icthyology of Museum of Natural History" having sent them "proof in a jar... Let us all praise jars." Hemingway considered keeping a diary of those months aboard *Pilar*, but rejected the idea as he figured, "head is best place to keep things and let them rot there." Out of that mental fermentation he would pluck the best bits, admitting, "I suppose if you are a writer, you're a writer till you die or it dies."

A few days after Gellhorn left their home in Cuba, Hemingway wrote on his birthday that the night before they had found, at the Floridita cocktail bar in town, "a little black dog… with a cut curled up over his back tail and a sweet loveing [sic] way" and brought him home. Her birthday telegram to him had arrived and he "woke up feeling awfully hoppy [sic]." At the end of the month he insisted, "it makes me so hoppy [sic] to get your lovely letters so please write whenever you are not too tired to. You know it is much easier on me this time you are away because the childies [sic] are here. But I always miss you as though all the best part of me were gone."

In these months apart there were dozens of letters between them, Ernest often introspective, confessing, for example, "I wish I would have been a better man all my life and treated everyone better; especially Hadley. It takes so damned long to grow up and even when it is granted to you to finally be grown up then you are probably dead." In that same September 5th missive, however, he also wrote, "Think Mr. Scrooby is going to die off from lack of use. Well he had a hell of a jolly life. So have I had really and read an awful lot of good books and written some too." He frequently praised Gellhorn's writing, observing that her most recent piece for *Collier's* "had some of the finest and loveliest writing you ever did and such a million dollar ear for the back talk. *Ni* [sic] Joyce [James] *ni* [sic] anybody any better ear than my Bong has now." At the end of September, he reminisced about being in Madrid with Martha in 1937 and how she had helped him write *The Fifth Column*, that they did not know "what we were getting into when we wrote that play." Loneliness is his touchstone and almost always his pets comfort him in Martha's absence, curling up by his pillow, knowing he "was in bod [sic] shape." He was worried that he might be away on the *Pilar* doing government work when Gellhorn returned to the finca and told her, wary of providing too much information for a censor, to "get in touch with me through the person whose name I will leave for you to call and I will fly from wherever first get word and we will rededicate bed."

MG to Ernest Hemingway

July 20, 1942
Hotel Citadelle
Port au Prince
Haiti

Dearest Bug,

This is the loveliest island you ever did see. From the window it looks like Naples and Hong Kong and like neither… The town is like a movie set, you know, sunny and wide and quiet and shabby with wonderful colors.

… I like Haitians. The people are gentle and the French is so sweet and courteous like children in a school play. There is not much of a story; just survivors and the internment camp; but I sit about and listen and ask questions and mainly I look at everything and I think that, out of all the island together, I will get a good bright story about how the subs have moved in where once there were tourists.

Tomorrow is your birthday and I hope your party is a great success and that you have a fine jolly time. I wish you many hoppy [sic] returns. Give my kotsies [sic] a good kiss and the childies too…

Have a good time Bughouse McGruder.

Your loving wife,
Marty

MG to Ernest Hemingway

July 23, 1942
Port au Prince
Haiti

Bug dearest,

It is now four o'clock and the mountains and the sea and the sky are all grey. This is the bad part of the day, waiting for rain. Now, if I can move my limp string muscles, I shall go to the *Charge d'Affaires'* house (he was in Prague when I was) and have cocktails with some people who run mosquitoe [sic] boats…

I have got together the things that interest me and it is more or less like stringing beads, no single place will be enough by itself…

I really have loved this place; there hasn't been a dull or useless moment and at any hour, even now, stifling in the grey heat, it is beautiful. If this job keeps up so well I will be a very lucky journalist. The war is really like a great pebble or a depth charge, thrown into the world at one spot and widening out from there… there are Germans here who have not been back to Germany since the last war. They sit in an internment camp and worship the Führer and believe every one of his lousy and repulsive theories, which they have studied by correspondence course, or learned through pamphlets and they are as ardent as if they were party officials in Germany. It was amazing to see them, and I also get the feeling they are insane, in a most dangerous way, because you cannot put a whole nation in the loony bin.

There are some wonderful little birds, which I think are swallows, though of course I don't know, playing in the sky like seals or pursuit planes. But oh my, how I love the South Seas, how I love to travel light and with no plans and have every day come as a surprise. It does not make for depth or wisdom probably but it keeps the mind light and limber and full of jokes. And I think I would rather feel young than be Jane Austen.

Love
Mrs. Bug

MG to Ernest Hemingway

July 26, 1942
The Condado Hotel
San Juan
Puerto Rico

Dearest Bug,

… Everyone knows your name everywhere. It is amazing. In Ciudad they had a very violent customs searching and full of red tape they made off with my typewriter. They said I could call for it at the Customs, where it would be interned, it was not a proper part of my baggage. I said it was as much my baggage as a toothbrush I was a *periodista* [journalist] from *Colliers* [sic]. That impressed them to a certain degree and they studied my passport. Then they said, are you related to the *gran escritor* [great writer]. I said yes. Then they said to each other, *chico* [boy], this is a scandal, her husband is one of the most great personalities of America, the great writer you know *chico*, we must do something about the typewriter. So they took it to the customs and returned it. I am embarrassed to profit by your fame, very embarrassed, and in Haiti, not wanting to get under false pretenses anything, I started off saying I was Miss Gellhorn. It was too complicated though; if that was my name how did it happen that my passport said Hemingway and after I explained, it still did not seem reasonable to anyone and in fact it seemed perhaps on the *louche* side. So I quickly gave up and said allright [sic] and then I sign Mrs. Martha Hemingway, still not wanting to impose, still not wanting to be specially considered due to a reflection from you, a thing I have not earned and do not merit. So then, inevitably I am asked if I am related to you, and people have seen my picture in the *Life* piece, and so I profit will-nilly. But I neither offer such information, nor ever use it myself first. Then one night I was made happy in Haiti eating in a restaurant; the proprietor was an Austrian refugee and he came up with my Prague book [*A Stricken Field*] and asked me to autograph it. I felt I was getting something due to my own work (a magnificent dinner and his amazing story thrown in.) But on the whole it seems to me I am getting something for nothing… How are you Mister Bug and how are my kotsies and the childies?

I love you,
Muki

MG to Ernest Hemingway

August 2, 1942
The Condado Hotel
San Juan
Puerto Rico

Bug beloved,

It is Sunday morning and it came just in time, so I can tidy my papers and my notes and my clothes and sit still and neither listen nor look. I have gotten too tired here…

The great problem is to buy books. I have run out pretty well. I have bought a pocket Bible (truly) in despair, figuring that if I am stuck on a schooner or somewhere it will at least take a long time to read and my time will not be wasted.

The story of Gigi [Gregory] at the shoot is a great story; I hope you will write it. You did write it, to me, in one paragraph, but write it truly…

This hotel behaves as if it had been under siege for two years; it is the dirtiest worst run place I almost ever saw and one of the most expensive. But anyhow, all is well with me now that I know you have not renounced me. Give my love to the childies… I will keep my eye out for birds for Mousie. Tell Gigi he is my hero. Give my love to Dog too. I'm very glad he's there. A woman should be able to take a cat with her, on her travels. If I had Winkie here, I wouldn't mind how boring people were, I'd talk to Winkie when I came home from work. I miss you my dearest Bug. There aren't any other men like you.

Love always,
Muki

Patrick and Gregory sent Martha a cable on August 3rd to Puerto Rico, the contents of which Ernest clarified. He "finally caught the rubber stopper that shoots up out of the mineral water bottle." He did so "while reading and the catch was clean and left handed." They must have had a bet that it was impossible, because he delighted in announcing that she owed him five dollars.

<hr />

Eleanor Roosevelt to MG

August 8, 1942
The White House
Washington

Dearest Marty,

I loved your letter and I read it to the President. He was delighted with it…

I feel as you do about Haiti, it is lovely and I shall be anxious to know what you think about the Virgin Islands, because they had some promise of working out when I was there.

Good luck to you and take care of yourself.

Affectionately,
Eleanor R.

<hr />

MG to Eleanor Roosevelt

Fall 1942
Finca Vigía
San Francisco de Paula

Yesterday the new copy of *TIME* came, and the first page is given over to complaints from important people about Americans (the common American) and his indifference to this war. Everyone is worried and angry it seems. But darling, I should think if this state of complacency exists in the public mind— you would all be wondering why and how it happened: and what to do about it. If the people think it is a "professional's war," it must be because that impression was given to them. If they do not know what Nazism means, if they do not have a clear flame of conviction, and a real fury against all that Nazism has done and can do, it is perhaps because things are not simple enough and straight enough yet. Surely that appeasing that still goes on must cloud the issues.

… The war dept thinks that woman's place is in the home, and they do not wish to transport females around to the areas of conflict, nor will they accredit female correspondents to the "armies in the field." I guess I can still get accredited to furriner's [foreigner's] armies all right so that part does not matter too much; but how to get anywhere? It is too late for me to do anything about being a woman, though I would gladly change my sex to be obliging, if it were feasible.

… Meanwhile, I am studying so that no time is wasted. I think I will be covering wars from now on, as I have been since 1936, and I think I might try to be a learned war correspondent. So I am slowly and painfully studying artillery, automatic weapons, tanks, planes, tactics and strategy, and working up to the rank of sergeant. It is very interesting, and later will be useful…

Ernest is writing. I wish I could. I feel too upwrought inside to be able to concentrate properly. He has always been better disciplined than I, and he is of course a better writer. (Better is a mild word.) Mother is working doubly hard (if that is possible) on the League of Women Voters, which is a fine job because they are the small all-over-the-place institutions of women for democracy, and it is certainly necessary to never abandon that subject for a moment…

I am homesick for mother, but she is too busy to come here and I don't like to leave E, who is my job. Maybe in the end, the only useful thing I will have done with my life is to have helped him (a little) to write.

… Darling, this started out as a little letter to say simply that I love you as always, and hate with passion the people who hurt you. But it has gotten into a very long letter. You won't even have time to read it.

Always,
Marty

MG to Ernest Hemingway   October 11, 1942
                                                        The Lombardy
                                                        New York City

Dearest,

Just spoke to Mouse. Like talking to someone in jail. Boys never allowed out except for dentist. I said I'd write headmaster he had to come in to dentist. But Pauline is here, so he said probably they'd check with her. Poor Mouse. No Thanksgiving. Now he's scared no Xmas, because of transportation (some new ruling)… He says school is allright [sic]—sounds horrible.

Lunch at Barberry Room (in your memory) with Teechie & King. Came home & slept. Now must hurry for dinner with Kitty & Walter [brother]. Very good day…

Kiss Gigi, Kotsies & little dog. Excuse dead-tired letter. My dearest dearest mos [sic] generous Bug.

Marty Bongo

MG to Ernest Hemingway

October 18, 1942
The Lombardy
New York City

Dearest,

… It was very funny at Dotty's [Parker] yesterday because a strange man was passed out in the living room. Like having a waxwork from Mme Tussaud's. No one knew his name. The girl who had brought him had gone home. It was like a really fine book by Gypsy Rose.

Max [Perkins] is one of the finest people in the world really. Now he wears an earpiece like a telephone girl. I do not write you everything because tired. But am remembering.

Do not do anything about Mousie until I see you. Would just make trouble for him. I will tell you all the angles. It's the Pauline situation. Sounds like bad place really. But I'd like someone to *talk* to Mousie. About school vacations. Some plan to stagger them so as not to clog trains in December.

Forgive awful letters…

Have everything of yours. Must buy some clothes to be pretty for you. Am having very interesting, very worthwhile time, but not gay. No one makes good jokes.

I love you.
M. Bongo

MG to Allen Grover

October 1942
The White House
Washington

Dearie dearie,

The reason I was so non-committal over the phone is that I do not imagine the phones are entirely un-monitored. I know that some kind of mysterious folk sit on the 3rd floor doing something electrical. See?

I told you I had Lincoln's room and how I felt ashamed to be in his bed, so I also told Woollcott who's up the hall in my former room (mine and Churchill's) and Woollcott said the bed had already been desecrated by Edna Ferber so what the hell.

I am sick in bed again and thoroughly fed up with myself and life and I think this cold is incurable like cancer. Living here is also like convent life; just Woollcott and me here alone and both ill and maybe the Lunts [actors Alfred Lunt and Lynn

Fontanne] to tea (if we can get them through the guarded gates) and nothing to do but cough and write notes on this costly paper…

What a trip. What *did* I do? I haven't even got a new dress. And meantime Allen, *how Rome burns.*

My love
Marty

Edna Gellhorn to Ernest Hemingway   November 9, 1942
                                                     On the Train

Dearest Ernest,

You are a saga, or whatever it is that is told by word of mouth from person to person. I hear more varied tales of your whereabouts than I, or even you, could or would invent. Now you are at *any* front depending on the latest press report. Again your [sic] are helping in the direction of *For Whom the Bell Tolls*, or at Sun Valley (old pictures revived) or on a "secret mission." But as far as I know you are "working hard" at Finca Vigía—you obviously did that for *Men at War*—thank you for the Introduction and also for the compilation that proves your text.

I have had happiest letters from Marty since her return to you and the Finca. Be glad, you two, and hug your happiness tight—it is the only treasure that nor time nor separation can take from you.

Your devoted Mother

Eleanor Roosevelt to MG   December 1, 1942
                                                     The White House
                                                     Washington

Dear Marty,

Many thanks for your welcome home. I did not get around very much alone, but I did see an enormous amount and I think with the training which Tommy and I have acquired in the past through traipsing around the country we got a great deal of what was underneath as well as what was on top.

It was deeply interesting and I am very glad I went. Toward the end I was pretty weary and only hope I can accomplish something, now that I am home, in the way of bringing about better understanding of the British war effort in this country.

I am glad you had a satisfactory time in the White House and I am sorry the Lincoln bed disturbed you but I thought you might get some historical interest in feeling the shadow of Lincoln.

I hope Ernest's work comes along well, and I know whatever role you are playing, you will do it satisfactorily.

I hope you do get the adult education started in the camp near you. I am sure that, if you begin in a small way, you will find it will grow.

I read your article on Puerto Rico and I liked it immensely. I must get the others so I can catch up.

Affectionately,
Eleanor R.

Gellhorn spent Christmas 1942 in St. Louis with her mother while Hemingway had his sons with him for the holidays in Cuba, so there are late December letters recounting home life, including the pick-up baseball games they played on the property, mentioning Gigi's "full size Joe DiMaggio bat which he can hardly lift." There are others where Hemingway is self-aware, noting that after 56 days at sea doing "crook factory" work with nine people "in closer quarters than in any jail cells," he ought to be "cooled out in a decompression chamber (as divers are) before you being exposed to me." He regrets that "all the good part of me (if there is some) stands by like someone watching a *grand guinol* in horror at how simply straight awful I am." He is embittered that he has not "written a word (except letters to you) for a year come next month," when being a writer is who he is. Yet, Hemingway hopes that he is "much better and kinder than I used to be," and he remembers "all the good things of you and of us and if you can put up with a no good Bongie for a couple of days you will see." He hopes that after the war is over, with the two of them once again writing well, they will make a "lovely honeymoon trip together with no hurry and all the fine part of the west that we do not know to learn about."

NINE

The View from the Ground

"Your letter came today… as a parachuted package of food
into the jungle, as a nice passing empty rubber boat
to what they call 'survivors.'"

—Martha Gellhorn, letter to H.G. Wells

1943

In January 1943, Gellhorn wrote to Max Perkins about the novel she was working on that she thought was "about love and loneliness, but who can say?" *Liana* was the first time she had "ever written all the time with pleasure… three weeks on it… were almost like a beautiful drunk." She continued that she "always used to see E. so tired but so happy when he was writing," whereas she was "usually just tired and doubting." She had been spending a couple of weeks in St. Louis with her mother while Ernest hosted his sons at the finca. In response to a despairing letter Martha wrote from the Palmer House in Chicago, Ernest chided her, "Pucker don't talk nor write wet like that." He hoped that if anything happened to him she would ensure that no incomplete manuscripts of his would be published and that she would "always be as nice as you could to the childies [sic]," worrying that, without Martha's attention, his three sons "would have no protection at all." The letters between them continued to be loving and full of daily life and worries. Martha worried about Edna's loneliness, and Ernest worried about Patrick and Gregory, his two youngest sons, usually referred to by their nicknames Mouse and Gigi.

Because the United States was officially at war, the mail was censored. Many of the letters from Ernest to Martha that remain in his papers at the JFK Library in Boston have a censor's number stamped on their envelopes. Hemingway lamented that because he had "gotten so used to writing letters that will be censored," he had "lost ability to put anything down." And yet, he always declared his love for her, writing "I love you very much dearest Bongie and send you the small part of my love that a letter can carry," and insisted that his life had "been brightened so much by you and the lovely light you bring."

Once the Hemingway boys returned to school, Ernest continued his "crook factory" work on the *Pilar*, looking for German submarines off the coast of Cuba, while Martha focused on her novel, hoping to finish it before she obtained accreditation papers again and *Collier's* sent her abroad to report on the war in Europe in October. Her mandate was to write 1,000-word pieces of "pure human interest, actual details of how people live," for which she would be paid $1,500 per article.

She sent chapters of *Liana* to Hemingway to read as she wrote them and he told her the book was "as vivid to me as this place." He regretted that he would not "have all the wonder of finishing it" with her, wishing, "Dear Mooky, *Viva* Book, your Bongie *El Rey de* Hugalug." When Gellhorn became discouraged by her progress on her novel, Hemingway reminded her that Tolstoy and Flaubert only wrote well for "3-4 days out of 7," while Dostoevsky "probably only got 1 out of 5." His advice was to "get exercise and write whether it is impossible or not. It is nearly always impossible." In one of his most affecting and loving letters to her he wished her, "a good trip and if it is to cold countries keep my heart always in your pocket and it will keep your hands warm."

He wrote to her late at night, typing when the water was calm enough, "a flashlight on ankle to light keys," pleading "please do not think that I am drunk r [sic] been drinking on acct of the typeing [sic]. It is a la ck [sic] of light and movement of boat." He worried that much of the communication between them had to be about the business of running the house and paying bills when he "would like it to be human and not all ju t [sic] money" because it was "really quite lonely in spite of many people" with him on the crew, insisting, "I am really *au fond* [at bottom] a much lonelier guy than you." He was always lonely for Gellhorn, "to see and feel and hear you and to see you so lovely asleep in the early morning and to hear you say intelligent and interesting things."

Before she sailed to Europe late in October, Gellhorn's "great secret illusion" was to have *Liana* selected for the Book of the Month Club. That did not happen and she was especially disappointed not to be able to have the money to give away to help out some of the people she loved: her brother Alfred, Gustav Regler and Cam Becket.

MG to Ernest Hemingway
January 10, 1943
Palmer House
Chicago

My beloved Bug,

You will get this after you have seen me. But I am writing it for the record… There was snow this a.m. in St. Louis & Mother was very happy thinking the plane would not fly…

The flight was smooth and I cried to myself the whole way so that tears splashed onto my bosom (which surprised me very much as I have never seen anything like this). I was crying about Mother & about leaving her. You see, I wasn't leaving her for you—as you will be away on your hunting trip—but for myself, for my story; and it seemed suddenly unbearably heartless & calculating & selfish. She sort of breaks my heart right now. And you know, she & you are all I really love in the world, so I have an enormous amount of love to divide, since it is not given elsewhere.

I don't know what I'll decide in the morning. But right now I think I am going home again. Why? Because it will haunt me otherwise. It doesn't matter anymore to you as I cannot possibly get home [to Cuba] before you leave on the 12th for your trip. You know how you said to decide between good and bad—what is good makes you feel good, what is bad makes you feel bad. And leaving Mother like this… makes me feel cheap & ashamed & cruel and very bad. And I'd go on feeling bad for a long time & it would make me hate the story…

So I think I'll go home Bug. I know you'll agree. I have to live with myself & I feel really ill & tormented about this. And I'll have a quiet week before you come back & I swear I'll work better for not having my heart so miserable about her. Besides, the story is really safe inside me. All that will be hard is the discipline of getting back to writing & I can and will do that.

… I love you my dearest. Goodnight. Your weary distressed sad loving and home-sick wife.

P.S. God we are lucky to live in the most beautiful house, in the sun. What a marvelous life we have.

P.S. If anything happens to you while I'm away, an accident or illness, I'll kill myself for sure.

February 16, 1943
Finca Vigía
San Francisco de Paula

Dear Max,

I could not work on my story today because our Persian has been having kittens and I was attending. I have never seen anything born before and I must say it has been an important day. The kittens, which at birth resembled squabs in a nightmare, started eating at once and have continued to do so. We built a nest out of shell boxes and heavy tomes on bullfighting and the mother purrs steadily and the kittens (one with an umbilical cord still trailing) crawl about, squeak and suck milk. I have seen a certain number of new dead, at wars (though I never actually saw the immediate thing where you watch what was upright fall) and what struck me, aside from any emotion, was the disorder. On the other hand, birth seems to be as disorderly as anything else: and perhaps disorder is the really profound quality of life. (There is no reason to go German and philosophical over the birth of kittens.) It is also instructive to notice how animal human beings are: either the cat is just like a woman, or women are just like the cat.

I wanted to write you about two things: to thank you for your letter with its cheering news about novel lengths. And the second is to thank you for sending Aldanov's book. The dust cover (please excuse me) was so horrible, something between a sunset and intestines, that I could not read it. But Ernest courageously broke through this obstacle and then I swiped the book from him. I have just finished it. There are various things wrong with it, I believe, and none so pitiful as that part about Spain. That does prove that a writer must either invent from experience or be a very solid and careful fact-finder. The Spain part is ludicrous (I am not talking about politics) but simply the idea of the old General wandering vaguely into an attack in University City and drawing his sword and scrambling forward to death with the milicians [sic]. It could never have happened: I wonder if Aldanov could not somewhere have learned the terrain of that city-front, the trench system, how attacks were made etc., without actually visiting Spain. But that is a minor criticism really, and though the book shows signs of fatigue at the end, it is beautifully invented and thick and solid and happily and excitingly unlike the mush that is so successful nowadays. I think the strongest and most exciting aspect of it is Aldanov's understanding of money: it is the book of a man who has been concerned with nickels for a long bitter time. But he is so right: and it is a thing writers tend to forget. The use of money or the lack of it, as a constant undercurrent, is wonderful: so is the use of age and sickness. And though both of us think he rang in the young murderer Alvera, the way strikes are dragged into

U.S. proletarian novels (and by the way, it is amazing how recurrent this callous poor cold-hearted young murderer is in modern European novels), we do think the actual scene of the murder was amazing and couldn't have been better or more convincingly done.

I am very grateful for the book: there's so little new to read and this one will be a good thing to have in one's mind for a long time. It is also an example and a sort of goad.

What are you people doing about it? I hope to God you are going to sell it. The writer deserves that; it must be a big book and it is a fine one, and it merits being read and he certainly has earned money. I have seen nothing about it yet but perhaps it is not on sale? Please struggle for it, Max. Right now there's only Aldanov and Algren who are worth struggling for.

I wish we could write the man and tell him how we admire him? Where is he? Is he alive and if so, what does he live on? Will you write and tell us whatever you know of him? My God, how the Russkis [sic] can write. He can write circles around Jules Romains of course but I don't think that's any overwhelming compliment; and when I think of Steinbeck and Katerina [sic] Anna [sic] Porter and our other Great, I am enraged that Aldanov isn't being Book of the Month and lolling over Connecticut vodka at the Ritz Bar.

My own book is in the painful process, like changing tires without a jack. (If possible: I guess not.) I was going along so happily and with such ease, pleasure and confidence that I said to myself: hell, there's nothing to this. So I wrote fifteen pages in that I-can't-go-wrong spirit and now, I bleed and burn—in the words of that Great Man—every morning, for hours, trying to rewrite that badness. It is more like draining a swamp and trying to make solid ground than like changing tires without a jack; but in any case, it is awful. I have been very anxious and monomaniacal about it, but Ernest gives me hell in doses like a cathartic and tells me that if one thing is worse than another it is a cowardly and doubting writer in the middle of a book. It will be a book finally: I hope it will be a good one.

Please write us about Aldanov. Please sell a hundred thousand copies of his book and make him both rich and warmed with proper appreciation. It would be heartbreaking if he ever doubted how good he is.

Yours,
Martha

Maxwell Perkins to MG

March 4, 1943
New York City

Dear Martha,

I was amused by your reference to writing letters as an excuse to defer working. But aren't you in truth happiest of all when you are working? Of course not when you are trying to work and are not able to make progress, but generally. It is the most curious thing how everybody shrinks from getting to work when they know perfectly well, that once they do it they will enjoy it. I do all my real work on Saturdays and Sundays, and I always go through exactly the same process. I put it off until late Saturday afternoon, and I begin it with a heavy heart, and then as soon as I get into it I like it and keep it up far into Sunday night because I have got absorbed in it. Why is it that a man shrinks from doing what he knows for sure he will enjoy? And he doesn't enjoy the leisure he gets by the postponement because his conscience bothers him. It's a funny thing.

I asked Charlie why he thought Aldanov was working in the library, though I really know that it was for purposes of research—But Charlie said it was probably because he had a wife. Anyhow, I am enclosing a piece that Wreden wrote for that Book of the Month Club bulletin which will tell you quite a bit about him.

We are publishing another book in the fall that I am pretty certain you and Ernest will like. Maybe I mentioned it before, "Indigo." The scene is India. IT [sic] has that wonderful quality throughout it that comes from nostalgia. The writer grew up in India, and left it some twenty years ago to marry a Boston man who had gone to India to hunt.

Yours,
MEP

MG to H.G. Wells

Spring 1943
Finca Vigía
San Francisco de Paula

Wells darling,

How are you getting on? Has [Somerset] Maugham sent you any more food packages?

I have just finished three books by Henry James. Never read him before because the type is always terrible. They are *The Americans, Portrait of a Lady* and *The Europeans*. I find them fascinating: James seems to me a classical Michael Arlen

[Armenian-born British novelist]. Classical not because his people are any realer or his situations more moving and true, but only because he writes with such unique care. I think the style is often ridiculous, don't you: and there is an old-lady quality to it that amazes me. Old lady, not fairy. I read *The Europeans* as if it were a thriller, so anxious to see what *became* of the people. Nothing becomes of them: you never know them, or else there is nothing to know… James reminds me very much of a philosophical discussion Ernest once had with Scott Fitzgerald. Did you ever read Scott? He wrote one fine book called *The Great Gatsby*. At least it was fine when I read it. Scott lived a great deal in Cannes and Antibes and was very much impressed by whatever he considered Society [sic]. He once said to Ernest, in an admiring, wistful way. 'The rich are not like us, Ernest.' And Ernest said, 'No, they have more money.' So that is the way James makes me feel too. The man was in love with aristocracy (his word, and his meaning); but I can never see how the aristocrats are so astounding, except that they talk very fancy and spend more money. Am I all wrong? Anyhow, James makes delightful war reading.

I am writing a book [*Liana*] that is nothing but a story. This is a new idea for me. I have gotten humble, or at any rate I have come to the wise conclusion that I do not know what I think, and that perhaps I never thought very well. I know exactly what I feel; but that is something else again. So this is a story about people, and a love story which is slowly working its way to a sort of frittering off ending. Not one of the love stories where everyone falls on a sword and dies. I like it and on the whole, except for bad stuck exhausted doubting periods, I have had fun with it. I would like, from now on, to write better if not bigger. It is quite an occupation and I am as absorbed as if I lived in the bottom of a beautiful well with no company except a typewriter.

This summer, maybe, providing *Collier's* and everyone else official agrees, I am coming to England. In August if I can arrange it. I want to write some things. Not that it appears there is much relation between what people write and what gets done. That curious hiatus between the written word and the urged deed must depress you sometimes, doesn't it? Depresses the pants off me. I miss you very much and send you a big juicy kiss.

Love,
Stooge

May 20, 1943
Finca Vigía
San Francisco de Paula

Darlings,

    … The social life here is limited but odd. The only people I have met of consequence are the pelota players. Pelota is the best ball game I ever saw and the pelota players are all Loyalists and mostly Basques, a fine folk anyhow. So about two nights ago I found myself with five of them, sitting in a café after the game, talking with the one who had played that evening, fast as wind, and by the time he reached us, sheet-pale and caved in. He was a lovely boy… who had fought for a year in the north in the San Andres Battalion, on that mountain which the German aviation set alight with thermite bombs, after they had practiced at Guernica. He retreated with his battalion back to Bilbao… and afterwards there was nothing to retreat into except the sea….

    I get on with my book [*Liana*]; it is more than half done Scroob [Hemingway] says it is good I hope he knows. He has often told me stuff stinks, so I do not believe he is just being a pal. I am worried all the time and will get drunk for a week when it is finished. What one needs is confidence: I can never be sure, for five minutes, that I have said what I wanted to say and as I desired. My own writing always seems to me peculiarly flat compared to anyone else's and my vocabulary bores me stiff. What keeps me going is the story (which I do not believe I will do justice to), and the background, which is the terrible and usual thing of a people on the march, the awful, now common, but unbearable and unbelievable flight of the refugees across Europe. Also what keeps me going is dog determination and pride. But by the end of every week, I feel light in the head and churning in the stomach, and the empty pages frighten me as much as the typed pages behind.

    Have you read Comrade Steinbeck's latest? I think it is very good. (It is not nearly as good as they say, but now the fashion is superlatives and no harm done.) Whenever Mr. S. confuses himself with God and writes like Tom Wolfe and the Saint James Version [Bible], seeing all, with a heart as big as a lake, it is pretty dead. But fortunately he has a story and comes back to it and tells it and his people are alive. At the end of course he goes off his rocker in a way that first takes your breath away and then makes you roll on the floor with laughter… Still, I keep wanting to write him to ask him how in hell he happened to do anything so lamentable and odd. He goes along fine, close to a truth, sticking very tight to his material and his people, remembering all the details which prove it and make it moving: and then he has to end up in a rain soaked barn, with a girl who has just produced a dead baby, feeding a starving stranger from her bosom.

I love you desperately. I don't know Auden, I know Spender. We saw him in Spain. He was always very upset about the dead and blood and what–not. Most people try not to think about these things, because there they are, and what can you do about it. But he thought and thought and wrote poetry. We heard him read it one night in Paris; we thought it was bad poetry but especially we thought he was being awfully gloomy about the war. I criticized him and Ernest said, "Well, he's a poet isn't he. Can't be too tough on him. I guess poets gotta be sensitive fellows."

Love to you pearls. This is a godawful letter. I have a headache and it is hot as stink.

Blessings,
Gellhorn

MG to Ernest Hemingway

June 3, 1943
Finca Vigía
San Francisco de Paula

Dearest,

What do you think? Cleaning up your room there were hundreds of lottery tickets. I must say I am a little cross with you about buying so many because it is such an off chance and there were about a hundred and twenty dollars [sic] worth. I copied down all the numbers and dates. Then I sent Juan in town to check the numbers and by God one of them came out; a cheap come-out, for the whole ticket only $60 but better than a poke in the face etc.

… I love you like mad; but am very brainy and bossy and horrid and ugly so do not mind these reports from GHQ. Will try to write a soft womanly letter some other time. I kiss you my pig.

Marty

MG to Ernest Hemingway

June 5, 1943
Finca Vigía
San Francisco de Paula

Bug dearest,

I got quite excited in my mind over some lines of T.S. Eliot quoted in the *TIME* review of his latest poems ("Four Quartets") Reading them again I am not so excited I think; I believed they had something about my book in them and greedily seized on a title. I guess not however.

These are the lines.

"At the still point of the turning world.
Neither flesh nor fleshless;
Neither from nor towards; at the still
piont [sic], there the dance is,
But neither arrest nor movement."

What I liked of course was: at the still point of the turning world. That seemed very right. The little remote lives so near the center that they don't move, and then catching by mistake into the turning finally and smally. I thought "The Still Point," but now it seems obscure and what the hell. We will have to do better I guess. There's a vast homesick attraction in the words: at the still point of the turning world.

I wrote all afternoon today and well and with some juice... If I have a good day tomorrow I'll be well along. I seen [sic] the end allright [sic] and clearly; it's just a question of getting it down in the right words...

I love you my pig.
M.

MG to H.G. Wells

June 9, 1943
Finca Vigía
San Francisco de Paula

Dearest Wells,

Your letter came today. It came (since these are the times we live in) as a para-chuted package of food into the jungle, as a nice passing empty rubber boat to what they call 'survivors.' I am so dying for talk. There is a big hollow longing for talk in me: you would find me a far better listener and learner and giver than I was that winter when you were like a snowed-in teddy bear with me in Connecticut.

… I am reading Stefan Zweig's *Autobiography* with such a passion of understanding and pity that I almost can't read it. It seems to me unbearable in every line, knowing that the man killed himself for no personal failure or despair, for no lonely human reason, but simply that without his arranging it, the world exhausted him and that he was actually driven too far. I do not know exactly why that seems so tragic that a Viennese Jew should kill himself in Brazil but it does; that is too far from home…

My own book [*Liana*] ought to be finished in a month. I don't know about it. Maybe it's all right. I must have a wide cowardice in me somewhere because I find confidence very hard to come by. It is difficult always to write with a doubt inside you: and the conviction that no matter what you do, you meant to do something much more. As for the love part, I do not believe these people are in love: my people that is… But the man is something like me, and I know damn well his job would come before his life (if you can call passion a life): so I think I guessed right in this case. I am very sorry for the girl in the book, but on the whole I am sorry for women. They are not free: there is no way they can make themselves free.

Wells, save me some time will you? Time to talk until all the saliva dries up, as well as the ideas. I also knew (or learned later) the meaning of the word Stooge. The meaning is wrong but the sound is different from the meaning, and a funny, amiable pleasant sound. If you prefer darling, I will however remain your adoring,

Martha

MG to Ernest Hemingway

June 13, 1943
Finca Vigía
San Francisco de Paula

Dearest,

I will not go to New York because

1. The picture [*For Whom the Bell Tolls*] may be awful, and by presence alone one approves it and it is hard to insult your hosts
2. How would I explain why you were not there? It would call attention and comment to your present occupation
3. I hate flashbulbs and interviews; I have no talent for being a celebrity even by marriage

4. I do not want to interrupt my life right now. I am really determined to finish the book [*Liana*]; if I start thinking about New York all is lost

5. I would not postpone or discommode Mother in any way

All these reasons are equal in value and when Mr. Mealand [Paramount Pictures executive] long distances tomorrow, as he wires that he would, I shall tell him very definitely nothing doing; but we would appreciate seeing the film …

I love you. Very tired. I missed my calling really; I should have been one of those organizing agencies, I have a talent for that.

Love,
Bongie

MG to Ernest Hemingway   June 14, 1943
Finca Vigía
San Francisco de Paula

Dearest Love,

It is raining which is nice for the planting and bad for Gigi and the new whitewash, which runs off like milk. This a.m. I packed the kids, so that is all settled.

… I love you. I am tired. Don't know why. But the end of the book is wonderfully clear in my head though I do not write. But every night I see it very clearly, and Liana is a poor woman really, a poor stupid lost woman without a place to live. So in a way it is a story of two men who finally go home, in their various ways, and a woman who has no home. If that is a moral?

Love,
M

MG to Ernest Hemingway   June 15, 1943
Finca Vigía
San Francisco de Paula

Bug dearest,

I worked today and now there is only one chapter left to do and I have said it over so often in my head that it seems impossible for it to escape me or present great towering difficulties. I would wish of course never to write a book again, the way I feel now; but I know how it is. The book creeps up on you, you suddenly find yourself started and there you are, in jail, until it is over.

Oh how I miss you. I miss you desperately and feel very sad and sort of lost. But it is better to stick this out and get everything done and then be free. You know what I thought: after Mother and the children go, in August, and I will be done with book and house, couldn't you manage to be here with me for two weeks alone and we will have a honeymoon before I leave. Could you? It would be very fine if you could. I'd rather have that than see you now, though I would certainly be happy if you walked in the front door this minute.

How do you find the children? Pretty wonderful aren't they? I guess they had a fairly ghastly time here with me alone but they will have forgotten that now.

Goodnight darling. I'm sweating and am going to take a shower. Then read John Whittaker's book and have a Martini [sic] and then to bed. I just live to write; simply waiting for the time to come around when I can write again. This is the bitter last period: it cannot end too soon for me.

Don't cut your beard; I want to see it as long as you can get it. We can always have that man from Dubi's come out and shave you. But I want to see it. Don't get too fat either darling; somehow don't. It will all just have to come off.

I so love you. Oh Bughouse. I give you a huge hug-a-lug, international style.

Bongie

MG to Ernest Hemingway

June 28, 1943
Finca Vigía
San Francisco de Paula

Bug my dearest,

How I long for you now. My cats are very good to me but fortunately or unfortunately they can neither read nor speak. I say to them: it is a good book; and they chase-chase over the table and roll with the electric wire and Friendless, with her dynamo purr, sits briefly on my lap.

I am enjoying Alicia who does the typing. She is surely the most unicellular female I ever had dealings with. Today she said, 'Martha, I hate men.' I believe it too: the way labor hates capital. She finds my books 'absorbing'; she loves Marc's 'reactions.' How odd it all is; how odd is life. Who ever would have thought that I, who started out with the dream of writing (and that dream at least never changed) and lived in a *maison de passe* alongside the Madeleine and romantically, self-consciously, bought a bunch of violets to wear, instead of buying breakfast, when I went looking for jobs (I was twenty), would end up here in this perfect safe beauty, finishing my fifth book. Alas, I do not want to grow old; not even if I write so much better, know more, and have an enviable instead of a rather shoddy uncertain life that only my posturing could dignify. I do not want to grow old at all. I want it so little that I would trade that wretched first book [*What Mad Pursuit*], right now, for this perhaps excellent fifth one: to have, included in the exchange, the fear and the surprise and the hope of twenty.

… I wish we could stop it all now, the prestige, the possessions, the position, the knowledge, the victory: and that we could by a miracle return together under the arch at Milan, with you so brash in your motor cycle [sic] sidecar and I, badly dressed, fierce, loving, standing in the street waiting for your picture to be taken. My God, how I wish it. I would give every single thing there is now to be young and poor with you, as poor as there was to be, and the days hard but always with that shine on them that came of not being sure, of hoping, of believing in fact in just the things we now so richly have. Well, shit. I am a fool.

… Marriage is a rare thing, since it happens everywhere in nature and always has, since it is more an instinct than otherwise, it must be good. But it is a brutalization too. You've been married so much and so long that I do not really believe it can touch you where you live. That's your strength. It would be terrible if it did, since what you are is very much more important than the women you happen to be married to, and certainly more important than this institutionalized instinct. But it is an odd performance. One is safe: two people live together and know they will find each other at certain hours within some kind of walls. And slowly, for each other, they become the common denominator: they agree without words to lay off the fantasy and passion, the difficult personal private stuff: they find some common ground, which is green and smooth, and there they stay…

I would like to be young and poor in Milan, and with you and not married to you. I think maybe I have always wanted to feel some way like a woman, and if I ever did it was the first winter in Madrid. There is a sort of blindness and fervor and recklessness about that sort of feeling, which one must always want. I hate being so wise and careful, so reliable, so denatured, so able to get one. Possibly why I have always been happiest at wars (and also because I have never been hit) is that war is the greatest folly of all and it permits the participants to throw away all the working paraphernalia of life, and be fools too. If that is being fools?

… I will almost bet twenty dollars that this letter makes you angry, my Bug. Doesn't it? What does she mean, you will say, complaining and crying for some other time and place and life? What the hell is the matter with that bitch: haven't I enough problems without her? But I am no problem, Bug, never think that. I am no problem. I have a brain locked inside the skull bones, as have all, and this is my affair. I only write to you as I know tonight I feel or think because why not: we cannot be so married that we cannot speak.

Marty

Aboard *Pilar*, immersed in "crook factory" work, Ernest explained that he was exhausted from steering the boat for "10-12 hrs a day," and he was sorry for boring her with daily accounts, but the nearest thing he had to privacy was "the chance to write to my Bong and so I just put down whatever comes into my head and it is a very dull head." He cautioned her that "where this letter is crabby or righteous or chickenshit just skip it."

Hemingway responded to her fantasy of repeating the past in Milan: "I think it would be wonderful. I loved Milan and you are who I love and never really loved anybody else and think how wonderful it would have been with you. But we are older and only fools are suckers for youth." He reminded her that he was "living in greater discomfort than I ever did" though admittedly not as bad as her boat trip around the Caribbean the previous summer. His only regret, "outside of lack of contact," was that he was "not there to be with you with your book at the end and to celebrate and enjoy it with you and be happy about it and help you in any damned way that I could." He worried about her plan to return to the European front because of his antipathy for wars, "for the people that die; that are enslaved; that are away from those they love; that are bitched; wounded; hungry; cold; oppressed; abused; and from the general chickenshit way they are bungled, run eternally fucked up by the idiots that handle them." He understood her need to report on the ordinary people living under extraordinary circumstances but he also respected her "head" and her "necessity to kick against whatever pricks," though he reserved the "right to say when" she just kicked from necessity, reminding her that "there are worse pricks than me."

Hemingway had anxiety dreams that he recounted in detail, like a sequence on July 6th when he was "expelled from the Havana Yacht Club (to which have never belonged)" and where "Mrs. Roosevelt on a visit to the front fired an anti-aircraft battery which shot into town and eight greek [sic] medlies [sic] came in and surrendered." He figured all of this meant that he had "better come home" to Martha.

Edna Gellhorn visited Martha at the Finca in August, and Ernest wrote to Martha about her need for intensity and that he hoped she would go easy on her mother and "rest her and not worry her." Hemingway knew that Martha had "all of Shakespeare" in her, "the comedies and the tragedies and the histories and the poems," but urged that she would give her mother "more of the comedy… and not that phony tragic shit that no one can ever be happy."

MG to Ernest Hemingway

July 4, 1943
Finca Vigía
San Francisco de Paula

My dearest Bug,

What a jolly ratfuck…

I love you; my God what a mess for you. I will spoily [sic] you very much…
Love Love Love. I will take care of you….

The house is now pink. I hope you will like it. I adore it. I feel very amused to
live in a pink house which temporarily (until rain and sun streak and mildew it)
looks like a sweet birthday cake…

I ate breakfast this a.m. on the back terrace looking at the view and it was cool
in the shade and quiet and beautiful with four cats romping on the lawn… Also
been getting big sunburn to counteract pasty end of book. Will you like me, short
and curly-haired, brown and thin? Sitting in front of our nice shiny pink house?
Hope so. Love to childies [sic].

Marty

Maxwell Perkins to MG

July 19, 1943
597 Fifth Avenue
New York City

Dear Martha,

I knew you would hate to write about your book, but I didn't see any way out
of it. And anyhow, it won't in the least affect my judgment or my enjoyment of
the actual manuscript. What you say serves the purpose very well, and the note we
have written will do nothing but good. It simply gives us a note, and the title—
and the title is all right, too—which at the moment is very important. I simply had
to ask you to do this though I know I was asking you to do something hard, and
something distasteful.

I don't believe that Ernest will like the picture [*For Whom the Bell Tolls*], but
just the same, as pictures go it is very effective, and extremely exciting. The funda-
mental trouble with it is that all the subjective part, of Robert's memories and
thoughts, which are really so essential to giving the true meaning of the book are
not there. But could they be there? I never saw a movie where they were—and
most writers simply accept the fact that the movie will never be the book. It
simply cannot be. But as a spectacle it is remarkable, and there are scenes in it that

nobody will ever forget. I suppose stars have to be stars, that the audience wants Gary Cooper to be Gary Cooper, and that the movie people do. But Pilar, and Pablo, and Anselmo, the old man, are unforgettable. I never saw any good book in the movies that really put the book into the terms of a dream. I doubt if it can be done, but superficially this one did follow the lines of the book much more than any other I know of—But superficially only.

I hope we shall see you soon, and the manuscript sooner.

Yours,
MAXWELL PERKINS

Maxwell Perkins to MG

July 27, 1943
597 Fifth Avenue
New York City

Dear Martha,

I finished the novel last night and with admiration. It seems to me a very remarkable performance, and to be successful to the veriest [sic] end. And I don't wonder that it was a great struggle for the material and the theme presented many difficulties and problems. But you mastered them, it seems to me. For instance, it is astonishing that one feels a loathing for Mark throughout the first part of the book, and ends with a liking and respect. Liana is made lovely and appealing and beautiful. One feels the whole quality of the place, the heat, the storm, and the sordidness of Liana's home. And one understands perfectly the way the young Frenchman feels about Liana and about France, and that he must fight for her again. That is the way it seems to me. A most unusual piece of work.

I am afraid I have made Charlie a little mad by sending the manuscript to the printer so quickly that he had no chance to read it. It came at the very end of the week, and I took it home, and sent all but the last two chapters off the first thing Monday morning so as to get going in view of the pressure of time. But I wouldn't have done it so hastily that Charlie couldn't see it except that I was sure, and so was he, that the carbon which you sent four days before the original, would arrive any minute. But it hasn't arrived yet. Surely it will come this week, and he can read that over the weekend. We'll get the proofs ready as fast as we can.

Anyhow, I think you have handled a most difficult story with amazing skill and success. I'll say no more now, for we can talk it all over when you come.

Yours,
MEP

Post–August 12, 1943
Finca Vigía
San Francisco de Paula

Dear Max,

I hasten to tell you the joyful news; I have found a title. We think it is good and I hope you will. It is: *"Share of Night, Share of Morning."* All of that. Does it scare you? It is only 7 syllables but it is a lot of words. I have been thinking how it would look on the cover; and I think it can be done, one word under the other, both on the back and the front hard cover. Thus:

> *Share*
> *of*
> *Night,*
> *Share*
> *of*
> *Morning*

Maybe without the comma if so printed. I dunno [sic]. You don't use running heads on the pages anymore, and on the title page of the book I think you could write it in two lines:

> *Share of Night,*
> *Share of Morning.*

It sounds quite pretty to say and it doesn't sound like anything else; I mean like any other title. It comes from a thing of Emily Dickinson (which should be quoted on the title page):

> "Our share of night to bear
> Our share of morning."

It is a very literary title but it is simple literary, instead of involved literary. It means something for the book too; I mean the book really is only about people and living and what you get if you live. And it is a very interesting idea (if I have understood the poetess) that you have to bear your share of morning too.

What do you think of it? Could you quickly write me? I am getting interested in this book again, after having gone through a dead-tired period when I could scarcely bear to remember it at all.

Am hurrying to get this off. Hope you are pleased with it.

Yours,
Martha

MG to Ernest Hemingway

September 8, 1943
The Berkshire
New York City

Beloved Bug,

It is 6:45 a.m. I went to bed at 1 a.m. & have been awake since 6. It is hard to sleep because there is no air in the room & very little in the whole city. I feel ill & gloomy. Have lived on my desert island for so long; and prefer same.

Yesterday had lunch with Colebaugh. He agrees to *all* my plans & suggestions, finds them very good. He says I'll be off in 2 weeks with good luck—longer with not so good luck, but in all cases no doubt about getting where I mean to go.

… Oh Bug I love you very hard & much & every minute and it seems a folly to be so far away. When this war is over let's go on a slow easy trip together all the time and not see *anybody*.

Do you know you can buy bubble bath powder for 5 cents in an envelope. I bought one & fixed it over the weekend & it would be perfect for you I think how fascinated the cats would be. I'll bring some.

Bug, I give you a big keep-you-company and love-you-always kiss.

Mooky

Edna Gellhorn to Ernest Hemingway

September 13, 1943
4366 McPherson Avenue
St. Louis

Dearest Ernest,

You must be very amused noteing [sic] how I keep you "abreast of the times" with clippings. If I were really your clipping bureau I should have to invest in bigger envelopes in order to forward that items that even I, rotten reader that I am, discover in papers and periodicals. Last night at a movie "The Invaders" Leslie Howard in playing host to a Nazi (Leslie didn't know at the moment that he had a viper in his nest) asked him, "What do you read? Hemingway?" So Leslie Howard belongs in our clippings.

According to our papers there have been some tereils [sic] in Cuba, but none in the West Indies according to "Caribbean Cuisine." I mean international part of tereils [sic]—Martha's letter from Paramaribo-Suriname was delightful—what a feast you and Martha will have of an evening telling tales in your wonderful living room—lamps lighted, music playing, drinks in hand and good talk—

My love to you.
Mother

MG to Ernest Hemingway

September 16, 1943
597 Fifth Avenue
New York City

My dearest,

My typewriter is broken so I am in Max's office while he is in Baltimore.

… Mousie [Patrick Hemingway] was here today… and we had a beautiful big luxurious breakfast at the old dining room of the Plaza looking out on the park and carriages and with the windows open. Then we rode through the park in a carriage and went to Mouse's doctor because he has to have a health certificate for school. The doctor said he had grown two inches but no extra weight.

[on *For Whom the Bell Tolls*]

… Bug, the reviewers are crazy. It is a fine picture… the most adult I ever saw. You cannot think of the book, it is another medium.

… Gary [Cooper] is wonderful… His love scenes with Ingrid [Bergman] are more beautifully done than anything he has ever done before; his hand on her hair is enough to make you cry. And my Christ her hair is a moving thing, so lovely, so lovely. He did with his eyes, his smile, his hands, as beautiful and restrained a piece of acting as I have ever seen. It is a tender love story, not the grab-all passionate fake of Hollywood.

… I so love you and so miss you and so admire you and am so proud of you. I am so glad you are not here in a specially made suit being noble in bars.

… More tomorrow. Yours really always and forever,

Mooky

MG to Ernest Hemingway

September 17, 1943
The Berkshire
New York City

Beloved,

It is 7 p.m. and I am going to write you & then go to bed and sleep 14 hours. I am *awful* tired. This a.m. I got your 3rd letter. I wish I were with you. You sound very sad. You do need me don't you. It's me specifically, too, isn't it? Please go on making such good care of your health and the cotsies, and we will be together again as soon as may be.

Today I lunched with Aldanov [Nobel Prize-nominated Russian writer]. He is not really the way I expected. He is jollier, surer, older, more worldly. He is unusually polite. He told me six times that "*votre mari est le plus grand écrivain de notre époque*." [Your husband is the greatest writer of our time.] He said he was perhaps he was the first Russian to appreciate you, 20 years ago in Paris when he first read you. He said you were *un homme de genie* [a man of genius] about the way Europeans do—it's a little embarrassing—and it always makes me feel like a profiteer, as if I profiteered on being your wife.

… Today I had my picture taken for Scribner's (I told Charlie he'd have to pay) and if one is good, will send it to you.

… I hope to go to Bryn Mawr to stay with Gertrude Ely [Bryn Mawr professor and head of the Pennsylvania branch of the League of Women Voters] tomorrow but I can't reach her, thus far by phone, so maybe she's away.

Oh dearest my beloved Bug, I give you such a homesick hugalug. We are a pair of little animalies who belong together on the Ark.

Bongie

MG to Ernest Hemingway

September 20, 1943
The Berkshire
New York City

Beloved,

I'm so sad for you. I'm sad about your mother dying and I'm sad about losing the gun which was like losing a really good friend. I couldn't have been decent about the gun. My dearest, I wish I could do something to help you. Is there anything I can do about your mother for you?

… I read the fall book list in the *Times* & my heart sank. So many of them, Bug. How can mine swim to the surface? Joe Chamberlain lists my book as follows (in his preview): "Martha Gellhorn's *Liana* is written by the wife of Ernest Hemingway." Ah well shit. If they want to do it that way, there is nothing I can do.

Last week I had the impression the book would be a success. But now I have no such impression. I resign myself; my last duty is to see that the dust jacket material is okay. And then I'll forget it. I don't want to break my heart over it being disappointed.

… I miss my bearded bear. Oh my God my Bug, how I think you are the only one.

M.

MG to Ernest Hemingway

October 1, 1943
Gladstone Hotel
New York City

My beloved,

Maury [agent] tells me, over the phone that Paramount is really seriously interested in the book; "if they can change the character." That means Liana. Make her white, I suppose… I find it all grim… and aside for the money I don't give a damn about it… There is no more brain or talent or courage in the theatre than in the movies. It is all shit. The way I feel is: all passes, books alone remain. A book is a hard beautiful unperishable thing.

… Louise Dahl Wolfe took a lot of pictures for me in Central Park and *Harper's* chose the best for their magazine. It is really very funny. It shows me reading a newspaper on a rock in a gale, with my hair blowing straight up from my head, and my old red coat buttoned sort of cockeyed around me. It is quite pretty and lively… It was hard to choose the right one for the book. I picked one which looked young, kind of pensive, and had a nice long row of park benches curving in to the background. Max liked one, very profile, laughing, much wind, but the hair in that distressed me, it looked so like Colette in her old age.

… Meantime nothing happens about England and I do not know what to do about it. And I worry over you. There haven't been letters for a few days so I am sure you have left… But Buggy, I meant what I said: I am yours first of all and you are my main concern, and if this is too hard for you, I don't want to do it. You tell me what you want and that is what I will do.

Now I must write Mother as I have not written her for a week and she is lonely too. I also must write Giggy and explain some books I sent him. I love you my darling. I love you more than I could put down in this public letter.

Always and always
Mooky

MG to Ernest Hemingway   October 4, 1943
                                                    Gladstone Hotel
                                                    New York City

Beloved,

   You must be away from home now because there are no letters. I wish you such
good luck and that everyone is happy *a bord* [sic] and that Sinbad works out well and
that everyone is eager and healthy. Oh my Bug, it is very bad not to be there; I find
it much easier to wait there than here; it is evident that men were made to go down
to the sea and women stay in the houses they left waiting for them to come back.
Waiting in a hotel where no one will come back is scarcely the role of any sex…

   We went to see *Farewell to Arms* because I had been too tired, curse-ridden to
go alone the night I planned… And Gary [Cooper] was awkward and ludicrous
in those riding pants uniform and such a poor actor, and everything phoney and
wrong and I wept with all my heart, weeping for your youth and everyone's youth
and remembering the book as I saw it betrayed before me, and weeping with
loneliness for you and for everything that I am ever lonely for. The only true line,
I thought, was in the hotel (never explained, the hotel), when Gary said, "I hate to
leave our fine house," and then I saw you like a big huge warm eyed loving bear-
like cobra, and saw all your always regret to leave whatever fine house one was in.
Oh Bug, how I miss you…

   Robert took a lot of pictures today so you will have those too as well as the
Dahl Wolfe proofs. I hope you will find something to keep you company in them
all. I need company awful bad too Buggy, and have your picture tacked right
alongside my pillow to say goodnight to.

I love you but surely you know that absolutely and well by now don't you dearest.
Marty

<hr />

MG to Eleanor Roosevelt   Early October 1943
                                                     Gladstone Hotel
                                                     New York City

Dearest Mrs. R,

   Tommy [Malvina Thompson Schneider, Eleanor Roosevelt's private secre-
tary] called and I feel very badly because, instead of coming at once when you
suggested, and when it was probably convenient for you, I said I didn't see how I
could. You see, there is a girl who is coming out of the hospital and I promised her

two weeks ago, before she had the operation (kind of as a consolation for having it) that I would go with her to the country for four days of convalescence. There isn't any substitute to take my place and though naturally I would rather see you, it would not be very fair. But if I miss you entirely that will be too grim…

I saw your pictures in the new *Life* and I think you look very pretty; tireder in some than in others but otherwise wonderfully well and handsome in the uniform. And with a smile like a blessing for the lonely people. I would like to tell you something in writing because I would never say it to you because of getting shy when one talks though not shy when writing. Yet it is hard to write because it should be exactly written. And anyhow it is that you are one of the really valuable people in the world because you stand for something, in yourself, in your heart, that is like a symbol of all the decency and generousness that the world longs for, and is sick and hungry for; and you are there like having it in person, as a model, and as a hope. I do not know whether I write it as clearly as I feel it but it is very true; and you must never change or die or anything because you are necessary. When one gets really discouraged, thinking of how the world works, there is you and then one is not discouraged.

Also I love you

Right now I have tetanus in my right shoulder and typhoid in my left and small pox on my leg, and I take a personally rather dark view of life. But this ought to improve tomorrow. If I can get passage on something or other I should be leaving in two weeks. It has been a long wait and I am very homesick for Ernest. I didn't even realize (the fine perceptions of a novelist) that I was after all a very ordinary and average woman who gets a gloomy wandering pointless feeling just because one man isn't near enough to shout at. But I do, and more and more, and if it keeps up like this in a few years I'll never be able to leave the man at all, and will be extremely surprised to find that freedom isn't such hot stuff in the end.

On the other hand, I can't see him anyhow, and had an odd mainly solitary year behind me so I guess the thing is to get through the war like the rest of the human race.

How I hope you can see me and how I hope you're not too tired of telling it to tell me some things about your trip and even if you are too tired I could just give you a big hug and leave you in peace.

Always,
Martha

October 8, 1943
Gladstone Hotel
New York City

My dearest love, how are you? Are you hoppy [sic]…

Today Charlie Scrib [sic] asked to see me and he wants to publish my book on Jan 9, but would publish sooner if I was disappointed. He said he could not publish until Nov 8 at earliest; won't have copies enough for ten days, then needs time to get to reviewers and stores and all deliveries very slow. Also said all stores would not re-order after Dec 1—would simply sell the stock they had because of being short-handed and crowded Xmas mails. He says my book is not Xmas book, and would be better to wait, build it up, put in for some good advertising space, have plenty of time for deliveries, and really make it the first big book on their list for the New Year. I said okay; did not seem possible to me for them to do any sort of proper job on it now. I do think Charlie would love to make a success of me and if he believes Jan 9 is better, I think I ought to agree.

… Bug I miss you waking and sleeping, every minute. I have gotten so used to being loved that I cannot feel alive if you are not there to love me. I want to tell you everything and show you everything and it seems very pointless to exist in a vacuum without you. I beg you to be very careful of you, for me, because you are all that I have got and I love you with my whole heart.

Goodnight dearest Bug.
Mooky

October 18, 1943
The White House
Washington

Dearest,

I must write you quick before it fades. You always say have a marvelous time, and I wasn't having, and I feel so sort of scared & lost because I wasn't & thought the ability to enjoy people was gone for good. But I am having a marvelous time now & wanted to tell you. I think it is because I have work to do (seeing all furriners [sic] to arrange my work in England) & enough extraneous attentive guys to take me out for meals & make me feel a life of beauty. (I was feeling like an old Bryn Mawr graduate)

Harry [Hopkins] said, "I bet Ernest is having a hell of an interesting time." And I agreed. No more. And yesterday I suddenly found myself telling Lillian Mowrer, who probably is too sympathetic to me, that I loved you so damn much I couldn't bear this being away.

... I'm dining with the Joyces tonight. They introduced me to some people in Bobby's former shop who made very fine contacts for me with representatives here.

I adore you & am so glad to write you a jolly letter for a change.

Love,
M. Bongie

MG to Ernest Hemingway

October 20, 1943
Gladstone Hotel
New York City

Just back from Wash [sic]—8 p.m. Found 3 letters from you. You are a good, generous uncomplaining man. How could we know it would work out so stupidly. I thought you'd be gone even before I left—2 or 3 months away at the least. I thought I'd wait 3 weeks—be abroad 3 months—and you'd be alone only 3 weeks in all & probably childies there at Xmas for company.

But now there is good luck for me & maybe it will be catching on to you. Harry [Hopkins] arranged things mainly because Mrs. R [Roosevelt] wanted him to, but also friendliness for us both also. And I am leaving (they say) from within 4 to 7 days. So... And now all I wish is that your luck gets good & you go quickly where you wish.

Mrs. R. showed *FWTBT* at the W.H. to a dinner party. Everyone said very fine things about it; but it drags like hell in the cave in the middle. Gives you squirms. Mrs. R. loved it, she said. I think she meant it. They all thought it was anti-fascist anyhow & Ingrid [Bergman] beautiful.

Everyone in the world asks for you & asks if I am related to you. I say *closely*.

... Please forgive dead-louse letter.

I will write you a good letter Bug when I have slept; this is a news letter. The main thing is that I see now I am going to do this job well & I see how to do it, and I feel confidence again (which leaked away in the waiting & in the disgust of watching people try to peddle my book). And since it has all been so poorly timed (through no fault of ours) the thing now is to carry it off as well & quickly as possible...

I so love you. And admire you. And wish you a quick get-away. Kiss all cotsies [sic] warmly.

Love,
Bongie

MG to Ernest Hemingway

October 21, 1943
Gladstone Hotel
New York City

Dearest Bug,

I just make talk to amuse us if we can. Just a little gossip from the Rialto. What I want to say is goodbye for while, Bug. Take care of yourself for me. Take good care. And have the great good luck that you have earned. And maybe come to me if that happens and if not I will come back to you; and in all cases, as you know, art passes all alone endure. And we are all alone. Please know how much I love you, how well, how admiringly. You are a much better man than me but I hope I am not too bad a wife, even if I have gone away when I thought you would be away too… I hate to leave you. And you are so good and generous and always want me to be happy and I feel ashamed of being happy unless you are. And tonight, just going, just feeling ahead already the strange places I am happy like firehorse. But like woman, and your woman, am sad: only there isn't anything final is there, this is just a short trip and we are both coming back from our short trips to our lovely home and our loving cotsies [sic]. And then we'll write books and see the autumns together and walk around the corn fields waiting for pheasants and we will go to all the places and be very cosy in them and we have everything both now and to come. I don't mean to write you any kind sad or dramatic letter or anything my Bug but I just want you to know how I love you.

Goodnight,
Mooky

Charlie Scribner told me a funny story today. He said Edmund [Bunny] Wilson had written a book, one long short story and some shorts, completely pornographic. Scribner's turned it down, couldn't publish it Charlie said with disgust. Bunny wrote Max a letter, citing paragraphs, situations and scenes in 5 of your books, saying you publish this of Hemingway which is much worse than mine.

October 27, 1943
En route to Lisbon

Beloved,

When I wake up, I don't know where I am. This was bothering in N.Y.—happening every morning or wherever I woke I the night—but now it is very fancy & one wakes in a panic, thinking: I'm late, I've overslept, I'll miss the plane. Not yet used to being truly on the way…

We flew very steadily, like in a rocking chair, to Bermuda. The berths are perfectly comfortable aboard & in the morning we landed with an enormous bounce on the famous swells of Horta. Such a bounce. I was loosely strapped in a chair opposite the chief steward and my feet went right over my head & we apologized to each other. Very funny. Felt like being a tennis ball.

… Seeing Azores at first gave me a big thumping beating of the heart—to see land that was almost Europe again, and I feel sort of choked in my throat & funny sick with excitement actually to be in Europe, in Portugal in another 2 hours.

I'm very happy now although a little punchy—you remember how this long plane travel sort of unhinges you even though it's completely comfortable. But you feel liverish and weary and a bit odd, anyhow. The company is regular (Spanish meaning) but as I sleep most of the time, do not see them anyhow. I miss you. Haven't read a book or magazine *en route*. My beloved Bug, I kiss you good.

Bongie.

October 29, 1943
Estoril Palacio Hotel
Lisbon

Beloved,

We have been here 2 days—maybe we will leave today or tomorrow or who knows when. The Estoril is a beautiful place, more like San Raphael than Cannes, and it is a little colder than one likes…

… I have danced 2 nights. I love that & find I am good at it again. I go about with a *cuadrilla* [gang] consisting of the Clipper captain, the co-pilot, a tall acne-masked gloomy young radio engineer & a very sharp young man from Montana who heads our scientific bureau in London (better ways to exterminate). Of these the Captain (who has a hideously scarred & deformed forehead—with a piece of that frontal bone obviously gone) is the only adult. But they are solid &

cheerful drinkers, good dancers & very attentive to your wife, and I have a fine brainless time.

Last night we went to a Russian place and the vodka was really beautiful. I never had better. There was a fine accordion man who went from table to table playing what you asked for… When the according [sic] came to our table I said play *The Last Time I Saw Paris*. It lilted out like a really marvelous insult to the heavy, weary, dead-faced men, and here it was, back again, defiant & wonderful in a marvelous song. Half the room applauded like nothing before; & they were silent. I almost wept with pleasure.

… I love you my Bug. I'm really very happy. I guess one's tastes change very little. I adore moving—I am a very superficial girl. The only real roots I've got, or want, are growing in you & mother. But do not think I do not love our home… It's just that it's such fun to see the world, at 250 miles per hour.

A big loving Portuguese kiss,
Bongie

TEN

The Face of War

"I scream for kindness. Let there be kindness.
There is bloody little and never at a high enough level."

—Martha Gellhorn, letter to Allen Grover

The morning after arriving in London at the beginning of November 1943, Gellhorn set out to buy her war uniform. There was a "C" for correspondent on the left jacket pocket and her army accreditation papers gave her the honorary rank of captain. From her temporary base at the Dorchester Hotel—where correspondents stayed in approximately two-week rotations—Gellhorn began to try to convince Hemingway to join her in Europe to cover the war. He resisted for months, while she reported on the young men flying the Lancaster bombers on dangerous night missions over Germany. Those planes "looked like enormous deadly black birds," but "somehow they looked different when they came back."

At the same time in Cuba, Hemingway wrote revealing letters to his publisher Charles Scribner and to Edna Gellhorn. To Scribner, he explained that Martha "was very discouraged because she said nobody could remember the title of her book (*Share of Share Of* [sic]) and that everyone called it *Liana*." He was "damned lonesome without her," so he went to "shoot all the time for more money than I can afford to lose" and to "keep from drinking nights and mornings," because it slowed him down. He tried a little dark humor, noting, "have eleven cats now and five dogs. I sleep on the floor with the cats and they hunt mice in my beard." To his mother-in-law, he was even more vulnerable, writing, "I'm just so damned lonely that I feel I'm dying a little each day like a tree that has been girdled." He believed that he "had learned how to be patient, to be understanding," but now he was "sick of it and would trade in my carefully taught and acquired virtue to have a wife… to love and cherish and go to bed with and talk to… and not a female war-correspondent [sic] who only comes home to get ready to go somewhere else or to write a book."

In January 1944, Martha wrote to Ernest, "I have to see before I can imagine. I feel and act like a hardworking stenographer and I feel kind of happy about it in a grubby hardworking way." Writing journalism was "an honorable profession… even when not pleased with what I write, I am immensely pleased with what I have understood." The January issue of *Harper's Bazaar* included a glamorous profile photo of Gellhorn, wearing a slash of carmine lipstick, a lit cigarette in her right hand, noting that she was "again right up front where the news is being made, as a *Collier's* correspondent in England." The magazine piece, however, did not allow Gellhorn or her work to be recognized on their own merit, as the copy also reported that "Home, when she is there, is a finca outside Havana, where her husband, Ernest Hemingway, is busy on his new book." That he wasn't busy on a new book—the case at that time—never occurred to journalists who wrote about him even in passing. Ernest sent a short response to Martha indicating that, although he was planning to finally join the war effort, he took "not the slightest interest" in where he was going and felt "no lilt nor excitement." Rather, it was as if he were an old horse, "being saddled again to race over jumps." He enclosed a review of *Liana* from Book of the Month Club, insisting that it revealed how Martha "wrote much better" than she knew before she "started ambulance chaseing [sic]." And, although they had been away from each other for five months, it felt to him "like that many years."

Her novel *Liana* was published at the beginning of the month in the United States and Hemingway wrote to publisher Charles Scribner on a copy of the *New York Herald Tribune* print ad that he was "furious that Scribner's is not doing more and better advertising." The first print run was 27,000 copies and, by February, half of those had sold. *Collier's* also profiled Gellhorn on March 4th and quoted Hemingway's perspective on her work as a foreign correspondent, which hinted at his problematic preference of viewing her as his wife first above all else: "She gets to the place, gets the story, writes it, and comes home. That last part is the best part."

Gellhorn returned to Cuba mid-March for a short respite. Hemingway had finally decided to go to the front as a war correspondent and to that end contacted *Collier's* and swiped his wife's accreditation. Each American print news outlet could send only one accredited journalist to the Western Front. Gellhorn had worked for *Collier's* as a foreign correspondent for seven years and filed dozens of pieces with them. Hemingway, who had previously freelanced for NANA—the North American Newspaper Alliance—could easily have found work with it, but he chose, out of spite, to approach *Collier's* in order to make Martha miserable. She was understandably furious, and when he announced he'd be flying to England, thanks to a favor from Royal Air Force attaché Roald Dahl at the British Embassy in Washington, she asked him to arrange her passage as well. He declined, claiming that no women were allowed on the flight. Later she learned that actress Gertrude Lawrence joined him on that flight. Instead of a quick flight, Gellhorn had to take a slow boat to England, one carrying explosives. She was the only woman and the only civilian on the Norwegian munitions ship.

MG to Ernest Hemingway

November 6, 1943
Dorchester Hotel
London

Beloved Bug,

It is really fine here… Ginny [Cowles] is a darling & completely helpful & I seem to have loads of pals & am having a marvelous time… Found out Leicester [Hemingway's brother] joined up here & is in the army & am going to write him & invite him to eat whenever on leave… I am only allowed 2 weeks in this hotel. It's a sort of room rationing system. No mail from you yet; please keep using the Embassy as address. I have my new war correspondent's card, with "assimilated rank of captain." And lots of privileges appertaining thereto.

It is hard to write because I'm so excited I can't sit still or think coherently. Everyone asks for you. Everyone. You are a big local hero & everyone speaks of your book & is very excited about soon seeing the movie. I'm dining tonight with some commando officers just back from Salerno & when they go off on a job they say they are "going bell-tolling." They all read your book as if it were a guide or a Bible & there are a lot of sound people who wish you were here to work with them. And I wish you were here. I think you'd love it Bug. It's so marvelous to be around with good sound tired people who make jokes & no shit. You would like them fine.

I've been seeing a mixed bag of nationalities & been very warmly impressed thus far. I am really & truly happy now…

I'm dining with [H.G.] Wells tomorrow night & going out with Ginny next week & probably starting off on the R.A.F. job. Such a dull letter my Bug. I give you a big hug-a-lug & a kiss for each cotsie [sic].

Always,
Mook

MG to Ernest Hemingway

November 20, 1943
9 Rex Place
London

Dearest Bug,

First I will make you a business letter with enclosures. Then I will make you a little letter written by a woman with a very awful cold in her head, who is also very awful tired. Then I will make you a hugalug by mail and also a kiss-kiss for the cotsies [sic]…

I found out that it was impossible to buy your books. I got mad and wrote Cape [Jonathan Cape, UK publisher] saying this is absurd. In the *Times* book store they said the only chance you had of buying anything of Hemingway was to get it second hand. However, you are I think more read and popular here than in the U.S. and people want your books. I told Cape to send a copy of *FWTBT* to a man who had once known you in Paris… Of course my book is completely unobtainable and he never printed the stories.

The extraordinary thing is how well people have read you; coming in last night on the train I started talking with an RAF officer; he knew everything you'd done, and specially loved *Farewell to Arms* and *Death in the Afternoon*. It is not the awful shitty literary talk; it is talk of straight and good people who have gotten a big happiness out of your writing. I am proud for you, too, but it seems a pity that I alone reap the benefit of this respect and admiration. It seems like a big imposition and horning-in and I am ashamed.

I have done my first piece called the "Bomber Boys" and when I have showed my only copy to the Air Ministry and to the Group Captain of the station I visited, I will send it to you. The censor cut out the best line, the best writing I mean, which saddens me.

… I have your pictures tacked to the wall by my desk [8 x 10 photos she kept always], and I try to remember exactly how you are from them, but I cannot. I've talked too much about you; that's the bad thing. I mean, not saying anything as you know, but talking of your books and so on, and what you like to do and how you look and in a way I've talked you away from me. Like talking away a story. I feel that I am just someone who happens to know, or is alleged to know quite well someone that everyone wants to know. The pictures straighten me out a bit and then I remember you are just Bug and that is lucky. Otherwise, at a distance, you become monumental and not quite human, and I am a sort of oddity—the very ordinary wife of a very extraordinary man.

... Where are you I wonder, and what doing. I love you and send you a fine diseased kiss-kiss. And, turning away the diseased kiss, a fine hugalug [sic] to keep you company.

Goodnight my Bug.
Mooky

Edna Gellhorn to Ernest Hemingway
November 27, 1943
4366 McPherson Avenue
St. Louis

My dear Ernest:

I've seen the film [*For Whom the Bell Tolls*] and was excited during every minute of it. You have not seen it? To get what is given in the film, one dare not set it alongside the remembrance of the book. Comparisons would destroy the film, but as movie art and acting it seems to me tops.

How are you? Have lots of things been claiming your thought and action? If so, all is well. One letter has come from Marty written just after arrival in London. Mr. Scribner sent me a copy of *Share of Night, Share of Morning* [*Liana*]—They've done a fine job, haven't they? I like everything about the looks of it. Has Bessie Smith's book come your way? *A Tree Grows in Brooklyn*. It bores me, but I must be wrong—it has had eight or nine printings—Does that prove everything? George is in the States. He is to be sent to sea to his great joy. More of this when I know more. He has spoken with me by long distance twice. I hope he can spend a week with me before he sets sail. Walter is in Washington with Ickes. What are the vacation plans for Patrick and Gigi? Will they have long holiday time with you?

My love to you.
Mother

MG to Ernest Hemingway
December 1, 1943
War Correspondent, Crowell Publishing
Force Headquarters, A.P.O. 887
c/o Postmaster, N.Y.

Dearest Love,

This a.m. the embassy phoned to say there was a cable and they read it to me and it said fifteen letters mailed love miss you. So now I feel fine though I doubt I will ever see the letters. You better just cable me from time to time so I know you are allright [sic] … I write you and have no belief you ever see the letters; it is sort of like Emily Dickinson putting her poetry in a bureau drawer.

Ginny [Cowles] is a boon to me. I see her every day and most evenings, when I get back very weary, and she is helpful and loyal and jolly and I am devoted to her. One does need a good close pal to count on and tell all one's stories too [sic], and she's it…

I had dinner with Koestler a few evenings ago and I cannot stand him. I almost never took a quicker and firmer dislike to anyone… He evidently thinks that he alone has a corner on the Light and the Way. I absolutely loathed him and made it clear, and the feeling was mutual. Now I am finished with writers, having met Waugh and Koestler: it's too disappointing. In future I will just read what they write…

Now I have to go back to bed. I feel too awful. My tummy has gone to bits also momentarily. Hell. You are always quite right in your judgments (unlike me) and what you say about staying where you are as you stayed in Spain when Joris went to China, is probably right. But if there were any reason to change that idea, you would come wouldn't you? It is also good to see this; you would see better than I do and understand better, as you always do. I think it is all going to go quicker suddenly, just a feeling as like everyone else I know nothing at all…

I send you a big kiss, carefully kissing you someplace where you won't catch flu, and a big hugalug and solidarity and wish you much luck and good fishing and a fine weather and everything you need.

Your loving wife,
Bongie

MG to Ernest Hemingway

December 9, 1943
Dorchester Hotel
London

Dearest Love,

Your second letter came today. It was dated Nov 12 and you had just got back from a trip and the cotsies [sic] had made a big fuss-fuss [sic] over you and you had found the short in Mother's room (you can't think how often those electrical comrades have failed to locate and dominate that problem, and you are a wonder and economical genius as well) I love you and I miss you and I wish you were here where you would be the darling of all… I so wish you could come. I think it's so vital for you to see everything; it's as if it wouldn't be entirely seen if you didn't…

I am a little fed up on London which begins to feel slightly like Valencia, and I am definitely weary of important people with big intellects. The hell of not being at a front is that you never really see anyone continuously or long enough or well enough to know much about them; even if you do run into fine guys at air stations it's just like being one of the reporters who stop people in the street and ask them what they think about communication with the spirit world. I like to have lots of time, and to live with the same bunch until I feel that I belong and understand them, and then write. But those are ideal conditions, and there isn't time. So what the hell.

When Ed Murrow went on that Berlin trip he went with my chaps that I had written about, and flew with one I knew, whom Ed and I both think is an absolute wonder. I'd have been scared to death; I simply couldn't do that. Planes really scare me.

… Well now I have to work my beloved Buggly. I can't bear to think of this article, about all the poor burned guys, and it has no shape in my head and I'm worried about it, and have those panics of thinking I'll never write another line. But I have to start and now is the moment. I wish you were here with my whole heart. Is there any tiny possibility? Goodnight dearest. Make a kiss kiss to all cotsies [sic].

Mooky

MG to Ernest Hemingway

December 13, 1943
Dorchester Hotel
London

Dearest Mucklebugletski,

Today I got four letters from you and it is a national holiday.

… I think you would like the cold long train rides, listening to the people talk. I think it is not disgusting to look at the world and at the war; because someone must see, and after all we have trained ourselves to see. It is an honorable profession. You are a very great writer and what you see gets pressed down and compact and one day it becomes a book. I am not a very great writer and function more like colonic irrigation, with things coming in and out at top speed. But I am on occasion very mildly pleased with my articles… pleased with what I have understood. My mind feels good now, lively and digesting with ease.

… I have to live my way as well as yours, or there wouldn't be any me to love you with. You wouldn't really want me if I built a fine big stone wall around the finca and sat inside it. I'm the same person who wrote articles for a steamship line trade paper to buy a third class passage to France in 1929. *I'll never see enough as long as I live.*

… Good night My Bug. God I am sleepy. The day isn't long enough nor is the night.

I love you,
Mook

MG to Ernest Hemingway

December 22, 1943
Dorchester Hotel
London

Dearest Buglet,

Merry Kissmiss [sic] and hoppy hoppy [sic]. I wanted to write you over the weekend when I was in a beautiful village, seeing life in village with charwoman, village groceress, plumber, policeman. I am too tired to write the story but it was fine there. The Thames is a tiny little river and reminded me of our place in France and the lock. I know what I want after the war: I want to travel on little rivers in Europe, never in a hurry. There were wild duck on the Thames and Spitfires over it and old land, gentle and smoky, and a winter sun. The village grew out in lanes, and each house was so like all the pictures one has seen of them that it didn't seem true. There was ivy on the old gravestones and a peace so solid that not even four years of war could change it. There was no haste; and the three dead boys of that town were mourned with a lasting unhurried grief. I wish you had been there. If you had liked nothing else and I often think you would not like it, you would have liked that place.

… Bed is "white cold and lonesome" (these are the words of a very young Dutch boy who was being scolded by his elders for never coming home) but it is sleep and not thinking or feeling. Today a Polish Jew, now in the army, came to see me; he had lived in the Warsaw Ghetto and worked in Europe afterwards. He was full of a tough iron dignity and he read me some things he had written about those times, so as to save my time. He had written it down to compress it, you see. It was almost more than I could bear, and I still feel the horror of it and the shame that I have helped no one and always been safe and lucky.

Well, so what. So I shall go on doing my stories. There must be some value in them since the people I write of are all pleased by what I write and perhaps just to give them pleasure is enough. I don't know anything, Bug. What do you know? Merry Kissmiss, my Bug. I am going to a very cold bomber station to keep the chaps company for Xmas.

I love you but my God you are far away. Cuba is the end of the earth right now and I cannot imagine it well. I think of you and the cotsies and you are real and my own, though very far away, but everything else—the kind good loving boring people and the life—is remote and somehow awful and I dread it. Please forgive me. When I think of it, it is like being strangled by those beautiful tropical flowers that can swallow cows.

I love you Bug. And am tired as hell. But so glad to know about other people even if I cannot help. Maybe just admiring them and loving them is a slight service.

Bongie

1944

MG to Ernest Hemingway

CABLEGRAMA
1944 JAN 1
ERNEST HEMINGWAY
HOTEL AMBOS MUNDOS HAVANA

DEAREST BUG HAPPY NEW YEAR AND FOR ALL OF US TO BE
TOGETHER IN IT STOP RECEIVED SEVEN LETTERS

FROM YOU STOP PLEASE IGNORE ANY BOSSY UNAPPRECIATIVE
SEEMING LETTERS WHICH WERE WRITTEN IN HASTE AND

MAINLY BECAUSE SO WANTED YOU HERE AND KNOW YOU ARE
MOST LOVED IMPORTANT THINK I HAVE KISS CHILDIES [sic]
COTSIES [sic] MISS YOU AND MISS YOU

MARTHA HEMINGWAY

Edna Gellhorn to Ernest Hemingway

January 9, 1944
4366 McPherson Avenue
St. Louis

Very dear Ernest,

Don't tear up the gloomy letters, send them. They won't make me happy, but I'd rather have them than keep wondering how you and the cotsies [sic] are managing. You don't know me very well, need I suppose. I don't know you really, you're not easy to know but I know enough of you to love you and to understand your loneliness.

Men generally can't manage loneliness. Women are generally better at it, perhaps because traditionally men have gone and women have waited, so we learn about being left from our fairy story times straight through our lives. The men go forth to fight dragons, lions, one another, or to bring home the bacon and women wait—so we're conditioned—well you're not, nor are others like you able to accept loneliness. I understand that much.

I hate to have you unhappy. How I wish I knew how to help. You don't want to leave your work there? Does Martha *ever* hear from you? She has had one letter from me. I've had four from her—she says she has sent her articles to you. I have my copy of "*Liana*" which is beautifully put together by Scribners [sic] and I am very proud to have in "for Edna Gellhorn." Here's hoping it gets some good reviews. Virginia & Walter F thank you for sending love. They wish to send theirs to you—oh darling you I love you.

Mother

On January 14th, 1944, Ernest wrote to Edna Gellhorn to tell her that he was planning to close up the finca and head north to New York City to "get a newspaper job to get across [the ocean] and join Martha" in London. He complains that he hates journalism "as much as Martha hates to miss excitement and world shakeing [sic] events," concluding that "this is what is known as a compromise I suppose." The letter is frank and reveals his emotional frangibility when he admits, "She really loves me, when she remembers it, but she has damned little imagination about what she does to me." He closes, resolved in his decision to go to England because it had been months since he had seen his wife. And, also, because Martha had shown him in her letters that he needed the experience on the western front for his future writing. But, he wonders, nevertheless, "... if I didn't need it, what about that?"

A month later Ernest writes to Edna again, this time worried about their "beloved Marty" from whom he has not had any word in the intervening days. He had tried to reach Martha through the U.S. Embassy in London, their friend Duff Cooper, and *Collier's*, all to no avail. He is yet in Cuba and wishes Edna were there to keep him company, insisting that he loves her very much. In a postscript he notes Martha's novel *Liana* "has had wonderful reviews all over the country. Several say that she is a better writer than me which should please her."

MG to Ernest Hemingway

January 15, 1944
Dorchester Hotel
London

Dearest Love,

It's been so long since I've written you that I am disgusted with myself. I have been ill again for nine days and just no energy to write letters because during same period had to turn out long difficult but I think very successful article on the Dutch. That's my fifth. Now I am writing my sixth and last on the Poles...

... My whole faith in the human race is re-established. I feel again, as I always used to, that however history works is usually cruel and bad, but the world is full of incredible people, such honorable and modest and jolly ones: and somehow people are better than the world they make or live in.

... I wish you could see me now; I am so thin it is amazing. I suppose I weigh about 123. I am told, because people are such goofs and so suggestible, that I look like Ingrid and I rejoice in an undeserved glamour because they believe I am the heroine of your book [*FWTBT*]. Being an honest type I disabuse them of this at once but it makes me feel very flattered and very glamorous. Also I wish you could see me in my uniform because that is too amusing...

Please give my love to all cotsies[sic]. Especially to my dearest wicked little Thruster. I loved your story about Graciella's little girl. My beloved Bug you are such a sweet and lovely man. It's so sweet about how you hadn't been courted for so long, so you were impressed. I'll court you until you are weary of it.

Always and always,
Marty

MG to Eleanor Roosevelt

April 28, 1944
Gladstone Hotel
New York City

Dearest Mrs. R,

Thank you very much for letting me come down. The White House is certainly a fine rest cure place, and I slept more than I have for weeks so returned here freshened up. Am now right back in the frantic stage, of endless errands and what-not. Actually I am getting almost sick with fear: the way it looks I am going to lose out on the thing I most care about seeing and writing of in the world, and maybe in my whole life. I was a fool to come back from Europe and I knew

it and was miserable about it; but it seemed necessary *vis-à-vis* Ernest. (It is quite
a job being a woman isn't it; you cannot do your work and simply get on with it
because that is selfish, you have to be two things at once.) Anyhow, due to Roald
Dahl—who has been angelically helpful—Ernest will get off to England at the
end of next week. But I have been shoved back and back, on the American Export
plane passenger list, and we do not know whether the RAF will consent to fly
me over (it's different for Ernest) and there I am. In a real despair and a real fear.
It's so terribly ironical too, because I had it all worked out, just how to cover the
Invasion, and during all the winter I was learning and learning so that when the
great time came I would be better able to understand it and now God knows what
happens. It will take an awful lot more humility and good sense than I now have
at my command to make such a great disappointment bearable, in case it all works
out for the worst. However. Anyhow Ernest will get there and he can always tell
me about it, as if that did any good.

Thank you again darling for letting me come down. I'm always happy just to
think of you, and what a person you are, and the good it does simply to have you
alive and going about being yourself.

Devotedly,
Marty

Eleanor Roosevelt to MG

April 29, 1944
The White House
Washington

Dearest Marty,

I am distressed that you are delayed and hope you will be able to get off soon.
Do let me know.

Much love,
E.R.

MG to Allen Grover

May 7, 1944
Gladstone Hotel
New York City

Darling, when I said I knew all about loneliness and it was just a thing people had
and should make a fuss of, and that I expected nothing anymore and could get

along fine, and all that other big talk, it was not so much whistling in the dark as it was positively screaming in the dark. It is all rot as you no doubt knew at once. And what I am, as all the other times, is sad and by myself and frightened. It seems very awful, if not unendurable, that you will not be there to make the going not so hard, to make it gay, to make it part of all the goings when you were there and I knew I would come back and you would be there too. I could never tell you what you mean to me. But I love you and that will always be true.

Marty

Gellhorn kept a diary, "Notes on a Sea Crossing," of the long days in May from the 9th through the 26th, when she was the only civilian and only woman on a Norwegian freighter run by 45 men and loaded with amphibious personnel carriers and dynamite, part of a convoy heading to England. As they sailed out of the harbor in New York "between a wall of black ships," shepherded by lit tugs "like water beetles" and "blinking buoys," she observed it looked "like a lit mountain—Hongkong [sic] or Mont St. Michel," a fat orange moon, strange in the beautiful night.

She knew she would miss Edna, recognizing that since her return to the United States and then home to Cuba mid-March, it had been a bad time, "with only Mother shining fair in it." The first morning at sea she saw the convoy through the porthole in her cramped cabin, looking "like a game for children—small grey ships in neat rows across the flat grey sea," the fog horns from other ships sounding "like lowing cattle." And, there was "Nothing to do for 20 days except live." Some meals she joined the crew and realized that "all conversations with Europeans now" had a new shape. When she talked about "marriage, divorce, new houses, jobs," they talked of "prison, confiscation, fines, torture." It was a lesson in perspective and comparative privilege, an apt reminder to Gellhorn that she was fortunate.

She passed the time sleeping, reading, writing letters and making up stories. Of the books she had with her, she enjoyed the anthology *Heart of Europe*, fiction from 1920–40, especially the pieces from Italy, and found Flavin's *Journey in the Dark*, a rags-to-riches story set in Chicago that would win the Pulitzer Prize in 1944, "a bad book," though she stayed up all night to finish it. Several days out of New York, she reflected that it was "really damn funny to be in a fog, with confused ships all slowly plodding about & a hold full of explosive," amused that the captain had told her not to bother to insure her luggage.

One morning the captain woke her to show her a swallow that had fallen on the ship, "worn-out from having flown too far, destroyed as a plane that crashes w. [sic] empty tanks. Beautiful rare & delicate w. [sic] the feathers so finely put together." Gellhorn worried that he was too attentive, observing that she was "right back into the wars again, 45 men & 1 woman." She knew firsthand how "proportion affects emotion." The captain's attention got her to thinking about Hemingway, which she tried not to do because she could not think about him "with kindness, but only with dread." That same day she was soon distracted from her worries, because "all of a sudden the sea was a mess of ships steaming around at odd angles, like people playing musical chairs."

At dinner one night a shipman reminded her of the "tyranny of money" for ordinary working folk, and she realized that she had "not written of it enough nor understood it enough." She hoped that the problems of her "very own tiny life" didn't "spoil the world" for her and blind her to everything that mattered.

On deck near the end of the voyage on May 25th, her grandmother's birthday, she saw "the land—murky lowish line of bluffs: Ireland to the right, Scotland to the left," and felt "such a feeling of wild happiness." Their convoy was now "a triple long line of ships, close enough to tow each other" through the Irish Sea. Her shipboard letter to Hortense Flexner richly detailed her psychological and emotional state during those days.

When Gellhorn's ship docked in Liverpool at the end of May after 17 days at sea, she was told that her husband had been in a car crash a couple of nights before after a blow-out bash for foreign correspondents at photographer Robert Capa's flat in Mayfair. Hemingway was in a London hospital.

Upon arrival at the London Clinic, Martha found Ernest holding court with his cronies, including Robert Capa, Irwin Shaw and William Walton, a crown of 57 stitches around his bandaged head, dead soldiers of booze bottles stashed under his hospital bed, *TIME-LIFE* correspondent Mary Welsh at his side. Within a couple of months, Hemingway began writing love letters to Mary Welsh, addressing her as "small friend" and "kitten."[15]

MG to Hortense Flexner

May 17 probably, 1944
At Sea

Teechie dearie,

God what a fine time I am having. I have just written seven pages of a short story that is going to be good; very good I think. Oh heaven help us, I hope it is going to be good. I am all sweaty and weary and feeling fine, the fine flying feeling, or as if one could walk on water. I hope it will be good. I hope I am not slick; I hope I do not make it work too easily. I hope this ease is the final result of having worked a long time, and being professional and knowing how to handle the tools; I hope it's not slickness.

… I have slept so much that days do not exist any more, there are just periods when I happen to be awake but it can be night or day. Yesterday it was clear (all the rest of the time fog) and suddenly there were three icebergs. So yesterday was Iceberg Day. The other days have no names. I had never seen an iceberg and they are more beautiful than you can believe and very wild. They fit into the ocean, they are wild and strange like something of another age before things got organized and spoiled. One of them, through the binoculars, looked like the wings of a white pigeon that had fallen head downwards to die, the wings peaked up and flaring. One looked like an enormous monumental Aladdin's lamp, with great high architectural sides, smooth and high and hard, made of granite if granite were diamonds. One was a great peak, a conventional iceberg, with a high fang of ice cutting up into the sky.

The convoy gets all mixed up, like musical chairs, when there is fog and when the fog lifts all the ships scurry about like children in grey school uniforms, trying to get on the chairs again. Sometimes, when it is in order, it looks like a toy, an enormous number of unlike little grey ships sewed to a big flat piece of cardboard. It so happens that this miniature tub on which I am the only passenger is carrying a great deal of stuff which would go BOOM if the very slightest thing happened. One cannot even smoke on deck. I think that is damn funny; one cannot smoke on deck and meantime we wallow around in this fog, blowing our whistle waspishly at everyone. (The whistle says, for *Christ's* sake don't run into me, you baboon, I'll explode.) It is the first place I have found for a rest cure in years. There never was so much sleep, so much time to read, dream, write, and just sit. The captain, who is the only person who talks to me, is a homespun Norwegian, a really kind and considerate man, and as he loves to talk and loves company I drive myself up to his sitting room for a while every day.

… I have read the first version of *Lady Chatterly's Lover* with a foreword by Frieda Lawrence. If you want to be made good and sick, read that foreword. Women are really too bloody awful. It is one of the most godawful tasteless mindless things I have ever read. The book is quite interesting, though for my money Lawrence cannot write at all. He is a dreadful writer. Dreadful and undisciplined. But I found the book this time a real book, quite a good psychological novel, a study in boredom and marital distaste. I wonder why he went on writing it until he got that highflown pornography at the end.

I am terribly happy you loved Ernest, as he deserves it. He is everything you said about him and he is more. He is a rare and wonderful type; he is a mysterious type too and a wise one and all sorts of things. He is a good man, which is vitally important. He is however bad for me, sadly enough, or maybe wrong for me is the word; and I am wrong for him. I don't know how it happened or why, as one does not know these things, they are some curious chemistry like the oddities that go on in one's blood cells. You must of course never speak of this. As far as I am concerned, it is all over, it will never work between us again. There may be miracles, but I doubt it, I have never believed in them. I am wondering now if it ever really worked; I am wondering what all these seven years were about exactly. I feel terribly strange, like a shadow, and full of dread. I dread the time ahead, the amputating time, I do not see how to manage it. I do not want the world to go dark and narrow and mean for either of us, and the world has been very unlovely in my eyes, and I very unlovely in it, ever since I got home from Italy. I wish there would be a beautiful mistake in compasses and this ship would deposit me in Italy instead of in England, so I would not have to go through anymore of the hardness and hurtingness. It is, note, my fault: I am the one who has changed. Or maybe I was changing all along, so slowly that it was like getting a callous; but now the callous is there where there ought to be softness and trust and love. And I am ashamed and guilty too, because I am breaking his heart. It is as if, quite unknowingly, he sharpened a sword and then it up and stabbed him. We quarreled too much, I suppose. He does not understand about that; he pays no attention to quarrels or to words said in anger. He expects each day to be new and the mind new with it. Unluckily mine is an old mind, which keeps all things about as they were; and the angry words have been ugly wicked little seeds which have taken root I guess and there is a fine harvest of mistrust to be reaped. It is all sickening and I am sad to death, and afraid, and as I said guilty and ashamed. But I cannot help it. I only want to be alone. I want to be by myself and alone and free to breathe, live, look upon the world and find it however it is: I want to escape from him and myself and from this personal life which feels like a strait jacket.

Well enough and enough for always. I want my own name back, most violently, as if getting it back would give me some of myself. Please use it always from now on, writing to me. And do not worry and do not feel badly. We are, basically, two tough people and we were born to survive.

Have a fine time, you two. You really do not know how lucky you are: having had the world's bad luck piled on you with a shovel, having been hurt by crooks and with God sending germs from time to time in order to make all easier: but you have the heart's good luck. It is the rarest kind surely, and without it I am not sure there is much value. There is a great deal of interest, fun, excitement, pride, triumph, I suppose; but there is a hollow as big as a house. There are no hollows in you two; you are all alive. There are no cold dead places. If there are any people to envy, then you are those people. Only not envy, Teechie dearest; you are two people to love and to thank God they exist and that, in a way, because they have such a home I have a home too.

Love,
Gellhorn

MG to Allen Grover   May 27, 1944
                                                           At Sea

Darling,

We've been out just a little longer than Columbus. Right now it is kind of spir-ited. There was, during dinner, a series of faint ship-shaking booms. Depths charges said the captain as he passed, with his mouth full, towards the bridge.

... I wish peace would be at least as purposeful and moving as war.

... Please never abandon me. Just be as you always have been, if you don't mind, a distant warmth, but always a warmth. It is a very odd feeling, at 35, to be begin-ning your life all over, sort of naked only rather tireder.

... It is pleasant to read and tell ourselves stories and write. And in some time there will be England and all the mess and doubts and hurts and difficulties to be gotten through, before one can simply lose oneself in work and in hurry. What an opiate hurry is. I have been taking it as dope my whole life.

Marty

Gellhorn gathered with other foreign correspondents for a briefing on the morning of June 6th at "9:46 or so," when they were informed that "In 5 sec [sic] the command will be given to the world. You may leave. Go." She jotted those details down in a tiny 2x4-inch notebook that she kept and labeled "Notes on D-Day." As she made her way around London that day, to Westminster Abbey, to Buckingham Palace, to the Prime Minister's residence at 10 Downing Street, people she asked about the invasion news thought it was only a rumor. All morning there was "no visible change except a small crowd jokingly trying to buy up regular noon editions."

She made her way to Southhampton where she observed "kids playing in bomb ruins," and it was there that she stowed away on a Red Cross hospital ship, waved aboard by an official when she claimed to be writing a story about the nurses. In a 1992 radio interview Gellhorn recalled that it was "a wonderful rap to say... it's a women's story, which is then regarded as of absolutely no interest at all and harmless." She locked herself in a toilet until the ship was on its way. All she did was "just write about it. What it was like day, night, day, on that ship. The inva-sion was one of the most amazing and extraordinary sights ever to be seen. And, the ship was very moving."[16] That night was "very blue with one star," and she was baffled about being "scared worried for E [Ernest]." Her first sight of France on June 7th was of "ships thick as ducks," and four roads "like brown scars up green cliff." She saw "sunk tanks with only wireless antennae showing above water" and "mines being exploded, one high thin like a fountain & the shrapnel like skipping stones on the water."

On June 8th, she went ashore—the only correspondent to do so; even Hemingway was confined to an amphibian craft—and helped to evacuate both Allied and Axis wounded, noting "grt [sic] speed & efficiency loading. Special tenderness towards colored wounded… Everyone watching in silence. No wounded speaking: too ill." Aboard in the ward for German prisoners, "cared for by a Jewish colonel who spoke no German," Gellhorn bellowed *ruhig*—be quiet—on a doctor's orders and another man repeated, "*du muss ruhig sein*" [you must be quiet] and they "were all instantly silent." She observed, "We are helpless against our own decency really."

Collier's published their pieces in the same issue later that July: "Over and Back" by Gellhorn; "Voyage to Victory" by Hemingway.[17]

MG to Colonel Lawrence

June 24, 1944
Dorchester Hotel
London

My Dear Colonel Lawrence,

I want you to know that I sincerely appreciate the understanding assistance of yourself and your staff, and that I am writing this letter not in criticism of persons but in criticism of a policy. As you know, General Eisenhower stated that men and women correspondents would be treated alike, and would be afforded equal opportunities to fulfill their assignments. This was later qualified to mean that, when American women, military personnel (in this case Army nurses) went to France, women correspondents would also be allowed to cross. As far as I know, nurses were working in France towards the end of the first week of the Invasion, but though eighteen days have now elapsed since the landing, women correspondents are still unable to cover the war.

There are nineteen women correspondents accredited; of these I know that at least six have had active war reporting experience, and at least two (of whom I happen to be one) have been war correspondents for seven years…

Speaking for myself, I have tried to be allowed to do the work I was sent to England to do and I have been unable to do it. I have reported war in Spain, Finland, China and Italy, and now I find myself plainly unable to continue my work in this theatre, for no reason that I can discover than that I am a woman. Being a professional journalist, I do not find this an adequate reason for being barred. The position in which I now am is that I cannot provide my magazine, and three million American readers, with the sort of information and explanation which I am sent here to obtain…

I must explain to my editor why I am not permitted to complete my mission here, and I trust that you will provide me with an official explanation which I can in turn send on to him. Naturally, since he has a very great obligation to the American public, he will protest this discrimination through channels in Washington. It is not the understanding of the Free American press that its representatives should be prevented from writing the news of a war which concerns every family in America...

It is necessary that I report on this war; the people at home need the most constant and extensive information, and my share of that work—humble as it may seem—is my obligation as a citizen. Since I am helpless to fulfill my obligation here I wish to return to Italy where I always found the greatest cooperation for the Press. Though Italy is now a secondary phase of the war, it is better to be allowed to work anywhere than to be refused permission to work at all... I do not feel that there is any need to beg, as a favor, for the right to serve as eyes for millions of people in America who are desperately in need of seeing, but cannot see for themselves.

Yours sincerely,
Martha Gellhorn Hemingway

MG to Hortense Flexner   August 4, 1944
                                                                  London

Teechie dearest,

I saw it all right. The takeoff as you say. What happened with me was that an airforce type popped into my bedroom at six a.m. or something and said it's happened and I said don't be silly, and he said no really. Then later I went languidly to the greatest press room of the world, where I was summoned (and they practically searched us) and we were locked in there while all the serious types pounded out a thousand words a minute saying nothing. Suddenly the doors were unlocked and we were allowed to pour out into the world like the germs from Pandora's box. I went out to my taxi and told the driver, he was the only person I could find quickly to impress. He said, it's not true, they wouldn't have started without telling me, why I'm on 24 hour duty. I then went around London looking for reactions. There were some American colored troops sightseeing in Westminster Abbey; they'd heard it and it was all one to them. There was a very old woman freezing outside the Abbey selling Red Cross pins, because it was the day of the Drive [sic] and she said she didn't think anything about it because it was very wrong to think anything about rumors. I got discouraged and went home to sleep.

The next day I went down to one of the embarkation ports. I saw the first prisoners arrive on the shores of England and wrote about it. They were a damn sorry master race. Everything was very lickety split and cheerful and you could get a ride to France easier than you could get a taxi. I went over myself the night of the second day on a hospital ship, and worked so hard I almost forgot to come up on deck and inspect the world. The wounded were very wonderful and I loved working not writing or looking, just working. I went ashore looking for wounded too and it was all sort of mad and ominous and dangerous and, in a way I can never explain to anyone, funny the way war always is funny. People rushed over and back and someone brought a bottle of French sand to the French girls who run a basement bar where all us folks hang out, and they tied red white and blue ribbon around its neck and wept and everyone was drunk as skunks.

After that red tape set in and I lost track. I got awfully cross because it appeared there were rules about women correspondents going to France. I had not heard of them and kept very silent…

I was bored and grumpy and couldn't find out what was happening and life was a dark thing until the pilotless plane which momentarily sped everyone's blood around enough. It did not frighten me, it seemed so much less than any secret weapon I expected. I slept without a quiver in my eighth or top floor room and sometimes when the noise was really too bad to sleep went up and watched them from the roof. Sometimes during the daytime they made you a little cold in the stomach. You couldn't hear them if you were in a cab and it was a shock almost to drive into one.

Then I left for Italy [setting for her play *Love Goes To Press*] which I had loved before and how right I was. This is the ideal theatre, it is successful and beautiful and the weather is good. Rome is very heaven; I cannot think why I did not know this before. Have been working very hard and having a marvelous time…

I'm now off on another fine exciting assignment, one I gambled on and which I look forward to with absolute joy. There never was enough time and there never was enough summer. But the spring and early summer this year were a time of such small grey eating sorrow that I can find nothing really very happy in them to remember. Now in July life has resumed its fine old pace, like a runaway train, like a comet, and it is funny and careless and all alive and I am happy again. I think I'll stay in this part of the world until the end of the war, but I think the end of this war is not far off. No later than November I should think and maybe sooner. And afterwards there is that wonderful thing I had forgotten and which Rome has reminded me of, Europe in peace. I want to see so many countries still and so many people. And I love this rare racketing job, which makes every day into a grab bag.

Yesterday I saw the worst thing I have ever seen in my life; it was so horrible that it passed the point where the mind or spirit can comprehend it. They are digging out of the catacombs the bodies of 320 hostages the Germans shot in reprisal for a bomb once thrown in Rome which killed 32 Germans. The smell was something utterly unimaginable and that garbage of human bodies, with nothing of human dignity left was the most ghastly sight I have ever seen. A great pit full of decomposing bodies which had melted into each other, and shrunken, and outside the people of Rome had made a sort of shrine and there were pictures pinned up, of real true people, imagined to be somewhere in that pit where nothing was real and nothing was people.

The Germans it seems are always very correct, only they shoot hostages every-where they go and Ginny [Cowles]—who is with me—tells me that in all the villages she has been going through in the north there are piles of hastily murdered unburied dead.

The war must also stop soon before all the lovely small old humble villages of Europe are smashed into grey rubble. And I think maybe the reason one is so very gay in a war is that the mind, convulsed with horror, simply shuts out the war and is fiercely concentrated on every good thing left in the world. A doorway, a flower stall, the sun, someone to laugh with, and the wonderful fact of being alive.

I love you both immeasurably. Take care of yourselves. We will all eat ourselves sick in Paris one day before we die.

Always,
Gellhorn

Days after Martha wrote to Hortense Flexner recounting her experiences aboard the Red Cross hospital ship during the Normandy landings, Ernest wrote to Martha from Mont St. Michel. He is even-tempered and encouraging, claiming he is "sure you will get good stories... and anyway liveing [sic] and being happy is better than stories." He tells her that he's planning to stay with the infantry division with whom he has been working, because he "would rather be with those who do the fighting in some useful capacity."

After Paris was liberated at the end of August 1944, Gellhorn returned to the city she had once called home, observing how it had changed since the German occupation, and spoke with Picasso, who said it had been a time "of little annoy-ances and big annoyances, but as they are now finished it is not worthwhile to speak of it." In her notebook she recorded, "Left Bank so much more warm-hearted—Poor restaurants—menus—no lights—people not minding," and people saying to each other, "What did you do during the war?"

In Paris, Robert Capa encouraged Gellhorn to telephone Mary Welsh's hotel room at the Ritz and ask to speak to Ernest, who was now romantically attached to Mary. She did. And set the gears in motion regarding a divorce. To her mother, Martha wrote, "I simply never want to hear his name again; the past is dead and has become ugly; I shall try to forget it all entirely, and blot it out as with amnesia. A man must be a very great genius to make up for being such a loath-some human being."

Even though Gellhorn had asked Hemingway for a divorce, a letter to his mother-in-law reveals that he not only sought Edna's emotional support in what he believed was Martha's mistreatment of him but also did not quite believe that it was over between them. He recounted to Edna his "bad skull and scalp business" from the automobile crash at the end of May in London, including the "headaches afterwards (worse than I knew there were)." There had been "flashes of politeness" between him and Martha, "but never any kindness." He hoped for "the prospect of a good, hardworking life ahead" with more "wonderful stuff to write," and did not want either opportunity to be destroyed by "good clean ambition and hatred of team play."

MG to Allen Grover   October 30, 1944
                                                              London

ON BRIEF REST FOUND YOUR CABLE STOP WHY NOT BRING YOUR BODY OVER AND WILL THERE ATTEND TO LOW MIND STOP FEELING PRETTY POOPED MYSELF ONLY SOLUTION IS CALL FOR LOUDER MUSIC STRONGER WINE STOP WRITE ME CARE APO 887 PLEASE DARLING AND DO COME OVER LOVE MARTHA GELLHORN

MG to Allen Grover   November 2, 1944
                                                              London

Darling, it is 8 o'clock and I have dined alone and am about to go to bed. This is revolutionary; in a year nothing like this has happened and God knows I have dined with fools. I feel myself very forlorn, since now returning to London after four months absence, I am so without hope that I will take no chances and will dine alone. It is like Dotty Parker, who sits and Suffers [sic] and never picks up the telephone.

Please come here soon and even at once. I need you. Is that enough (I would not think so). Who shall I talk to and who will tell me why I am doing what I am doing. Darling, it seems to me I had better get divorced. There is no one to marry, and if God has any benevolence for me he will spare me further horrid errors of the heart, when one tries to make permanence. I wish only to be unmarried; it seems neater. I am so free that the atom cannot be freer, I am free like nothing quite bearable, like sound waves and light. But I think it is disorderly to be so free and officially, legally, attached. There is a kind of theatre about this deal which is displeasing. I resent being asked after my husband and pleasantly lying: he is well, with the First Army... when I have no husband and it is all fake, and I want no husband, and why ask me.

On the other hand I want a child. I will carry it on my back in a sealskin papoose and feed it chocolate milkshakes and tell it fine jokes and work for it and in the end give it a hunk of money, like a bouquet of autumn leaves, and set it free. I have to have something, being still (I presume) human. But how does one work that out? My God who made it so hard to live, or does one weave this out for oneself every morning like a spiderweb (useless spiderweb catching no flies.)

Darling are you tired? My Christ I am tired. It's got me at last, I cannot bear anyone else dying. Though no doubt it is worse if legs and private parts get blown off by mine, and still one lives. Certainly worse. I can bear none of it. Nor the very pale big-eyed faces of children too small to talk, wounded in hospitals (in the cellars where they keep them since the town is still shelled).

I do not even know what I scream against, except the barbarousness of the human animal. I scream for kindness. Let there be kindness. There is bloody little and never at a high enough level.

What shall I do with myself? It is not enough to suffer for everyone, to have everyone's story like one's own personal guilt, to wake in the night sick for the people you know and do not know but can well imagine. (The ones I know are all dying; it is not worth while making dates.) One cannot stop anything or help anything and only finds oneself a little mad—with always the fine shrewd disgusting self protection that halts madness before it becomes heroic—and lonely and afraid not of the usual things, but of the unseen things, the dark series of days, the long days and the long years and all the time ahead which will be no better than this time.

... I feel too fiercely to write, even to talk. It is no good to be alone either; though one makes no noise the screaming is all there.

And what happened to the fine gilded hopes when one expected to be like other people, with a place to come back to, someone to trust, someone to whom one could say anything without shame: what happened to the desired never existing always comforting loving trusting arms that were to be guarantee forever against nightmares. What a shitty business: who invented marriage since it fails.

I am in good health, you will be interested to hear. I am a witty dashing woman who can vamp any young man (specially if he is at the front and there are no women for miles around and no tidy small mouthed boring decent little girl who is exactly his cup of tea but now, due to high explosive, lacking from the scene). Oh Allen come and hold my hand and I will hold yours. Life is as long as war.

I do love you and always did.
Marty

MG to Edna Gellhorn   November 14, 1944
                                                              London

Matie dearest,

It's been weeks since I wrote you. This will be such a bad letter that I wonder whether it is right to bother. I got your sweet one of October 27, my birthday letter; it was full of talk and silences. It is as if you made the talk to cover up the silences and that would not surprise me. There is really so little one can speak of nowadays without misery.

I've been at this business too long; maybe this business is simply living and maybe I've done that too long too. I went to England almost three weeks ago, to sleep and think. I was so tired I thought I was going to die and so I slept a lot and got sadder and sadder. At the end I went to a doctor and found out that as usual my blood pressure was abnormally low, accounting for the fatigue (which is still with me). One takes vitamins and thyroid and what does one take for the mind or the spirit. No pills are available.

If only my own life was a mess and a sort of boring dismal failure, that would be bad enough; but I cannot separate anything and my horror about the war has gotten beyond the place where I can control it. There is no use going into that: writing of it only makes it worse and there is no sense in dumping it onto you. But every dead [sic] seems to me to be part of me, and I can have a feeling of such absolute and unutterable despair that I can scarcely handle it. The Catholics brand despair as a mortal sin, and they are right. For them, it is to despair of the Lord, to be without faith: but my kind of despair is a loss of faith in life and it is surely as bad.

I do not want to stay here and I do not know where to go. I would like to go home and there is no home. Home is something you made yourself and I have not made one. I feel so rootless now that it is fantastic; one cannot be as free and live. You are my only link I think with life, because I believe in you and you go on; but since no one can help me, except myself, I must find my way out of this alone. Perhaps writing is the answer; I shall try.

This is a long wailing; if you can believe me, I wail for the world. For myself I do not know what to do, not even wailing seems to have any point. E. and I will get divorced now, I feel sure: he is not here but will soon return and I shall talk to him before going off on the next job (Toulouse and a story about the Spanish, and so tired that it gives me horrors to think of going anywhere but as it also seems horror to stay anywhere what does one do.)

There is something you must not repeat to anyone at all: Bum [Jack aka Bumby Hemingway] has been wounded and captured. It is pretty awful isn't it. I think E must be at wits [sic] end and hearts [sic] end. He has a girl [Mary Welsh] not a good one unfortunately, but she will seem so and he will try to make a life with her. I wish him such luck. I have grown so queer that I really wish to see no one and I do not know how to make time pass. Well this is the worst letter yet and will not send it. And how I love you every minute of every day.

Marty

ELEVEN

The Heart of Another

"I think I have learned all there is to know about amputations;
one has to learn all the time, doesn't one?"

—Martha Gellhorn, letter to Ernest Hemingway

In January 1945, Gellhorn wrote to Allen Grover about her loneliness, something with which she had struggled for years: "When I'm alone sorrow drowns me. This is a grief I did not know I could feel and it is very hard to bear." So, she focused on work, and followed Mauriac's imperative of *"travail: opium unique."* Work was her chosen opiate. In spring 1945, Gellhorn traveled with the U.S. Army's legendary 82nd Airborne unit to research the piece she was commissioned to write for the *Saturday Evening Post*.[18] Under the command of General James Gavin, they joined the Allied forces' push across Germany and actively engaged in fighting. British troops liberated Bergen-Belsen, one of the Nazi concentration camps, on April 15th, with Edward R. Murrow observing, "I have reported what I saw and heard, but only part of it. For most of it I have no words."

Gellhorn remained in Europe, reporting on the war for *Collier's*, including the liberation of Dachau in May 1945.[19] Forty years later she'd say that "Dachau completely darkened my hopes or feelings about the perfectibility of man. It, by the way, was not the worst concentration camp, it was the first.[20] And, it was my private war aim to see it opened. That such a thing could be, that there were plenty of people demand such a thing, I just thought we are imperfectible. There is something wrong with us." She felt as if she had fallen over a cliff and "suffered a lifelong concussion without recognizing it." She wrote about those hours at Dachau—her visitor's pass permitted her access to "the camp and compound from 1600 to 1800"—in her war novel *Point of No Return*.[21]

Gellhorn spent August 1945 in St. Louis with her mother, where she wrote to Hemingway about making arrangements to send her possessions from the finca. She'd bought a little house on South Eaton Place in London that she would use as home base for the next couple of years as she continued to report on the war and its consequences for *Collier's*. It wasn't habitable when she arrived at the end of September so she joined James Gavin, with whom she was now romantically involved, in Berlin where he was stationed. In the meantime, Edna Gellhorn continued a genuine friendly correspondence with her son-in-law, and Hemingway, in turn, wrote back, intent on seeking her approval about the legal settlement of his divorce from Martha. He told her about the progress of his writing, the health and happiness of his sons, and his relationship with Mary Welsh, who had moved in with him in Cuba.

Gellhorn's divorce from Hemingway was finalized in the states of their birth, Missouri for Martha and Illinois for Ernest, on December 21, 1945. That winter in Paris she received her final letter from Hemingway and they never spoke or saw each other again. She later said, "I loved him as long as I could and when I lost all respect for him as a man—not as a writer—I said so and withdrew and that was that." Ernest, nevertheless, continued to correspond with Martha's mother Edna, and Martha, for her part nurtured relationships with his sons.

Continuing to file human interest pieces for *Collier's* as she trailed American armored columns across Germany, Gellhorn wrote "We Were Never Nazis!" and radioed it from Germany where she said in the opening paragraph, "No one is a Nazi. No one ever was… Well, there weren't really many Jews in this neighborhood. I hid a Jew for six weeks. I hid a Jew for eight weeks. All God's chillun [sic] hid Jews." She insisted that all of the townspeople she spoke with whined about the bombs, how they had suffered, that they had done nothing wrong and "were never Nazis." And, that "to see a whole nation passing the buck" was not "an enlightening spectacle."

Close to Cologne, she met a burgomaster who claimed that if the Americans did not occupy Germany for 50 years, "some man, with a bigger mouth than Hitler, will come along and promise them everything and they will follow, and there will be war again." When she got to Cologne, Gellhorn noted that the physical damage was devastating, though the soldiers and reporters were "not shocked by it, which only goes to prove that if you see enough of anything, you stop noticing it." What she did notice, however, was a little pushcart between "two mountains of broken brick" where a vendor was selling tulips, narcissus and daffodils. Such a juxta-position was typical of Gellhorn's prose. Especially when she also included the personal losses the German flower-seller had endured. "His family, forty-two of them including his grandparents and parents, his wife and children, his sisters and their children and husbands, had all been buried in one cellar during one air raid." In a poignant gesture of human contact, the stranger "brought pictures out of his wallet" to show them to her.

1945

MG to Cam Becket
Post–July 16, 1945
London

Dear Cam,

… Will you forgive me for being a damn bore and hounding you to death? I do not forgive myself as you look plenty weary without having all my nonsense piled on to you. But I shall leave in a few months and then you will not be bothered for a long time I trust.

… I have mailed the letter to E [Ernest] and we shall see what we shall see. I don't care much; it is clear to me now that he does intend to divorce me one day; I will have to be represented and my lawyer will see that (ultimately) he returns my possessions to me (as listed in the previous letter to you) and that he does not give some grim reason for divorcing me which would embarrass Mother. That is the essential.

I think really my residency problem is the main one around now; didn't you get the impression that E was sincere and one day I would be free (whatever that means, I'm as free as air if heavier right now.)

Mother and I are in Lyme. It is an okay place I guess and the main thing is that we are together… and it is wonderful to be seeing her like this, all alone, so that I can concentrate entirely on my good fortune in being related to her.

Darling, I write you about the scrubbiest dreariest notes imaginable; there seems almost no room in my addled mind for anything except this kitchen work of life. I am anxious beyond anything to have it finished; to be settled somewhere, to have the play [*Love Goes to Press*] settled; to have money matters settled; to have all this fixed up and forgotten and start writing.

I hope you are enjoying the summer season in your palace and that you are not too driven by work. If all your friends are as noxious as I am, you won't have a day's rest. Give my regards to your handsome family.

Love and always more gratitude than I can ever tell you. I don't quite see how I would ever have handled my life if you hadn't walked into it about twenty years ago.

Marty

That Gellhorn and Hemingway were planning to divorce was no secret. In fact, it was newsworthy. One item quoted Gellhorn directly in St. Louis on July 25, 1945: "Martha Gellhorn, magazine war correspondent and wife of author Ernest Hemingway, said today she planned to get a divorce this fall. Miss Gellhorn, who reported the war in Europe for *Collier's* magazine, said she hoped to return to Europe in mid-September 'because I want to see what's going on in Germany and the other countries.' She said she had no future matrimonial plans." A few days later the *St. Louis Post-Dispatch* reported their divorce under the heading "The Bell Will Toll."

MG to Cam Becket

August 10, 1945
4366 McPherson Avenue
St. Louis

Dearest Cam,

... Enclosed a lamentable royalty statement from Scribners [sic]. Am feeling poor: just had to spend an extra $600 on some gloomy rugs for my London house; that little establishment is slowly eating away my fortune. I only hope I like it when I have it; at the moment I am sick of it. Also generally sick of everything. Fine day to be sad, with the Japs [sic] asking for surrender—if only we will overlook Hirohito, which is exactly like overlooking Hitler. Anyhow the war is almost over, all the wars, and that's a damn fine thing. In the pall of weariness, one can at least be relieved and happy about that.

... I am going ahead on my own to ask Ernest to return my possessions; a pal in Cuba says he will and that it's okay and it's the proper way to do it anyhow. I am waiting for energy to write that letter; between us Cam this whole business makes me sad and a little sick and very very tired...

Take care of yourself son.

Love,
Marty

P.S. Will save check books; and mail all of same to you before leaving the country. There's no sign I'm to be divorced for some time, so I think my non residence here will stick for this fiscal year. Of course England is a stinker still, but they can't charge me retroactively as a resident, during a fiscal year that I have paid taxes in America, can they? So I should think that, however it turns out, I'll be paying taxes to one or the other country as of Jan 1, 1946 anyhow that is what I hope.

The following letter was written from Gellhorn's family home in St. Louis before she travelled back to London, where she continued to report on the aftermath of the war for *Collier's*. Full of grace, it is a testament to what a remarkable person she was. It may well be her final correspondence with Hemingway; it remains rife with their idiosyncratic, intimate diction. She did see his sons again as well as correspond with them as adults and was especially close to Patrick for the rest of her life.

MG to Ernest Hemingway

Dear Bug,

A notice has come that my clothes are in the customs; Mother will pick them up today. I am very grateful to you for sending them so promptly. I see that the weight is 165 pounds, which must have cost a fortune by air express so please let me know what it was so I can send you a check. And thank you again very much, and I hope it wasn't too much trouble.

I have found out how to ship my things to London. They should be packed and turned over to the Railway Express in Cuba; the Railway Express sends them to the American Express in NYC and thence they are shipped across to London. The way this works is to get a professional packer who will, if possible, put everything— including barrels of china—into one big crate (as it costs less and is less likely to get lost in transit, if it is one package). Then this crate should be addressed: Martha Gellhorn, Dorchester Hotel, Park Lane, London, W.1. via American Express, 65 Broadway, NYC, and marked ATTENTION MR. PLUNKETT. Mr. Plunkett is the citizen at Amer [sic] Express who is handling all my stuff for shipment to London. It should be insured, overall risk, for $3000.00 *plus* shipping charges. That means that the insurance also covers the shipping charges: if crate is lost not only the value of the items but also the freight expenses are covered. In making out the customs [sic] declaration (the crate goes through NY in bond and only is subject to customs [sic] in England) the crate should be declared as containing used household furnishings and personal apparel etc. I know this is scarcely a job for a healthy man but I feel sure Joy Kohly would supervise the packing and even round up the items if you give her the enclosed list. The packing should most certainly anyhow be done by a company, who specializes in that stuff, or everything will arrive broken. So just turn it over to her, (how do you like being a housewife, poor darling) and forget it.

You will see by the enclosed list that the things I want are the possessions or presents of my family, and my clothes, papers, typewriter. My whole house wouldn't be big enough for my room furniture; but as I can easily imagine Mary would be much happier in a room designed by and for her, whenever you get ready to change that furniture let Mother know, and she will take over. (It will be a question of having it crated and shipped to a storage company in NY, but won't bother you with names and addresses now. She will tell you all that, whenever you get ready to change that room.)

My dear Bug, I may not have been the best wife you ever had, but at any rate I am surely the least expensive, don't you think? That's some virtue. As for the rest, whatever

I had a share in (the ceiba tree because I found it and even when, at the beginning you said, "Well if this is where you live, I guess this is where you live," I did know it was lovely—do you remember what a stinker that house was, fresh from the D'Orn's [sic] and painted poison green) I give it to you as a wedding present and hope you are always happy there and that this marriage [to Mary Welsh] is everything you have been looking for and everything you needed. And I hope you go on writing wonderful books there, and if you do the finca will one day become a national monument and be tended by a grateful and admiring government. And meantime it also makes a fine place for Mousie [Patrick] to paint; I think often of the colors and the African view over the hills and the palm trees and think he must be doing lovely things. It is a sorrow not to see Bumbi [Jack], not to see Mousie's work, not to hear Gigi [Gregory]: I really expect I will never see any of them again. However; I think I have learned all there is to know about amputations; one has to learn all the time, doesn't one? I never want to learn again; it seems to me a terribly enduring kind of knowledge.

Take care of yourself and good luck.

Love,
Mook

1) SILVER

I think all the silver, except the *Normandie* prize cup, and two Gary Cooper ciga-rette boxes, is stuff from my family: the table silver (flat silver); silver plates, coffee service, candlesticks, little cocktail shaker (birthday present from Mother) etc.

2) LINEN

All the monogrammed or embroidered sheets and pillowcases, all the monogramed [sic] towels—hand towels and bath towels—mats and washrags (these are sets), all the damask table linen and napkins and embroidered or monogrammed table mats and napkins, all the lace doilies.

There is plenty of ordinary new stuff which I bought in Cuba, sheets, towels, mats etc., which can stay there. The other is easy to distinguish because it is mostly old and otherwise has my initials on it.

3) CHINA and GLASS

The white and gold dinner service of my grandmother, the pretty odd old plates of varying types and colors (not sets of them), the Chinese stuff (keep half if you want it), the swedish [sic] glass wineglasses and water glasses if any of them are left, the glass carafes—white and gold, very thin, the two small hurricane lamps (the big ones came from Clara Speigel as a wedding present and are yours), the blue Mexican wine glasses, the champagne glasses you gave me as a present, so you had better keep them; you're more apt to have champagne anyhow.

There are two modern dinner or rather general use sets which I bought, one yellow with flowers and one dead white, which can remain for use until you improve on them.

4) CLOTHES and PAPERS

My typewriter, most important, and all the clothes—can give away very readily in England any extras, and all my papers. I believe there was a tin trunk or a very big suitcase in the basement under the little house, which was full of papers I had not kept in my desk; I would like that too please. I think all my clothes—even the winter ones—were packed in my various closets or drawers, do not remember anything stored in the little house basement. It's really impossible to divide books, not knowing what was mine and what yours, so we'll just have to leave that. Anyhow I ordered a second hand Encyclopedia [sic] in a burst of enthusiasm so can read it for the next twenty years, quite happily.

I do very much want Cuco to have my gun. That's like a bequest. It might not even know how to shoot in England, and maybe I won't shoot there anyhow. I don't know any shooting folks at present, and I have plenty of time anyhow to find another somewhere. It's got a special kind of sentimental value, which is perhaps not a sensible kind to carry around with one. The other old things, rounded up by Mother for me, from many family sources, have not only—to me—great beauty and a sort of irreplaceability [sic], but a feeling of continuity. They will make me feel at home, I hope, and someday will go to little Martha, Alfred's child, which is suitable.

MG to H.G. Wells

August 25, 1945
4366 McPherson Avenue
St. Louis

Wells darling,

You are the greatest man in the world. There was probably no reason to doubt this and you will not be surprised by this statement, but the atom bomb has convinced me once and for all. As you are right in everything, I am not looking forward gloomily to living underground in an air-conditioned artificially lighted tunnel eating vari-coloured pills (instead of spam and brussel sprouts as it used to be in the fine old days).

I have a house in South Eaton Place and am returning to it on the Clipper on September 21st. If London after the war is as wonderful as it was during the war it seems to me a place where a permanently rootless one might take roots, for a while at least.

Did you know that E and I were getting divorced? Change and decay in all around I see, in case that is the accurate quotation. How are you darling? I wish you could foresee something agreeable for the world, as you seem to have influence with history.

Love,
Stooge

In August, James Gavin was given command of the American forces in Berlin where Gellhorn visited him that fall. In her diary she wondered, and rightly so, "what shall I do when this easy comradely life goes to pieces? Am really unsuited for anything else."

James Gavin to MG

September 5, 1945
Hqrs 82nd Abn Division
APO 469 c/o PM NY NY
Berlin

My darling Marty,

I am most anxious to write you tonight, principally because I want to talk to you. I have talked about you a lot lately so it does seem time I talk to you. The Capa has been with us for the past few days. Making up a few dollars poker winnings I suspect in preparation for his impending and long threatened trip to Hollywood. [To be with Ingrid Bergman.] He had been staying at the press camp but moved into the house today. He is a good influence around the damn place. I have been just simply busy as hell. To begin with I still have to exercise some paternal supervision over my own 14,000 Cherubs. Now in addition since Parks has returned to the states on a leave I have his crowd of about 22,000 plus all of the US sector. The Kommandatura [sic] apparently makes me mayor of our six bezirkes [sic] including some 887,000 very hungry but rather docile krauts [sic]. So, nothing can be done to completion or satisfaction. The day seems to consist of checking and rechecking sketchily on everyone else to be sure that things are going well. This is not my best nor happiest technique, I'd certainly much sooner be doing. But if they aren't to starve nor riot too much they must be fed and cared for. Our food consumption is now 600 tons daily which is a hell of a lot of potatoes and uses a lot of trains. The fuel looks disasterous for the coming winter but it may work out somehow. This morning I have 1500 Krauts turning out to cut trees in the Grunewald forest, it sounds fine and would be except that I have about six saws and not more than a dozen axes. But I have a line on more and I'll get them. This all must sound screwy as hell to you, I never thought that it would happen to me. I resent that it has, I believe, but now that it has I am going to make it work…

Darling, all of this doesn't mean a damn thing if I know that you are going to be here. So please, hurry.

I love you beautiful.
Your Jimmie

Edna Gellhorn to Ernest Hemingway

October 23, 1945
4366 McPherson Avenue
St. Louis

Dear Ernest,

I have thought countless letters to you and finally it seems to me that I had better put something in the mail. Let's begin where we are—namely, that I am in St. Louis enjoying wonderful Indian Summer days, with the trees aflame in their red and yellow leaves, almost as beautiful as the flamboyante of your country (probably I've got the name and the spelling quite wrong, but you know the tree I mean). Martha is in Berlin, as far as I know. At any rate, some-where in Europe. The London house was not nearly ready for occupancy so she left for the continent to see what she could see. The month of August Martha and I were together in St. Louis. You know she would rather be almost anywhere else than St. Louis but it's where I belong and so she endured the locale and made up for her disliking by enjoying with me our togetherness. We talked often, as you may well know, of you, and I want to make sure that you know that it was always with appreciation of the many good times the three of us had had together…

This has been a long story about me, so let's turn to you. I hope you are writing and writing happily. The world is waiting for what you have to tell. Is Cuba beautiful at this season, and are the house and the place lovely as you want them to be? You remember I have two volumes of clippings that have been carefully entered chronologically. Shall I keep them until you are in the States where they could easily be forwarded to you, or shall we take a chance and have them go to you at the Finca? They are carefully put away and I am delighted to take care of them, but it is always possible that the house may burn down or blow away.

Do you and Mary sometimes have liqueur? If so I want her to have those lovely jade liqueur cups that you brought me from China. I should like to know that you and she are using them. They are certainly lovelier than anything else I could find to send you.

With affection and all good wishes,
E.G.

[Added in handwriting:] Dear Cam [Becket, MG's lawyer] There's no harm in me having sent this letter to E., is there? I thought it followed out your idea of expect the best. I love you very much. Edna Gellhorn

In response to Edna Gellhorn's recent missive with the news that Martha was in Berlin and her wish that her son-in-law was "writing happily, the world waiting" for what he had to tell, Ernest wrote a ten-page letter rife with the details of impending divorce. That November first rambler revealed not only the legal matters but also how much Hemingway genuinely respected Edna and he waxed nostalgic about their shared memories of happy times together with Martha, like "when we came through [St. Louis] from Sun Valley that late fall, and on the boat [*Pilar*] and breakfasts down at the [finca] pool." Actually, he claimed to remember "every time I ever saw you."

Edna had asked about his sons and Ernest told her that both Patrick and Gregory were "coming along in their heads" and good company, while his enlisted son Jack, an army captain, was recovering from two bad wounds and six months in a prisoner of war camp where he survived "on a diet of soup once a day."

Holding himself accountable to Edna, Hemingway insisted that he was exercising self-discipline by cutting out "all drinking in the night no matter how lonely or bad things seemed." He also ran and swam every day and "got down to 202 and haven't gone above 205," a healthy weight for him. That October he had written steadily on his new book [*The Old Man and the Sea*] in Edna's bedroom at the finca, working "on a system of nobody to disturb for anything in a.m. until work done." Headaches plagued him when he worked too long, but he reassured her that they "are normal from the repeated concussions but will disappear finally."

At the heart of his letter, Ernest explains that his lawyer advised him that even though he and Martha had lived as husband and wife in Cuba that they could be "divorced only according to the laws of the states in which they were born:" Illinois for him, Missouri for her. The grounds by which they would be divorced was *abandano*, that is, desertion, "simply technically ceasing to live with a person." Martha had authorized Ernest in writing to divorce her on those grounds, since the others mandated in their states—"habitual drunkenness, committing a felony, the wife being pregnant by another man"—did not apply. Neither one of them would have to appear in a Cuban court, nor would any evidence have to be presented by a lawyer, "except an allegation that we did not live together for a year," a fact that could be readily proven by Martha's "*Carnet de Extranjera* (Foreigners identity card)."

The divorce business explained, Ernest's tone shifts and, trusting Edna as he always did, he admits, "I did not enter into marriage with Martha lightly. I had no idea it would ever terminate and I am sure that for her to have wished it to terminate I must have grave responsibilities." In a moment of self-awareness Ernest confesses, "I think writers are awful difficult bastards to live with and much more difficult when you stay away from them." He insists that he is trying "to make people happy instead of miserable and weed out my worst traits and still write well giving it full and complete importance."

He pleads with Edna to "write me or wire me when you get this as I told the lawyer I would not tell him to proceed until I heard from you." He promises to send Martha's lawyer, her friend Cam Becket, all of the necessary legal information in order to speed the process, understanding Martha's desire to have their divorce finalized as soon as possible, "to please you, to please me, and to please whatever there is instead of God." Hemingway concludes by rejecting Edna's offer of the jade liqueur cups as a gift for him and Mary, insisting, "They were for you and are for you. You have given me more than anyone else ever did and don't need tangible objects to remember it. Much love."

James Gavin was a thoughtful fellow, as this cable sent on Gellhorn's 37th birthday to her new home in London proves.

James Gavin to MG

8 NOV 45
MACL1347 JEFFERSONCITYMO 21 7 455P
NLT GELLHORN 21 SOUTH EATON PLACE LONDON
YOU ARE MY JOY AND PRIDE REMEMBER THIS ALWAYS WITH MY
LOVE HAPPY DAYS

According to Gellhorn's handwritten note in the Boston archive, "The letter addressed 'Mook' is to me—the last communication I had from Hemingway—in Paris, winter of 1945—and the only letter of his I possess. Returned, at his request, all I had with me (the rest were in my room in Cuba); he was to return mine, which he never did. Great irony—perhaps he feared that one day I would write about him. I seem to be unique in the world; I'm the only one who *never* will write. This final note failed to move me. I doubted E.H.'s 'decent part' by then; and thereafter, & before."

Hemingway confesses, "no matter what hatred or justifiable contempt you feel for me I tell you truly it cannot be as much as that I feel for myself." It's true that he behaved badly toward Gellhorn several times following the liberation of Paris in August 1944, with their shared friends Robert Capa and William Walton reliable witnesses. He apologizes for his "hate rage," admitting that he's "just no good." Furthermore, "from the fine box-seat the decent part of me occupies at all my performances," he did not "admire the delivery." Hemingway signs the letter "Bong," one of the many affectionate nicknames Martha called him over their eight years together.

James Gavin to MG

23 DEC 45
K6223 WASHINGTON DC 16 21
NLT MRS MARTHA HEMINGWAY
DORCHESTER HOTEL LDN
=ARRIVED SAFELY MISS YOU VERY VERY MUCH LOVE JIMMIE

TWELVE

Love Goes to Press

"How can people write autobiographies?
How can they remember the strangers they were?"

—Martha Gellhorn

Gellhorn reported for *Collier's* on the Nuremberg Trial, where she recorded in her notebook, "the pictures of concentration camps simply ignored; all lies." The Nazi leaders on trial were "interested only in their own lives & problems—no moral concept possible." It became apparent that "the point was only: *not* to lose the war." She also published pieces with the *Saturday Evening Post* including "82nd Airborne, Master of the Hot Spots." And, although Gellhorn did not parachute out of a plane with the storied 82nd, she flew with the crew many times and understood the risk. She observed, "the long, last waiting" when the men's faces and eyes were blank, concerns "entirely private" before the "red warning light flashed" and they jumped with 100 pounds of equipment—"ammunition, grenades, land mines, first-aid packets, rations and maps, perhaps a radio"—to carry on the ground.

In February, she wrote to *TIME/LIFE* correspondent Robert Sherrod, who had previously introduced her to contacts in the Far East, that she was "all shredded up inside" from war and from her split from Hemingway. She despaired about "the pale empty color of the future." She traveled in March 1946 to cover the Japanese surrender in Bali, observing in another letter to Sherrod that Indonesia was "hopeless and shitty. Give the country back to the ants, I say."

Back in London, for ten fallow days near the end of April, Gellhorn wrote a satiric play called *Love Goes to Press* with fellow American correspondent Virginia Cowles, who reported for *Hearst* newspapers and whom Martha had first gotten to know in Madrid in 1937. They set the play in a press camp that they knew during the Italian campaign in July 1944.

Still in the city in June 1946, Gellhorn attended the 50th anniversary dinner for the *Daily Mail*, kitted out in the black backless Schiaparelli gown that she'd first worn at the London Economic Conference in 1933, when she'd interviewed Hitler's translator. She wrote to a friend that her spine "was the most visible thing in the room," where she "got waved at, drunk to, and talked about," snarking that if her bosom had been bare she no doubt would "have been made a peeress."

The "jokey play about war correspondents" she wrote with Virginia Cowles featuring two female leads that "were caricatures of Ginny and me" was in production with the "odious title, '*Love Goes to Press*' tacked on by whoever bought the script." The play ran for several weeks at the Embassy Theatre in Swiss Cottage, the equivalent of off-Broadway in London's West End, and then moved to the Duchess Theatre in July, where it opened to rave reviews. *The Tatler and Bystander* critic noted that "Miss Irene Worth would seem to have a genuine flare for character" in the authentic "story-stealing atmosphere of the Press camp," the writing itself, although biting satire, had "enough laughter to salve any wounds." Typically pragmatic, Gellhorn later recalled, "Laughter was lifesaving escape. Theater tickets were inexpensive, and a theater was warm because of all the bodies in it." When the play transferred to Broadway in January 1947 and closed after four performances, Gellhorn noted, with wry amusement and self-deprecation, "There you are: some jokes, like some white wines, do not travel."

Gellhorn was having an affair with James Gavin, the celebrated general of the 82nd airborne who had also dated Marlene Dietrich. Of their relationship Martha wrote as an introduction to his correspondence in her Boston papers: "This is a record of the only completely physical passion of my life—ending really in boredom. And it now seems to me incredible, not so much comic as loony. But it's as near autobiography as I'd ever be able to manage. How *can* people write autobiographies? How can they remember the strangers they were?" Gavin doted on Gellhorn and of the two of them was decidedly more in love.

James Gavin to MG

Western Union
Cablegram

1946 JAN 2 PM 4 32
ML 1 NEW YORK 15 2 901A
MRS MARTHA HEMINGWAY HOTEL DORCHESTER
LDNW1=

HAPPY NEW YEAR MISS YOU VERY MUCH LOVE
=JIMMIE

William Walton was a fellow war correspondent who trailed the 82nd Airborne with Gellhorn. In September and October 1944 he was with Hemingway at the Battle of Hürtgen Forest. Walton claimed that Hemingway saved his life then, pushing him out of the jeep they were riding in to the safety of a ditch when he recognized the sound of a German plane about to strafe them. A close friend to the Kennedys, Walton also convinced Mary Welsh to donate Hemingway's papers to the JFK Library in Boston. A *TIME/LIFE* colleague of Welsh's in the 1940s, Walton helped the final Mrs. Hemingway get the accreditation she needed to return to Cuba to reclaim all her husband's papers after his 1961 suicide. He'd been one of the inner circle at Hemingway's hospital bedside at the London Clinic in May 1944. A father himself, he became a wonderful emotional support when Gellhorn adopted an Italian orphan in 1949, in spite of the fact that their affair was coming to a close. His letters to Martha are among the most amusing that she kept and reveal how she was, indeed, considered one of the chaps. She called her affair with Walton "sweet and safe and jolly."

William Walton to MG

February 2, 1946
Time & Life Building
Rockefeller Center
New York City

Darling pie,

Al Grover [VP at *TIME*, former paramour to Martha, lifelong friend and correspondent] phoned me the first two lines of a limerick which has now become:

Bulletin from Belgravian:
Marty's gone to Batavia
With a guy named van Mook
Who can't even fook,
Which is most unusual behavia!

So you can see how constantly you are on our minds, but never so often as that wonderful windy day when our little friends of the airborne came prancing up Fifth Avenue with all the city going wild around them. Naturally we all were in the grandstand. Capa sat next with a woman he'd warned me about beforehand so I wouldn't make any cracks in front of his aunt.

Every other day was cold and gloomy, but the 82nd's luck was customary and streamed down, planes zoomed and the crowds cheered—millions of them clogging air traffic for an entire day which was a holiday. And you would have wet your drawers if you'd seen James [Gavin] striding in the lead, his helmet held on by his jumpers' [sic] chin-cup, and the staff in line-abreast behind him, every button and ribbon gleaming, eyes right and heads high… everybody whose [sic] still alive.

… Then the city gave a huge dinner at the Waldorf, then Capa, Charles and I entertained the staff at the Stork (a pretty penny, my puss). James brought my watch along and shyly asked me in to the men's can for presentation, but on second thought just slipped it to me under the table. One of his usual heart-breaking little speeches was whispered and as usual I was moved to tears. We drank toasts to you and ignored the ugly wives and courted the pretty ones. And batted off Bill Hearst who kept trying to horn in…

Now as long as Leaky Pipe Collingwood is so proud of his venereal complaints, I've decided to enter the running (no pun) and have come back from Europe with an ugly testicular ailment which turns out to be ringworm or Jock Strap Itch, as my doctor puts it. Charles is mad with jealousy because my entire abdomen, geni-talia and thighs have been painted with iodine—a rather skillfully drawn pair of livid shorts. Of course, one has to be careful to turn off the lights before taking off one's clothing or it would scare people. So they just think one is extremely modest. AS [sic] one sometimes is.

Capa spent a couple of weeks among us and now has gone to Hollywood as has Charles too, so I am feeling very lonely. Capa has a thing with Ingrid Bergman, but insists it isn't serious and is writing a book about Pinkie [Capa's previous girl-friend]. I think she really broke his soft Hungarian heart. Absolutely no news from Cuba [about Hemingway].

And none from you, but then I suppose you're being the White Queen of the Dutch Indies, sipping gin in some marble-floored villa, sleeping with a bolster (named van Mook) and looking ravishing instead of ravished as you should.

I long for you.
Walton

Bertrand de Jouvenel to MG

April 10, 1946
2 place de l'Église
Chexbres
Switzerland

Marty,

When your letter came I did not open it at once. I knew it was yours: when I try to understand why, I tell myself tis [sic] because I can recognize your typing as surely as your writing, and because inside the envelope your paper is folded in a certain way that belongs to you; but possibly there is no reason.

Before I read, sprang into my mind the cable you sent me after I'd come to America in 35, and been very stupid, because I was wounded: that cable said: I will always be waiting on every pier. And it has been true: in all those eleven years you have never failed me. At the end of every road I have seen you, just as you were when I came to you in 31, standing in your blue linen dress, with your bare arm raised in greeting.

I remember walking by your side on the wide wild beach of Grande Isle and feeling terribly shut off. And again the same walk, the same feeling along the coast of Lavandou. While we lived together I suffered very much from that barrier I fancied you erected against me, and which, possibly, was thrown up by my very eagerness, even as the sea builds against itself a rampart of land. But since we have walked so far apart, the wall has vanished.

I am very glad that you have taken a little house in London. It is a strange thing that I managed to settle down only when the world unsettled itself and that I have found quietness in the midst of the sound and the fury. I felt quiet inside me since the disaster of 40: possibly my secret work helped as it severed me from people, even as I saw them. But probably it was something deeper: the knowledge that something had to be saved: France as I thought then, or something beyond France as I feel now. I wonder whether you can only save it by loving it. There is in fighting a destructive virtue which extends to the very thing you are fighting for: also you get absorbed in the struggle, amused by the game, sucked down into the means, diverted by the incidents. I became quietest when I was hunted in such a manner as to become useless and helpless. Among the places of hiding I was driving to there was a monastery, where I lived among the monks, submitted to their discipline, which includes absolute silence. You can hardly imagine how liberated one feels when the constant babble of humanity is entirely stilled. When I came out to slip into Switzerland, voices to me were like blows. And the obligation to speak was torture. There is nothing to say; there never is anything to say and only true intercourse is with the dead.

Everyone is dead now. Martial Brigouleix has been shot, my chubby red-faced, red-haired, jolly sentimental captain of the war and the organizer of the Armie [sic] in Corrèze and Pierre is dead. I loved him dearly. I mean Drieu, of course. We had fallen out on the matter of the collaboration. I had been in Switzerland not for very long when he came there, and called up to ask whether I would see him. Then he stayed with me three days. Quietly and sweetly Pierre explained to me he had to go back to Paris because he must be killed. As you know, they did not want to kill him, so very quietly he killed himself.

… I can understand your making your home in England. One feels it is the only country which does not defile its own image, does not deny everything one loves it for, does not betray itself. If something can be saved of Europe, twill [sic] be by rallying around England.

You asked me whether you could do anything for me. Yes. I would like you to find out what has become of a major Hanau who lived in Belgrade before the war and at the beginning of the war, and was a representative of Vickers. I would like him to know how much I like him and how I have never forgotten him.

And another thing: if you should come across any copy of Shakespeare, send it to me. I went all through the war with one and I miss the company.

Nothing else. As you probably know, I wrote a heavy book called "*Du Pouvoir*" which is at present out of print. I cannot send you another copy if the copy sent to Cuba did not reach you. It got an unexpectedly generous review in the *Times Lit Suppl* [sic], and I understand Hutchinson's are thinking of publishing it. These things will take care of themselves.

… It is a pity you should have left *Collier's*. You got a lot of money for work which did not take all of your time and left long periods of leisure. But probably it will turn out to have been a good thing. After roaming the world, one needs to remain very still and digest it all. One must know that one cannot be mobilized at a moment's notice. The months must stretch ahead, empty: gloriously empty.

As for me there is nothing I wish to do, there is no place I want to go to. I am content to stay and think. The articles I write for a living are just like flies I swat from time to time … I am not interested in being read. People buy my books at their own peril.

I feel deeply that the awfulness we have seen is only the beginning of the end. Our civilization is going up in a column of smoke and mud and smell. It is quite impossible for things to settle down when there is such turmoil in the minds and hearts of men.

… This is turning into quite a long letter. Yet I have said almost nothing. I was deeply grieved when I heard about you and Ernest. I was happy that you had found happiness. I looked upon him as achieving what I had not achieved, and I was grateful to him for it. You are wrong though when you say that he has replaced you. No one can replace you, ever, my dear.

It is quite inconceivable that one should stop loving you.

What E. has probably done is to take to himself a woman who falls into her place as a woman. That was never your place. You matter far too much. When you laugh, all one's other interests dissolve into dust; and when you frown, the whole world becomes bleak.

Write books. There was great beauty in *Liana*. I could not buy it then: a good Samaritan bought it for me. I was glad it came to me as a subtle gesture of friend-ship. What was not good was the part about France. I am sending you a novel, of no literary value if I am a judge, but which gives a good picture of France under occupation. People's feelings were far more complicated. The best of the book were the parts where nothing happened. "Nothing ever happens": you never meant it in the way of Heming. [sic] "Nothing ever happens" in your own work is your true theme. The best in the book about the unemployed was the couple playing the harmonica sitting on a tree trunk. There are no events. The books I love: Kathleen Coyle's *Flock of Birds*, Sackville West's *As Passion Spent* give that feeling of something beyond the reach of mere events.

Do you see Morgan [E.M. Forster] sometimes? I love him: *The Voyage*, as a work of art, as a novel, was possibly inferior to the others. But as an expression of what he means, it was far more perfect, and I, for one, feel enormously indebted to him. When his hero goes into the prison to quell the mutiny with peace in his heart, that is the truest picture I have ever read of the way one feels in action.

This is far too long. Give my love to all. 21 South Eaton Place… I wonder, isn't that where Philip Baker lives? I was great friends with him in the far past and then we fell out or rather he fell out with me. I feel very friendly towards him—but possibly towards a man who is no more. Either people die or they alter. Mostly they die. As you must have realized I was not insensitive to Jean Luchaire's tragic end. We had been friends so long. I tried very hard to stop him. Possibly not hard enough. I feel the tragic pull of those destinies of men who at one time were so near to me.

Darling Marty, write again.

Yours, as you know.
B.

MG to Cam Becket

Late April 1946
21 South Eaton Place
London

Darling,

… Our play [*Love Goes to Press*] is actually going to be put on at the Embassy that means we get a good show case, possible bids from movies or other managers, and anyhow three weeks [sic] royalties which will be several hundred pounds per. Also I sold $1200 worth of articles to *Satevepost* [sic]. Also I sold my car in Paris and a rug here and that helped.

I sent a proud and casual note to Chenery [editor at *Collier's*], answered his letters, saying I'd do 4 stories a year if I could choose time and place and subject matter, and got a cable in return saying hooray: so I shall get a real contract… and have $6000 a year earned income assured, plus two free months a year while I live on expenses.

… Darling, I want to get my name back legally, on my passport and etc. I went to the Embassy in my innocence and said change my passport bud and they said, you have to have your name changed in your divorce decree and failing that it's a legal problem. I can't do more now than insist that everyone call me Miss G., but as I have to sign everything MGH it does create a confusion. And I have a sort of funny horror about anything that says H; like a shell shock case.

I love you and you are a pet and I give you a large loving kiss and make myself a fiesta to see you again.

Marty

MG to Robert Sherrod

May 4, 1946
21 South Eaton Place
London

Dear Beautiful Robert,

… Last night I was trapped into the 50th anniversary dinner of the *Daily Mail*. Representing the US were Mr. Luce [magazine publisher Henry Luce] and Miss Gellhorn. None others. I saw him from a distance, looking old and with skin like blotting paper and was full of pity mixed with contempt. Everyone was rich and famous and there was not one good warm generous mouth in the gathering, plus a very strong odor of decay. I had a great personal success (though I was so busy saying SHIT that I scarcely had time for it) due to wearing a 12 year old backless Paris evening dress; from the speaker's table talked about by Mr. Churchill who said, "Ah so it's Farewell to *his* Arms."

Next week however I am going to America. Isn't it silly? I want to see Mother and Jimmy Gavin (because I must straighten that up; I can't go on being romantic and wasting his time). Also a favored nation treaty with *Collier's*—4 stories a year, my own time, place, subject matter—because I have to have papers to live here… The trip is free and I shall be gone 3 to 4 weeks and then return for the opening night of our play which comes out on June 18 at the local version of the beginnings of the Theatre Guild… After that, by Christ, I am going to write, as I have been a nonsense for long enough and it is giving me sort of ulcers (soul as well as stomach).

But the happiness that had to come, has come. With the spring, and with this house, and with a sort of feeling that the past—good, bad, and mediocre—has past, and I am fit to live and not really frightened about anything. I hope this lasts, as it is heaven itself.

The news is not to be pursued for a while; one's body and heart and spirit need some kind of strengthening. I would wish for you exactly what I have; a bit of dough in the bank and an inexpensive life. (I live well for less than $80 a week). And in one's mind a good warm feeling towards everybody but no desperations.

Brother, be calm. Your spring is bound to come too. I send you an avuncular kiss. Martha

---

Hortense Flexner to MG   May 4, 1946
                                                          Bryn Mawr
                                                          Pennsylvania

Darling Gellhorn,
    ... So, you're coming home. Was that good news? Oh boy—and the play going on. My God, you may not be excited, but I am—and the house all that you like plus solitude. Who would mind solitude I ask, with James [Gavin] in mind? That's not solitude, Baby. That's just enjoying the intermission. But as for your being a writer—I'll never give you any peace until you do write a book, exactly in the style of my letter—full of warm-heartedness which is you, wit, which is double-you and all the old-fashioned virtues of loyalty, sweetness, fun of a very wonderful kind—yes, all of this must be in it, no matter what kind of plot it has.
    ... Must stop now darling as I have just had a really sweet letter from Mrs. E.B. White of *New Yorker* about a poem, serious too, that I'm trying to sell them. Have to do a little tinkering, so the editors can understand it—the dim-wits. Call us up, come at any hour. The dog-wood is out, the fruit trees in bloom, magnolia petals blowing like dirt in New York and the willow waving. A big hug, darling. After wig adjustment I'll just read your letter and step out like Eliz. Arden.

Teechie

Bertrand de Jouvenel to MG   May 5, 1946
                                                         194 rue de Rivoli
                                                         Paris

Marty darling,
    you [sic] were teaching me to love your American land, I was in the rapture of that new life with you in a new world. Then, one night, you counted the weeks before my child was born, you found the true date of his conception in bed. I found nothing to say and indeed it was a blunder I had made for which I paid all my life and will pay as long as I live.

How well I remember that wire we got from Marcelle when we were, I think, in Florence, planning our future. It said she was with child and recalled me. And she met me in Grenoble and I was sorry for her and wanted to be nice. And being nice was fatal. What had not been true then became true. And it parted us for a time. And it killed the child you were bearing. How can you ever have forgiven me. And though I staid [sic] with Marcelle I staid [sic] with resentment, and was impatient all the time, waiting, waiting to join you whom I loved as I have never loved and will never love.

Then Marty, the years which followed from October 34 till the war were nothing but waste. Follies in the realm of both public and private life. Nothing mattered anymore. False moves, false emotions, false ideas. I was quite rudderless.

Hélène proposed to reclaim me. She wanted to set me on my feet. And for two and a half years I lived with her in complete seclusion, worked, was very happy to have my little girl.

I thought I was doing rather well. But I was deeply worried about my little boy. Marcelle would not let me have him alone, just the two of us. I did have him three days. Three days in almost fifteen years of his life. Three days last summer during which we cycled together through Switzerland.

But he had little chance to know how I thought of him and loved him. She thought I wanted to take him away from her.

… It is silly to recount these things. No words, and surely not my clumsy colorless words, can convey the heartbreak. D'you know I have seen of course war, but it is the first time I watch the last moments of a human being slowly dying. And it is my very son. My son whom I never saw at such continuous length as I did in his last two weeks of earthly existence. Practically I learned to know him on his death bed.

Beloved I am rambling aimlessly. You will see from this letter that alas I have not changed.

Oh had he grown up to be a man, how I would have explained to him my faults, my mistakes, my idle attempts! How I would have stressed to him the importance overriding all else, of a private life, built on the rock of a good and careful choice, of a great unfaltering love.

… Rabbit, it was wonderful to hear your voice. You have never really known and you can never really know and now it can never matter that you should know or not, how it glows within me when I just hear your voice.

forever,
Smuf

MG to Eleanor Roosevelt

May 16, 1946
South Carolina

Dearest Mrs. R,

What a schemozzle I got things into. Will you please forgive me? It seems to me I had you sending as many telegrams as if I were a congressman on the verge of voting for something, and then I got into such superb knots I couldn't get out. Please please forgive me; I'll never be such a nuisance again.

Are you taking some vacation this summer? I hope so. You know I always think it is unfair for you to work steadily for everyone else in the world, and never look after yourself. And I remember the vacation you took with Tommy and the two gents near Miami and that you looked so well and rested and loved it. Is Tommy going to kidnap you? Please tell her I hope so.

Mother and I are off on a grand wild outing. We have her car which is seven years old, a small Plymouth. We both love it because it is like a steady old horse, and neither of us has any idea what goes on inside a car, what its hopes and fears might be. In this charming antique we are driving to Mexico. Every once in a while we look at the Atlas and add up the mileage and having now discovered that it is farther than crossing the Atlantic we are very impressed. At the same time, we are not especially go-getting about driving, and have a tendency to settle down as soon as we see a nice place. This is apt to happen every three days. For after three days at the wheel (and it's an enormous day if we go 300 miles) we feel we have already crossed the country in a covered wagon.

At present, we are taking up the squatters life at Myrtle Beach, South Carolina, and adoring it. There's a huge white sand beach, and a huge grey-to-blue sea and we found a hotel which seems to us divine, being clean comfortable quiet and cheap. So here we camp: I have been writing an article, Mother has been reading, in between times we walk along the beach collecting shells for grandchildren, attend the local movies, and gossip together. We have a portable travelling cocktail shaker, and every night sit cheerfully on Mother's bed and have our evening drinks, and launch forth to dinner giggling like a pair of Peter Arno charladies. It is a very good life and I will be astounded if we get to Mexico before June. Mother, to the delight of her children, is at last taking a sabbatical year and high time too. She is going to be with me until later September and then with the brothers in Englewood and she is apparently enjoying it. I am the enemy of the consciences of you and Mother, because I think you have too much of same, and just because you are both the noblest animals the Lord ever created is no reason for you to carry the white man's burden all the time. None of this sounds new to you, does it?

In a moment of madness, I seem to have bitten off the most godawful assignment for next winter and I am already dreading it. I told *Collier's* I wanted to go from Finland to Greece—Poland, Czecho, Jugoslavia [sic], as way stations—and report on how people really live behind what the press is pleased to call "the fringes of the iron curtain." As I am thoroughly and heartily sick of the idea that people necessarily eat babies just because they don't operate on the basis of free enterprise. Maybe they do eat babies, but I want to see it for myself before I'll believe it. And it occurred to me that all we ever hear is the solemn badinage of statesmen and I want to know what ordinary humans are saying and feeling, shop clerks and college professors and plumbers and truck drivers and farmers. Not that I believe such as they, the majority of the earth, control the policies that make war and peace. But for my own hope and sanity, I prefer to keep in touch with them, for on the whole I have found them good. It always beats me that there is such a difference between life and politics, and between people and those who represent them. On the other hand, the thought of plowing through snow up to my neck, all winter long, gives me the horrors: and also, unluckily, I never really believe that my reporting does the slightest good or informs or educates anyone.

And I've got a novel [*The Wine of Astonishment* aka *Point of No Return*], written once but badly, which has to be done over and finished this summer. This is the only work I really care about, so I'm delighted. I've been panic-stricken about it several times, and decided to abandon it, because whereas men apparently have no nerves in writing about women reverse is rare, and I found myself launched on writing about men as if I were one. Suddenly I said to myself, come, come, you might as well admit you aren't and then the panics set in. But Max Perkins, of Scribner's, who seems to have a sort of literary divining rod, tells me I better do it, and as the highest compliment, "I wouldn't have thought a woman would have written it." Now why that should please a female writer, I don't know. Perhaps it's because I've never lived in a proper women's world, nor had a proper woman's life, and so—feeling myself to be floating uncertainly somewhere between the sexes—I opt for what seems to me the more interesting of the two. Or is that right? Women are just as interesting as men, often more so, but their lives seem to me either too hard, with an unendurable daily exhausting drab hardness, or too soft. The home, in short, does not look as jolly as the great wide world. Anyhow, I am going to try to get the novel right, and if I don't there are always matches available wherever one is, and a manuscript burns very nicely.

I find that the story of my life fits easily into two paragraphs and does not make absorbing reading. So will stop.

Darling, please take a rest, please have fun. Perhaps, in the fall, you'd get into a car and come off on a weekend with me. I was astounded by New Jersey,

Pennsylvania and Maryland, as we drove through them, with everything bursting into flower and the little towns so clean and sound and gentle; and I thought, if this is what they mean by the American Way of Life, they have something to talk about. (Then of course we hit the coastal part of the Carolinas, a garbage country if there ever was one, and doubt set in.) But if you could spare the time, what fun to set out and find a pretty place for a couple of days. However, that sounds like a dream as I write it. Anyhow, will find you the moment we return and come and gratefully grab whatever minutes you can afford.

I love you enormously as you know, and think you are an absolute blooming wonder, as you also know.

Always,
Marty

James Gavin to MG

May 20, 1946
Fort Benning
Georgia

Beloved,

It is good to be able to talk to you. You know, of late I have been thinking for the first time in my life I can share my life, my thoughts, my likes and dislikes, with someone who is fundamentally sympathetic—no matter how odd they may seem or how good or bad they actually are, because I believe you love me. You know in your heart that it is wonderful that you returned, it is the best thing that could possibly have happened to us both. You were writing, "perhaps it is all being done with mirrors" now I know that we have found otherwise... As a matter of fact I have never known what it was like not to be lonely until I met you, which reminds me that you told me in Berlin once that you were a bit lonely with me. I hope that you have gotten over that because I know what you mean...

No matter where I go or what I am doing I will be thinking of you.

I adore you.
James

June 12, 1946
Fort Benning
Georgia

My darling Marty,

It is now 10:30 and I have just come in from a two hour talk by Gen. Groves on atomic development. Movies were shown on Hiroshima and Nagasaki and were quite impressive. You must be a war correspondent if the shooting ever starts again. The safest place will be with the combat divisions. All that you have said of the destructive power of the bomb is more than true. Frightful. If people ever use them against each other in retaliatory fashion one war will be enough. Incidentally I think well of Gen. Groves. I have talked to him during the past several days and he is a very intelligent, and rather sensitive and kind man. He has taken a severe pushing around from the press and many pseudoscientists anxious to get their names in the headlines. He is now about to be reduced to BG [Brigadier General] by congressional action as though, apparently, he has done something wrong. Although you will not agree with me it is entirely a matter of press relations. Handled in a different manner it is quite possible that he would be made a Lt. Gen. instead by God he gets the axe and he cannot say a thing about it to anyone. Oh the sadness of it all. Darling no letter from you yet. I hope that you are well and happy and miss me—a bit as I miss you. I have been very busy and it is good that I am. I have thoughts of no one or of anything but you. Derwood reported in this afternoon and I questioned him exhaustively about your trip to the airfield. I must talk to someone about you. Be happy and please love me. I love you dearly, mountains and mountains.

Your James

James Gavin to MG

June 28, 1946
Fort Benning
Georgia

My beloved Marty,

It is a hot Saturday afternoon, over my shoulder to the west it is clouded and there is a distant rumble of thunder so it may rain. I am in the office.... Your letter has been on my mind all day. I feel that I could write a volume about it. Then at noon today I had another letter. They are so wonderful, I love your letters. You know Marty we have something that few people ever know, I love you so and I am so happy in loving you. I would like to go around telling everyone how much I love you. You are the purpose of my life, you have become my life itself...

God knows where I will go in the service or how long I will stay in it. Christ, I don't expect you to marry the army.

... Darling, why in your letter do you presume to tell me that our love is entirely on a sexual basis. Is this so? Even if it disappoints you my love I must tell you that far from it I love you madly for many reasons besides sex. You are wonderful with me and as far as sex goes I never want to look at another woman. But I love your mind, I love to talk to you and I love to listen to you talk to other people. I am so proud of you that I literally feel at times as though I will pop at the seams. I love to go to the galleries with you and go walking with you; to find things to giggle about and talk about. In short, I adore you and am madly in love with you.

I did not know that you had another brother Cam [Becket]. You seem to have a brother for every purpose although I must admit that your doctor brother [Alfred] was poor competition for the Pope. And the more they all disapprove the more I am convinced that it will work. The best judges are our closest mutual friends and they are almost as happy with us being in love as we are being in love. Capa, Walton, and Charles think that it is wonderful and who in the entire world could be better judges.

... I love you. I love you. I love you.
James

James Gavin to MG

July 11, 1946
Fort Benning
Georgia

My darling Marty,

I am beside myself with worry and unhappiness. The only good thing in this life is that you love me... I have written you almost daily for weeks. Yesterday I received your second cable saying that no rations were forthcoming and I cannot understand it. Could a mistake have been made and they are being sent by boat?

... I have had two wonderful letters from you. It may take several letters to answer them. You cannot speak of your writing like that, you cannot write shit. Please ask me some of your questions and not the drunken ill-mannered type you met at Averell's. Darling you remember there are three infantry battalions in our regiments and they are numbered one, two and three. Only the separate battalions, for example tanks, artillery, tank-destroyer etc. have separate numbers.

What darling, in gods [sic] name were you doing on television. I do not want to lose you and you are far too beautiful to expose to ten million people and their covetous scrutiny. I love you and I am proud of you. My beloved, everyone in the division keeps coming into my office to ask silly questions about nothing at all but still they are an interruption.

I love you and I adore and please do not be unhappy. I cannot stand to think that you are. It is good to have this love, without it now I couldn't live.

Yours, ever
Jimmie

James Gavin to MG

August 2, 1946
Berlin

Hi darling,

What a day, gee I wish you were here. Well most of the day was spent on reconnaissance of potential training areas, browsing around the woods looking at hills and valleys and imagining what would or could reasonably happen in such a setting then forming some kind of a plan, figuring how to get the troops in and out.

… Darling, have you received my letter asking about PJs, if you do not take better care of me than this now what can I expect after we are married. Here I am working over a hot stove all day frying the damn pork chop and you will not even get me a pair of pajamas. You know, you would hate Berlin now, all of the loot is gone. On second thought that is when you are at your best, when no loot is in sight and you always find it. The future looks interesting, for at least a month, perhaps a week. Gee, I wish that you were here. I am just waiting for you.

Thought you would like the enclosed. It was taken about a week ago. We were having a wonderful time. I guess I mean I was, the troops were probably bored to death but I don't believe it. I love you very much.

Your Jimmie

James Gavin to MG

August 9, 1946
Berlin

Another day of this and I am going to die. I know it, as surely as I am here I will be as dead as one of your smelts if I do not get a letter from you.

To keep my mind off my misery I just about knock myself out at athletics. At the present rate I will be a mass of muscle at the end of another six weeks, and then what.

This one sided conversation gets me a bit astray at times, like a shipwrecked sailor soon I will be talking to myself. If my own answers to my questions appear unexpectedly in my letters you will have to understand.

Had a call from Miss D [Dietrich] last evening. She arrived in Hollywood and intends to stay there even though her astrologer advised differently. There is a three months [sic] picture in the offing. I only mention this because we were inclined to believe that she would show up at Bragg. By now she must be convinced beyond any doubt that I love you to the exclusion of all else in this world…

I adore you my goddamnedest woman but you must write.

All of my love,
James

James Gavin to MG

August 10, 1946
Berlin

My beloved,

A wonderful letter from you yesterday and then another entirely of clippings. Darling, why the clipping about Bacall and Bogart? I did appreciate them all, the article by Sumner Wells is, as you would coyly put it *shit*. The Germans must be permitted some government of their own creation…

I am dopey this morning. Last night Bob Capa brought Ingrid Bergman and Jack Benny by the house for coffee about eleven. We sat up and talked until about two. Bob had been rather anxious to bring them by for several days I thought, I haven't been able to understand quite why [Capa's affair with Bergman!], but I avoided it in order to comply with the latest thought on USOers in the ETO. Generals are positively not to entertain visiting celebrities and so deny the GIs of their time and company. And that's that. Now instead of being an obligation that one, in some cases, reluctantly fulfills, it is an opportunity to enjoy surreptitiously the pleasure of doing something that is absolutely forbidden. Both parties find it far more pleasant, perhaps that was the intent of the order.

… Capa says that he is leaving his car for you in Paris. Darling, I want to hold you in my arms again so badly, hurry.

I love you very much. I'm waiting for you.

Your Jimmie

MG to Cam Becket

September 7, 1946
London

Darling,

How are you doing with getting my name legally changed to Martha Gellhorn? I am starting my travels again (briefly—to Paris & Nurnberg [sic])—& the passport with Hemingway thereon is an infuriating nuisance.

Am doing short stories, pretty good ones, & hope to have a book of same by February.

And you?

Love
Martha

MG to Cam Becket

September 12, 1946
21 South Eaton Place
London

Darling,

Thank you for your long letter. Life is a package of trouble isn't it? I am off to Nurnberg [sic] and Paris in two days, for two weeks, hoping to make some money (knowing it: $3000 and expenses) I am really broke and realize to my horror that since March I have spent $10, 500 and all on this house, for myself I am just about walking around barefoot. Isn't it appalling; and again I am worried. I think I shall have to work more than I want for *Collier's* this year, as the finances are lamentable.

… The play was a financial failure; it is apparently going on in NY where it probably won't make money either.

But I work for myself all the time, and that is both wrong and satisfying. I keep the wolf from no door but my own, and slave for no cause except the cause of my own prose style. And beyond that, there is this dismal question of being in love, a phrase I handle with extreme caution as if handling six snakes and a live wire. For in the end, how do I know what love is, and where sex starts and ends, and love (for me always an operation done with the biggest fanciest mirrors in the world) comes true and is not my own invention, invention of need and loneliness and the terrible boredom of looking after oneself. James [Gavin] is coming to me next month; and I am hoping that something will be clearer; but I doubt myself terribly, and in a way I doubt life. I have E to thank a bit, for there was such an investment of illusion and it paid off so shabbily, that I am frightened and doubtful, and everyone who touches me must suffer. I should dislike, more than anything, hurting James, who in no way deserves it.

How are you my lamb and how is the law, which you practise so wisely and well, like the family doctor, which is the only real way for anyone to live or work. I bet you my brother Walter would be happier if he used the law as you did, to help the human heart quite as much as earn a living or propound knowledge.

Much love, always,
Martha

MG to James Gavin

Fall 1946
London
[handwritten on envelope: For Jimmy Sad Letter]

Dearest Love, dearest Jimmy and darling; I have thought of nothing but you all these days and everyone and everything seems very flat in comparison. I think of you any number of ways: and I mistrust myself and I fear all this deeply. Because you see, you will fall more in love with me as I am more and more in love with you; I know this is so and unavoidable. And I will make a wonderful story of you in my mind, making you into many people you are not (as well as the person you are), and I will live with that story and count on it. Meantime, you, being more intelligent, will simply count on me. I suppose love is like this: done with the most beautiful mirrors in the world. But when I can make any sense, which is not often nowadays, I recognize this all for folly and very dangerous.

I simply could not be a good army wife. I'd be dreadfully bad at it, I know: it is sickening to realize that two people alone are not a world nor even a life; we live in a fixed specific world (I, on the other hand, am only happy if living in every available world and obeying the rules of none), and we live with countless people. I am too definite and too old and too spoiled and too intolerant to be a good wife when good wife principally means good mixer: and though I could take you anywhere with me—for all my world would be enchanted by you—you really would find me burdensome in the end. If not a good deal sooner. I'd be bad for you, and I'd be bad because I'd get bored and impatient: I'd only like the wives I liked and see no reason, finally, to act otherwise.

This is an effort to be honest for us both, and as a warning. I write it when I love you so much that these days are rather fuzzy dreams and I am living suspended in time, waiting for you to come. All my desire is to follow you, so I can be where you are, where your voice is and your funny face is, and all the things that delight and surprise me about you. But really, I ought to let you go entirely. I cannot see, now, where I belong; I think possibly I am doomed to live alone because there is no place where I can imagine living. But I am already depressed by this life I see ahead of me; the best that can be said for it is that it will not irritate me: it may easily freeze me to death. My feet are cold every night, without you, and presently I suppose I will be cold throughout.

I am trying to say that nothing short of perfection is good enough for either of us now; I would have to believe I could guarantee it, and I fear that I cannot. We don't really need to make a Big Plan: the Big Plan is already made, we have made it with the years of our lives. We may always be in love, some way; but we won't be able to make a partnership that will last day after day after day after day.

And I love you and kiss you.
M

1947

From January through March, Gellhorn was in Portugal, beginning to work on the novel she would call *Point of No Return*, a phrase that she'd heard used in 1943 British airforce briefings denoting the specific limit a pilot could reach before turning around "or else the plane would be unable to fly back to England." Even though the phrase was "spoken as a necessary fact," she found it "powerful and chilling," so it stayed in her memory "waiting to be used." She wrote to Max Perkins, "My life is a beauty: I find myself without visible means of income, on the verge of bankruptcy, in a second-rate hotel some place by the sea in Europe; alone, and writing as if the whole house were burning down."

She arrived in Lisbon on January 4th and noted in her journal "the release, the joy of getting back to where people talk out loud, kiss each other, laugh, show off," and how it contrasted with "the real horror of that self conscious English reserve." She stayed in Praia da Rocha in the Algarve, admitting that she was excited about being in a strange place and felt well, even with a "*Gotterdammerung* wind roaring in over this claptrap resort." The CIA kept a file on Gellhorn, and of this time a censored report dated May 16, 1947, stated that "Martha Gellhorn HEMINGWAY, the divorced wife of Ernest HEMINGWAY" was "running a communist network which had its headquarters at Badajoz in Spain" in southern Portugal. As Gellhorn said, that was surely "some black joke."

She looked about her, observing "the fatal way that hotels have of being peopled with solitary women. There are 4 here (I'm one)" and recognized how such women had "to go through the appearance of being alive." She also noted the two little boys "in smocks (one with a cap) who are always playing with their excretal functions, alongside the wall that borders the first sardine factory. One day studying with interest an enormous caca, the capped one had made: the next day making a river of pipi [sic], with loud delight." She saw them daily on her walks when she daydreamed, telling herself "beautiful stories of happiness." Local children played with stones, a game like marbles, and "kicked an orange peel in semblance of soccer," and were "ecstatic with excitement" because she wore slacks.

William Walton to MG

January 5, 1947
Time & Life Building
New York City

Darling Miss Gellhorn,

On the assumption that you are not overly sensitive about your current dramatic success [*Love Goes to Press*] I'm sending this clipping to show you how careful you girls must be if you don't want to be responsible for a wave of suicides.

You remember how awful the composer of Gloomy Sunday felt after half of Budapest took poison upon hearing his song? Well, be careful. The division history has just reached me and if it weren't for you, it would be the dreariest little scrapbook ever pasted together by a PRO. Your pieces do lend it some distinction, but when you see what some of the other divisions have done it makes you rather sad, knowing that these guys had the most terrific material ever available. Well, just don't tell James [Gavin] what we think. On re-reading one of your letters—which I do at odd moments—I realize you've told me rather definitely that you're no longer in love with said James. But it must have been a rather quiet, easy-to-take ending because you seem unruffled, only nostalgic. And wasn't it a mad idea to ever think of marriage? You are a wise one, my pretty, and somehow I never worry about you because you always get along and suffer just so much and then don't any more.

I think.

Your loving,
Walton

William Walton to MG

January 27, 1947
New York City

Lovely hunk of despair, I was about to wire you frantically because no word filtered through from your rainsoaked cabin. And then this grudging letter came today, so I'm bundling up my old magazines, just like we used to do for Near East Relief in 1923, and packing them off to your desert.

Have you heard about the new Multi-Purpose Food which obviously was designed to end all your difficulties? Well, here's a small sample and I shall send more just as soon as I can find some. It is made of soybeans and was invented to help the starving Chinese, the starving Poles, the starving Finns and all the other starving peoples of the world—costs 1 cent for a day's sustenance. And though they didn't have starving blondes in mind, it will see you through the winter, I think. Just boil this and add to any other food you have around the house and there you'll be all fixed up with everything you need except vitamin C. And certainly they still have a few oranges in Florida which will provide you C.

So we've taken care of your health and by this happy device and your mind with these old magazines. And if I can find a little dry ice package I shall send you a small vial of semen. And then you will be just as good as new.

... Now about the book [*The Wine of Astonishment*]. I've decided it doesn't matter whether its [sic] any good or not because I've read all of *The Heart of Another* and it's so damned good it never matters whether you write another one or not. You've done it. "Portrait of a Lady" and "Good Will To Men" are absolutely perfect, not an unnecessary word or thought, and everything is there. I wish I'd read them long ago because maybe I understand you a tiny bit better after reading them... they're so full of you and your wildness and vitality and despair and everything.

... Otherwise I am devoting myself to flower catalogues which are filling my mail and planning my diminuitive garden as though it were a mere eight acres. We must simply buy some land, you and I, I mean. You buy it and I'll take care of it, better than anyone you know. As for my buying it, Jesus, my taxes went up $2,500 as a result of my last burst of income and my lawyer has sent me a bill for $1,000 more and the school tuition is due. So I ask myself......

But if we had a tumble down house like Luigi's [MG's story "Luigi's House"], think of what fun.....

I still miss you and wish I had a better picture.
Bill

On February 21st Gellhorn reflected on the emotional and psychological lay of the land for herself, making two detailed lists:

What I now know
1. I have lost my credit at *Colliers* [sic]. To have a job there, I shall have to start over and earn it, as if I were beginning.
2. I cannot live in London (Therefore my house is worthless) unless I have a regular fulltime job which keeps me there.

3. I was happy about "Jacob Levy" because of the *act* of writing. [protagonist of her war novel *The Wine of Astonishment* aka *Point of No Return*, the final one that Perkins edited] (As escape from all problems) I wanted to do a novel because a novel meant the chance of fame (more than money) and showing Ernest.

4. A lot of my thinking & acting has been based on showing Ernest. For fear that I reached my ugliest point, with & through him, and that in every way I am only sinking into obscurity little by little.

5. I need a personal anchor because I need a human place in the world. And because, truly, I lack continuous judgment & guts & confidence. This is the purely selfish side of it.

What I am going to do:

1. Ignore entirely for now: a) *Colliers* [sic] & job problem b) money problem c) personal future d) Mother & summer

2. Finish this book of short stories, as soon as possible, but not driving it. Make it the *best*.

3. Think of myself as someone new; with no credit balance. Ignore the debit balance; people's memories are short. Must remember not to torment myself about past failures and mistakes. Consider everything is to be earned, as of now.

4. Also get over the last-chance feeling. Work steadily, modestly, sincerely—but not desperately. It is not that I have all the time in the world: it is that panic will ruin the remaining time.

Maxwell Perkins died unexpectedly of pneumonia on June 17th. Not only had he been Gellhorn's editor at Scribner's for *The Heart of Another* (1941), *Liana* (1944) and *The Wine of Astonishment* (1948), but he had also been a friend to her and to Ernest throughout the years they were together.

Bertrand de Jouvenel to MG

July 1, 1947
2 place de l'Église
Chexbres
Switzerland

Marty darling, where are you I wonder? … I hope your divorce with Europe lasts long enough for me to find you in the States when I get there as I hope in the second half of September. I expect to spend a month, more or less. The thrill is never absent, when I think of getting there as it always calls to my memory my first landing when I saw your arm raised over your blue linen dress on the pier.

… I would love to know whether you're working, and on what. I wonder if you could stand the alienation after all those years of freedom. It may be that your problem will be solved for you, as so many other people's problems, by the next war, which seems to me almost unavoidable.

… There are possibly situations in public as in private life where you can't go right. Whatever you chose brings a train of disaster. We may well be at a stage of history when the downward plunge of civilization cannot be arrested by human agencies.

… Dear little Marty, how are you! I don't really want to talk to you about the state of the world? I want to Know [sic] whether life is being kind to you. Or to put it more accurately whether you've come to terms with it. The answer seems to be to shut oneself up in a room with the window open giving upon a vista of trees. Just as I am now.

Where are you? I would like to picture you. Please send an address to which I can send all these books I'm bringing out. Not that I want you to read any of them, God forbid. Except possibly the *Last Year* which may stir memories.

I bet you've lost my address. Or you would have written. Images stir. I can see you writing in that little hotel we stopped at when we hiked over from Italy into Switzerland, going to Sils Maria. You so liked writing letters so you wrote me letters of introduction to people in Paris you were going to see with me soon after. I like to remember that even then I was conscious of storing up memories for all my life, and as I like to think, more lasting than life.

… D'you remember that all our correspondence has always been tinged with the expectation of war. It is the great shadow always overhanging everything. There was a letter of yours once from some island in mid-Pacific. You'd found machine guns in marvelous lagunas. And you said: surely the answer is sun-bathing for all, not a machine gun in every nook.

… We are fronted with moral problems that can be overlooked only by people in bad faith. The Germans are held all guilty of horrors going on in their country, which they ignored. But the French today ignore the horrors that are going on in their country. We condemn the people who tried to come between the invader and the population to alleviate the situation. But if the Russians should come, we'd be pleased, at first, to have people come between them and the population. We'd also hold it against them, afterwards.

Marty darling, it's a mess. I hope my letter won't depress you. I'd rather you had one of these fine flares of indignation. But especially I wanted to tell you I'm listening all the time, through space, to your breathing and heartbeats, anxious to know your temper and tempo.

your old Smuf,
B

Eleanor Roosevelt to MG

September 30, 1947
29 Washington Square West
New York City

Dearest Marty,

I can just imagine how sick the Dies Committee made you.

Do not worry about anything that is said about me. There is nothing I would like better than a chance to appear before the un-American Affairs Committee. They are such despicable people I should enjoy trying to put them in a hole.

Time does slip by and I hope very much that you will not come to New York without letting me know and I am sure we can find some time to get together.

Do not get too discouraged. Human nature is not as bad as you think. Here and there one discovers some very good traits!

I think you should come up and visit the UN and hear a few of us make futile speeches.

Affectionately always,
Eleanor Roosevelt

THIRTEEN

Point of No Return

"Where are you this very minute… when I am in Rome,
thinking how dreadful it is the way one loses the people one loves."

—Martha Gellhorn, letter to Eleanor Roosevelt

Throughout 1947, Gellhorn worked on her novel about Dachau, which was published by Scribner's in 1948 as *The Wine of Astonishment*, a more benign title—and one lifted from the 60th Psalm as suggested by her editor Maxwell Perkins—than the one she had selected, *Point of No Return*. She sent an early draft to Allen Grover for substantive feedback. He'd been a trusted first reader of her fiction since 1935 when she wrote *The Trouble I've Seen*, portraits of all generations of disenfranchised citizens who'd been hit hardest by the Depression. The novel was published that fall to rave reviews. It was a Book of the Month Club selection, the reviewers observing that "the grueling life in the infantry in Europe in the last war is presented here with remarkable insight… and a sad, brutal power." Gellhorn's characters revealed "a deep disillusioned wisdom about life, love and death." Another reviewer named *The Wine of Astonishment* "one of the very best World War novels," because its author got "below the surface to the motives, thoughts and feelings of men in battle." She understood the psychology of men at war, and the novel stood as an indictment of human brutality. It was a story of how people were "made and unmade in the torment of war," and how they grasped "for life and happiness," managed "to laugh, suffer, fear, struggle against deadly fatigue" and, yet, continued to hope.

Martha was making plans to adopt a war orphan on her own, having visited more than 50 grim Italian orphanages and witnessing firsthand the desperate need of the children whose losses were collateral damage from the conflict on which she had reported since 1939. The process itself was frustrating as she was neither a Roman Catholic nor a believer, and a single woman, to boot, so she found a local lawyer to help her navigate the system. Enlisting the special support of Eleanor Roosevelt, a respected figure worldwide, Gellhorn persevered, and on her 41st birthday in November 1949 she was notified by her Florentine lawyer that she could go to the Protestant foundling home in Pistoia to pick up her 19-month-old son, Alessandro.

1948

Allen Grover to MG
January 28, 1948
New York City

Dear Marty,

Herewith a valuable packet—Chapters 21-25 [*The Wine of Astonishment*]. You will find almost no suggestions on them.

As to Dachau, I *think* it comes off. I don't know for sure. The reason why I don't know for sure is that as [protagonist] Jacob Levy goes from one horror to another, stunned and unbelieving, there is no interpolation by the author of what is happening in his mind.

I know you haven't time to do it without changing pace and technique, so you mustn't do it.

Then he is sick, gets in his jeep, and suddenly runs over the civilian krauts. I hope it's all right psychologically. Temporary insanity is a well recognized state of mind. But have you checked that afterwards it's all right for him to be sane and to defend his act to himself (as well as the outside world)? Jake was a boy who all through the book has had a marvelous balance. You make the unbalance real to the reader, but is it psychologically okay for him to go on?

Chapter 25 I think does come off beautifully. Perhaps that's all one needs to understand him emotionally—but is it sound medicine?

… You don't say about when you expect to be back, though I gather it's around the middle of February. Let me know as soon as you know and keep well.

Ever yours,
A.

MG to William Walton

December 25, 1948
Avenida del Parque 14
Cuernavaca

Darling,

Christmas got itself over in record time this year. I imagine (it is six p.m. of Dec 25) that you are now surrounded with your young, making that train run. And snow, by God. Whereas I spent the morning, after feeding my three animals and doing the housework, sitting naked in the sun, wearing a large sunhat and reading a very frivolous novel.

And yesterday, Xmas eve, I had an amazing experience. I could scarcely believe it. As I had forgotten what it means: to be moved to tears…

I went to a tiny church near the market, called the Church of the Mats, the smallest I've ever seen, all white and red and gold and pink and lovely dressy saints and a modern square grandfather clock (you know with different colored woods). Outside there was a throng of little boys; at the front there was a handmade rickety litter carrying the figures of Mary on a *burro* [donkey] and Joseph dressed up like a Spanish grandee. Two little boys, in red dresses and white surplices, with candles bigger than themselves, stood in front; and right by the church door there were about ten little boys, clustered around a dirty printed paper, on which words were written and they were singing. Wonderful voices and wonderful music, tremendously gay and easy to sing and yet with that great thing songs sometimes have, the thing of being like water flowing. The boys' voices rose, singing the simple wonderful words: "My wife is feeling very poorly, please let us come in." From inside the church other boys' voices rose in answer, so that the church and the courtyard were light with sound: "We are very poor and we have no room, we cannot." Finally, outside the boys' voices climbing up the night, said the great words: "But my wife is the Queen of Heaven." And all over, singing and singing, while the Holy Family was carried to the altar by two little creatures looking like Huckleberry Finn. And I stood in the back of the church, weeping. I who have never dound [sic] anything in a church except architecture, and sometimes (Midnight Mass at St. Étienne du Mont in Paris) the great beauty of the music, the organ. But I never really felt that anyone loved God and Mary and the Infant Jesus and even poor old Joseph; and suddenly here they were, being loved like members of the family.

… I find us quite wonderful people, you and me together; because I don't quite see how we could have done that, what we felt like, what was suitable, and carried it off without any anguish or embarrassment or anger between us. Men and women aren't generally sound with each other (and that may be why you and I will certainly love each other until we die, faithfully, through everything: which is somehow different from the pain and folly and fireworks and also joy of being in love, a thing which—for me—can never be maintained, as it burns too hard and bright.) We know this now: what we have we will always have, we will have no more and we should have any less. It's a very good quality. I am richer because of it.

And I will always be there, year after year, certainly the best gin-rummy-part-ner-in-bed that a man can find, don't you think?

I'm writing again, and think I'll have a book of short stories ready for next fall, though I don't care if I do or don't. I want to do a very long story, and am brooding about it ineffectually, on Ernest and the cats. I've got a wonderful picture growing in my head, a composite man, which would delight me to get down; but I haven't seen the woman yet. I'll write that just as long as I want it, letting it find its own size as it goes.

… Goodnight darling. I hope you have the happiest new year imaginable and that everything you want, happens.

Love always,
M

1949

Cam Becket to MG

January 3, 1949
Lakeville
Connecticut

My dear,

I've been year-end thinking or musing & trying to orient this legal microcosm into the second-half of the twentieth century… What fascinates and horrifies is the certain knowledge that the future holds far less chance of spiritual growth & physical well-being, far less possibility of a golden age—of culture & scientific advances joining hands to make mankind whole, free from poverty, war, disease, than it does for a third world conflict.

You have seen the destruction to man & his works, the disintegration of a race that could accept Buchenwald and gas chambers & genocide without a moral quiver, & will know better than I how much worse the next war must be… At what an expense no one can conceivably calculate. And another generation of war-nurtured children, fed on revenge & nationalism, while the Christian doctrine, for good or ill, has never come close to them. Lately, the few evenings the office has merely beckoned not summoned, I've been reading the bible [sic] & books about it. But 'tis a late hour for Father Becket to begin this study of the golden rule, late enough to make me weep for my stupidity.

You & I—it's good we met so long ago, yesterday it seems to me, and good we have each other even at long range. You mean something to me no one else ever has or ever will—see what a responsibility you have to take good care of yourself!

C.

Hortense Flexner to MG

January 18, 1949
Bronxville
New York

Dearest Gellhorn,

I wanted to write all week, as your letter, funny and wonderful, made me feel like it. But needless to say, Kinglet came back from the hospital with a virus bug in his throat and was terribly sick for five days. The house vibrated with nurses, penicillin, even doctors—and Teacher, between teaching, cooking, persuading a low Irish taxi driver to get me up the hill, felt like one of the dancing dervishes. I've now served notice on King. Yes, he is attractive as you say—he has many quite good points, but unless he can pull a little health out of his pocket, I am going to start a movement to remove from the marriage oath, "In sickness and in health." Poverty and wealth is O.K., although only love could swallow that one. But good god—sickness and health! Someone should take a stand. However, now when I am ground down to a gray piece of talking rubber, up bobs King, feeling fine and so—all is really well.

"The story of your life" is part of the story of Gellhorn. She took all of life's dares, including the most risky one. The human pattern must be good or it could never have held so many and so diverse a group as this earthly family. But I can't imagine any more hampering article than an infant, especially to a writer, though doubtless a nurse would take care of certain aspects of the problem. And the interest would be intense, and your procedure was very original. Wyncie says you are very serious about this and that he understands why you are. In a way, I do—but only in a way. Maybe I want to talk to you about it all—and certainly I envy the baby, whoever or wherever it comes from. I think of you as going in for this, as you went to the war—partly because you have convictions about the duties of people in a time like this, and partly because you want to see and experience the whole story for yourself. And that is right. Of such are the creative people made. I was too old when I married to O.K. the pattern aside from having a positive dislike of it, and Kinglet and I, in our rich days were too busy making up for what we hadn't seen and known to think of future generations. I was lucky we felt alike on this issue. I'm sure you must be right—only it's something I've never quite associated with you. And yet, as I get used to the idea—I'm sure I'll like it, and will understand (since K. is already persuaded) that it is the good way, for you. Now I expect to be peeled alive—but you see this was quite a hurdle for Teacher to take, as it was completely out of her imaginative range.

Are you in Florida—is the book going well? I know it is. I know by the way you talked of it. We are having great fun with Mr. Roberts, just ideal for this time in our lives. Yes, Wyncie's stories are always beautiful, and if he could write them, he would start a new school of lit. They are so squared by the stars and the big eternities, and there is absolutely no falseness nor pride in them, but an artist's deep burning interest in humanity. That is why he cannot be interested in technique— he measures it all against the standard performance, the real virtues in art. And we have lived in a time when nothing is as tarnished as these virtues and when his kind of absolutely true, difficult individual work can go quite unnoticed—just because the right little tin-horns have not backed him. And this he too accepts, which it would be better if he did not—but he can't get interested in persuading them of what is so evident to him—and so, here he is doing mechanical stuff, and all of his originality being really wasted. That is what breaks me down—that is what I cannot bear, for of course in the end, it does something to his work too. When I see him listening to the fools, as he always does quite attentively and without any sense of superiority, I just want to die but then anyhow you and I do know. And I was mighty glad you wrote that letter to him at this time—it was what you have always done—been there when needed.

Goodbye and good luck in all creative ventures. As ever, Teacher.

Think often of "Point of No Return"—and believe the idea is true. Look at Spender's new book, *Poems of Dedication*. You may find your quotation right there.

MG to Eleanor Roosevelt

June 22, 1949
c/o American Express
Rome

Dearest, dearest Mrs. R,

I talk of you so often, think of you so much, love you so greatly, and I never see you or hear from you. It makes me sad. I wish you weren't always so far away and that I never knew anymore what you're thinking and feeling. Where are you this very minute, I wonder; half past twelve on a hot summer's day, June 22, when I am in Rome, thinking how dreadful it is the way one loses the people one loves.

Have been in Italy for two months, working most of that time on one article about Italian children, the ones who paid, are paying, will always pay for the last grown-ups' war. It was heartbreaking work and I don't know what good it is; the readers of the *Saturday Evening Post* may feel slightly heartsick on the subway—but what else, what more? Look at the world, I think, with special attention to the incredible beauty thereof. And in the fall I go home, to Cuernavaca, and the sun and the silence. It's a very privileged life, really, and I am almost too lucky.

All I want really is children of my own; about six of them, I think. I don't feel I have to bear them, just have them around, and worry about their eating and sleeping and having shoes. It is such a fierce bore to worry about oneself, only.

Please please write. It is more than a year, I think, since I've heard from you.

Love,
Martha

Eleanor Roosevelt to MG

July 3, 1949
Hyde Park

Marty dear,

It was wonderful to get your letter. I was not really surprised to find you are now in Italy, though your rapid changes of domicile take my breath away.

I shall watch with interest for your article on the Italian children, but I wish you would tell me when it is going to appear. I am sure it was heartbreaking to see the Italian children who have suffered as have children all over the world as a result of their elders [sic] war. I am sure what you write will do good. All of it adds up to better understanding on our part of what happens to people in other parts of the world.

I wish I could hope to go to Mexico because I would like to know the place to which you return with such joy, but I am fairly sure I will be back on the UN in the fall and stuck in New York City for three solid months.

Your quota of children should not be difficult to find if you really want them. You might pick one out from various parts of the world to see if they could get on together and if they could be taught to do so!

You cannot be accused of worrying much about yourself. You are always out for some cause or other.

I worked hard this spring on the Human Rights Commission and on the adjourned session of the General Assembly, and on getting thin, which seemed to be essential—all of which have been moderately successful. I am just as well as possible and concentrating now on spending the summer at Hyde Park and acquiring as many children and a few older people to help me enjoy my possessions.

I count on you to let me know if you are anywhere near and either come to Hyde Park or to the apartment in New York.

I would love to hug you so be sure to let me know when you are coming through.

Much love,
ER

MG to Eleanor Roosevelt

Summer 1949
c/o American Express
Rome

Darling Mrs. R,

Your good long letter arrived; it is something to be in touch with you again, even only via the mails. And I'm glad to know you're going to have some rest in the summer because, if my changes of domicile startle you, your work schedule fills me with dismay. No one ever anywhere worked as much, I think, and it seems an unfair division of labor. Also how did you get thin? I have gained about 10 pounds in Italy and look like a sausage and am wondering what to do about it, aside from starve. Did you lose a lot? Was it hard to do? Does it depend, as I am afraid it does, simply on discipline and not eating anything one likes?

I am writing you in the middle of a hot afternoon, in a dismal hotel room, and I have been in a state for two days—a state bordering on despair. This is due to my efforts to adopt a child. I seemed to be getting nowhere with it because Italians think it is mad to adopt children, as they produce their own in unheard quantities and forget the others in overcrowded orphanages. One has the feeling (I have had it) that they don't want to change anything. I write this badly because I am tired and weary and hot and discouraged. But the point is, darling, I need your help and hope you will give it to me. I have been talking with two Italian women (good ones, who assume their duties in the country) and both agree that I must have backing from my own country. I am going to get a letter from the Embassy here, certifying that I am a respectable American citizen. But there is no one here who is an old friend. I wonder if you could dictate a letter addressed "To Whom It May Concern," saying that you have known me for years and know my family and know that we are sound decent people and that a child would get a good education and care and all the rest. If you could do this, very quickly, I would appreciate it more than I can tell you and I hate to bother you. But of course everyone here knows and admires you, and that would be the best sort of guarantee that I am not a crazy rich American (there is a tendency here to think all Americans are crazy and rich) who just has a whim for adopting children.

I think, maybe, the reason I am so depressed is that I have been thinking of adopting a child for four years; have waited; have been afraid; have thought and thought of every possible angle and eventuality—from finances to whether I could be a good enough person—and at last have decided that I can certainly give a child a better life than it will ever get in one of these really ghastly orphanages which I have been seeing now for two months. God knows I have not made this decision lightly and God knows it is quite a big one; so it horrifies me to run up against this sort of dead unmoving attitude here. If I had the money I would want to take ten, and get them out of this life, and put them in freedom and air and laughter and hope and a chance to grow bodies and minds. But I must start humbly with one, and then if possible take another next year. I am asking for a chance to give a child a life, to build a life with a child, and in a way you would think I was asking for the Victor Emmanuel Monument as a present. Ah me.

So if you can do that, I thank you endlessly. And now I have to go on and do some more worrying and fussing. I have found a little boy of five, who I dote on, but I doubt if I will get him. His mother is alive (he is an illegitimate child) and very likely, although she can't keep him and has a new man who doesn't want him, she won't give the child up. He's such a tough-spirited little boy; I can hardly bear to think how he will grow up, slowly being crushed by the wet-towel sort of discipline at the orphanage, all so grey and dreary, all directed towards making the children obedient and humble and colorless. However. If I can't get him, I must get over him.

This is a grim letter; please forgive it. I love you very much,
Martha

William Walton to MG

July 5, 1949
Stone Ridge
New York

Dearest Travelling Mate,

For days the sun has been baking our countryside to a crisp brown but late this afternoon a storm swept down from the mountains and torrents of rain miraculously turned everything green again, cooled the air and soothed my soul. Now the children are tucked in their beds and the night is so still the sound of my typewriter seems to stop dead in the dripping green foliage. As usual I'm thinking about you and conducting my usual conversations with you. Very witty, I must confess, and very profound, too. What a pity you're missing them. Probably this is the 33rd such chat we've had, or I've had, since we parted in that golden city on the Tiber. But if you have any doubt about the persistence of your influence over me, consider this: I haven't YET had my hair cut. And now it curls down over my collar, makes great wings that meet at the back of my head and is so weird that people turn in the street. I don't know what to do. For some reason I feel getting it cut would be unfaithful to you, as though I were sneaking when you couldn't see, after I'd promised faithfully not to. Still, I know I can't go on like this.... will you please, please release me from my lightly taken vows? Think of my children? What will their friends say? Think of my career, if I ever decide to have one again. Think of the discomfort in this baking, blighted American summer. Just a little trim would make it so much easier to emerge from the pool without looking like a drowned circus freak. In the meantime, I shall stay hidden away in this odd piece of New York State, with Aunt Emily, two of her girl friends of 75, a parrot named Albert (he can sing *Little Brown Jug* in a cracked tenor) the children and endless time on my hands. This state of affairs will go on until the end of July when the children and I, without Albert, will proceed on to Provincetown where life will be simpler, more to my liking for sun and sand and no clothes.

But to begin where we left off... so many thousands of miles, I don't know where to begin. Two hours of waiting at the Rome airport... Next day I joined my little party of second-rate newspapermen and we flew off to Normandy where the beaches looked lovely from the air and the Renault factory had sent a fleet of little cars to entertain us for three days. That meant transport was perfect and I buzzed all over Normandy, seeing the terrain around Ste. Mere [sic] Eglise [sic] that Jimmy [Gavin] and I knew so well and watching certain [D-Day] anniversary ceremonies in the village with disdain knowing that I was the only American present who had been there five years ago. Gave one a lofty feeling, and then again a rather ghostly one of returning to a page in history that people had in any real way forgotten, or never known and only read about, a feeling of coming from another era and another race of men. Shiver. Lunched one day at Mont St. Michel which teemed with French, not American, tourists. And motored to Paris with a rather nice bovine guy named Walter Cronkite. Used to know him in the war.

I'm never quite prepared for that first sight of Paris. Everything always happens all over again, the slow turning over of the heart, the painful wrench of the river and the bridges and the domes and the Place de la Concorde. God, I'm unfaithful to Rome already. Paris was shopping for gifts (lovely little ones) and staying at Teddy White's flat opposite the George V, and cocktails at the embassy (dandy new ambassador and wife I've known before) and a drink with M. Le President de France (all of us) and a beautiful medal ceremony in the Court of Honor of the Invalides. The medal, of course, was tenth rate, handed out by the bureau of Tourism, but the French do such ceremonies up with style even though their tongues are in their cheeks… the Garde Republicain, the Star Spangled (off key), and the Marseillaise more stirring than any other anthem. Lots of old newspaper pals were in the bars and life couldn't have been cosier. Then off by air to Luxembourg. This time the Army sent cars from Germany for us to use (at the taxpayers' expense) and we revisited Houffalize and numerous other villages and I unveiled a bronze tablet on the hotel staircase where you so haughtily refused to sleep with me on New Year's Eve 1944, silly girl…

I, of course, arrived in NY in that one heavy dark suit which I had donned the afternoon before for an embassy cocktail party and by the time I flew on to Washington, the suit and I had become one. Surgery was required to get it off. Washington looked weedy and lovely, snoring in the summer, but very friendly and fine. The house was in good shape, the garden wall is all done and the roses were even in bloom. Pausing only to reload my camera, I flew on to St. Louis, picked up the children and motored to Jacksonville. And if you aren't tired by merely reading this itinerary you are cruel and insensitive.

… Now for what little news I could glean during a week in our capital. Buck [Lanham] had just returned from Cuba. Three weeks of fishing. Pappa [Hemingway] is drinking more than Buck has ever seen him drink, which means a Titanic quantity. He was rather cagey about the subject but I gather the book [*Across the River and Into the Trees*] is neither finished nor going well. He says Pappa has aged considerably and he (Buck) is worried.

My relations with the children are quite satisfactory, improved if anything by their winter in St. Louis. As for my relations with you, dear heart, I have thought about them long and often. I don't understand anything except that I'm deeply and permanently attached to you and I miss you every day. A thousand times on this scatty journey I wanted to show you something or tell you who said what, and it wasn't half as much fun without you there, searching eternally for your *gabinetto* [toilet], groping for your electric pad, groaning about the stupidity of women who press your clothes. I find you dear and silly and comfortable and endlessly stimulating. And I find myself incomplete without you…

My own *fetruccini* [sic], please write about your gay doings for I shall be rusticating in this green landscape which is full of tennis flannels, polite conversation and a deep nostalgia for the days of Henry James.

Your loving,
Bill

Please stay away from Janet Flanner [legendary lesbian expat journalist in Paris]. In

your present mood, I don't know what might happen. I would rather go on being
jealous of an electric pad than find you in the arms of that Messalina.

My address till Aug 1 is Stone Ridge, Ulster County, N.Y.
Then General Delivery, Provincetown, Mass.

MG to William Walton
July 16, 1949
Rome

Beloved, distant Pronto,

You take your time all right about communicating with the outside world but
when you do, no one can kick. I had just about decided to send you a 300 word
cable collect, to teach you not to plunge into silence. And then your wonderful
letter came, which I have memorized, and I do not feel that you have been gone
for ten years (previous feeling) and that no less than eight oceans separate us.

I hardly know what to tell you about here so will begin with the joyous news
that my Capri article which was a solid mass of shit was described as excellent by
the *Satevepost* [sic] and bought. Thus I am solvent…Was robbed by the hotel and it
was there that I started getting bored. I know now how this works. At some point
I stop seeing or hearing people (really) and of course a huge boredom sets in. I
also stop everything else and go about in a slightly soured daze. Now I am deep in
that and Rome is so hot (yes) that it makes me both sick and angry.

But the real thing is the adoption business and I am keeping a detailed record
of it and someday I am going to write a honey of an essay. The Eyeties [sic] act as
if I wanted to eat the baby and not adopt it. This is due to being a non Catholic
foreigner, both states being regarded as willful criminality. Today, when I was
nearly in despair I discovered the Italian Protestants and all may be well. If you can
believe it, these lambs have been lurking around in the Piedmonte mountains for
about six centuries, being absolutely completely and determinedly Protestant. I am
of course drawn to them like anything, with my usual tenderness for minorities.
They think it is lovely for me to adopt a child if only they have one I like. So that
is the next step. I am going to try to be named guardian of the child—quicker
process and more chance of winning. Later, any number of years, it will also be
easier to adopt; a sort of *fait accompli* [done deal] angle. But I am tired and bored
and it is drab work.

… I am going to Florence to see the Mooreheads and Protestant orphans in four
days; thence up to Piedmonte; thence to Venice to a palazzo. I do not know how
long I can stand it and am longing to get to England, sell everything, see everyone,

and return to my delectable white house in the mountains. Am homesick. I hope I will wake up again and be able to look at the world around me. I have done no sightseeing here, and am a lump. But this adoption thing obsesses me.

... The only good thing is my car which I better go and garage before it is pinched. I do love it and it makes a great difference. Not trapped anymore. But it does not replace you; what I want is you and the car. I also resent the idea that you find me comfortable, but am delighted with your other remarks. Do you really miss me? Do you really prefer me (at least spiritually) to all those girls with huge breasts? I feel sure you will marry some chit of a girl (such a hideous expression) and forget me and our *amour d'automne* [late-in-life love affair] will go up the creek. But you know I love you; you last.

M

P.S. What do you think Ernest has done now? He told the Mooreheads he paid me $500 alimony a month, which explained why I travelled and had such a fine life. You know, he may also be quite quite crazy.

MG to William Walton   Summer 1949
                                                                      Rome

Dearest *Vietato Fumare* [No Smoking],

I realize that, since you are gone, I have *looked* at nothing. How lucky that you were here at all; otherwise I should finally leave Italy (a fairly welcome day, whenever it comes) without having seen any more than if I had spent four or five months in Oshkosh, Wis. [sic] It is terrible and criminal and I feel at once ashamed of myself, bewildered and helpless. I drive blindly through the country; I struggle in this heat (how fragrant and cool my tropics are, by contrast) and am a mono-maniac with no room for the things of the spirit or spert [sic], as we say in the American Express.

But, out of this, something has come; I've found my child. At last. I calculate I have seen about 52 orphanages and institutions for children. In Pistoia, which is a small boiling town 25 miles from Florence, there is a shabby Foundling Home and therein dwells my heart's desire. His name is Allessandro [sic]. His age is either 14 or 17 months; the birth certificate will have to be verified. He is as fat as two sausages, blonde like Botticelli folks, with grey eyes, a snub nose, a deli-cious mouth, and bow-legs. He is covered with prickly heat and normally dressed in an old UNRRA [United Nations Relief and Rehabilitation Administration, founded in 1943] flour sack. He walks, waving his arms and grunting with pleasure, like an old gent who has palsy. His smile is not to be believed; it looks as if he had invented the whole idea of smiling. He waddles forward and clutches my knees. The other day I was passing a happy morning with him on the floor; we were playing a distinguished game of tossing his rubber teething ring back and forth. All of a sudden, he found this so absolutely perfect and satisfying that he sighed with delight, a huge fat sigh, clapped his hands, and lay down to laugh better. I cannot tell you how I dote on him. He may grow up to be very short and stout and of a moderate brightness; but I think he is always going to be happy, and sow happiness around him. He's a complete optimist. And in this tragic jungle of warped children, with sad pinched little faces, who either scream all the time or compete like fierce animals for love and attention, he alone is serene and generous and taking it easy.

Legal complications have set in. I felt my mind going; it's been so long and so depressing and so exhausting a search. So I have fled for a few days to the home of the Gherardesca family, and you would adore it. I miss you doubly because it would be such a pleasure to giggle with you. They live in a renovated antique, which has housed their line for 1100 years. It burned down in the 19th century and like fools they put it right up again. It is so dark at all times that you feel your way along the corridors.

... Italy is a huge sweat box, with a wind like hair driers [sic], and the land bakes brown and mosquitoes the size of ponies. Not a leaf stirs. And at night, what air there is cannot enter the endless 14th century windows. I hate these houses; I have never been more uncomfortable than at the Villa Diana (where I stayed a week with the Mooreheads who are plainly angelic and whom I dote on) and here and the glamorous country houses in England. I am so homesick for the comfort of Cuernavaca that I could weep. But the plan is just to hang on and hang on until I get that child, and make plans from there. Anyhow someday I am going to get him, and put him under my arm, and jump into a plane, and settle down in my walled garden. It's all I want. I think I may have to come via New York and maybe should stay over and take the baby to a first rate doctor to be sure he is okay. If so, will you come to NY to see him. Such a dreamboat. I love you. I miss you.

M.

MG to Eleanor Roosevelt

August 1, 1949
American Express
Florence

Dearest Mrs. R,

Your letter to Professor Biondi arrived this morning. (The American Express in Rome was sitting on it, as upon an egg.) We went out to Pistoia at once and used it within three hours, on the local judge. I hardly dare say this for fear of bringing bad luck, but it looks as if it had worked, like pure beautiful desperately needed magic, and all is going to be well.

You know how I thank you. I never needed help like this before; I never wanted anything as much as the child I have at last found. And you, darling, have very likely made it possible to have him.

… I'm already afraid of loving him too much, of being the lowest sort of mother who has heart attacks if her child crosses a street. Will have to fight against that. He needs care and good care and quickly, as his diet is a scandal and he had rickets and arrived at the Foundling Home, aged six months, almost starved. But if only I can get him I know I can make him strong and well, and I think happiness is built into him, I think he will carry it with him wherever he goes, and share it.

Oh such a child.

You can't know how grateful I am for your letter. It was up until now a heart-breaking search…

If I can't get this child I give up. I don't want any other.

Bless you. There's no way to thank you.

Is the heat destroying you? It is apparently worse there than here and here it is nearly unendurable. I hope you're keeping cool in the pool and getting some rest.

It's terrible never to see you but please know that I love you every day I live whether I can tell you so or not.

Always,
Martha

William Walton to MG

October 2, 1949
Provincetown
Massachusetts

Dearest…. Indeed indeed it is all true, that I haven't written in weeks and how I wish it weren't. But the simple fact is that I HATE writing letters, perhaps because

I do it badly, or vice versa, who knows. Now you, you are able to do it magnificently and I imagine it is easy, because you always manage to catch something of yourself in every letter, no matter how short, what you are thinking and how you are looking and everything important....

Now I will report on several aspects of existence.

PHYSICAL: suddenly I find I have lost 15 pounds. Bingo. So I'm so slim you'd never believe it, even bony, and how it happened I haven't the faintest idea. Making clothes fit is a problem, but I shall eat a great deal and gain it back again, unless it is some wasting disease which has no other symptoms...

PRIVATE: the brief start made in painting has been carried through. Actually the accomplishments are negligible, but so many things are floating through my head that I'm sure I shall carry on and maybe even paint something I like. A picture of a Victorian house will be yours as soon as I can get a better idea of what you want---oil or water-colour, size (miniature or mural) colourful or monochromatic, an old one or something of the new Walton era. I don't know whether your house has much color in it or not. White walls, I'm sure, but what else is there that a picture must get along with? Old scarlet shawls, a tinny Modernage radio-phonograph, or what? Just hint a few things.

EMOTIONAL: I think of you so often that really I was almost positive I had written often until I checked myself very carefully. It is the imaginary conversations in which I engage frequently that have given me the illusion of complete rapport with you. Do you believe in telepathy and Extrasensory [sic] perception, the way I do? Now that the October days are turning golden I miss you more than ever because this is the time you were in Washington and the time we were happiest together. Maybe the happiest I have ever been. Then or since.

... Tell me more about the fake Cap d'Antibes set swirling around your base. Tell me more about everything.

Do you suppose the reason we were so happy that Fall and find the October days particularly nostalgic is because ours is an *amour d'automne*?

Your loving sere and yellow leaf,
Bill

December 1949
Avenida del Parque, 14
Cuernavaca

Darling, darling,

The trip was terrific, marred of course by work, which I have grown away from. I cannot stand going about asking strangers questions; it seems such an intrusion. And of course I know the absolute folly of journalism which at best reflects the vision of one person, and pretends to give an 'over-all picture.' And I hate to write it; and only want to do short stories.

Israel was bliss. Sun, to begin with, and without which I find no life valuable. And there was Capa, standing at the bar of the hotel when I arrived. It reminded me of Spain, of all my youth; one worked so hard, leaving every day at dawn, returning every night late, exhausted, but still ready to go out and look, listen, drink, laugh. It's a hard uncomfortable country, with one million individuals in it; you'd never have known how many different kinds of Jew there are, until finally there is no such thing as a Jew. But their stories, ah William, this affects me as the sight of Italy affected you; a gold mine of stories, the equal of which I've never before seen. And then they're brave, or they wouldn't be there and alive… I laughed more than I have in years and my mind reeled, between the glories of Crusader ruins (history, there, is so tangible that you feel yourself really moving, not dislocated, but small and inevitable, in a procession of centuries) and the corrugated tin huts springing up on Mount Carmel. I want to go back. If I could, sometime, when Sandy's older, I'd like to live there a year and collect those stories; although now is the time to go. Because the stories will become legend, not immediate fact, and be dimmed or lost. But what a place. If I had to move from here, I'd only want to go there; I like drama or sleep, and nothing much in between.

I fell in love with no one, anywhere, which saddens me—surely part of a journey, of tourism, ought to be falling in love. But I can't any more. I was also appalling homesick, sorrowing because I missed the sudden changover from babyhood to boyhood in Sandy. And thrilled to be home, here, where I still love life best, in this green flowering place, living quite separately among all the small quiet lives. The child is a grandeur, always more beautiful, more exciting, more charming. And he's happy, always, so that it is like having the sun built in to one's private world.

I love you and wish you a *very* happy New Year,
Martha

December 14, 1949
Avenida del Parque, 14
Cuernavaca

Dearest Mrs. R,

We have been home two and a half weeks, Sandy, Mother and I. I think about you steadily with gratitude. I doubt if I'd ever gotten Sandy out of Italy (and with no Catholic strings attached) were it not for your fine convincing letter. He is a dream of a baby, lovely to look at, strong, funny, intelligent and with double jointed thumbs (which Mother swears are a sign of adaptability). He is chums with everyone and now, at last after the desperate upsetting beginning, he seems settled in, completely happy, eating like a pig, sleeping well and long (at last, I thought I would go mad with his wakefulness); and only hampered in that he has no language. He was starting to speak Italian, and he has survived everything without any change to his existential soundness; but the language change has him bewildered, if not saddened. He makes himself well understood with pointing and babbling and he knows a few words, such as BAY ★ BAY-BYE [sic], which apparently means farewell since it is accompanied by a wave. And "mama" which he shouts steadily. And "papa" which means food oddly enough, and Babo [sic] which means Daddy and is how he addresses all men, with a ravished smile. I dote on him and he has been a backbreaker.

… We have a dream nurse, who I trust will love us as I love her (and, as Sandy does) and he is serene and we, finally can sleep and call our souls our own for a few hours a day. He is worth it, every bit of it; but I doubt if I would undertake such a journey again, as a brand new mother with a 19 months' old child.

I have learned a lot already. In the first place, I have such respect for women, I can hardly stand it. Imagine them all of them or at least the great majority of them, handling children steadily, as if it were perfectly easy. I think they are colossal. I am still partially dead from my first month and a half, and only now beginning to see the light with plenty of people to help me. Secondly, I have fallen into the errors I have always deplored in mothers; I am obsessed and can think of nothing else but this child; what he eats, how he sleeps, his now waning bronchitis, his diaper rash, his character, his hair-washing. I am a colossal bore, and I am the first to feel it. Some nights I keep myself awake to read, thinking I will go crackers unless I think of something besides Sandy. And when I shall ever get the time to write again is a mystery. But never mind, this one is what I want and if he keeps up at his present rate he will fill my life too full. If we ever get a picture taken (we haven't any talent for mechanics, therefore cameras) I shall send you one. In the meantime, I mainly wanted to bless you for your letter and say it finally turned out after eight months;

and we are here; and well and safe; and the baby belongs to me and me to him, as if, in fact, I had produced him in the usual way. So that is the end of the first chapter anyhow.

How are you darling? I never see newspapers here and so do not know what you are doing. How is Tommy? I have not read your book because I haven't had a chance to get to it, but I shall soon. One thing is sure: you are vastly busy. I hope also you are well and happy, and I admire and love you every day I live, with each and every breath drawn.

Always,
Martha

Afterword

Commissioned by the *Saturday Evening Post* to write a piece about the belea-
guered process of adopting her son Sandy—"Little Boy Found"—Gellhorn recalled
that she "could not say exactly when, or where, or why" she started to think of
adopting a child. "It was after the war… beginning in Spain. There had been too
much dying and destruction; there had been enough to disgust the mind and
break the heart. The only hope was to take care of life. It is not enough to look
after one's own life; it is foolish and a bore." She visited dozens of Italian orphanages, understanding that the "patched-up peace would not be good to them,"
because most of the world had "forgotten its hurt and homeless children." As a
single parent, she got her "baptism of fire in the diaper-changing racket high over
the Alps" on the long journey home. She did everything awkwardly; sometimes
handling baby Sandy "like rubber and sometimes like Venetian glass." She hoped
that there would be "space in America for all the homeless children American families would want to welcome and share their safety with. A country isn't big enough
if it has no room for children." A wish that remains true today.

In the early 1950s, Gellhorn and toddler Sandy settled into the beautiful,
sleepy community of Cuernavaca, Mexico. She later referred to those years as
her "private golden time." There she was visited by Leonard Bernstein, Dorothy
Parker, her friends Hortense Flexner and Wyncie King, and for long stretches by
her beloved Edna. Edna had continued to correspond with Hemingway after the
divorce, and he had sent her as a gift the manuscript of *The Old Man and the Sea*.
Edna returned it to him saying, "thank you, dear, but I've already read it." A letter
Hemingway wrote to Edna in March 1953 remains in Martha's papers with a handwritten note explaining, "From Hemingway to my mother—don't know why she
sent it on or why I pushed it in with other letters. Here it is, anyhow—and I think
he loved her, so much as he knew about love." In it, he insists that Edna was "the
finest and the loveliest woman" he had ever known.

Ernest reminisces about their shared time at the finca in Cuba, at her house in
St. Louis, at Sun Valley, and during their car journeys to Kansas City, "all the road,
where we ate, what we said about the League of Women Voters… and how lonely

it was. Very, very lonely." He tells her about his hope that Spencer Tracy will star in *The Old Man and the Sea*, but he is tired of the indecision of the film producers and "will not wait around much more." As always, Hemingway discusses his work: "writing is harder to do all the time. I thought it would get easier. But it doesn't." He wonders if that is the way everything is and suggests, "Maybe I should stop… but I am still sure I can take it further if I have good luck."

Gellhorn continued to correspond with Eleanor Roosevelt, their letters always revealing how each cherished the other, even though they rarely managed to meet face-to-face. By 1954, married to Tom Matthews (retired editor of *TIME* and a T.S. Eliot enthusiast, who wrote a biography of him, *Great Tom*), Gellhorn was living in London and trying unsuccessfully to embrace what she referred to as "the kitchen of life," the domestic drudgery of running a home. She knew that she was not made for "shared daily life, only shared joy." Like Gellhorn, T.S. Eliot had spent his childhood in St. Louis, and he had known her uncle who was of the same generation. She met the poet in London and they discovered that they "rode in the same streetcars dreaming of other places" where they wished to be. But she "didn't particularly take to him."

In fall 1961, her teenaged son Sandy at boarding school, she traveled to Jerusalem to report on the Eichmann Trial, after most of the world's press had gone, apparently weary from the many months of evidence. She raged, "Does it by any chance bore us to hear of the agony of a people?" It seemed to Gellhorn that there was "nobody there in the courtroom except Israelis." It was as if "a whole country was having a combination of mourning, education and a sort of nervous breakdown." It was not news to Gellhorn what was revealed over those days because she had also been to the Nuremberg Trial. It was nevertheless "a darkness on the record of humanity, because in a way everyone had guilt." She could not comprehend why fleeing Jews were not allowed into other countries or why there was not an "enormous protest made by other countries immediately." By reporting on the gruesome details, she hoped to "wake minds" to the realities of the Holocaust, "the single greatest crime that has ever been done." She wanted people to understand "the absolute necessity for a country like Israel, a haven for people who had been persecuted for no reason whatsoever except what they were born."

On her 54th birthday in 1962, she woke to the news of Eleanor Roosevelt's death and wrote the following letter to Adlai Stevenson, who had been the Democratic Party's presidential nominee in 1952 and 1956, a "dear man" to whom she had been introduced by Eleanor Roosevelt.

November 8, 1962
20 Chester Square
London

Dearest Adlai,

This is a day when it would have mattered to be together. To weep. All the weeping for Mrs. R. should have been done years ago, starting seventy years ago. Not for her, now; she'd have never have been afraid of dying and would have hated to live, ill and dependent. I always thought she was the loneliest human being I ever knew in my life; and so used to bad treatment, beginning with her mother (she spoke of her mother with love; I hated her mother) and going right on that it did not occur to her to ask for anything for herself. Not ever. I've wept for her often; and been shaken with anger for her too; and I never liked the President, nor trusted him as a man, because of how he treated her. And always knew she was something so rare that there's no name for it, more than a saint, a saint who took on all the experiences of everyday life, an absolutely unfrightened selfless woman whose heart never went wrong. And her hunger to give love—she who had never gotten it when she should, from those who should have given—is hardly to be remembered; you will find it mad that I felt she was younger than I, and I was twenty-five when I first knew her and felt it then.

Today we can weep for ourselves. I feel lonelier and more afraid; someone gone from one's own world who was like the certainty of refuge; and someone gone from the world who was like a certainty of honor.

Words are no use. Weeping's no use either. There it is. I know you feel this too; I wish I could have spent some of this day, which happens to be my birthday, with you.

Hands across the sea, dear boy; from one in need to another, helplessly.

Love,
Martha

By the mid-1960s, divorced from Tom Matthews, Gellhorn made visits to St. Louis to be with Edna, then in her 80s, and to Washington and New York City to see friends including William Walton, former fellow war correspondent, by then an abstract expressionist painter and appointed by President Kennedy as Chairman of the Commission of Fine Arts. After visiting the Library of Congress to read through some of James Michener's papers and laughing "like a drain" at what was included, she decided to make arrangements to donate her own papers to the Boston University archives. She made the first gift in early 1965, noting that "at some distant day—when we are Pompeii—it would be interesting (providing any papers remain) to know how people managed, in terms of the gold that bought them the time to write. This lot is a joke and a beginning."

In May 1965, she attended a UN Security Council meeting to hear her friend, then-US Ambassador to the United Nations, Adlai Stevenson speak, and passed handwritten notes there with Lauren Bacall, wondering, "Why did they take pictures of us? If we've been bugged, it's glorious." Bacall responded, "TV perhaps—otherwise I don't know—who are the sinister gentlemen on either end of room?" Gellhorn had to leave to make another appointment, and asked Bacall to be sure to thank Stevenson for arranging her seat. Two months later, Stevenson suffered a fatal heart attack while walking to Grosvenor Square in London. It was a neighborhood Gellhorn knew well from the 1940s when she strode along those same streets from the Dorchester Hotel to file her war reporting with the U.S. censor's office. As she yearned for the moral leadership of Eleanor Roosevelt after her death, so she "deeply missed" Stevenson, noting "how different the world" would be with them in it, "instead of the dime store minds and spirits now ruling."

To Hortense Flexner she wrote, "Someday, and very soon I feel, instead of pursuing a lifelong folly, the passionate desire to find someone to communicate with, I shall simply write. I will at last admit to myself that it is a mug's game, there is no one to hear and no one to talk back, and the last and good resort is the white page and the faceless strangers who may or may not hear. I will talk to myself on paper; I have been talking to myself, in my brain, silently, all my life."

The war in Vietnam enraged Gellhorn. In August 1966, she decided to go there to report on it for the *Manchester Guardian*. Before she left, she wrote two letters, to her mother and to her son Sandy, as well as one to her lawyer brother Walter. They were to be mailed in the case of her accidental death in Vietnam. She had felt keenly Robert Capa's sudden death in May 1954 when he stepped on a Vietminh landmine in Indochina, insisting, "I miss him every day, it only grows." In the letter to Walter she asks for "the silver baby's mug" on her desk in which she kept pencils "to be given to Cam Becket with my love. I want him to know that I value his lifelong kindness to me, deeply." The letters were never sent, because she did not die in Vietnam. Here is the one written to Edna.

August 9, 1966
London

My best beloved, my dearest little Fotsie, my one lifelong companion: I hope you will never get this letter and I do not think you will. But I am nearly thirty years older than when I went to Spain and far tidier: if by some accident I did not return from Vietnam I would hate to leave you without a word. Especially as I shall have been deceiving you, for the first time in my life and only for your own good and peace of mind, by *not* telling you that I am going to this evil, insane war. And I feel guilt about this, and guilt about going for your sake (though one can always drown in a bath-tub); but I believe you will understand why I must.

I reviled and despised those silent Germans who saw what a menace their government was to their own people and as an obvious sequence to the world. I cannot live with the sense that I have not done all I could (and small enough it will be) to protest against the war in Vietnam, protesting on behalf of the Vietnamese, Americans and finally on behalf of the human race; since now folly and wickedness are more terrible than ever: there is a way to make a Third and Last of All Wars. It may be that the human race is on the way out, a failed species, and anything one tries to do is futile. But I think that even if I knew that was true, I would still believe that each individual is responsible for his conscience; and must live by his standards of right and wrong, as long as he breathes. All I know how to do is write: the only way I can write with any authority, in the hope of influencing even a very few people is to write from firsthand knowledge. You will understand this, and respect my motive; but that won't make it any easier for you. So I ask you to understand and forgive, should you ever get this letter; and know it is not any lack of love for you that allows me to take chances with my life. It's that I cannot live it, feeling, thinking and fearing for the future as I do, and *not* take the only action open to me.

I love you best of anybody; I always have. I'll love you as long as I live, and admire you wholeheartedly out of the whole world, and be more grateful to you than I can ever say, because you are yourself.

Your,

M

In "A New Kind of War," published on September 26, 1966, Gellhorn wrote about the Qui Nhon provincial hospital that was "crowded to bursting with wounded peasants, men, women and children of all ages." A doctor took her to show her a "small-blackened cavern" that was the kitchen, "flanked by six latrines," four of which were boarded up, "totally blocked by excrement," the facilities "for the families." They continued on to the ward where there was a small child burned by napalm, "a little piece of something like cheesecloth" covering his body. It seemed that "any weight would be intolerable but so is air." His hand was burned, "stretched out like a starfish; the napalmed skin like bloody hardened meat in a butcher shop." Yet again, Gellhorn looked, while others looked away.

After her reports ran in the *Manchester Guardian*, Leonard Bernstein wrote to her, "Darling Marthy, I don't write letters these days (or notes of music either, or read or study them, or anything much involving the medulla oblongata) but at the moment I can't sleep and I keep thinking of you & your glorious three pieces... You're a good girl, & a brave and imaginative one, and a loving though despairing one, and you must suffer and do more, though it afflicts you."

A letter from a stranger in 1968 delighted Gellhorn. On it she has scribbled, "There are still a few pleasing jokes left in life, aren't there?"

June 7, 1968
Kirkwood
Missouri

Dear Martha Gellhorn,

In recognition of your outstanding contribution to American literature, you have been unanimously elected.

A DAUGHTER OF MARK TWAIN

All cordial esteem,
Cyril Clemens
Editor
Mark Twain Journal

Throughout the 1970s, Gellhorn spent time in Kenya at the remote cottage she had built in 1968, halfway up a mountain, she said, in order to be near the giraffes. In her 80th year, one early March morning she wandered down the path from her modest house to the beach, a habitual walk. At the bottom of the steps, she was knocked down and raped. Her attacker ran off, and she returned home to drive her car into Mombassa to seek medical treatment. In a letter she wrote, "women have been raped all over the world since time began. Simply because I was involved does not make the case special." She continued, that she would not let fear change her attitudes and actions, insisting that the "Ugly Event on the steps" not spoil the genuine, lasting pleasures of Nyali.

Gellhorn continued to report on American politics. Writing about the 1972 presidential campaigns of Nixon and McGovern, she observed that a "President is sold like toothpaste or detergent; money puts the message across. Without money, a campaign is crippled. We talk of one man, one vote, the basis of our great democracy, when we know that cash and more cash is essential to get out that vote, cash down to the lowest level, for stamps, telephones, even campaign buttons. Why do we accept this insane distortion of the electoral process? Or do most Americans believe that money is righteousness; money is all, the having and the getting; and he who speaks for money, with money, speaks our truth?" Those words remain true almost five decades later. So does her final question: "Who will explain to the young that the conscience of America cannot be reached, for lack of money?"

In January 1977, Gellhorn returned to Washington to cover the inauguration of Jimmy Carter for *The Observer* in London. With her press kit from those days she included the note, "I came to see my man inaugurated. The U.S. will regret chucking him in 1980." Her prediction was right. And, the wider world took notice when Carter was awarded the Nobel Peace Prize in 2002, "for his decades of untiring effort to find peaceful solutions to international conflicts, to advance democracy and human rights, and to promote economic and social development." At one of the inaugural parties, where "all the races and classes of America mixed easily," a man grabbed her by the shoulders and said, "Carter is THE man. You know why? Because he's one of us, he's the people. And he's gonna get us outa [sic] all this junk we've been in! Happy Inauguration!" Waiting to flag down a taxi later, another fellow said, "You tell them in England we've got hope again. Tell them we're full of hope." She agreed. Hope was "bursting out all over."

When *The Paris Review* published an interview with poet Stephen Spender, who claimed as fact apocryphal anecdotes about her and Hemingway, Gellhorn wrote a blistering letter to its editor George Plimpton.

August 27, 1980
72 Cadogan Square
London

Dear Mr. Plimpton,

Where on earth are you sending your letters? Mexico, Africa? Suddenly I realised that the second had followed the first into oblivion and time is running out, if I wish to state that Mr. Spender is an ass. He was always an ass but a timid type ass. In his advanced years he has become a pompous ass, which is deplorable. All true believers (in anything) should unite in war on pomposity.

So now I am going to write what I suppose must be a letter to the editor of the *Paris Review* and you will have to fill in the gaps, since I haven't anything except our transatlantic chat to go on.

Sir: An article in your issue of date (title of article) has come to my attention and caused me amazement. Therein is a short short story by Mr. Spender, as follows. (Here quote in full the bit you read me on the telephone.)

Someone could make a riveting book entitled Hemingway Apocrypha Anthology, filled with fishy tales by famous names. If people feel that they gain luster through inventing encounters with Hemingway, that is their problem and no business of mine. But I dislike being included in the nonsense.

So:

1) I never knew Mr. Spender had a first wife.

2) I never had lunch in Paris with Mr. Spender and his unknown first wife; therefore, logically, neither did Hemingway. I wonder whether Mr. Spender ever had lunch with Hemingway anywhere; they did not seem faintly compatible during a brief meeting in Spain. This is not a criticism of either of them.

3) I did not know there was a morgue in Madrid, but upon reflection now, I see that there must have been one, as there is one in every big city. The only morgue I ever frequented was in Albany, NY as a cub reporter on a Hearst newspaper in my distant youth. I assumed that someone buried the dead in Madrid where of course many died from the unnatural cause of war.

4) The very idea that anyone visited a morgue anywhere daily before breakfast proves that Mr. Spender has a weird and wondrous imagination.

But Mr. Spender muffed the end of his short short story. To make it really powerful, he should have said that he then knocked Hemingway down for insulting his first wife while I stalked out, indignant at the slur upon my courage. Much better ending.

It is risky to suggest that someone is a liar, but it can do no harm to suggest that someone is a silly juggins.

Yours,
Martha Gellhorn
Over to you, Mr. P.

In her 70s, Gellhorn embraced aging and solitude, remarking in a letter to her friend Bernard Perlin that she loved the silence of the Welsh countryside where she had a cottage and "the empty days." Musing where this preference might lead, she suggested, "You read about recluses found dead in a mass of old newspapers with half a million in gold under the rotting mattresses; I think, without newspapers and gold, that's probably me." In an unpublished piece about traveling as a pensioner, she remembered "when forty seemed senility," and that now young eyes must view her "as a robust corpse." She felt, nevertheless, "invisible and therefore free." It no longer mattered how she looked or what she did, because nobody noticed. She was comfortably "a voyeur, watching others through a one-way mirror." It was a new and unexpected freedom that she embraced.

After her friend Rebecca West's memorial service in April 1983, she wrote how astounded she was that Tolstoy had been alive when West was born, and that fact gave her "a thrilled sense of the continuity of life." As a result, Gellhorn reflected on the "vastness of change" in her own life and how history crept up on her day by day because she was living it. Changes did not daunt her; it was "the repetition that daunts" and "seeing stupidity, the root source of evil, repeat itself."

At 81, Gellhorn strapped on a knapsack and headed to Panama to report on the U.S. invasion, "an act of war, a surprise attack from the air, sea and land on a sovereign state. It killed and wounded thousands of civilians (poor people), flattened their homes (tenements) and caused widespread commercial ruin from three days of unhampered looting." She believed that from its "overkill start in 1989 until its end in April 1992, with the sleazy seven-month trial and conviction of Manuel Noriega," this operation "Just Cause" would "not shine in American history." For *The Guardian* she wrote about the working class district of Chorrillo that was blitzed, shelled and flattened by U.S. Army bulldozers. In that piece, "The Damned of Panama City," she noted that the "Spanish word for totally destitute is *damnificado*." The citizens who ran from "their burning collapsing houses in Chorrillo, with the clothes on their backs, saving their lives and nothing else, were *los damnificados de Chorrillo*." She wanted to hear their stories. In reporting their "small exact messages," Gellhorn hoped that readers would recognize "the small exact trouble of a stranger," and feel something "understandable, personal, real." They would connect, "as E.M. Forster meant it."

In November 1993, Gellhorn celebrated her 85th birthday with friends at Groucho's Club in London, wearing a tiny nametag of white card stock on which she had written in black ink in her sure, looping hand "Jolly, old." She kept a telegram that Laurance Rockefeller sent then. He had been "her best, longest and last love." They'd seen each other seldom, in "stolen hours" over 30 years and he made her laugh. He was "some sort of golden gift of good fortune, bringing excitement, glamour, fun, a long love affair by telephone across continents and ecstatic meetings whenever possible."

November 12, 1993
New York City

KEA7748 NKY501 2749611 WUF-F 1389 N-9331609699279 12 NOV 1993/1515

TELEGRAM
MRS MARTHA GELLHORN
72 CADOGAN SQUARE
LONDON SW1

MOST EAGER TO HEAR NEWS OF PARTY. HOPEFULLY A TRIUMPH
SUCCESS. WHERE ARE YOU AND WHY CAN WE NOT REACH YOU BY
PHONE. PLEASE CALL COLLECT IF NECESSARY. LOVE LAURANCE

She began to revise her thoughts on aging, turning to memories of what fun her friendships had been, "a joy and a necessity." And that sadly, her peers and her "beloved elders and betters" were dead. She missed them "more now than ever before," those "companions of the road" who had lived through the same history, knew the same things, spoke a language they each understood, without explanations. Her mother had died in 1970; Bertrand de Jouvenel in 1987; Cam Becket and Leonard Bernstein in 1990; Allen Grover in 1993; and William Walton in 1994. She was the oldest person she knew, noting that only her 80-year-old brother Alfred shared with her "this peculiar experience of old age." By telephone between Wales and New York City, they laughed "like drains over the latest signs of change and decay" in their own bodies, a "kind of absurdity in falling apart like an old car." Alfred was her last equal, to whom she could "truthfully and mockingly" talk about her "handicapped progress on this last short piece of the road."

There were other books—novels, short fiction and nonfiction, including a selection of her "horror journeys" in *Travels with Myself and Another*, and collections of both war and peacetime reporting, which she promoted at Toronto's International Festival of Authors in her 84th year: *The Face of War* and *The View from the Ground*.

More manuscripts remain in her Boston papers, yet unpublished, from *Ways and Means* (written in the mid-1930s and inspired by Bertrand de Jouvenel and his family), to *Peace on Earth* (completed in 1937 and "judged useless after a year's work"), to "Two False Starts" on novels circa 1952, to an African novel "never shown" from 1964 and many more. In one she called *Meaningless Question*, "a novel in embryo," Gellhorn's protagonist Mrs. Farnham mused about writing an autobiography in the form of a "thorough private letter." Of all her departed friends, she "missed the letter writers most." There were "letters of conversation, for pleasure, hundreds of letters received with delight, and answered when she felt like it, at equal length."

In her papers, there's also a "Diary for Paul Theroux," an extended letter scribbled over a hundred pages in a reporter's notebook, chronicling her return to Cuba one bitter February 40 years after she left her life there at the finca in 1945. She visited Gregorio, then 87 and "the vague shape" of the man she once knew, who talked about "E.H. absurdly, lovingly," all the while wondering why Mary Welsh did not give him any money from the estate. She visited the home she had shared with Hemingway from 1939 until 1945, "impressed by the driveway lined with palms," and bemoaned the loss of the glorious ceiba that had been killed when cement was poured on its roots during a repair of the front steps. Painted white, no longer the blushing pink it had been, the house looked to her "like a sanitorium." Inside, it was hideous: "animal horns and heads everywhere. Ghastly material on sofas." In Ernest's room, over his desk, there was a huge buffalo head, which she'd take "as Mary's joke, revenge, were it not for the miserable nothingness of her room." She was delighted by the pool, never having realized its immensity before, and noted that "*Pilar* will rest where the tennis court was." She was especially struck by "the solemnity of the caretakers."

Gellhorn submitted her final piece of investigative journalism in 1996, about the murdered street children of Salvador, Brazil. On a draft of it in her Boston papers, she wrote: "an historic document. It is my last and worst article. It was written without being able to see what I wrote. I could see the large letters on the typewriter keys but not the words on the page." The pages had to be read back to her and corrected verbally. "This process was done 6 times. The result is unsatisfactory to me in every way. I cannot possibly continue to work in this manner." It is particularly moving to know that just as she found her narrative voice writing about the most disenfranchised citizens in post-Depression America in the 1930s, she finished her career doing the same more than six decades later. In the end, she felt that she had "done nothing, except note what happened." And the records she had made were "partial and brief, and they were hampered by [her] own lacks and also by being fitted into a form." The pieces never satisfied her, because "they never told enough."

Aging became a burden, and, at 88, Gellhorn told her friend Mary Blume, "I am really too old, I have outlived my life. I've never had anything life-threatening, only life-demeaning." To Nicholas Shakespeare, she said that nothing interested her anymore except the natural world because it had the most to teach. At his home in Wiltshire, only days before her death, the snowdrops had come out and "she wanted to hear about them."

And, yet, in her 89th year, she traveled alone to the south of France, still beguiled by the world around her. This handwritten letter to her friend Betsy Drake, one of the last she kept, reveals a new vulnerability that is particularly poignant.

> June 30, 1997
> New Hotel La Baume
> Nîmes

Dearest Betsy,

This is my 6th day in France & for 5 days there was no sun anywhere in the country. Like a Biblical curse. Clouding now again. I spent 3 days on trains moving south from city to city & decided to settle here. Nîmes is adorable, last seen over 50 years ago. It remains small & quiet, a Roman city with splendid ruins but otherwise not on tourist beat. Little streets & low houses & big trees on the few boulevards. This old small hotel is ideal & I plan to sit here & wait for summer. When it finally comes I'll find a hotel with pool in the countryside. No hurry about getting back. I fear this is my last launching into the blue journey. The talking books make my suitcase on wheels too heavy for me. Legs very wobbly. Sight too bad. I miss the world around me. Other infirmities. Nice chance to lie on a bed in Nîmes, with a little veranda on the roof top, & listen to books— change from same life in Cad Square.

I bought carnations for my room & cherries, figs & peaches for me. I walk badly & with medium pain & have little energy but I'm feeling happy here. The people are sweet & unspoiled by *tourisme*. I've hardly seen anything of Nîmes & think I may stay several weeks or until my books & nappies run out. Hope you are getting mobile.

Love,
M.

Everything in order, fresh white tulips in a jug on her bureau, a recently published book by Sebastian Faulks unspooling on her audio cassette player, Gellhorn readied herself for her final sleep on February 14th, 1998, swallowing a pill she had kept for this purpose. As if death were just another destination, a previously unexplored place to journey.

In her will, Gellhorn asked that there be a gathering of her friends at her Cadogan Square flat, to raise a glass or two of Famous Grouse whiskey and to tell stories about their shared moments. On March 6th, her stepson Sandy Matthews hosted that evening, attended by her 84-year-old brother Alfred, her son Sandy Gellhorn and several of her cherished "chaps," including Victoria Glendinning, John Pilger, Laurance Rockefeller, Nicholas Shakespeare and Paul Theroux. Many of them met each other for the first time that night, but all of them were full of delight in their friend Martha. She was life for them, their "moral, true north" as her mother had been for her. She was, they agreed, "the great non-con-formist journalist," a genuine maverick who "wrote truthfully and pursued things truthfully." Nicholas Shakespeare suggested that "anybody who knew her was fortune's favourite kid." Alfred, recalling the "Star of Survival, First Class" that his only sister had created for their mother on her 90th birthday, recognizing "lifelong and unfailing gallantry, generosity and gaiety, with an added citation for beauty," insisted that Martha be its second recipient.

The next day, Alfred and the two Sandys tossed her ashes as she'd requested into the Thames for her "last travels," returning her to the natural world with which she had remained so beguiled. Her instructions ended, "if it's inconvenient, what the hell."

Appendix

Requiem by Martha Gellhorn (circa 1931)

"Dr. Brandon's office?" the girl inquired of the elevator boy. Steel gates clanged shut. The car mounted slowly. There were little pools of tobacco-stained saliva on the floor. She wondered who else besides Dr. Brandon had offices here.

"Eighth floor," said the boy. Was he looking at her curiously? Was he smiling? She pulled her collar up about her face. This is the time to wear a veil, she thought. How vile being afraid that someone will guess. How sordid it is. No use thinking about that. The real thing is: get my lies straight. I'll say my name is "Allen;" might as well say, "Miss Allen." What else? Probably better say I was attacked in the woods by a stranger. The nastiness of that. Cheap lies. But I can't tell the truth. If I did, I'd hate it. And if I hate what really happened, I'd go mad. People don't go mad. She stopped to despise herself. Don't make drama out of it, she instructed herself; low and lousy it is, to be sure, but some things sometimes happen this way. Stop thinking; you're a spineless idiot.

The nurse was a girl with painted lips and darkened eyes; rather young and pretty and very friendly. "Come in, dear" she said. No names asked. That's funny, thought the girl, how do they run this place anyhow?

In the waiting room the nurse said, "The doctor will want to examine you, just take off your step-ins or anything else like that you're wearing." The girl was surprised. How do they know what to examine me for, she wondered? They seemed to know. No one bothered with questions. The examination was revolting to her. The nurses chatted to each other about Marlene Dietrich, who was playing in a film at the movie-house next door. The doctor said to her, "Loosen up, girlie." She trembled, loathing it all. The oldest nurse said, "Get dressed now and we'll have a little talk." As if they were going to a tea party together; it was too much, this air of intimate and cheerful secrecy.

"Doctor says," began the oldest nurse chattily, "that you're pregnant and you've got a right nice little start, too." Am I supposed to be pleased, thought the girl, am I supposed to say something funny. Her voice failed her. She was silent. "Now this is how we do it," the nurse continued, "we put in a dressing in the afternoon and you have the operation the next morning." "Oh," said the girl. Then, remembering her plans, she asked, "Can you take me at once; I must get this finished as soon as possible." "Well," said the nurse, "We're very busy; doctor really can't take care of all his patients; but we might make a special arrangement for you." "How much does it cost," said the girl. "Two hundred dollars," said the nurse. The girl drew the bills from her purse. "We'll take you right away. Get undressed again."

In the operating room the doctor was washing his hands. The young nurse admired a ring the girl was wearing. The doctor collected his instruments with a bored gesture. The girl couldn't see what was happening. But as the pain sharpened she began to think of stories she had read—people died like this—there was Brieux's play "Maternity," for instance. There were all sorts of references to just this, in literature. The pain became like a hydraulic drill, a steel spike gouging its way up through her stomach into her breast. This isn't me, this can't be me, she thought. Things like this don't happen to people like me. We aren't in places like this, and we aren't murdered by fake doctors. It can't be. I don't believe it. The pain surged suddenly to the back of her head. She thought, I must be going blind; no—mad. Great God, what has happened? This isn't life, this isn't real. She put her teeth through her lip; you couldn't scream in front of people like this. "She's sweating," said the young nurse with interest.

It was over. The doctor smiled at her. He has a great many nice gold teeth, she thought. There are fools who get themselves into this mess, pitiful fools, and then he buys lovely gold teeth—as monuments. Shut up, she thought, needn't sentimentalize. Besides this man is saving your whole future. If he kills you, you're not losing much anyway.

"Never been in this condition before, have you?" said the doctor brightly. "No," she said. "Never going to be again, are you?" She said "No," with fervor. There was no sense in being here; life itself was not worth this ugliness. "Well, don't lose my card," the doctor went on, "most of my clientele comes back."

The older nurse said, "You won't sleep very well; but just stay in bed, and don't take out the dressing unless you can't stand it."

Her room at the hotel was quiet. There was nobody in the room who would ask questions; nobody to lie to; nobody to act for. She tried to read. I mustn't think; there's nothing left to think about. The book blurred. She was crying, aching tears. Just crying about yourself, are you? she jeered. Well, who got you into this? Who's a plain fool? What are you crying about? Because your own mind is a rotten instrument? Oh, God, give me peace. I don't want to be hurt anymore. I don't want to be hurt. Oh God, I'm so tired. Well, she mused, so I'm praying. That's a new idea.

The night was slow. Every hour she turned on the light. Only an hour between these hopeful glances. She tried everything she knew, to still the pain. She laughed at one moment, wildly, crazily, and then calmed herself by saying, "Now don't act, you fool. This is your own mess; try to behave with some courage. Do you suppose soldiers got hysterical about their wounds? Do you imagine that his is as bad as the War? Well, it isn't; and you're a gutless coward and that's all."

The young nurse greeted her like an old friend. She felt that she was going on a treasure hunt or something mysterious and gay. Why were these people so fiendishly amiable? She was taken into a room and told to undress. With terror, she realized that there were other women there. Bodies huddled under army blankets. Six of them. She could see some faces. The pallor of them was too frightful; they looked dead. They lay without moving. One of them muttered something and stirred. They were all young. They all looked alike. They had the same expressions of strain and suffering and patience. She was so horrified that she found herself growing cold. I'm going to be sick, she thought. Then she argued tensely with herself, "Look here, it isn't so terrible for you because it's just as bad for them." The logic of this wasn't especially fine, but it helped to get into her nightgown.

The older nurse took out the dressing. It seemed endlessly long. Its ends were twined around her heart. She felt them pulling. Her breath wouldn't come. Her heart was choked in twisted, bloody gauze. The nurse gave her an injection. "Twilight sleep," said the nurse, "now just you lie quiet and snooze for a bit." She slept. Later they waked her and jabbed a heavy needle mercilessly into her arm; more twilight sleep. Well, well, she thought, what amateurs they are; you don't stab a person to death merely to give an injection. Her arm throbbed. She slept again.

The older nurse waked her. "Just lean on me," she said. They hobbled like drunken dancers into the operating room. Everything was soft and lovely. She would sleep. No more pain. If she died it didn't matter. Nothing mattered. Only sleep. "It won't hurt?" she asked dreamily. "No," said the nurse.

Then the doctor appeared. There was a moment's lull. Something suddenly happened to the world. It quivered and blazed. The walls bent in on her. She closed her eyes. Her breath beat her lungs like a whip. This pain. She should be asleep. Twilight sleep. They gave it to women when they were going to have babies; real babies that they could talk about. It must be good. She was dreaming this silent, burning hell. No, this pain was real. Nothing had ever been real before. Only this. Her breath groaned out of her in sudden bursts of released agony. "Loosen up, girlie," said the doctor, "You're resisting. You're making it harder." Christ, how could she relax when the man was tearing open her body. "Stop, stop, oh for God's sake stop," she screamed. The walls collapsed. She closed her eyes again and the world was red and hot. A long knife turning slowly. "Stop stop oh doctor please stop for the love of God how much longer I can't stand this please please for God's sake." She heard this scream through a red haze of madness, pain, that knife. She couldn't let them tear away her heart. It had touched her heart; it was all over her body; cutting her; scraping her bones; her nerves writhed. Her mind was a little crystal box balancing on the edge of a precipice. One more lunge of that knife and the box would fall; it would be broken to pieces in a great dizzy darkness, a darkness made hideous and shrieking with pain. The knife jabbed suddenly. No! No! you couldn't kill people this way, not slowly and cautiously, not while they lay with all their senses crying out for mercy. You couldn't. It didn't happen. She screamed again. The young nurse said, "shut up. Do you want to bring the police in?" The older nurse said, "I thought you were going to be such a fine girl." She sobbed, "I'm sorry. I'm sorry. I don't want to scream. I want to be brave. Oh please oh doctor I can't stand it I can't stand it—I didn't know—please please." She was sobbing; her body retching up shapeless, gasping cries. The doctor said, "Give her another shot and put your hand over her mouth; we can't have her bellowing this way." Time, time: time like a leering dream that couldn't be driven away even by consciousness. Must keep the crystal box safe; mustn't let it smash. That's all that counts. Take the knife away. I never did anything to deserve this. I only wanted to make a man happy. Take the knife away! "Please doctor stop!" Her voice rose. The nurse put her hand hard over her distorted mouth. "Shut up," she commanded fiercely. God, you know I did this because I thought it was fine and honest. God, why must I have this, as the end. The crystal box trembled. There was darkness.

Another pale, sleepwalker was led into the operating room. They carried the girl back to a wicker couch. An army blanket was wrapped around her. She looked like the other huddled lifeless bodies. Her face was like theirs; strained and quiet.

They woke her several hours early. "Sorry to hurry you, dearie," said the young nurse, "but we've got such a jam here. Go on back home and sleep. You'll be alright." The girl didn't answer. She was so tired. Could she walk, she wondered, or would they take her in an ambulance. The nurse helped her to dress. She staggered. "Pull yourself together," said the nurse, "there's nothing wrong with you. You've just got rotten nerves."

On the way out, they passed the operating room. The older nurse and doctor were eating lunch off the operating table; heavy, fat sandwiches and two bottles of milk stood on the leather surface. The girl laughed. The doctor said, "Goodbye, kid, don't forget my address." She didn't bother to tell him that her only wish was to forget everything; the past and the future, her name, life—only to sleep and forget.

The pretty nurse held out her hand. "So long," she said, "if you have any girlfriends who'd like to know about our place, tell them the address. We won't say you've been here." She stared at the nurse. Was she crazy? Did the nurse really think that people usually came to places like this. Oh, it was too comic, too enormously, magnificently comic. "I'll tell them," she promised. Sleep, sleep; sleep before the laughter that was strangling her broke loose; sleep so that she could forget. The young nurse became confidential. "Are you going to marry your man?" she asked. "No," said the girl. Why talk about him. What had he to do with all this. What had he to do with her, with this person stumbling out of Dr. Brandon's office. She wanted to forget him, too. Only sleep. "Well," said the nurse, "I guess there's something to free love but it's not very safe."

The girl felt her way along the wall to the elevator. She rang the bell. There was a mirror between the elevator doors. She looked at herself. Like wearing a mask, she thought; I'd recognize the face, but I'd say, "Dear, dear how that girl has changed." She began to sway on her feet. Christ, what an ugly face; white and gaunt and old. Pooh, what's in a face. Will this elevator ever come? Do they want me to faint on the floor? That wouldn't help their trade.

The elevator came. The boy recognized her. The doors clanged shut. They were alone in the car. The boy smiled, "Doing anything tonight, kid," he asked.

Timeline

1908   November 8, born in St. Louis

1929   June, leaves Bryn Mawr after completing junior year
June–October, fact checker at *The New Republic*
November–December, cub reporter Albany *Times Union*

1930   March, arrives in Paris, works for Dorland Advertising Agency,
then *Vogue*
July 14, meets Bertrand de Jouvenel
December, returns to St. Louis

1931   January, has abortion in Chicago
April, tours Texas, New Mexico, California, Nevada, writing for
Missouri Pacific Railroad
June–July, tours Mexico for Missouri Pacific R.R., meets
Diego Rivera
September, meets Bertrand de Jouvenel in NYC; they drive
through the Southern states, taking odd jobs, ending in New Orleans
at Christmas

1932   January–May, works as an extra in Hollywood and begins writing
first novel, *What Mad Pursuit*
June 30, returns to Europe

1933   January–March, works at *Vogue*
June, reports on World Economic Conference in London,
interviews Hitler's personal translator
July–December, travels with Bertrand through France, Spain, Italy

1934   January, travels to Germany with young French political activists;
novel *What Mad Pursuit* is accepted by publishing house
Frederick Stokes
June, mother Edna Gellhorn visits France

October 10, returns to U.S., begins working for Harry Hopkins, reporting on the treatment of the unemployed for Federal Emergency Relief Administration (FERA)

1935	January–August, reports for FERA

January–August, reports for FERA

August, begins writing *The Trouble I've Seen*

September, loses FERA job for inciting a riot among the unemployed in Idaho

October–November, lives in the White House at the invitation of the Roosevelts; meets H.G. Wells

December, continues writing *The Trouble I've Seen* in Connecticut

1936   January 25, father George Gellhorn dies in St. Louis

June, stays with H.G. Wells at 13 Hanover Terrace, London; writes lynching piece, "Justice at Night"

July–September, travels through France, Germany, Austria, researching novel *Peace on Earth* (never submitted for publication)

December, visits Key West with mother Edna and brother Alfred; meets Ernest Hemingway

1937   March 30, arrives in Madrid, stays at Hotel Florida

May 2, stops in Paris *en route* to NYC

June 4, attends Writers' Congress at Carnegie Hall

June–July, works on *The Spanish Earth* documentary

July 8, screens *The Spanish Earth* for the Roosevelts at the White House with Ernest Hemingway and Joris Ivens

July 17, *Collier's* publishes first piece of war reporting, "Only the Shells Whine," about bombing in Madrid

August 14, sails on *Normandie* to France

September–December, reports from Spain, stays at Hotel Florida

December 25, spends Christmas in NYC

1938   January, lectures across the U.S. to raise funds for Spain

March 31, returns to Spain

May–June, visits Prague to report on the German-Jewish refugee crisis

July–August, in Paris writing *A Stricken Field*

November 18, travels to Barcelona

December 2, returns to Paris, *en route* to NYC

1939 February 18, arrives in Cuba

March–July, writes *A Stricken Field* at the Finca Vigía, San Francisco de Paula

July, mother Edna visits Cuba

August–September, lives at Sun Valley, Idaho, with Ernest Hemingway; Gary Cooper, Dorothy Parker and Alan Campbell visit

November 19, sails to Finland to report for *Collier's*

November 30, arrives in Helsinki where war has started

December 10, arrives in Stockholm, Sweden

1940 January–September, stays in Cuba

November 4, Ernest Hemingway divorces Pauline Pfeiffer

November 21, marries Ernest Hemingway in Cheyenne, Wyoming

1941 January 4, leaves for Far East with Ernest Hemingway, to report for *Collier's*

June, returns home to Cuba, works on short stories published in *The Heart of Another*

1942 July–September, tours Caribbean, reporting for *Collier's*

1943 In Cuba, writing novel *Liana*

November 3, arrives in London to report on the war for *Collier's*

1944 January 27–March 17, reporting from Italy for *Collier's*

February 17, novel *Liana* has sold 17,000 copies

March 21–May 2, in Cuba

May 10–May 27, takes slow boat to England from NYC

June 6–10, on Red Cross hospital ship, helping to care for D-Day wounded

July–September, reporting on war for *Collier's*

September 20, arrives in Paris

1945 March–April, follows armored division

May 7, visits Dachau in the days following its liberation

December 21, divorces Ernest Hemingway

1946   July, play about women war correspondents, *Love Goes to Press*, is performed at London's Duchess Theatre

1947   March 4, receives War Department Citation

June 17, editor Maxwell Perkins dies

1948   Novel about Dachau, *The Wine of Astonishment*, is published

1949   November, adopts son Sandy from an Italian orphanage

1950   Lives in Cuernavaca, Mexico

1954   Moves to London, marries Tom Matthews

May 25, Robert Capa dies in Vietnam

1963   Divorces Tom Matthews

1966   August, travels to Vietnam to report on the war for *The Guardian*

1968   Builds home in Kenya

1970   Buys London flat, 72 Cadogan Square

September 24, mother Edna Gellhorn dies

1977   January, reports on the inauguration of President Jimmy Carter for *The Observer*

1990   June, reports on the U.S. invasion of Panama for *The Guardian*

1993   November, celebrates 85th birthday at Groucho's Club, London

1996   June 7, files final investigative piece about the murdered street children of Salvador, Brazil

1998   February 15, dies by suicide in London, aged 89

Selected Further Reading

Gellhorn, Martha	*A Stricken Field*
Gellhorn, Martha	*Liana*
Gellhorn, Martha	*The Face of War*
Gellhorn, Martha	*The Heart of Another*
Gellhorn, Martha	*The Honeyed Peace*
Gellhorn, Martha	*The Trouble I've Seen*
Gellhorn, Martha	*The View from the Ground*
Gellhorn, Martha	*The Weather in Africa*
Gellhorn, Martha	*The Wine of Astonishment* aka *Point of No Return*
Gellhorn, Martha	*Travels with Myself and Another*
Gellhorn, Martha and Cowles, Virginia	*Love Goes to Press*
Baker, Carlos, ed.	*Ernest Hemingway Selected Letters 1917-1961*
Bruccoli, Matthew, ed.	*The Only Thing That Counts: The Ernest Hemingway-Maxwell Perkins Correspondence*
Capa, Robert	*Slightly Out of Focus*
Hemingway, Ernest	*For Whom the Bell Tolls*
Hemingway, Ernest	*The Fifth Column*
Hochschild, Adam	*Spain in Our Hearts: Americans in the Spanish Civil War, 1936-1939*
Kellen, James	*Hemingway's Spanish Earth*
Kert, Bernice	*The Hemingway Women: Those Who Loved Him~the Wives and Others*
Moorehead, Caroline	*Martha Gellhorn: A Life*
Moorehead, Caroline	*Selected Letters of Martha Gellhorn*
Rhodes, Richard	*Hell and Good Company: The Spanish Civil War and the World it Made*
Vaill, Amanda	*Hotel Florida: Truth, Love and Death in the Spanish Civil War*

Acknowledgments

Each of the chapter titles is lifted from Gellhorn's published writing and the title itself comes from her closing in an early letter to lifelong friend Cam Becket.

This book would not exist without the kindness and generosity of Martha Gellhorn's literary executor Dr. Alexander Matthews, who provided access to her restricted papers in Boston as well as encouraging words along the way.

Thank you to Lionel Koffler for giving the book a home at Firefly and to Michael Worek for his keen editorial eye, both of them matching my enthusiasm for each new discovery. Gratitude also to designers Noor Majeed, Hartley Millson and Jacqueline Raynor; to George Walker for the glorious endpapers; and, to publicist Melissa Zilberberg, whose work was essential in launching *Yours, for Probably Always*.

My many weeklong peregrinations through Gellhorn's papers were a treat every time thanks to the support of archivist Sarah Pratt. Her ebullience for the material equals my own. I appreciate also the work of Stacey Chandler, Eliza Gilmore, Maryrose Grossman and Megan Woods at John F. Kennedy Presidential Library, Maurice Klapwald at NYPL and Sandra Bossert and Squirrel Walsh at Princeton University.

The Ontario Arts Council provided essential funding and I am grateful especially to Sarah MacLachlan at House of Anansi Press, Liz Johnston at *Brick: A Literary Journal* and Barry Callaghan at Exile Editions for believing in my work on these remarkable years of Gellhorn's life. And, a longform piece about Martha Gellhorn's enduring friendship with Eleanor Roosevelt, commissioned by Haley Cullingham at *Hazlitt*, was a concrete nod to a potential audience.

All of the following fine folks listened patiently as I rambled on in person or in letters about my research and made me feel that this story mattered: Cheryl Andrews, Stephen Ardill, Cary Barbor, Martha Brooks, Glenda Burgess, Wayson Choy, Bernard Conlon, Anne Margaret Daniel, Shivaun Hearne, Helen Holtby, Alison Hurst, Tim Hutton, Douglas Jamieson, Christine Kalkanis, Martha Kanya-Forstner, David Kent, Pat Keresteci, Owen King, Florence Minz, Rex Pickett, Erin Prendergast, Denise Quinn, Erika Robuck, Shelagh Rogers, Jennifer Walcott and Sue Williams.

Special thanks to Rob Burdock in Fife, Scotland, who kicked the stone along the path several years ago by suggesting I read *Selected Letters of Martha Gellhorn*. To Sandra Rabinowitz for providing a copy of a radio interview Gellhorn gave to Eleanor Wachtel. And to Adam Hochschild for a life-changing conversation about *Spain in Our Hearts: Americans in the Spanish Civil War, 1936–1939* in fall 2016.

I hope all of you who have found your way to this book will seek more of Martha Gellhorn's own words. She remains a wonder.

Janet Somerville
Toronto

Letter Citations

ACSS	Archives of Charles Scribner's Sons, Princeton University	
CCPC	Crowell Collier Publishing Company Records, NYPL	
EHPP	Ernest Hemingway Personal Papers, John F. Kennedy Library	
MGPP	Martha Gellhorn Personal Papers, Howard Gotlieb Archival Research Center, Boston University	

Chapter 1: Nothing Ever Happens

March 1930	MG to Cam Becket	MGPP-013-008
5 April 1930	George Gellhorn to MG	MGPP-019-002
3 May 1930	George Gellhorn to MG	MGPP-019-002
21 June 1930	Edna Gellhorn to MG	MGPP-018-001
Fall 1930	MG to Bertrand de Jouvenel	MGPP-008-008
February 1931	Cam Becket to MG	MGPP-013-008
26 February 1931	MG to Cam Becket	MGPP-013-008
May 1931	MG to Cam Becket	MGPP-013-008

Chapter 2: What Mad Pursuit

January 1932	MG to Bertrand de Jouvenel	MGPP-008-008
22 January 1932	MG to Bertrand de Jouvenel	MGPP-008-008
26 January 1932	MG to Bertrand de Jouvenel	MGPP-008-008
29 January 1932	Bertrand de Jouvenel to MG	MGPP-008-008
January 1932	MG to Bertrand de Jouvenel	MGPP-008-008
May 1932	Bertrand de Jouvenel to MG	MGPP-008-008
12 May 1932	Bertrand de Jouvenel to MG	MGPP-008-008
Late May 1932	MG to Bertrand de Jouvenel	MGPP-008-008
June 1932	MG to Bertrand de Jouvenel	MGPP-008-008
17 June 1932	Bertrand de Jouvenel to Edna Gellhorn	MGPP-008-008

3 October 1932	MG to Bertrand de Jouvenel	MGPP-008-008
21 October 1932	Bertrand de Jouvenel to Edna Gellhorn	MGPP-008-008
Early March 1933	MG to Bertrand de Jouvenel	MGPP-008-008
Early March 1933	MG to Bertrand de Jouvenel	MGPP-008-008
Early March 1933	MG to Bertrand de Jouvenel	MGPP-008-008
30 March 1933	MG to Bertrand de Jouvenel	MGPP-008-008
June 1933	MG to Bertrand de Jouvenel	MGPP-008-008
June 1933	MG to Bertrand de Jouvenel	MGPP-008-008
Late June 1933	Edna Gellhorn to MG	MGPP-018-001
Fall 1933	MG to Edna Gellhorn	MGPP-018-001
31 December 1933	Edna Gellhorn to MG	MGPP-018-001
Early 1934	Bertrand de Jouvenel to MG	MGPP-008-008
27 February 1934	MG to Bertrand de Jouvenel	MGPP-008-008
Early March 1934	Bertrand de Jouvenel to MG	MGPP-008-008
20 March 1934	MG to Bertrand de Jouvenel	MGPP-008-008
23 March 1934	Bertrand de Jouvenel to MG	MGPP-008-008
7 April 1934	Bertrand de Jouvenel to MG	MGPP-008-008
29 April 1934	MG to Cam Becket	MGPP-013-008
7 May 1934	Bertrand de Jouvenel to MG	MGPP-008-008
May 1934	Edna Gellhorn to MG	MGPP-018-001
Early June 1934	Edna Gellhorn to Bertrand de Jouvenel	MGPP-018-001
25 June 1934	Bertrand de Jouvenel to MG	MGPP-008-008
29 June 1934	Bertrand de Jouvenel to MG	MGPP-008-008
4 July 1934	Edna Gellhorn to MG	MGPP-018-001
10 July 1934	Edna Gellhorn to Bertrand de Jouvenel	MGPP-018-001
29 August 1934	MG to Cam Becket	MGPP-013-008
24 October 1934	Bertrand de Jouvenel to MG	MGPP-008-008

5 November 1934	MG to Harry Hopkins	MGPP-021-005
15 November 1934	Bertrand de Jouvenel to MG	MGPP-008-008
26 November 1934	MG to Harry Hopkins	MGPP-021-005
2 December 1934	MG to Bertrand de Jouvenel	MGPP-008-008
8 December 1934	Bertrand de Jouvenel to MG	MGPP-008-008

Chapter 3: The Trouble I've Seen

6 February 1935	Eleanor Roosevelt to MG	MGPP-004-121
8 February 1935	Bertrand de Jouvenel to MG	MGPP-008-008
26 February 1935	Percy Philip to MG	MGPP-010-010
18 March 1935	Bertrand de Jouvenel to MG	MGPP-008-008
6 April 1935	H.G. Wells to MG	MGPP-001-001
10 April 1935	MG to Hortense Flexner	MGPP-002-037
Early April 1935	H.G. Wells to MG	MGPP-001-001
April 1935	H.G. Wells to MG	MGPP-001-001
23 April 1935	Bertrand de Jouvenel to MG	MGPP-008-008
25 April 1935	MG to Harry Hopkins	MGPP-021-005
26 April 1935	H.G. Wells to MG	MGPP-001-001
14 May 1935	Bertrand de Jouvenel to MG	MGPP-008-008
25 May 1935	H.G. Wells to MG	MGPP-001-001
Late May 1935	Bertrand de Jouvenel to MG	MGPP-008-008
July 1935	Alfred Gellhorn to MG	MGPP-021-004
1 August 1935	George Gellhorn to MG	MGPP-019-002
Summer 1935	Allen Grover to MG	MGPP-024-004
13 August 1935	Allen Grover to MG	MGPP-024-004
17 August 1935	H.G. Wells to MG	MGPP-001-001
4 October 1935	H.G. Wells to MG	MGPP-001-001

12 October 1935	Bertrand de Jouvenel to MG	MGPP-008-008
14 October 1935	H.G. Wells to MG	MGPP-001-001
Fall 1935	Allen Grover to MG	MGPP-024-004
Fall 1935	Allen Grover to MG	MGPP-024-004
31 October 1935	Bertrand de Jouvenel to MG	MGPP-008-008
8 November 1935	Journal entry	MGPP-001-007
27 November 1935	H.G. Wells to MG	MGPP-001-001
12 December 1935	H.G. Wells to MG	MGPP-001-001
23 December 1935	MG to Eleanor Roosevelt	MGPP-004-122
27 December 1935	Eleanor Roosevelt to MG	MGPP-004-121
5 January 1936	H.G. Wells to MG	MGPP-001-001
9 January 1936	Bertrand de Jouvenel to MG	MGPP-008-008
21 January 1936	Bertrand de Jouvenel to MG	MGPP-008-008
28 January 1936	H.G. Wells to MG	MGPP-001-001
29 January 1936	MG to Hortense Flexner	MGPP-002-037
30 January 1936	MG to Eleanor Roosevelt	MGPP-004-121
31 January 1936	H.G. Wells to MG	MGPP-001-001
4 February 1936	Eleanor Roosevelt to MG	MGPP-004-122
7 February 1936	MG to Eleanor Roosevelt	MGPP-004-121
2 March 1936	Bertrand de Jouvenel to MG	MGPP-008-008
20 April 1936	H.G. Wells to MG	MGPP-001-001
2 May 1936	H.G. Wells to MG	MGPP-001-001
9 May 1936	H.G. Wells to MG	MGPP-001-001
26 June 1936	Eleanor Roosevelt to MG	MGPP-004-122
7 July 1936	Eleanor Roosevelt to MG	MGPP-004-122
12 July 1936	Edna Gellhorn to H.G. Wells	MGPP-018-001
2 August 1936	Edna Gellhorn to MG	MGPP-019-002

5 August 1936	MG to Allen Grover	MGPP-024-004
6 August 1936	MG to Allen Grover	MGPP-024-004
7 September 1936	MG to Allen Grover	MGPP-024-004
12 September 1936	Edna Gellhorn to MG	MGPP-019-001
16 September 1936	"My Day" Column by Eleanor Roosevelt	MGPP-001-002
25 September 1936	Alfred Gellhorn to MG	MGPP-021-004
4 October 1936	MG to Allen Grover	MGPP-024-004
9 October 1936	Eleanor Roosevelt to MG	MGPP-004-121
15 October 1936	Alfred Gellhorn to MG	MGPP-021-004
24 October 1936	Review, *The Trouble I've Seen*	MGPP-010-021
6 November 1936	Alfred Gellhorn to MG	MGPP-021-004
7 November 1936	Eleanor Roosevelt to MG	MGPP-004-121
8 November 1936	Bertrand de Jouvenel to MG	MGPP-008-008
11 November 1936	MG to Eleanor Roosevelt	MGPP-004-122
30 November 1936	Eleanor Roosevelt to MG	MGPP-004-121
10 December 1936	Eleanor Roosevelt to MG	MGPP-004-121

Chapter 4: The Spanish Earth

17 December 1936	H.G. Wells to MG	MGPP-001-001
28 December 1936	Eleanor Roosevelt to MG	MGPP-004-121
8 January 1937	MG to Eleanor Roosevelt	MGPP-004-122
12 January 1937	Allen Grover to MG	MGPP-024-004
13 January 1937	MG to Eleanor Roosevelt	MGPP-004-122
14 January 1937	MG to Pauline Pfeiffer	MGPP-013-008
16 January 1937	Eleanor Roosevelt to MG	MGPP-004-122
26 January 1937	*N.Y. Herald Tribune*	MGPP-010-021
30 January 1937	MG to Mrs. Barnes	MGPP-013-008

January 1937	MG to Ernest Hemingway	MGPP-024-022
8 February 1937	MG to Cam Becket	MGPP-013-008
8 February 1937 MGPP-013-008	MG to Ernest Hemingway and Pauline Pfeiffer	
9 February 1937	MG to Eleanor Roosevelt	MGPP-004-122
12 February 1937	Eleanor Roosevelt to MG	MGPP-004-121
15 February 1937	MG to Ernest Hemingway	MGPP-024-002
1 March 1937	Eleanor Roosevelt to MG	MGPP-004-121
2 March 1937	MG to Ernest Hemingway	MGPP-024-002
Early March 1937	MG to Allen Grover	MGPP-024-004
March 1937	MG to Cam Becket	MGPP-013-007
23 March–25 April 1937	Spain Journal	MGPP-001-007
Early May 1937	MG to Ernest Hemingway	MGPP-024-002
Late May 1937	MG to Ernest Hemingway	MGPP-024-002
Late May 1937	MG to Ernest Hemingway	MGPP-024-002
1 June 1937	Eleanor Roosevelt to MG	MGPP-004-121
9 June 1937	MG to Eleanor Roosevelt	MGPP-004-122
14 June 1937	Eleanor Roosevelt to MG	MGPP-004-121
Post-14 June 1937	MG to Eleanor Roosevelt	MGPP-004-122
17 June 1937	MG to Ernest Hemingway	MGPP-024-002
Mid-June 1937	MG to Hortense Flexner	MGPP-002-037
24 June 1937	Eleanor Roosevelt to MG	MGPP-004-121
30 June 1937	Eleanor Roosevelt to MG	MGPP-004-121
3–4 July 1937	MG to Eleanor Roosevelt	MGPP-004-122
8 July 1937	MG to Eleanor Roosevelt	MGPP-004-122
Late July 1937	MG to Ernest Hemingway	MGPP-024-002

Chapter 5: High Explosive for Everyone

27 November 1937	Edna Gellhorn to Cam Becket	MGPP-018-001
19 December 1937	MG to Ernest Hemingway	MGPP-024-002
23 December 1937	MG to Ernest Hemingway	MGPP-024-002
24 January 1938	MG to Eleanor Roosevelt	MGPP-004-122
31 January 1938	Eleanor Roosevelt to MG	MGPP-004-121
1 February 1938	MG to Eleanor Roosevelt	MGPP-004-122
8 February 1938	Eleanor Roosevelt to MG	MGPP-004-121
Post-23 March 1938	MG to Eleanor Roosevelt	MGPP-004-122
5 April 1938	Eleanor Roosevelt to MG	MGPP-004-121
24/25 April 1938	MG to Eleanor Roosevelt	MGPP-004-122
25 April 1938	Journal Spain	MGPP-001-007
23 May 1938	Eleanor Roosevelt to MG	MGPP-004-121
26 May1938	MG to Edna Gellhorn	MGPP-010-010
13 June 1938	MG to H.G. Wells	MGPP-001-001
17 June 1938	MG to Eleanor Roosevelt	MGPP-004-122
29 June 1938	Eleanor Roosevelt to MG	MGPP-004-121
4 July 1938	MG to Edna Gellhorn	MGPP-010-010
7 July 1938	MG to H.G. Wells	MGPP-001-001
14 August 1938	MG to Eleanor Roosevelt	MGPP-004-123
25 August 1938	MG to Edna Gellhorn	MGPP-010-010
31 August 1938	Eleanor Roosevelt to MG	MGPP-004-121
7 October 1938	MG to Edna Gellhorn	MGPP-010-010
19 October 1938	MG to Eleanor Roosevelt	MGPP-004-122
22 October 1938	MG to Charles Colebaugh	CCPC-316-024
15 November 1938	Eleanor Roosevelt to MG	MGPP-004-121
3 December 1938	MG to Eleanor Roosevelt	MGPP-004-122

6 December 1938   MG to Charles Colebaugh   CCPC-316-031

1 January 1939   MG to Eleanor Roosevelt   MGPP-004-122

Post-8 January 1939   MG to Eleanor Roosevelt   MGPP-004-122

26 January 1939   Eleanor Roosevelt to MG   MGPP-004-121

5 February 1939   MG to Eleanor Roosevelt   MGPP-004-122

18 March 1939   MG to Eleanor Roosevelt   MGPP-004-122

11 May 1939   MG to Eleanor Roosevelt   MGPP-004-122

17 May 1939   Eleanor Roosevelt to MG   MGPP-004-121

4 August 1939   MG to Eleanor Roosevelt   MGPP-004-122

8 August 1939   Eleanor Roosevelt to MG   MGPP-004-121

Late August 1939   MG to Eleanor Roosevelt   MGPP-004-122

Fall 1939   MG to Eleanor Roosevelt   MGPP-004-123

11 September 1939   President Franklin D. Roosevelt, on behalf of Martha Gellhorn
MGPP-004-121

27 September 1939   Eleanor Roosevelt to MG   MGPP-004-121

16 October 1939   MG to Ernest Hemingway   MGPP-024-002

Late October 1939   MG to Charles Colebaugh   CCPC-316-039

Chapter 6: Death in the Present Tense

Pre-19 November 1939   MG to Allen Grover   MGPP-024-004

19 November 1939   MG to Allen Grover   MGPP-024-004

30 November 1939   MG to Ernest Hemingway   MGPP-024-002

4 December 1939   MG to Ernest Hemingway   MGPP-024-002

31 December 1939   MG to Ernest Hemingway   MGPP-024-002

19 January 1940   MG to Ernest Hemingway   MGPP-024-002

31 January 1940   MG to Eleanor Roosevelt   MGPP-004-122

9 February 1940   Eleanor Roosevelt to MG   MGPP-004-121

7 March 1940   "My Day" Column by Eleanor Roosevelt MGPP-001-002

8 March 1940	MG to Allen Grover	MGPP-024-004
10 March 1940	Hortense Flexner to MG	MGPP-002-037
11 March 1940	Allen Grover to MG	MGPP-024-004
12 March 1940	Eleanor Roosevelt to MG	MGPP-004-121
13 March 1940	MG to Charles Colebaugh	CCPC-316-054
17 March 1940	MG to Eleanor Roosevelt	MGPP-004-122
Mid-March 1940	Hortense Flexner to MG	MGPP-002-037
19 March 1940	MG to Allen Grover	MGPP-024-004
21 March 1940	Charles Colebaugh to MG	CCPC-316-056
22 March 1940	Eleanor Roosevelt to MG	MGPP-004-121
23 March 1940	MG to Allen Grover	MGPP-024-004
26 March 1940	Hortense Flexner to MG	MGPP-002-037
29 March 1940	MG to Hortense Flexner and Wyncie King	MGPP-002-037
3 April 1940	MG to Charles Colebaugh	CCPC-316-058
17 May 1940	MG to Hortense Flexner and Wyncie King	MGPP-002-037
7 June 1940	MG to Eleanor Roosevelt	MGPP-004-122
8 June 1940	MG to Hortense Flexner and Wyncie King	MGPP-002-037
7 July 1940	MG to Charles Scribner	MGPP-021-004
20 July 1940	MG to Eleanor Roosevelt	MGPP-004-122
24 July 1940	MG to Ernest Hemingway	MGPP-024-002
Late July 1940	MG to Hortense Flexner	MGPP-002-037
2 August 1940	Eleanor Roosevelt to MG	MGPP-004-121
23 August 1940	MG to Charles Scribner	MGPP-021-004
25 August 1940	MG to Hortense Flexner and Wyncie King	MGPP-002-037
6 September 1940	MG to Allen Grover	MGPP-024-004
Post-21 October 1940	Hortense Flexner to MG	MGPP-002-037
24 October 1940	MG to Eleanor Roosevelt	MGPP-004-122

26 October 1940   MG to H.G. Wells   MGPP-025-026

29/30 October 1940 MG to Charles Scribner   MGPP-025-026

30 October 1940   MG to Hortense Flexner   MGPP-002-037

8 November 1940   Eleanor Roosevelt to MG   MGPP-004-121

9 November 1940   MG to Eleanor Roosevelt   MGPP-004-122

9 November 1940   Alan Campbell to MG   MGPP-010-020

5 December 1940   MG to Eleanor Roosevelt   MGPP-004-122

18 December 1940   President Franklin D. Roosevelt, on behalf of MG
MGPP-004-121

27 December 1940   MG to Eleanor Roosevelt   MGPP-004-121

30 December 1940   Charles Colebaugh, on behalf of MG   CCPC-316-085

Chapter 7: Mr. Ma's Tigers

6 January 1941   Eleanor Roosevelt to MG   MGPP-004-121

24 January 1941   Eleanor Roosevelt to MG   MGPP-004-121

1 March 1941   MG to Charles Colebaugh   MGPP-021-004

8 March 1941   MG to Alexander Woollcott   MGPP-010-020

2 June 1941   MG to Allen Grover   MGPP-024-004

3 June 1941   MG to Eleanor Roosevelt   MGPP-004-121

10 June 1941   Eleanor Roosevelt to MG   MGPP-004-121

18/19 June 1941   MG to Hortense Flexner   MGPP-002-037

21 June 1941   MG to Charles Scribner   MGPP-025-026

July 1941   MG to Allen Grover   MGPP-024-004

15 September 1941 Eleanor Roosevelt to MG   MGPP-004-121

22 September 1941 MG to Hortense Flexner   MGPP-002-037

23 September 1941 MG to Eleanor Roosevelt   MGPP-004-122

1 October 1941   Eleanor Roosevelt to MG   MGPP-004-121

17 October 1941   MG to Maxwell Perkins   MGPP-021-004

17 October 1941   MG to Eleanor Roosevelt   MGPP-004-122

10 November 1941 Eleanor Roosevelt to MG   MGPP-004-121

17 November 1941 MG to Eleanor Roosevelt   MGPP-004-122

Chapter 8: Messing about in Boats

22 January 1942   MG to Alexander Woollcott   MGPP-010-020

3 February 1942   MG to Charles Colebaugh   MGPP-021-004

8 March 1942   MG to Hortense Flexner   MGPP-002-037

30 April 1942   Allen Grover to MG   MGPP-024-004

22 May 1942   MG to Ernest Hemingway   MGPP-024-004

23 May 1942   MG to Ernest Hemingway   MGPP-024-004

25 May 1942   Edna Gellhorn to Ernest Hemingway
EHPP-IC09-002-007

26 May 1942   MG to Ernest Hemingway   MGPP-024-004

29 May 1942   MG to Ernest Hemingway   MGPP-024-004

30 May 1942   MG to Ernest Hemingway   MGPP-024-004

1 June 1942   MG to Ernest Hemingway   MGPP-024-004

14 June 1942   MG to H.G. Wells   MGPP-001-001

29 June 1942   MG to Ernest Hemingway   MGPP-024-004

29 June 1942   Eleanor Roosevelt to MG   MGPP-004-121

10 July 1942   MG to Eleanor Roosevelt   MGPP-004-123

15 July 1942   Edna Gellhorn to Ernest Hemingway
EHPP-IC09-002-008

16 July 1942   MG to Charles Colebaugh   MGPP-21-004

20 July 1942   MG to Ernest Hemingway   MGPP-024-002

23 July 1942   MG to Ernest Hemingway   MGPP-024-002

26 July 1942   MG to Ernest Hemingway   MGPP-024-002

2 August 1942   MG to Ernest Hemingway   MGPP-024-002

8 August 1942	Eleanor Roosevelt to MG	MGPP-004-121
Fall 1942	MG to Eleanor Roosevelt	MGPP-004-123
11 October 1942	MG to Ernest Hemingway	MGPP-024-002
18 October 1942	MG to Ernest Hemingway	MGPP-024-002
October 1942	MG to Allen Grover	MGPP-024-004

9 November 1942   Edna Gellhorn to Ernest Hemingway
EHPP-IC08-002-011

| 1 December 1942 | Eleanor Roosevelt to MG | MGPP-004-121 |

Chapter 9: The View from the Ground

10 January 1943	MG to Ernest Hemingway	MGPP-024-002
16 February 1943	MG to Maxwell Perkins	ACSS-275-008-007
4 March 1943	Maxwell Perkins to MG	ACSS-275-008-010
Spring 1943	MG to H.G. Wells	MGPP-001-001
20 May 1943	MG to Hortense Flexner and Wyncie King	MGPP-002-037
3 June 1943	MG to Ernest Hemingway	MGPP-024-002
5 June 1943	MG to Ernest Hemingway	MGPP-024-002
9 June 1943	MG to H.G. Wells	MGPP-001-001
13 June 1943	MG to Ernest Hemingway	MGPP-024-002
14 June 1943	MG to Ernest Hemingway	MGPP-024-002
15 June 1943	MG to Ernest Hemingway	MGPP-024-002
28 June 1943	MG to Ernest Hemingway	MGPP-024-002
4 July 1943	MG to Ernest Hemingway	MGPP-024-002
19 July 1943	Maxwell Perkins to MG	ACSS-275-008-018
27 July 1943	Maxwell Perkins to MG	ACSS-275-008-021
Post–12 August 1943	MG to Maxwell Perkins	ACSS-275-008-025
8 September 1943	MG to Ernest Hemingway	MGPP-024-002

13 September 1943   Edna Gellhorn to Ernest Hemingway
EHPP-IC09-002-018

16 September 1943   MG to Ernest Hemingway   MGPP-024-002

17 September 1943   MG to Ernest Hemingway   MGPP-024-002

20 September 1943   MG to Ernest Hemingway   MGPP-024-002

1 October 1943   MG to Ernest Hemingway   MGPP-024-002

4 October 1943   MG to Ernest Hemingway   MGPP-024-002

Early October 1943 MG to Eleanor Roosevelt   MGPP-004-123

8 October 1943   MG to Ernest Hemingway   MGPP-024-002

18 October 1943   MG to Ernest Hemingway   MGPP-024-002

20 October 1943   MG to Ernest Hemingway   MGPP-024-002

21 October 1943   MG to Ernest Hemingway   MGPP-024-002

27 October 1943   MG to Ernest Hemingway   MGPP-024-002

29 October 1943   MG to Ernest Hemingway   MGPP-024-002

Chapter 10: The Face of War

6 November 1943   MG to Ernest Hemingway   MGPP-024-002

20 November 1943   MG to Ernest Hemingway   MGPP-024-002

27 November 1943   Edna Gellhorn to Ernest Hemingway
EHPP-IC09-002-015

1 December 1943   MG to Ernest Hemingway   MGPP-024-002

9 December 1943   MG to Ernest Hemingway   MGPP-024-002

13 December 1943   MG to Ernest Hemingway   MGPP-024-002

22 December 1943   MG to Ernest Hemingway   MGPP-024-002

1 January 1944   MG to Ernest Hemingway   MGPP-024-002

9 January 1944   Edna Gellhorn to Ernest Hemingway
EHPP-IC09-002-020

15 January 1944   MG to Ernest Hemingway   MGPP-024-002

28 April 1944	MG to Eleanor Roosevelt	MGPP-004-123
29 April 1944	Eleanor Roosevelt to MG	MGPP-004-121
7 May 1944	MG to Allen Grover	MGPP-024-004
17 May 1944	MG to Hortense Flexner	MGPP-002-037
27 May 1944	MG to Allen Grover	MGPP-024-004
24 June 1944	MG to Colonel Lawrence	MGPP-001-009
4 August 1944	MG to Hortense Flexner	MGPP-002-037
30 October 1944	MG to Allen Grover	MGPP-024-004
2 November 1944	MG to Allen Grover	MGPP-024-004
14 November 1944	MG to Edna Gellhorn	MGPP-010-020

Chapter 11: The Heart of Another

Post 16 July 1945	MG to Cam Becket	MGPP-013-007
10 August 1945	MG to Cam Becket	MGOO-013-007
13 August 1945	MG to Ernest Hemingway	EHPP-IC09-003-007
25 August 1945	MG to H.G. Wells	MGPP-001-001
5 September 1945	James Gavin to MG	MGPP-008-008
23 October 1945	Edna Gellhorn to Ernest Hemingway	MGPP-018-001
8 November 1945	James Gavin to MG	MGPP-008-008
23 December 1945	James Gavin to MG	MGPP-008-008

Chapter 12: Love Goes to Press

2 January 1946	James Gavin to MG	MGPP-025-002
2 February 1946	William Walton to MG	MGPP-010-020
10 April 1946	Bertrand de Jouvenel to MG	MGPP-010-020
Late April 1946	MG to Cam Becket	MGPP-013-008
4 May 1946	MG to Robert Sherrod	MGPP-016-005
4 May 1946	Hortense Flexner to MG	MGPP-002-037

5 May 1946	Bertrand de Jouvenel to MG	MGPP-008-008
16 May 1946	MG to Eleanor Roosevelt	MGPP-004-123
20 May 1946	James Gavin to MG	MGPP-025-002
12 June 1946	James Gavin to MG	MGPP-025-002
28 June 1946	James Gavin to MG	MGPP-025-002
11 July 1946	James Gavin to MG	MGPP-025-002
2 August 1946	James Gavin to MG	MGPP-025-002
9 August 1946	James Gavin to MG	MGPP-025-002
10 August 1946	James Gavin to MG	MGPP-025-002
7 September 1946	MG to Cam Becket	MGPP-013-007
12 September 1946	MG to Cam Becket	MGPP-013-007
Fall 1946	MG to James Gavin	MGPP-025-002
5 January 1947	William Walton to MG	MGPP-010-020
27 January 1947	William Walton to MG	MGPP-010-020
1 July 1947	Bertrand de Jouvenel to MG	MGPP-010-020
30 September 1947	Eleanor Roosevelt to MG	MGPP-004-121

Chapter 13: Point of No Return

28 January 1948	Allen Grover to MG	MGPP-013-008
25 December 1948	MG to William Walton	MGPP-010-020
3 January 1949	Cam Becket to MG	MGPP-013-007
18 January 1949	Hortense Flexner to MG	MGPP-025-026
22 June 1949	MG to Eleanor Roosevelt	MGPP-004-123
3 July 1949	Eleanor Roosevelt to MG	MGPP-004-121
Summer 1949	MG to Eleanor Roosevelt	MGPP-004-123
5 July 1949	William Walton to MG	MGPP-010-020
16 July 1949	MG to William Walton	MGPP-010-020

Summer 1949	MG to William Walton	MGPP-010-020
1 August 1949	MG to Eleanor Roosevelt	MGPP-004-123
2 October 1949	William Walton to MG	MGPP-010-020
December 1949	MG to William Walton	MGPP-010-020
14 December 1949	MG to Eleanor Roosevelt	MGPP-004-123

Afterword

8 November 1962	MG to Adlai Stevenson	MGPP-025-026
9 August 1966	MG to Edna Gellhorn	MGPP-002-065
7 June 1968	Cyril Clemens to MG	MGPP-004-110
27 August 1980	MG to George Plimpton	MGPP-016-002
12 November 1993	Laurance Rockefeller to MG	MGPP-025-026
30 June 1997	MG to Betsy Drake	MGPP-025-006

Notes

[1] The British Library acquired a rare copy of *What Mad Pursuit* (1934) in 2012. It may be read there on site in London.

[2] Other pieces Gellhorn considered short fiction, which present as nonfiction, include "Justice at Night," "Rondo," "Vie de Bohème," "Return of the Foreign Correspondent" and "Portrait of a Power." "Requiem" appears in its entirety in the Appendix.

[3] From Gellhorn's *Memoirs: A Bare Beginning* (unpublished)

[4] *Memoirs: A Bare Beginning* (unpublished)

[5] *Memoirs: A Bare Beginning* (unpublished)

[6] Caroline Moorehead, *Martha Gellhorn: A Life*, p. 67

[7] Martha Gellhorn, *What Mad Pursuit*, p. 7

[8] Martha Gellhorn, *What Mad Pursuit*, p. 61

[9] *Peace on Earth* opens, "It was six o'clock. They walked up the rue de Provence to the rue de Lafayette. The shop girls were leaving the Galeries Lafayette and the Printemps. The pastry shops and the insurance offices on the rue Taitbout had just closed. Even the little cobblers and the cleaners and dyers scattered humbly from the rue Lepelletier to the rue de la Chaussée d'Antin were bringing down the shutters, locking the doors and wondering whether there were any late customers to miss. The patron of the Camarades Interalliés, at the corner of the rue Drouot and the rue de Provence, wiped off the zinc bar, getting it dry and ready for the gentlemen who would stop in for a bock or a vermouth or a *fine*, on the way home. The small black women and the small black men pushed and hurried, converging on the metro. It was the end of the day and it was almost spring."

[10] Caroline Moorehead, *Martha Gellhorn: A Life*, p. 127

[11] When Sotheby's auctioned this letter in 2008, it was believed then to be one of only two surviving letters from Ernest to Martha—the other dated August 6, 1944. Some months before her death in February 1998, Gellhorn—according to her adopted son Sandy Gellhorn—went through her correspondence files, feeding much of it, including her letters from Hemingway, into her fireplace flames. Sandy Gellhorn was able to interrupt the process, saving two letters from Ernest to Martha and ten letters from Hemingway to Edna Gellhorn, Martha's mother, from destruction.

This provenance is no longer accurate. There are in Gellhorn's papers two more letters from Ernest to Martha and both are included in this book. One is from winter 1945, a letter that Gellhorn knew was in her papers when she donated them to the Gotlieb Archive in Boston; the second, dated "February First," and written in 1937, was stuffed in a file called "Letters from Friends." Neither letter has been published before.

Furthermore, when Gellhorn and Hemingway divorced in December 1945, she returned to him, at his request, any letters she still had in St. Louis and London. There are dozens of those that were made available to read in Hemingway's papers beginning fall 1998 at Boston's John F. Kennedy Library. Mary Welsh, Hemingway's final wife, donated those letters and made Gellhorn's death a condition of their release.

When Gellhorn learned of the stash of her letters to Ernest that was included in his papers, she requested that the originals be returned to her. They were sent to her *via* the Gotlieb Archive in Boston, where photocopies of them remain.

[12] According to her authorized biographer Caroline Moorehead, Gellhorn spoke excellent French, adequate Spanish and some German. *Martha Gellhorn: A Life*, p. 175

[13] Gellhorn was reticent to join the Scribner's stable of writers in 1940 because it was Hemingway's longtime publisher. After her editor Maxwell Perkins died in 1947, Gellhorn took her work to other publishing houses, including André Deutsch, Penguin, Simon & Schuster and Granta Books. Her final book, *The View from the Ground*, a collection of peacetime reporting, was published in 1989.

[14] The stationery that Gellhorn and Hemingway shared from 1939 through 1945 had FINCA VIGÍA SAN FRANCISCO DE PAULA CUBA in red ink across the top. *Finca Vigía* translates as "the Watchtower," an apt moniker for a place that stood on a hill and looked down to the sea. Gellhorn found the property through a 1939 advertisement in a local paper and paid $100/month in rent. Hemingway purchased it outright for $12,500 in December 1940 with some of the Paramount Pictures option money for *For Whom The Bell Tolls*.

[15] In Hemingway's personal papers at the John F. Kennedy Library in Boston, his love letters to Mary Welsh from "Big Friend" to "Small Friend" begin in July 1944. Gellhorn and Hemingway divorced on December 21, 1945, and he wed Mary Welsh in Cuba in March 1946.

[16] Recorded interview with Eleanor Wachtel, Toronto, CBC Radio's *Writers & Company*, 1992.

[17] There is a different version of "Over and Back" than *Collier's* published. Gellhorn included "The First Hospital Ship" in her papers at Boston University.

[18] "82nd Airborne: Master of the Hot Spots," *Saturday Evening Post*, February 23, 1946, 22–33.

[19] "Dachau: Experimental Murder," *Collier's*, June 23, 1945, 16, 24.

[20] Originally opened by Himmler in 1933 and intended to hold political pris-oners, Dachau served as a model for all later concentration camps and a school of violence for the S.S. men who worked there. According to the Dachau Concentration Camp Memorial Site, 41,500 people were murdered there. See www.kz-gedenkstaette-dachau-de

[21] *Point of No Return* was first published as *The Wine of Astonishment*, a title Gellhorn's editor Maxwell Perkins insisted was less alienating to readers. Gellhorn reclaimed her preferred title in subsequent editions.

Photo Credits

EHPC: Ernest Hemingway Photo Collection, John F. Kennedy Presidential Library
and Museum, Boston, Massachusetts

MGC: Martha Gellhorn Collection, Howard Gotlieb Archival Research Center at
Boston University

Cover: June 1937, MG in silver fox fur at Carnegie Hall EHPC 5580 (top),
1943, MG with R.A.F. pilots in front of a Lancaster bomber
MGC-019-002 (bottom).

Endpapers: All of the correspondence may be found in the Martha Gellhorn
Collection, including the Wyncie King illustrations. The letters were
written by Campbell Becket, James Gavin, Edna Gellhorn, Allen
Grover, Bertrand de Jouvenel, William Walton, and H.G. Wells.

193: 1916, League of Women Voters event, St. Louis   MGC-019-002

194–195: 1931, letter to Cam Becket   MGC-013-008

196: 1932, Bertrand de Jouvenel, photo by Martha Gellhorn   MGC-019-002

197: 1933, Hadley Hemingway wedding invitation   MGC-018-001

198: Circa 1936, portrait of MG   MGC-019-002 (top)
March 1940, Wyncie King illustration   MGC-002-037

199: February 12, 1937, letter from Eleanor Roosevelt   MGC-004-121

200: Spring 1937, MG in Spain with Ernest Hemingway   EHPC 2981
June 1937, MG in fur jacket with Ernest Hemingway at Carnegie Hall
EHPC 5580

201: January 16, 1938, *St. Louis Post-Dispatch*   MGC-001-007

202: May 1938, MG in Prague   MGC-019-002

203: 1939, Ernest Hemingway's passport photo   MGC-021-004
December 1939, MG, speaking with an officer in Finland   MGC-019-002

204: 1939, MG standing on the ledge of the pool at Finca Vigía, Cuba   EHPC 5589

205: 1939–1940, MG, with Ernest Hemingway on Leicester Hemingway's sailboat
EHPC 5629
1940, MG with her mother Edna Gellhorn, Finca Vigía, Cuba   EHPC 1039N

206: November 1940 wedding invitation   MGC–011–024

207: 1940, MG with Ernest Hemingway and his sons at Sun Valley, Idaho, photo by Lloyd Arnold   EHPC 4869

208: November 14, 1940, Cabin Creek Party, photo by Lloyd Arnold EHPC 4861

241: December 18, 1940, letter from President Franklin D. Roosevelt MGC–019–002

242: Early 1941, MG with Ernest Hemingway, Stork Club, NYC   EHPC 5582

243: Circa 1941, MG, steering *Pilar*   MGC–011–024
Early 1941, MG and Ernest Hemingway wearing leis, Hawaii MGC–019–002

244: MG's 1941 passport   MGC–019–002

245: 1941, Chinese soldiers crushing gravel barefoot   MGC–021–004
1941, MG with Madame Chiang in China   MGC–021–004

246: 1942, MG with Caribbean crew   MGC–019–002
1942, MG with U.S. airmen in Puerto Rico   MGC–019–002

247: 1942–1943, Ernest Hemingway   MGC–019–002
1944, MG in uniform on the Italian Front   MGC–008–009

248: 1943, MG with R.A.F. pilots   MGC–019–002

249: "Martha Gellhorn, London, England 1943" © Lee Miller Archives, England 2019. All rights reserved. www.leemiller.co.uk
1945, Wyncie King illustrated envelope   MGC–019–002

250: May 7, 1945, Dachau Concentration Camp Visitor's Pass   MGC–019–002
1945–1946, Robert Capa and James Gavin in uniform   MGC–008–009

251: September 7, 1946, letter to Cam Becket   MGC–013–008

252: 1947, War Department citation   MGC–019–002

253: 1948, William Walton   MGC–019–002

254: 1949, Wyncie King stork illustration   MGC–002–036

255: Early 1950s, MG, with Sandy Gellhorn   MGC–019–002

256: 1980s, MG, leaning on a globe   MGC–019–002

Index

Dear love, this just a line to say I'm most t...
My mind ra... I become insane when I'm jea...
I'm a... ...linquished 'worldly...
...you. That a...
blind with
...cause on
...o (and
...hand

Monday 7th
Feb.

darling - There are some
naive aspects to your
character. Such as that we are
out of touch with each other
because we don't write - or at
least I don't, much (and you don't
either). Actually we are not. A day
rarely goes by that I don't think
of you, wherever you are, just
watching the day unfold - or
chasing a war. Recently I've been
rather busy, and uncommunicative,
because, as I explained one day
on a banquette at the Brussels.
I've been thinking. You've been
thinking a lot longer than I and
some fruits of it were rather beautifully expressed in your last letter.
My thinking takes me into somewhat
different paths because, unlike you,

15/4/35

John Pickett, Castle Hill, Windsor. No. 3591

This space may be used for

No letter from you.
I'm working 27 hours
on this films.
Read my article in G...
please. They are hastily
written but I believe they
say something very important.
Tell me how they get you.
Please.
...cking...
...up myself
...again y.
go back to
I fee...
...keep,

6 april.